Essentials of U.S. Taxation:
What Every Executive Must Know

♦ **HBJ MILLER** ♦

Essentials of U.S. Taxation: What Every Executive Must Know

William A. Duncan, Ph.D, CPA

HBJ Miller Accounting Publications, Inc.
a subsidiary of

Harcourt Brace Jovanovich, Publishers
San Diego New York London

> This publication is designed to provide accurate and authoritative information in regard to the subject matter covered. It is sold with the understanding that the publisher is not engaged in rendering legal, accounting, or other professional service.

HBJ Miller Essentials of U.S. Taxation: What Every Executive Must Know is a trademark of Harcourt Brace Jovanovich, Inc.

Copyright © 1992 by HBJ Professional Publishing Division of Harcourt Brace Jovanovich, Inc.

All rights reserved. No part of this publication may be reproduced or transmitted in any form or by any means, electronic or mechanical, including photocopy, recording, or any information storage and retrieval system, without permission in writing from the publisher.

Requests for permission to make copies of any part of the work should be mailed to: Permissions Department, Harcourt Brace Jovanovich, Inc., 8th Floor, Orlando, Florida 32887.

Some material derived from *A Review of Essentials of Taxation*, 1990 edition, by Ray Sommerfeld.

Printed in the United States of America

ISBN 0-15-601726-1

To

Ray Sommerfeld:
Teacher, thinker, mentor, friend.

TABLE OF CONTENTS

Chapter 1: The Law of U.S. Federal Income Taxation	1.01
Origins of Statutory Tax Law	1.02
Organization of the Code	1.04
Administrative Interpretations	1.11
Judicial Interpretations	1.14
Secondary Authorities	1.19
Chapter 2: Income as a Tax Base	2.01
Income: Definitional Issues	2.02
The Concept of Realization	2.05
Recognition Rules	2.06
Chapter 3: Calculating the Tax Liability	3.01
Exclusions	3.02
Deductions	3.06
Tax Rates	3.10
Tax Credits and Prepayments	3.12
Chapter 4: Taxpayers and Tax Rates	4.01
Individual Taxpayers	4.02
Corporate Taxpayers	4.08
Fiduciary Taxpayers	4.12
Other Business Entities	4.15
Two Major Problem Areas	4.20
Chapter 5: Accounting Periods and Methods	5.01
Accounting Periods	5.01
Accounting Method	5.03
Aggregating the Income of Separate Legal Entities	5.10

ESSENTIALS OF U.S. TAXATION / ix

Chapter 6: Special Rules for Individual Taxpayers	**6.01**
Deduction Options	6.01
Personal and Dependent Exemption Deductions	6.08
The "Kiddie Tax"	6.09
Business Income	6.11
Chapter 7: Property Transactions	**7.01**
Measuring Gains and Losses	7.01
The Capital Gains Provisions	7.08
Some Nontaxable Exchange Provisions	7.12
Chapter 8: Losses	**8.01**
NOLs or Net Operating Losses	8.02
PALs or Passive Activity Losses	8.04
Capital Losses	8.10
Personal Losses of Individual Taxpayers	8.11
Other Losses	8.13
Chapter 9: The Compliance Process	**9.01**
Filing Returns	9.01
The Audit Procedure	9.04
Interest and Penalties	9.05
Assessing a Tax Expert	9.07
Chapter 10: Tax Planning	**10.01**
Fundamentals of Tax Planning	10.01
Two Examples of Tax Planning	10.03
Limitations to Tax Planning	10.12
Glossary	**11.01**

Preface

Does your position require that you know just a bit more than you already do about the U.S. (federal) income tax? If so, this book is probably for you. Almost everyone knows something about the one tax that already produces over $500,000,000,000 in government revenues each year, and that figure continues to grow! Yet very few people know as much about the income tax as they should know. The minimum federal income tax payable on a business venture or a property transaction may change dramatically depending on your understanding of general rules that determine specific tax results. The purpose of this book is to bring you up to date on the most important recent changes in federal income tax law. If you have never studied the U.S. income tax law, or if most of your study was completed before 1986, then you almost certainly can benefit from reading this book.

This overview of U.S. income tax provisions should be helpful to many individuals in very diverse circumstances. Included in that disparate set of individuals are business owners and managers, those who make investments in U.S. assets, and those who study business phenomena in general. In short, whether your specific job title is business owner, investor, manager, adviser, attorney, accountant, editor, realtor, student, or any of several others, you are likely to be interested in tax-oriented insights that can be achieved with minimal effort. Although this short book will not be of much help if and when you fill out your own income tax return, it certainly will help to explain the basics of the largest tax system in the world.

The IRS recently reported that 822 individual taxpayers, each with adjusted gross income of $200,000 or more, legally avoided paying any U.S. income tax. Of those individuals, 731 paid no income tax to any country in the world. Another 835 individuals would also have escaped the income tax had there been no alternative minimum tax (AMT). During the same year, however, the most highly compensated 1% of all U.S. (individual) taxpayers actually paid nearly 25% of the $400-plus billion collected from individuals by the U.S. government. The intent of this book is to help you understand how the income tax can have such disparate results in one year.

Phoenix, Arizona   *William A. Duncan*

THE LAW OF U.S. FEDERAL INCOME TAXATION

For most business professionals, a detailed knowledge of the tax law is not necessary. What is essential is that professionals have a grasp of key issues and potential opportunities sufficient to assure that the right questions are asked of the professional tax adviser. And, most importantly, that such questions are asked in a timely manner. This is because minor changes in the structure of compensation arrangements, property transfers, and many other transactions, can make tax-free what might otherwise be currently taxable. But what may be easily accomplished during the negotiation stage is frequently impossible in hindsight. We will begin with the basics.

The federal income tax in the United States is imposed and collected on the authority of statutory law that is compiled in a document technically known as The Internal Revenue Code of 1986. Like all statutory laws, the tax Code is subject to constant interpretation by numerous administrative and judicial authorities as well as by millions of taxpayers and their expert advisors. Because of the complexity of the law, a minimal tax library requires literally hundreds of volumes, many of which must be constantly updated. Locating, reading, and correctly interpreting the portion of the tax law that applies to a specific situation is often an extremely difficult task best left to professional advisors. Nevertheless, some general knowledge of the authorities on which experts base their own opinions is helpful in both understanding and assessing their technical advice.

The objective of Chapter 1 is to explain the various tax authorities in general terms so that the reader will be better prepared to understand the tax experts' questions as well as to evaluate their opinions and advice. Chapter 1 is subdivided into five major parts. The first part explains the legislative process that converts proposed bills into tax laws. The second part details the organization of the tax law in the Code. The third part examines the most important administrative interpretations that expand the original statutory law. The fourth part reviews the judicial interpretations that concurrently (a) resolve specific conflicts in the interpretation of tax law and (b) modify the law itself. The fifth part concludes this introduction with a brief description of the numerous secondary authorities that are often helpful in understanding tax issues. An appendix to Chapter 1 explains and illustrates the format of citations to the administrative and judicial interpretations of the law.

Origins of Statutory Tax Law

It is important to keep a wary eye cocked for any sign of proposed legislation that could affect a planned business transaction. If your tax adviser is an integral part of the planning process, he or she should keep you advised. If not, the popular press will often provide the first warning that some element of the tax law may be changed. Pending legislation adds a new and decidedly unwelcome element of uncertainty to business decisions and it is possible that a transaction will have to be accelerated, abandoned, or deferred in the face of such legislation. The decision on how or whether to consummate a transaction depends on the potential tax cost, the effective dates, and the likelihood of passage. Each of these items deserves comments and suggests the need for professional advice.

First, the tax adviser should compute the tax cost under existing and proposed law (and the business executive must understand the fluid nature of the proposed law in the midst of the legislative process and the need for ongoing revisions of those tax cost estimates). Second, effective dates need not correspond to the date the legislation is signed into law. They are sometimes linked to the timing of the original proposal or some other significant event. In other words, the law as eventually enacted may be retroactive to the date the proposed legislation was first offered, when public hearings were first held, or some other date prior to completion of the legislative process. Finally, legislation is a very human process and assessing the likelihood of passage is a difficult task with a high probability of error for even the most knowledgeable tax adviser.

It is helpful to understand the lawmaking process for several reasons. Perhaps the most obvious is that proposed tax legislation has an increased probability of enactment the further it has advanced through the legislative process. Second, a number of documents are produced by the process that indicate the intention of Congress in enacting the law. These documents provide guidance to taxpayers and sometimes tax relief. Third, it is possible for taxpayers, usually through trade or business organizations, to influence legislation at critical junctures, especially effective dates. Hence, a review of the lawmaking process is presented below.

The Constitution of the United States provides that tax bills must originate in the House of Representatives, the larger and more populist body of a bicameral legislature. Once introduced, tax bills are referred to the Committee on Ways and Means. House rules generally give committee chairmen almost complete authority over the subsequent disposition of matters pending before their committees. The Chairman of the House Ways and Means Committee is, therefore, a very influential player in the U.S. government. Although the Chairman can effectively pigeonhole most routine bills introduced by fellow members of the House, major bills that have the backing of the Administration are virtually assured serious attention.

Major bills ordinarily receive their first public exposure in hearings conducted by the Ways and Means Committee. The first witnesses to testify are typically those invited by the Chairman. In the case of bills sponsored by the Administration, the Secretary of the Treasury is usually the first person to speak. Following invited guests, others with interest in the proposed legislation are allowed to make oral remarks and/or submit written comments. These hearings may be published by the Government Printing Office. They have no special significance, however, because they simply compile the views of interested parties, none of whom can enact legislation.

The *Report of the Committee on Ways and Means* that accompanies a tax bill when it is reported out of committee is, on the other hand, a potentially valuable source document. It contains the views of the committee members and gives a general explanation of the reasons they had for recommending this legislation to the entire House of Representatives. Their views may be important when one is subsequently trying to determine "the intent of Congress." A taxpayer, for example, may argue that the Internal Revenue Service (IRS) is interpreting a statutory provision in a manner that is both detrimental to the taxpayer and contrary to the intent of Congress. If, by citing a Ways and Means Report, the taxpayer can convince a judicial authority of the legitimacy of that contention, that document has served a very important role in the process of taxation.

The House of Representatives generally votes on tax bills under a "closed rule." This means that the members of the House are not free to amend a tax bill. They generally must accept or reject the bill in its entirety, as submitted. If a majority rejects the bill, it dies; if a majority accepts it, the bill proceeds to the Senate, the smaller chamber in the bicameral legislature.

Tax bills received in the Senate are referred to the Senate Finance Committee. The Chairman of the Finance Committee now has power and authority over tax legislation similar to that previously ascribed to the Ways and Means Chairman. The Senate Finance Committee largely repeats the procedure of its House counterpart when it considers tax legislation. Consequently, any published *Hearings of the Senate Finance Committee* are less significant than the *Report of the Senate Finance Committee*. The latter is the second document that may contain the "intent of Congress." The Senate, unlike the House, generally permits its members to amend proposed tax bills during floor debate. Because amendments occur after the Finance Committee's Report is printed, any record of the intent of Congress concerning an amended provision must be found in a third publication, the *Congressional Record*, a daily tabloid of the events that transpire on the floor of Congress.

If the Senate approves a tax bill, the bill typically varies significantly from the version originally passed by the House. To reconcile the two versions of the same bill, a Conference Committee is appointed. Conferee appointments are made by the Chairmen of the House Ways and Means and the Senate Finance Committees, giving those two positions still greater importance in the legislative process. The Conference Committee generally does not hold additional hearings; but it does conduct negotiation sessions—sometimes behind closed doors—to hammer out a final version of the tax bill, which is eventually submitted to both houses of Congress for ratification or rejection, usually with no possibility for further amendment. The *Report of the Conference Committee* that accompanies a final bill is the fourth source for uncovering the intent of Congress. A record of the Conference Committee's negotiation sessions, commonly called the *Blue Book*, is the fifth and last document that may provide that insight.

After a tax bill has been approved by a majority of both the House and the Senate, it is sent to the President for approval or rejection. Major tax bills are rarely vetoed even though the final version of the bill may be quite different from the version supported earlier by the Secretary of the Treasury. This political process, however cumbersome, is supposed to reflect the will of the people and thus legitimize the taxes imposed by the statutory rules.

During its journey through Congress, a tax bill is assigned a separate House Report and Senate Report number; for example, HR 1321 and S 642. A bill approved by Congress will also be given a title (for example, the Tax Reform Act of 1989) and a Public Law number (for example, PL 100-492). After enactment each tax act will be integrated into the current Code to facilitate the taxing process. The section numbers assigned to various provisions in a tax act are *not* the same as the section numbers assigned to those provisions once they become part of the Code.

Organization of the Code

References to "the Code" by tax professionals are a source of irritation and confusion to non-tax experts just as the use of Latin by medical professionals is disconcerting to those of us with no medical training. But the Code is organized in a fairly straightforward manner, and since professional opinions will continue to reference the law by Code section, it is helpful to have some idea of how to interpret these references. The Internal Revenue Code of 1986 is the third Code in U.S. tax history. The first Code (the IRC of 1939) covered the period from 1939 to 1954; the second Code (the IRC of 1954) spanned the years from 1954 to 1986. Prior to 1939 there was no single compilation of the then-current federal tax law. In those days individuals had to look to the several independent tax acts previously approved to determine the law applicable to any specific situation. However difficult our current Code may be, it is clearly an improvement over the earlier circumstances.

Subtitles and Chapters

The Code is presently divided into nine major divisions called "subtitles," which are separately designated by the English letters A through I. Subtitle A contains the income tax law; Subtitle B, the estate and gift tax law; Subtitle C, our employment tax law; etc. These subtitles are further subdivided into "chapters" designated by Arabic numbers. Subtitle A (the income tax) includes six chapters, titled as follows:

Chapter 1:	Normal taxes and surtaxes
Chapter 2:	Tax on self-employment income
Chapter 3:	Withholding of tax on nonresident aliens and foreign corporations
Chapter 4:	Rules applicable to recovery of excessive profits on government contracts
Chapter 5:	Tax on transfers to avoid income taxes
Chapter 6:	Consolidated returns

Chapter 1 is of more general interest than are the other five chapters.

Subchapters

Chapter 1 of the Code is currently subdivided into 20 "subchapters" designated by the English letters A through V; Subchapters R and U have been repealed. Subchapter designations are frequently used as a shorthand form of communication among tax professionals as well as a technical frame of reference within the Code itself. Consequently they are detailed below.

Subchapter A:	Determination of tax liability
Subchapter B:	Computation of taxable income
Subchapter C:	Corporate distributions and adjustments
Subchapter D:	Deferred compensations, etc.
Subchapter E:	Accounting periods and methods of accounting
Subchapter F:	Exempt organizations
Subchapter G:	Corporations used to avoid income tax on shareholders
Subchapter H:	Banking institutions
Subchapter I:	Natural resources
Subchapter J:	Estates, trusts, beneficiaries, and decedents
Subchapter K:	Partners and partnerships
Subchapter L:	Insurance companies
Subchapter M:	Regulated investment companies and real estate investment trusts
Subchapter N:	Tax based on income from sources within or without the United States
Subchapter O:	Gain or loss on disposition of property
Subchapter P:	Capital gains and losses
Subchapter Q:	Readjustment of tax between years and special limitations
Subchapter S:	Tax treatment of S corporations and their shareholders
Subchapter T:	Cooperatives and their patrons
Subchapter V:	Title II cases

Even a cursory reading of the subchapter titles reveals that some are of general interest, while others are only of special interest to select taxpayers. For example, the contents of Subchapters A, B, E, O, and P are of general interest, while Subchapter F is of primary interest to churches, schools, and other tax-exempt organizations; Subchapter H, to banks; and Subchapter L, to insurance companies.

The contents of some subchapters are aptly described by their "titles" or "headings" (Subchapters E and O are good examples), while the titles of others fail to describe their content. Subchapter C is a classic example of the latter category. A literal interpretation of "corporate distributions and adjustments" implies a set of corporate tax rules that would be of interest largely to corporations in limited circumstances. As a matter of fact, Subchapter C contains the rules that govern the tax consequences of nearly all transactions between a corporation and its shareholders, in their role as shareholders. Because shareholders exist in a variety of species (e.g., individual, corporate, trust, and partnership shareholders are all commonplace) this subchapter is of much more general interest than its title suggests. Incidentally, Subchapter K similarly provides the rules that govern the tax consequences of transactions between a partnership and its partners, in their role as partners. Since the term *partners* includes individuals, estates, trusts, corporations, and other partnerships, Subchapter K is also of widespread interest.

Parts

Most of the subchapters of the Code are further broken down into "parts," designated by Roman numerals, as required. Subchapter A, for example, is divided into seven parts, numbered I through VII; Subchapter B, into eleven parts; and Subchapter C, into seven parts. These subdivisions can be important for one of two reasons. First, a Code provision may impose an internal limit by cross reference to a part. For example, Sec. 317 provides a statutory definition of the word "property." That definition begins, however, with the following words: "For purposes of this *part*, the term property means..." [emphasis added]. Accordingly, the definition of property in Sec. 317 is valid only when that word is used in Part I of Subchapter C; i.e., in the part of Subchapter C in which Sec. 317 is located.

A second reason for looking at the subdivisions known as parts is that their descriptive titles may provide a helpful overview of what is located there. The seven parts of Subchapter C are good examples. They read as follows:

Part I:	Distributions by corporations
Part II:	Corporate liquidations
Part III:	Corporate organizations and reorganizations
Part IV:	Insolvency reorganizations
Part V:	Carryovers
Part VI:	Treatment of certain corporate interests as stock or indebtedness
Part VII:	Miscellaneous corporate provisions

If one is trying to locate the tax rules that govern the creation of a new corporation, it would be wise to begin that search in Part III of Subchapter C. Rules governing dividends, on the other hand, will likely be found in Part I.

Subparts

Some parts of the Code are subdivided into still smaller units, called *subparts*, which are again designated by capital English letters, as required. Parts I and II of Subchapter C, for example, include subparts as follows:

Part I: Distributions by corporations
   Subpart A: Effects on recipients
   Subpart B: Effects on corporation
   Subpart C: Definitions; constructive ownership of stock

Part II: Corporate liquidations
   Subpart A: Effects on recipients
   Subpart B: Effects on corporation
   Subpart C: Collapsible corporations
   Subpart D: Definition and special rule

These headings can be useful in locating pertinent statutory authority. For example, anyone looking for the rules that apply to a shareholder *receiving* a dividend distribution would be well advised to examine the sections found in Subpart A, of Part I, of Subchapter C. Anyone searching for the definition of a corporate liquidation might well begin with the sections found in Subpart D, of Part II, of Subchapter C.

Sections

The unit of the Code most frequently referenced in both the popular and technical literature is, notwithstanding all of the prior explanation, something known as a Code section. When the drafters of the first Code designed their numbering system, they created a nonrepetitive system *at the section level*. Part I of Subchapter A was allocated Sections 1 through 10; Part II, Sections 11 through 14; etc., with no number being used twice. To allow room for subsequent modification to the Code, they deliberately did not use all numbers immediately. Hence there is, for example, no Section 6, 7, 8, 9, or 10 to this day. Because of the frequency of amendments in recent years, we have run out of numbers in some areas. Therefore, even though it was originally envisioned that a section number would consist of only an Arabic number, a growing number of sections today contain both an Arabic number *and* an English capital letter. For example, Part IX of Subchapter B—the portion of the Code that deals with items that are *not* deductible—was originally allocated 20 section numbers (from 261 through 280). Over the years Congress modified this portion of the Code so frequently that the original 20 numbers proved to be insufficient. Rather than readjusting all subsequent section numbers to allow more numbers in Part IX of Subchapter B, the drafters began adding English capital letters to expand the Code as needed. Therefore, we now have a separate Sec. 263 and another Sec. 263A; a Sec. 269, another Sec. 269A, and yet another Sec. 269B; as well as Secs. 280, 280A, 280B, 280C, etc., through 280H.

Because section numbers are used only once, they provide a convenient cross reference. After sufficient experience, a person discovers that any section numbered between 301 and 399 is part of Subchapter C—i.e., part of the tax law that governs the tax consequences of transactions between corporations and their shareholders, in their role as shareholders. Similarly, experts soon discover that sections in the 700 series govern transactions between partners and partnerships, while sections from 861 through 999 are of interest only to taxpayers engaged in a multinational business (or, in other words, to those interested in Subchapter N).

Any reference to a section number only is assumed to refer to the section in the then-current Code. For example, a simple reference to Sec. 482 found in a current journal article is assumed to refer to Sec. 482 of the 1986 Code. On the other hand, an article published in 1952 with a similar reference would, of course, refer to Sec. 482 of the 1939 Code. If an author of a current article desires to make reference to a section in either the 1939 Code or 1954 Code, it is incumbent on the author to make explicit the Code intended.

Further Subdivisions

Code sections may be further subdivided into *subsections*, identified by lowercase English letters in parentheses; into *paragraphs*, by Arabic numbers in parentheses; into *subparagraphs*, by capital English letters in parentheses; and eventually into *subsubparagraphs*, by lowercase Roman numerals in parentheses. To illustrate, consider the subdivisions of the statutory law found in Sec. 11, which reads as follows:

The Law of U.S. Federal Income Taxation

section	Sec. 11. Tax Imposed
subsection	(a) Corporations in General. A tax is hereby imposed for each taxable year on the taxable income of every corporation.
subsection	(b) Amount of Tax
paragraph	(1) In general: The amount of the tax imposed by subsection (a) shall be the sum of
subparagraph	(A) 15 percent of so much of the taxable income as does not exceed $50,000,
subparagraph	(B) 25 percent of so much of the taxable income as exceeds $50,000 but does not exceed $75,000, and
subparagraph	(C) 34 percent of so much of the taxable income as exceeds $75,000.
	In the case of corporation which has taxable income in excess of $100,000 for any taxable year, the amount of tax determined under the preceding sentence for such taxable year shall be increased by the lesser of (i) 5 percent of such excess, or (ii) $11,750.
paragraph	(2) Certain personal service corporations not eligible for graduated rates. Notwithstanding paragraph (1), the amount of tax imposed by subsection (a) on the taxable income of a qualified personal service corporation (as defined in section 448(d)(2)) shall be equal to 34 percent of the taxable income.

Subsection 11(a)—written as Sec. 11(a)—is the operative part of our statutory law. That is, it is the subsection that *imposes* an income tax on corporations in general. Subparagraphs (A), (B), and (C) of paragraph (1) of subsection 11(b)—written as Sec. 11(b)(1)(A), (B), and (C)—provide the corporate income tax rates for most corporations; the remainder of paragraph (1) provides (in effect) a 5 percent surtax for corporations earning between $100,000 and $335,000. Paragraph (2) of Subsection 11(b)—written as Sec. 11(b)(2)—provides a special (flat-tax) rate of 34 percent for a certain kind of corporation, specifically for personal service corporations, as defined in Sec. 448(d)(2).

Although the various subdivisions of the Code may appear to provide nothing but confusion, they actually provide a convenient shorthand for tax experts. The simplicity is attributable to the fact that no citation generally is needed for any level above the section designation.

Summary Example

The portion of the Code that imposes a flat tax of 34 percent on a personal service corporation's taxable income could correctly be cited as IRC of 1986, Subtitle A, Chapter 1, Subchapter A, Part II, Section 11, subsection (b), paragraph (2). Fortunately, however, that cumbersome cross reference is wholly unnecessary. A simple citation to "Sec. 11(b)(2)" does the job equally well since no section number is utilized more than once. Individuals wanting to determine the other identifying subdivisions of any Code reference can do so by consulting the index to the Code, usually located at the front of the Code volumes.

Unfortunately, understanding some Code sections proves to be a more difficult task than learning how to cite those sections correctly. The next several pages will explain administrative interpretations in general.

Administrative Interpretations

After Congress has enacted a tax law it is the duty of the Treasury Department to issue administrative interpretations necessary to implement the new law in a reasonably efficient manner. Those administrative interpretations range from very general pronouncements, intended for large numbers of somewhat diversely situated taxpayers, to very specific interpretations, intended for only one taxpayer.

Treasury Regulations

The most general administrative interpretations of statutory tax law are known as Treasury regulations. The authority for a regulation can derive either from the longstanding general authority given to the Treasury Department in Sec. 7805 or from specific authority granted in a particular Code section, such as Sec. 469(l), a section concerned solely with the problem of "passive activity losses." In fact, the latter are often referred to as "statutory regulations." The distinction between the two authorization sources is important because the courts are more likely to find regulations issued under general statutory authority as incorrect interpretations of statutory law than they are regulations authorized by specific authority. This should not be taken to suggest that the regulations may be easily flouted. The courts are very reluctant to overturn either type of regulation. Moreover, the taxpayer must bear a very heavy burden of proof in such cases, and the possibility exists that substantial penalties could be imposed on the taxpayer.

The procedure the Treasury Department follows in issuing regulations generally involves a substantial amount of input by interested parties. In most instances Treasury will first issue **Proposed Regulations** and invite commentary on those proposals for a period of 60 to 90 days. At the end of that period, Treasury will consider the responses received and take one of three actions, namely:

1. issue Final Regulations with the same or some relatively minor modification in wording;
2. withdraw the Proposed Regulations and issue a revised set with relatively major changes; or
3. withdraw the Proposed Regulations and do nothing further by way of interpretation for a longer time period.

In rare instances Treasury will allow a set of Proposed Regulations to remain outstanding for a prolonged period of time even if the Proposed Regulations provide administrative guidance that is directly in conflict with permanent and final Regulations previously issued. A good example of this existed with the regulations issued in the interpretation of Sec. 355, the Code section that authorizes a tax free distribution of a subsidiary corporation's stock by the parent corporation. Numerous provisions in Final Regulations, issued in 1955, were directly in conflict with Proposed Regulations, issued in 1977. The Proposed Regulations were outstanding for more than 10 years. Treasury did not resolve obvious conflicts between the two until January 1989 when it made the Proposed Regulations the (new) Final Regulations. Fortunately, this does not happen very often.

The frequency of modification to the statutory tax law has accelerated substantially during the past 10 to 15 years. Because Treasury has been unable to issue all of the regulations called for by these frequent new laws, Treasury has increasingly relied on Temporary

Regulations. These administrative interpretations generally do not call for the same external input as is common with Proposed Regulations. As a result, complaints and disagreements from taxpayers and tax advisors are more common with Temporary Regulations than with Proposed (and/or final) Regulations. On the other hand, many individuals appreciate the early guidance provided by Temporary Regulations, even when they disagree with the administrative interpretations. It is important to note that Temporary Regulations are legally binding and should not be confused with Proposed Regulations, which are not.

Revenue Rulings

Revenue rulings are issued by the IRS, a subdivision of the Treasury Department responsible for the day-to-day administration of federal tax laws. Revenue rulings take one of two basic forms known as **published rulings** and **private letter rulings**. Both forms derive from taxpayers' requests that the IRS issue an administrative interpretation of tax law as it applies to their specific circumstances. If the IRS considers a ruling to be of significance to numerous taxpayers, it will "sanitize" the request—i.e., guarantee privacy by removing all information that would identify the taxpayer who made the original request—and publish it for the general direction of all taxpayers. Private letter rulings are similarly sanitized before they are released for circulation by commercial publishers. Private letter rulings are not intended as guidance to anyone other than the taxpayer submitting the original ruling request. Although the IRS agrees to follow a private letter ruling addressed to a specific taxpayer—assuming the information submitted in the request was complete and accurate in all details—the IRS need not reach the same conclusion in identical circumstances encountered by other taxpayers. In spite of this limitation of private letter rulings, many tax advisors subscribe to commercial tax services that publish those rulings because they believe the rulings reveal the general attitude of the IRS toward current issues. Incidentally, the IRS may withdraw a private ruling if the ruling request was incomplete or incorrect.

There are three additional points worth noting about Revenue Rulings. First, Revenue Rulings are issued by the IRS rather than the Treasury and do not carry the same weight of authority as do Regulations. Second, the IRS is free to revoke published rulings, even retroactively, although this latter step is infrequently employed. Finally, published rulings do provide valid precedent for taxpayers whose fact situation is substantially identical to those set out in the ruling, and provide a valuable planning tool for taxpayers in structuring transactions to achieve certain tax treatments. This is because a published and outstanding ruling represents the official position of the IRS and, as a result, it will frequently be more convincing to an IRS agent than a court case or other source of interpretation of the law.

Other Administrative Interpretations

The Treasury Department issues other interpretations to aid taxpayers in complying with the statutory law. Among the other items are revenue procedures (abbreviated as Rev. Proc.), technical information releases (TIRs), technical advice memoranda (TAMs), etc. Revenue procedures generally explain administrative procedures within the IRS and give guidance on such diverse matters as depreciation procedures (e.g., Rev. Proc. 87-57) and a checklist of information to be included in certain ruling requests (e.g., Rev. Proc. 83-59).

The IRS also publishes a multiplicity of forms and instructions to accompany those forms. A few of the more important forms are identified in Chapter 9. Finally, the IRS issues various "publications" intended to help groups of taxpayers such as farmers, small business ventures, executors of estates, etc. Anyone interested in getting a copy of these secondary interpretations should pay a visit to their local IRS office.

Judicial Interpretations

The U.S. income tax operates on a self compliance basis. This means that, once Congress has enacted the law, it is the taxpayers' responsibility to comply. As a practical matter, approximately half of all taxpayers attempt to comply on their own; the other half utilize some form of paid assistance. Regardless of how compliance is accomplished, it is not surprising to discover that disagreements over the correct interpretation of the Code are commonplace. The IRS has established a considerable administrative machinery to reconcile as many differences as possible without resorting to the courts. Nevertheless, several hundred disputes between taxpayers and the IRS proceed to litigation every year. Consequently, a substantial body of judicial law has evolved over the years.

Once a taxpayer decides to litigate a dispute with the IRS, the taxpayer must decide in which of three alternative judicial forums to proceed. Those options are (1) the Tax Court, (2) a federal district court, and (3) the Claims Court. If a taxpayer initially refuses to pay the amount assessed by the IRS, a case will automatically fall within the jurisdiction of the Tax Court. If a taxpayer pays the additional assessment under protest and files a claim for refund, jurisdiction will lie with either a district court or the Claims Court, at the discretion of the taxpayer.

Appeals from the Tax Court and the district courts go to one of 12 circuit courts of appeal, based on the geographical residence of the taxpayer. Appeals from the Claims Court go to the Court of Appeals for the Federal Circuit. The party losing a tax dispute at the circuit court level may file a **writ of certiorari,** requesting the Supreme Court to hear the case, but there is no guarantee that such a request will be granted. In most years the Supreme Court hears no more than six to eight tax cases. Those accepted often involve interpretations in which the appeals courts are in disagreement. Exhibit 1.1 shows the courts in which a taxpayer may file suit and the path that appeals would take.

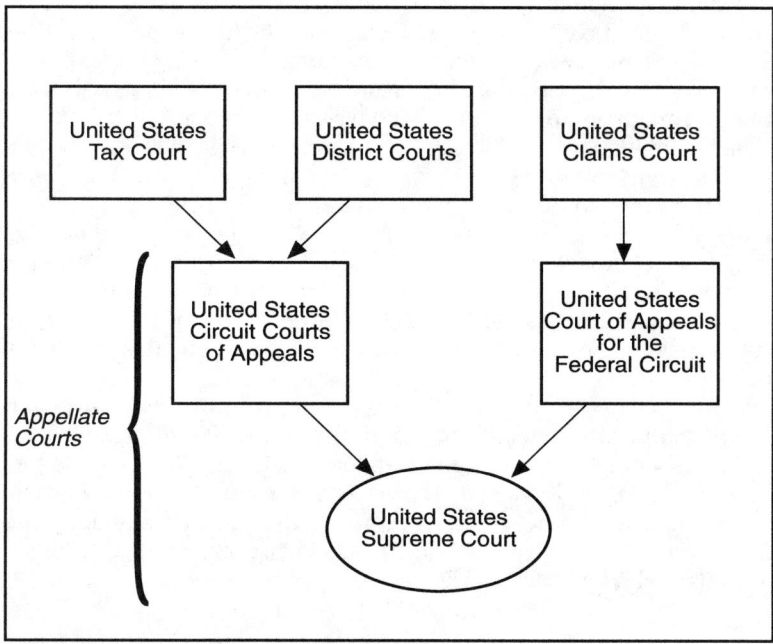

Exhibit 1.1 Federal judicial system

Tax Court

The Tax Court's jurisdiction is, as its name implies, restricted to tax issues. Although headquartered in Washington, D.C., Tax Court judges routinely hear cases in most of the larger cities throughout the United States. As a federal court, it has no smaller geographical boundary; however, it will—under the **Golsen rule**—honor decisions of the circuit courts on issues previously resolved by that court for taxpayers residing in the circuit court's geographical jurisdiction. Hence, when opinions of circuit courts differ on the same issue, the Tax Court will render different decisions on the same issue for taxpayers residing in different parts of the United States. Because of their limited subject-matter jurisdiction, Tax Court judges are best able to resolve the most complex tax issues.

In most instances a single Tax Court judge will independently hear and resolve all issues brought before the court in a given case. However, before the decision of any one Tax Court judge is released, it is reviewed by the Chief Justice. In this review, the Chief Justice makes two critical decisions: One concerns the need for additional judicial input; the other evaluates the general importance of the case as legal precedent. If the Chief Justice decides that a case is of sufficient importance and complexity, the decision of the judge that heard the case will be reviewed by all, or some panel of, the 19 Tax Court judges. "Reviewed decisions" are resolved by majority vote; dissenting and concurring opinions may be written by the minority.

The Chief Justice also decides whether each decision is of sufficient value as legal precedent to justify its publication in the Tax Court reporter series. If a case simply resolves a factual dispute (such as the "fair market value" of property) in a well-settled area of law, the Chief Justice almost certainly will classify the decision as a "memorandum" decision rather than a "regular" decision. Only regular decisions are published in the Tax Court reporter series. Memorandum decisions are reprinted and sold by two commercial tax publishers.

Within the Tax Court there is also the opportunity for a taxpayer with a small claim (the current maximum is $10,000) to proceed in a much less formal way to resolve a dispute with the IRS. Issues taken to the small claims division are heard by a Commissioner, rather than a Tax Court judge; no written record of the proceedings is maintained; no appeal can be made by the losing party; and no legal counsel need be present to represent the taxpayer.

District Court

The federal judicial system in the United States operates on a geographical basis. Although the basic subunit is the 50 states, the more populous states are further subdivided into "districts" to facilitate the work of the court. Therefore, in district court citations, you will frequently discover a cross reference to an eastern, western, northern, or some other district of a federal court located in a particular state. For example, (W.D. Okla.) identifies the Western District of the federal court in Oklahoma; (C.D. Cal.) identifies the Central District of the federal court in California.

Judges appointed to federal district courts hear all matters brought before them. They are not, therefore, specialists in matters of federal income taxation, although they do render decisions in tax refund cases. The procedural rules of the district court allow a litigant the right to demand a trial by a jury of peers. Juries can, however, decide only questions of fact. Questions of law must be resolved by the court. Because appellate courts rarely overturn decisions of fact, the selection of the court of original jurisdiction is often a matter of substantial importance. Incidentally, the district court is the only court of original jurisdiction in tax disputes that authorizes a trial by jury. Because of the potential importance of this fact, skilled and experienced legal counsel should always be engaged before a taxpayer proceeds to litigate a dispute in any court.

The Claims Court

The Claims Court is limited in its jurisdiction to claims against the government of the United States. It is headquartered in Washington, D.C., and operates without geographical boundary, other than national boundaries. Judges of the Claims Court will, on some occasions, sit to hear a case in cities outside Washington, D.C. However, a majority of the cases that it hears are litigated there. The number of tax cases litigated in the Claims Court each year is relatively small. It has only a chief judge and four associate judges. Most cases are originally heard by one of 15 commissioners.

Circuit Courts of Appeal

Appeals from both the Tax Court and the district courts go to one of twelve circuit courts of appeal (CCA). Eleven of the twelve circuit courts are "numbered"; the other one serves only the District of Columbia. The geographical jurisdiction of the twelve courts can be summarized as follows:

Court	Geographical Areas Included
CCA-1	Connecticut, Maine, Massachusetts, New Hampshire, Puerto Rico, Rhode Island
CCA-2	New York, Vermont
CCA-3	New Jersey, Pennsylvania, (U.S.)Virgin Islands
CCA-4	Delaware, Maryland, North Carolina, South Carolina, Virginia, West Virginia
CCA-5	Louisiana, Mississippi, Texas
CCA-6	Kentucky, Michigan, Ohio, Tennessee
CCA-7	Illinois, Indiana, Wisconsin
CCA-8	Arkansas, Iowa, Minnesota, Missouri, Nebraska, North Dakota, South Dakota
CCA-9	Alaska, Arizona, California, Guam, Hawaii, Idaho, Montana, Nevada, Oregon, Washington
CCA-10	Colorado, Kansas, New Mexico, Oklahoma, Utah, Wyoming
CCA-11	Alabama, Canal Zone, Florida, Georgia
CCA-DC	District of Columbia

Judges of the circuit courts of appeal are not tax specialists; nevertheless, they collectively hear a significant number of tax cases every year. Hearings are typically conducted by a panel of three judges.

The Court of Appeals for the Federal Circuit

For many years the decisions of the Claims Court could be appealed only to the United States Supreme Court. Since 1984, however, those decisions are appealed to the Court of Appeals for the Federal Circuit. The significance of this court in tax matters is limited because of the relative infrequency of tax cases brought before it.

Supreme Court

The United States Supreme Court is the final judicial authority on all issues. Its decisions must be followed by all lower courts. Consequently, new tax legislation is sometimes required following a decision of the Supreme Court. The Court has one Chief Justice and eight Associate Justices.

Each year some 5000 cases are appealed to the Supreme Court. In a typical year it will agree to review about 200 of the 5000 cases. As noted earlier, the number of tax cases actually heard in an average year typically varies from six to eight. The entire Court ordinarily sits in judgment on all cases.

In summary, then, the tax law of the United States derives from three primary sources, namely, statutory, administrative, and judicial law. Because of the length and complexity of the Code itself—it currently is available from commercial sources in two volumes, with approximately 4000 pages of relatively fine print—and the large number of administrative and judicial interpretations required to interpret the Code, it is not surprising to discover that literally thousands of volumes of secondary authority have been published to compile, summarize, and/or explain the primary authorities.

Secondary Authorities

Secondary authorities in tax matters vary from highly reliable to virtually worthless. They represent a marketplace in which the maxim caveat emptor (let the buyer beware) prevails. Some of the most reliable secondary authorities are best described as "tax services." They bring together the Code and the related regulations, along with a synopsis of (and cross reference to) the more important administrative and judicial pronouncements on either a Code-section or a topically-oriented basis. They may also provide editorial comment. These tax services are available in both hard copy (i.e., printed volume) and via electronic transmission from computerized data bases.

The differences between, as well as the advantages and disadvantages of, the various tax services are both difficult to summarize and relatively subjective. Therefore, in the limited space available here, the author has elected to simply list those tax services that he has found most helpful on different occasions.

There are, of course, many additional secondary authorities in tax matters including some that could be classified as general-purpose legal services. In addition, there are hundreds of reference works, textbooks, periodicals, newsletters, and pamphlets intended to help a taxpayer understand the law of federal income taxation.

Printed Services

Common "Reference"	Actual Title	Publisher	General Organization
BNA	Tax Management	Tax Management, Inc. (Bureau of National Affairs)	Topic
CCH	Standard Federal Tax Reports	Commerce Clearing House	Code Section
Mertens	Mertens' Law of Federal Taxation	Callaghan & Co.	Topic
P-H	Federal Taxes	Prentice-Hall, Inc./ Research Institute of America	Code Section
RIA	Federal Tax Coordinator-2d	Research Institute of America	Topic

Electronic Services

Trade Name	Publisher
LEXIS	Meade Data, Inc.
PHINET	Prentice-Hall/Research Institute of America
WESTLAW	West Publishing Co. (a general legal data base)

Key Points to Remember

❏ The primary authority that governs most federal income tax issues is the Code—specifically The Internal Revenue Code of 1986—as amended. This statutory law is subject to constant interpretation by the Treasury Department and by various federal courts.

❏ A Code section number is the most common and appropriate reference concerning the law of federal income taxation. (Paperback copies of the Code can be purchased in campus bookstores, especially those located near large universities.)

❏ Most disputes between taxpayers and the Internal Revenue Service are resolved through relatively informal administrative proceedings. However, a smaller number proceed to formal litigation every year.

❑ There are three possible courts of original jurisdiction in federal income tax litigation: the Tax Court, a federal district court, or the Claims Court. The taxpayer controls which court will be utilized in any given dispute.
❑ If the meaning of a new tax provision is vague, tax experts may attempt to determine the intent of Congress in enacting that provision by reviewing the official documents that accompanied the proposed law through the legislative process.
❑ If the meaning of a tax provision enacted some years ago remains vague, its meaning can generally be determined by a thorough search of existing administrative and/or judicial law. That search is best made by a tax expert; however, an expert's findings and recommendations should be understandable to anyone who reads this text.

Appendix to Chapter 1

This appendix explains and illustrates the format of the more common citations to administrative and judicial interpretations of statutory tax law. It provides useful information for anyone trying to read or to locate technical tax publications.

Administrative Citations

Regulations are numbered in a distinctive manner consisting of at least three separate sets of numbers. The first set is separated from the second by a period or decimal point; the second set is separated from the third set by a dash. In conceptual fashion, these three parts of a citation to a regulation can be illustrated as shown in Exhibit 1.2.

The first set of numbers designates the nature or general subject matter of the regulation. The most frequently encountered first set of numbers can be summarized as follows:

Number	Designation
1	Income Tax
20	Estate Tax
25	Gift Tax
31	Employment Tax
48	Excise Tax
301	Administrative and procedural rules

The Law of U.S. Federal Income Taxation

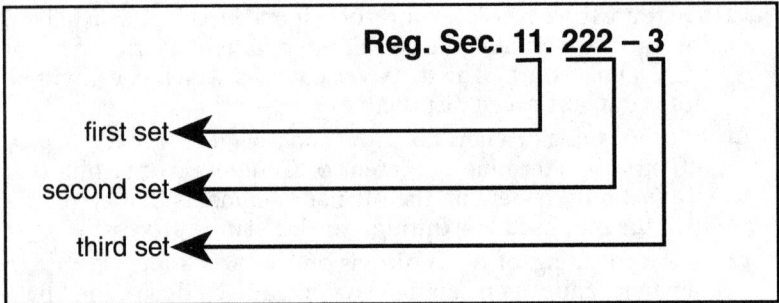

Exhibit 1.2   Citation to regulation

The second set of numbers refers directly to the statutory Code section being interpreted. The final set simply provides a numerical sequence for multiple regulations interpreting the same section. For example, a citation to Treas. Reg. Sec. 1.301-4 reveals immediately that it refers to the fourth (final) Regulation interpreting Section 301, an income tax provision. Proposed Reg. Sec. 301.6611-1, on the other hand, refers to the first (proposed) Regulation issued in the interpretation of Section 6611, providing some form of administrative or procedural rule.

Published revenue rulings (along with Temporary, Proposed, and final Regulations, and other administrative pronouncements) are first published in the weekly *Internal Revenue Bulletin*, cited IRB. The same pronouncements are subsequently republished by the Government Printing Office in a semiannual bound volume known as a *Cumulative Bulletin*, or CB. The citation to a published revenue ruling consists of two parts separated by a comma, the first providing a simple numbering system, the second a publication reference. Thus a citation to an imaginary Rev. Rul. 89-19, 1989-2 I.R.B. 6, would refer to the nineteenth published ruling issued in calendar year 1989, one that can be located beginning on page 6 of the second weekly IRB published in 1989. A later reference to this same imaginary ruling might refer to 1989-1 C.B. 30, suggesting that it now appears in the more permanent volume one of the 1989 *Cumulative Bulletin*, beginning on page 30.

Judicial Citations

Most judicial decisions on tax matters are published in one or more court reporter series. The standard format for a citation to a judicial decision consists of three distinct parts, in addition to the name of the litigant(s). The first set of numbers ordinarily designates a volume number; the letters that follow identify the reporter series; and the final numbers indicate the page on which the decision begins. To illustrate, consider the following imaginary citation:

Tax Essentials, Inc., 91 TC 302 (1989)

This imaginary case involves a dispute between a corporation named Tax Essentials, Inc., and the IRS Commissioner (the identity of the IRS Commissioner is implicit in a Tax Court case). The report of the decision can be found in volume 91 of the Tax Court Reporter beginning on page 302. The year of litigation is indicated in parentheses at the end of the citation. The most common court reporters in tax matters can be summarized as follows:

Abbreviation	*Reporter Series*	*Publisher*
TC[1]	Tax Court	Government Printing Office (GPO)
F. Supp.	Federal Supplement	West Publishing Co.
Cl. Ct.	Claims Court	GPO
F. 2d[2]	Federal Reporter,	West Publishing Co. 2d Series
U.S.	U.S. Supreme Court	GPO
S. Ct.	Supreme Court	West Publishing Co.
AFTR 2d[3]	American Federal Tax Reporter, 2d Series	Prentice-Hall, Inc./Research Institute of America
USTC	United States Tax Cases	Commerce Clearing House

1. Prior to 1942, the Tax Court was known as the Board of Tax Appeals, and the court reporter series was abbreviated BTA.
2. Prior to 1925 this series was designated simply as the Federal Reporter, Fed.
3. Prior to 1954, this was simply AFTR.

Because of competition between publishers, many decisions appear in more than one reporter series. Hence multiple citations to the same case are common. To illustrate, suppose that our imaginary corporation, Tax Essentials, Inc., lost its dispute in the Tax Court and appealed that decision to the Third Circuit Court of Appeals. A decision of the appellate court could be cited in the following manner:

Tax Essentials, Inc. v. Com'mr., 76 F.2d 614
(CA - 3, 1990), 43 AFTR 2d 149, 60 USTC 309

This citation suggests that you can read the identical decision in any one of three reporters—the F.2d, AFTR 2d, or USTC series—at your option. The duplication in citations is deemed to be a convenience to readers; i.e., they can locate and read a case in whatever reporter series is readily available.

For most recent years, the coverage of the various courts in the several reporter series can be summarized as follows:

Court	Reporter Series
Tax Court	TC only (except for "advance sheets" available in certain commercial tax services)
District Courts	F. Supp.; AFTR 2d; USTC
Circuit Courts of Appeals	F. 2d; AFTR 2d; USTC
Claims Court	Cl. Ct.; F.2d; AFTR 2d; USTC
Court of Appeals for the Federal Circuit	F.2d; AFTR 2d; USTC
U.S. Supreme Court	U.S.; S. Ct.; AFTR 2d; USTC

Citations to "memorandum" decisions of the Tax Court are to one of two separate reporter series. The Prentice-Hall (P-H) series of memorandum decisions is cited as P-H TCM; the Commerce Clearing House (CCH) series, as TCM. The formats of these two citations differ slightly from that suggested above for most other judicial decisions. An imaginary example will illustrate the differences:

John Doe, 1989 P-H TCM ¶88,101;
   T.C.M. 1988-1442

In the Prentice-Hall series the year in which the decision is rendered appears in lieu of a volume number, and a paragraph reference replaces a page number. In the CCH publication the year and page number are combined and follow the reference to the reporter series.

INCOME AS A TAX BASE

Virtually all economically developed countries impose some form of an income tax today. The relative dependence of various countries on that one tax varies, however, from a low of less than 20 percent of total tax revenues to a high of over 50 percent. Of the group, the United States is among the most reliant on income tax; we collect nearly half of all tax revenues from the income tax. The widespread use of income as a tax base is probably attributable to the facts that (1) it can produce relatively large amounts of government revenue; and (2) at the same time, it can be designed in a way that concurrently achieves a host of specified social and economic objectives. In other words, the income tax can both "pack a big wallop" and be finely tuned.

The fine-tuning of the income tax is most frequently achieved by changing the definition of **taxable income**. At some times and in some jurisdictions the statutory definition of income has been so contorted that the residual legal quantity subject to tax has only a minimal resemblance to the economic quantity called income, at least as that word is commonly understood by accountants, lawyers, and business persons generally.

The objective of this chapter is to explain the fundamental income concept that is utilized in the United States federal income tax. Chapter 2 is subdivided into three parts. The first part examines some of the more important definitional nuances implicit in the word "income." The second part elaborates on the realization criterion that importantly modifies the more general concept of income for tax purpose. The final part introduces certain recognition rules that further explain some of the many differences between income in general and taxable income in particular. Before there can be an income tax liability, a taxpayer must respond affirmatively to each of three distinct questions. They are:

1. Was there any *income*?
2. If so, was it *realized*?
3. If so, must it be *recognized* immediately?

Income as a Tax Base

Because a negative response to any one of these three questions relieves a taxpayer of any income tax liability, it is imperative that we define each of the three critical words—income, realization, and recognition—in an operational way. It is very important to note that the mere presence of income is not, by itself, sufficient to trigger an income tax; that consequence requires both realization and recognition as well.

Income: Definitional Issues

Economists, accountants, and lawyers frequently disagree on the meaning of the word "income." For tax purposes, however, it is imperative that we somehow resolve those differences because the Code very clearly imposes a tax on (taxable) **income**. The initially critical word is found in both Secs. 1 and 11, the two operative statutory provisions in the imposition of the federal income tax. They read (in part) as follows:

> Sec. 1: "There is hereby imposed on the taxable *income* of... (every individual)... a tax..." [emphasis added]
>
> and in Sec. 11: "A tax is hereby imposed for each taxable year on the taxable *income* of every corporation." [emphasis added]

The meaning of the adjective **taxable**, and its role in the modification of the noun *income*, is the heart of Chapter 3. For the moment we should concentrate our attention on the meaning of the word *income*.

Sections 61 through 67 (which constitute Part I of Subchapter B) purport to offer the definitions required in the computation of taxable income. Sec. 61, which defines **gross income**, is the conventional starting place. It reads in its entirety as follows:

Sec. 61.   Gross Income Defined.

(a) General Definition: Except as otherwise provided in this subtitle, gross income means all income from whatever source derived, including (but not limited to) the following items:

  (1) Compensation for services, including fees, commissions, fringe benefits, and similar items;
  (2) Gross income derived from business;
  (3) Gains derived from dealings in property;
  (4) Interest;
  (5) Rents;

(6) Royalties;
(7) Dividends;
(8) Alimony and separate maintenance payments;
(9) Annuities;
(10) Income from life insurance and endowment contracts;
(11) Pensions;
(12) Income from discharge of indebtedness;
(13) Distributive share of partnership gross income;
(14) Income in respect of a decedent; and
(15) Income from an interest in an estate or trust.

(b) Cross References: For items specifically included in gross income, see part II (sec. 71 and following). For items specifically excluded from gross income, see part III (sec. 101 and following).

As definitions go, this effort is sophomoric at best: it simply says that "income means all income." That is not, obviously, an operational definition.

In spite of its many shortcomings, a careful reading of the statutory definition of income found in Sec. 61 clearly supports the expansive interpretation given it by the various administrative and judicial authorities. Four critical phases are:

1. except as otherwise provided,
2. income means all income,
3. from whatever source derived, and
4. including (but not limited to).

Each of these four phases clearly supports the conclusion that, if you have any doubts, resolve them liberally. In other words, if something even remotely smells like income, you had better assume that it is income for tax purposes. If you follow this general rule, you will almost certainly be right more times than you are wrong.

So far, so good; but we still have not *defined* income. To get directly to the point, it is the author's personal conclusion that, for federal income tax purposes, the economist's traditional definition of income comes closer than any other to the definition of income followed by a majority of tax authorities. That definition postulates that **income is equal to any increase in net worth, between two moments in time, plus the value of any items consumed during that same time period**. This is, obviously, a very broad definition, a conclusion consistent with the general tenor of Sec. 61.

Income as a Tax Base

To illustrate the breadth of this definition, determine whether or not X has any income in each of the following ten scenarios:

1. X mows your lawn once for $20 cash.
2. X mows your lawn weekly for board and room all summer.
3. X finds a $20 bill on a city sidewalk.
4. X babysits your child in exchange for your promise to prepare X's tax return next April.
5. X buys your ring for $100 and quickly resells it for $150.
6. X discovers oil on his property; this discovery alone increased the value of X's property by $500,000.
7. X discovers buried ancient gold coins on his property; the coins are worth $500,000.
8. X buys your ring for $100 and promptly resells it for $100.
9. X borrows $500 from a bank.
10. X embezzles $200,000 from his employer.

If you apply the economist's traditional definition of income correctly, you will conclude that X has some amount of income in each of the first seven scenarios. X has no income in scenarios 8 and 9 because he has neither (1) an increase in net worth nor (2) consumed anything. (In scenario 9, X's liabilities increase by the same amount as his assets.) Scenario 10 is very difficult to call. On the one hand, X legally owes his employer the $200,000 that he has embezzled; hence X has no real increase in net worth and, until he spends some of it, has no consumption either. On the other hand, X probably has no intention of repaying his employer, hence the status of the liability is questionable.

When the Supreme Court was first presented with the essential facts of scenario 10, it concluded that X had no income. (See *Comm. v. Wilcox*, 327 U.S. 404 (1946).) This holding can obviously be viewed as one that "encourages" the antisocial behavior of embezzling. Largely for this reason, the Supreme Court several years later overturned its prior decision and concluded that proceeds of embezzlement do constitute gross income. (See *James v. U.S.*, 366 U.S. 313 (1961).)

The purpose of the ten examples is simply to get you (the reader) to think about the definition of income. The examples suggest that many things that one might reasonably question probably do constitute income for federal tax purposes. For example, this definition clearly implies that many employee fringe benefits, bartered rights, mere increases in property value, illegal gains, and "windfall" profits are all within the domain of income as that term is generally defined for U.S. federal income tax purposes. Item 10 on the list is included solely to illustrate how judicial decisions can and do extend and/or contract statutory provisions. Item 10 also illustrates why all general rules should be viewed with caution in practical applications. At least in tax matters, logic sometimes yields to reason.

To proceed, we must remember that the presence of income is only one of three necessary conditions to the creation of an income tax liability. Realization and recognition are also required.

The Concept of Realization

The economist's definition of income clearly has no realization requirement; that requirement derives largely from accounting and legal traditions. The statutory language of Sec. 61 does *not* patently demand realization; it provides only that income must be *derived*. (That is, Sec. 61—as quoted above—simply states that ". . . income means all income from *whatever source derived. . .*" [emphasis added].) There is, however, a long and impressive list of administrative and judicial authorities to support the conclusion that unrealized income will not immediately be subject to taxation. To investigate those authorities would lead us far from the primary objective of this book; we will, therefore, resist the temptation to undertake an interesting intellectual exercise in the annals of income taxation.

To state that realization is a necessary condition for taxation once again begs the critical definitional issue. What, exactly, does the word "realization" mean as used in this context? The outer boundary is obvious: If X buys common stock for $800 on February 3 and that common stock increases in value to $1000 by December 31, the $200 increase in value may represent income to X (because of the increase in net worth), but it most certainly will not be subject to tax until it has been realized.

Again, so far so good. But how can we operationally define the verb "to realize" for federal income tax purposes? To the best of the author's knowledge, no really helpful, authoritative, and brief definition exists. Therefore, he has coined his own definition as follows:

> For federal income tax purposes, realization appears to require: (1) a significant change in the form or the substance of a taxpayer's property or property rights and (2) the involvement of a second taxpayer.

The list of administrative and judicial authorities that have led the author to reach this conclusion must once again remain outside the confines of this "essentials" text. Although the intellectual exercise of

Income as a Tax Base

proving the author's postulate would be challenging, the ability to apply it is critical.

To test your understanding of the above definition of realization, reread scenarios 1 through 7 on page 26 and determine which of the seven satisfy the realization criterion of federal income taxation. If you apply the definition correctly, you will conclude that X realized some amount of income in every scenario except number 6. The change in property rights is readily apparent in all seven situations; the involvement of a second taxpayer in scenarios 3 and 7 is less obvious. A careful study of property law would support the conclusion that some (unidentified) person may also have certain rights to the $20 bill and the gold coins found by X. It is this difference that apparently justifies a different result between scenarios 6 and 7.

The author's definition of realization is, obviously, nothing more than a potentially useful general rule. Like all general rules, it has exceptions. The three exceptions that appear to have the greatest importance can be summarized as follows:

1. borrowing against (i.e., mortgaging) an appreciated property,
2. making a gift of an appreciated property, and
3. transferring an appreciated property at death.

In each of these three exceptions, the increase in the property value (i.e., the meaning of appreciated property) provides income as defined above. The change in the taxpayer's property rights is equally obvious in all three situations. And the involvement of the creditor, donee, and heir (or devisee) respectively, appears to satisfy the requirement of a second taxpayer. Nevertheless, in each of the above circumstances there is primary authority to support the conclusion that no income has been realized. Except for these three situations, the author believes that his definition of realization is operative. Incidentally, each of the three exceptions to the general rule embodies a tax planning opportunity.

Recall, however, that even if a taxpayer has realized a given amount of income, that still does not necessarily mean that the taxpayer must immediately pay an income tax. A third and final requirement must also be satisfied. It involves what tax experts refer to as "recognition" rules.

Recognition Rules

The verb to recognize, as used here, means to report for federal income tax purposes. In general, a taxpayer must recognize income for federal income tax purposes in whatever tax year it is realized. There are, however, three broad categories or classes of exceptions to this general rule. Income will not be recognized for tax purposes when it is realized if

1. the income has been specifically excluded by Congress from the income tax base,
2. the taxpayer properly reports the income in some other year following a method of accounting that is acceptable for tax purposes, or
3. the transaction is one that is subject to a special statutory "nonrecognition" rule.

Each of the three general classes of exception to the immediate-recognition rule will be introduced briefly in the remaining pages of this chapter and will be explained in greater detail in later chapters of this book.

Exclusions

The word **exclusions** in income tax parlance simply means those income items that Congress has deliberately elected not to tax. The correct presumption is that all income is taxable unless you can find good authority to exclude it. Fortunately, most of the statutory provisions that authorize an exclusion are neatly collected in Secs. 101 through 140; that is, in Part II of Subchapter B of the Code. This part is clearly titled as "Items Specifically Excluded from Gross Income." Among the statutory exclusions are interest on most state and local government bonds, gifts, bequests, life insurance proceeds, and a host of other items to be explained in greater detail in Chapter 3.

Accounting Methods

The Code specifically authorizes several different accounting methods including the cash method, the accrual method, the hybrid (part-cash, part-accrual) method, the percentage-of-completion method, and the installment method. If a taxpayer is concurrently engaged in more than one trade or business, a different accounting method may generally be used in each business. There are, however, numerous restrictions for certain taxpayers and varying circumstances that will be explained in greater detail in Chapter 5.

Income as a Tax Base

For the moment we need only understand why an accounting method rule may cause income to be recognized in some period other than that in which it was realized. Perhaps the easiest example to understand involves the sale of an investment asset by an individual taxpayer. Most individuals are cash-basis taxpayers. For tax purposes this means that they will report their routine items of income—such as salary, interest, rents, and dividends—whenever they are received in cash. It definitely does *not* mean that they have no income unless and until they receive some amount of cash. To emphasize this important conclusion, consider again the scenarios numbered 2 (lawn mowed for room and board), 4 (babysitting in return for tax preparation), and 7 (finding gold coins), earlier in this chapter. In each of those situations X would have to pay an immediate income tax on the "fair market value" of the income received. The fact that an item is difficult to value does not excuse a taxpayer from the need to pay the income tax. If it were not for this rule, a literal interpretation of the cash accounting method for income tax purposes would quickly convert a large part of even the most economically advanced nation into a barter economy overnight. In other words, if people could legally avoid taxation that easily, they would almost certainly do so en masse.

For all nonroutine items of income, a cash-basis taxpayer must generally report as income the "cash equivalent" or "fair market value" of any noncash income items received. Thus, if an individual were to sell or exchange an investment asset and realize a $5000 profit, that individual would generally have to report the entire profit immediately. If, however, the sale qualified under the installment sale provisions for tax purposes, then the taxpayer would be allowed to report the $5000 profit on a pro-rata basis, as the installments are received.

To illustrate, assume that a tract of land, which cost the taxpayer $20,000 four years ago, was sold today for $25,000. Income of $5000 would be realized immediately, without regard for payment details. If the sales contract called for $5000 down plus $10,000 payments (with interest) in each of the next two years, this sale might well qualify for the installment sale accounting method. If so, the taxpayer could report $1000—or 20 percent of the $5000 received (i.e., $5000 profit spread over the $25,000 sales price)—as income this year, and 20 percent of $10,000 (or $2000) as income in each of the next two years. In the event the sale does qualify as an installment sale, the individual taxpayer will have **realized** the entire $5000 profit this year, but will be authorized to **recognize** it over a period of three years. In summary, this example illustrates how accounting provi-

2.08 / *ESSENTIALS OF U.S. TAXATION*

sions may sometimes defer the **recognition** of some portion (or all) of the income that has been **realized** in the current year.

Nonrecognition Rules

In addition to the exclusion and accounting provisions, the Code also contains a significant number of statutory nonrecognition rules. Some of these provisions are neatly collected in Secs. 1031 through 1042—that is, in Part III of Subchapter 0, entitled "Common Nontaxable Exchanges"—while others are scattered throughout the Code. Because it is impossible to cover all of the nonrecognition rules in this book, the reader must rely on expert assistance for guidance in real-world situations. In Chapter 7 we attempt to alert the reader to the general circumstances most likely to trigger a nonrecognition provision.

When a nonrecognition rule does apply, the general intent is usually a mere postponement of recognition. In other words, if a taxpayer realizes a $100,000 gain today in a transaction that is subject to a nonrecognition rule, the probable result is that this $100,000 gain will simply be postponed until the taxpayer subsequently disposes of the property acquired in a taxable transaction. This result is accomplished through a basis adjustment, a procedure that will be better understood after reading Chapter 7.

To summarize, there can be no income tax unless and until a taxpayer

1. has income
2. that has been realized and
3. that must be recognized immediately.

Income can be operationally defined as an increase in net worth between two points in time *plus* consumption. Realization can generally be defined as any change in a taxpayer's property or property rights with the involvement of a second taxpayer. And recognition will be simultaneous with realization barring an exclusion provision, a special accounting rule, or a nonrecognition section.

Key Points to Remember

❑ Income is often defined very differently for financial accounting purposes than it is for federal income tax purposes.

Income as a Tax Base

- ❏ There can be no federal income tax liability unless
  1. Income is present;
  2. The income has been realized; and
  3. The income must be recognized immediately.
- ❏ Income can be defined as an increase in net worth between two moments in time plus the value of anything consumed during that same time period.
- ❏ Realization can be defined as a significant change in the form or the substance of a taxpayer's property or property right and the involvement of a second taxpayer.
- ❏ Subject to three major exceptions, income generally must be recognized for federal income tax purposes in whatever year it is realized. The major exceptions concern
  1. Exclusions;
  2. Accounting methods; and
  3. Special nontaxable exchange provisions.
- ❏ Gross income is assumed to include all items of income unless you can identify good authority for a contrary conclusion.

CALCULATING THE TAX LIABILITY

Every tax liability is determined by multiplying a tax rate by a tax base. In the case of the federal income tax, the tax base is a quantity known technically as **taxable income**. The emphasis in Chapter 2 was on the noun, *income*. In this chapter we will concentrate most of our attention on the meaning of the adjective, *taxable*. In other words, in this chapter we will examine the statutory provisions that first convert income, broadly conceived, into taxable income, and then examine how a taxpayer's actual tax liability for a year is calculated.

The four remaining steps used to determine an income tax liability can be stated very simply as follows:

Measure income broadly conceived

Step 1 *Subtract "exclusions"*
Equals gross income

Step 2 *Subtract "deductions"*
Equals taxable income

Step 3 *Multiply by the tax rate(s)*
Equals the gross tax liability

Step 4 *Subtract prepayments and credits*
Equals the net tax liability

The organization of Chapter 3 generally follows the steps in this outline. Because we completed our study of the general income concept in Chapter 2, the first major part of this chapter examines the exclusion provisions; the second part, deductions; the third part, tax rates; and the fourth part, prepayments and credits.

In this chapter we are not concerned with details that may become important at an entity level. This means that we will ignore, to the maximum extent possible, provisions that apply only to individual taxpayers, corporations, insurance companies, or any other special entity. The most important of those details will be covered in various other chapters, most notably in Chapters 4 and 6.

This overview of the tax calculation permits us to emphasize one very important aspect of the U.S. federal income tax. That is, there is really only one federal income tax, not two or three. Because of the way government revenues are reported and the way most college

Calculating the Tax Liability

textbooks approach the subject, many people come to believe that there are two separate income taxes—one, a tax on individuals, and the other, a tax on corporations. In actuality the Code makes no such distinction. Instead, it simply defines taxable income and then identifies three entities as taxpayers. The three taxable entities are individuals, corporations, and fiduciaries. Although some exclusion and deduction provisions are specifically restricted to one or two of these taxable entities, the vast majority of all Code sections apply equally to every taxpayer.

Exclusions

As noted in Chapter 2, the word *exclusion* means those items of income that Congress deliberately decided not to tax. Because the general presumption is that all income is subject to tax unless you can find statutory authority to exclude it, you are well advised to begin your study with a cursory review of the section titles found in Part III of Subchapter B, the subdivision of the Code that harbors most of the exclusion provisions. Those titles read as follows:

Sec. 101.	Certain death payments
Sec. 102.	Gifts and inheritance
Sec. 103.	Interest on state and local bonds
Sec. 104.	Compensation for injuries or sickness
Sec. 105.	Amounts received under accident and health plans
Sec. 106.	Contributions by employers to accident and health plans
Sec. 107.	Rental value of parsonages
Sec. 108.	Income from discharge of indebtedness
Sec. 109.	Improvements by lessee on lessor's property
Sec. 111.	Recovery of tax benefit items
Sec. 112.	Certain combat pay of members of the Armed Forces
Sec. 115.	Income of States, municipalities, etc.
Sec. 117.	Qualified scholarships
Sec. 118.	Contributions to the capital of a corporation
Sec. 119.	Meals or lodging furnished for convenience of employer
Sec. 120.	Amounts received under qualified group legal service plans
Sec. 121.	One-time exclusion of gain from sale of principal residence of individual who has attained age 55
Sec. 122.	Certain reduced uniform services retirement pay
Sec. 123.	Amounts received under insurance contracts for certain living expenses

Calculating the Tax Liability

Sec. 125.	Cafeteria plans
Sec. 126.	Certain cost-sharing payments
Sec. 127.	Educational assistance programs
Sec. 129.	Dependent Care Assistance programs
Sec. 130.	Certain personal injury liability assignments
Sec. 131.	Certain foster care payments
Sec. 132.	Certain fringe benefits
Sec. 133.	Interest on certain loans used to acquire employer securities
Sec. 134.	Certain military benefits
Sec. 135.	Income from United States Savings bond used to pay higher education tuition and fees
Sec. 136.	Cross reference to other Acts

Even a cursory reading of these titles reveals that many of the exclusion provisions are of limited scope. Four, for example, apply only to military personnel; one, to the clergy; one, to students.

The exclusion provisions of most widespread interest are those that apply to employee benefits. Because of these provisions, employees can receive a limited number of genuine economic benefits free of the federal income tax. Fortunately, as we will learn later in this chapter, the employer is generally able to deduct the cost of those same benefits. From a tax point of view, obviously, that is the best of all possible worlds. It has, in fact, been a primary reason for the incorporation of many small businesses. So long as owners operate their businesses as either a sole proprietorship or a partnership, the owners are not employees; they are, instead, the sole proprietor or partners of the business. Following incorporation, however, a corporation can hire its own stockholders and thereby make them employees as well as owners. The high-water mark in this tax scheme occurred in the decade of the 1960s when many professionals incorporated their various practices primarily to obtain the tax benefits of employee pension plans. Additional details on these and other employee benefits will be explained briefly in Chapter 10.

For now, simply note in passing some of the employee fringe benefits that can be excluded from gross income.

- Sec. 101 allows the heirs of a deceased employee to exclude up to a maximum of $5000 in certain "death benefits."
- Sec. 105 permits employees to exclude only certain payments received under a health and accident insurance plan. Excluded payments include payments for loss of a body member or body function; injury payments, so long as they are computed *with-*

out regard to the time an employee is absent from work; and medical expense reimbursements.
- Sec. 106 excludes from an employee's income the value of a health and accident insurance plan provided by the employer.
- Sec. 119 authorizes an employee to exclude the value of required meals and lodging provided on the employer's premises, for "substantial noncompensatory" business reasons, with no election to take cash or other property. Under the right circumstances, this provision can provide major tax benefits for owner-employees.
- Sec. 129 excludes up to $5000 worth of employer-provided care for an employee's dependents, under prescribed circumstances. Moreover, properly structured, this exclusion will also be available to self-employed individuals and to partners in a partnership.
- Sec. 132 allows employees to exclude from their gross income four kinds of fringe benefits. They are (1) no-additional-cost services; (2) qualified employee discounts; (3) working condition fringes; and (4) de minimis fringes. The definition of these statutory terms is best left for a handbook of current provisions.
- Sec. 125 authorizes an employer to give its employees the opportunity of picking and choosing from among several fringe benefits without losing the tax advantage.

A general requirement for virtually all excludible employee benefits is that they must be provided on a nondiscriminatory basis. In other words, if any employee benefit is restricted to owner-employees, to highly-compensated employees, or to any other subgroup of the rank-and-file of all employees, it cannot be wholly excluded.

Although most of the statutory exclusions are found in Secs. 101-135, a few are tucked away in other portions of the Code. Two of the less visible exclusions of general interest to employees are found in Secs. 79(a) and 911. Sec. 79(a) permits an employee to exclude from gross income employer-paid premiums on up to $50,000 in face value of *group-term life insurance*. And Sec. 911 authorizes an employee to exclude up to $70,000 of *foreign-source earned income per year*, if the taxpayer remains outside the U.S. for a sufficiently long period of time.

One exclusion provision that applies equally to all taxpayers is Sec. 103. It is the statutory authority permitting taxpayers to exclude from their gross income the interest received on state and local bonds. Note that the authority of Sec. 103 extends only to the interest on certain bonds, not to any gains attributable to increases in the value of those same bonds. The general exclusion of Sec. 103 is also subject to numerous restrictions in Secs. 141, 148, and 149. Those limitations apply to certain "private activity bonds," "arbitrage bonds," and "bearer bonds" issued by state and local governments—three subjects that must remain largely undefined in an "essentials" book. Suffice it to observe that the interest exclusion granted to state and local governments is partially proscribed when those governments attempt to act as an intermediary supplier of capital for largely private investment projects.

Four of the exclusion provisions of general business interest are Secs. 108, 109, 111, and 118. They can be summarized as follows:

- Sec. 108 generally permits a taxpayer to exclude a reduction in debt from gross income if it occurred in a title 11 case (a special bankruptcy provision) or if the taxpayer is insolvent. This section goes on, however, to cause a taxpayer to reduce certain beneficial tax attributes—such as depreciable basis in property, loss carryovers, and business credits—by an amount equal to the exclusion.

- Sec. 109 allows a lessor to exclude from income the value of any improvements made on a leased property, so long as the improvements are not made in lieu of rents.

- Sec. 111 authorizes a taxpayer to exclude from gross income the recovery of any item deducted in a previous year, but *only to the extent* that the deduction was of no tax benefit in that earlier year. To illustrate, suppose that a taxpayer deducted $18,000 last year but, because of some limit on that deduction, only $12,000 of the deduction was effectively utilized to reduce last year's tax liability. If this year the taxpayer were to recover $10,000 of the $18,000 deducted last year, $6,000 (of the $10,000 recovered) could be excluded under Sec. 111 because it was of no tax benefit.

- Sec. 118 excludes capital contributions made to a corporation from gross income. In general this section applies to capital contributions from nonshareholders; Sec. 1032 applies to contributions from shareholders, at least those made in exchange for stock. Sec. 118 would, for example, exclude a governmental grant made to a corporation as part of a business-inducement plan. As with Sec. 108, however, the corporation must generally reduce the depreciable basis of assets by the amount excluded under Sec. 118.

Calculating the Tax Liability

Two final observations concerning exclusions are necessary. First, the exclusion of gifts and inheritances in Sec. 102 does not extend to any income earned on a gift or an inheritance. Furthermore, it is often very difficult to distinguish between a true gift and disguised compensation. Whether a transfer is in fact a gift is supposed to turn on the true intention of the donor, and the courts have not hesitated to look through the form of many apparent gifts to determine their true substance. If an alleged donor has any kind of business relationships with an alleged donee, the likelihood increases greatly that a purported gift will be recast as compensation for services rendered.

The arithmetic difference between a taxpayer's income (broadly conceived) and exclusions is technically known as **gross income**. This residual quantity has only limited significance in tax matters. However, it is the quantity that determines whether or not individual taxpayers have to file a return. As explained in Chapter 9, individuals with a sufficiently small gross income need never file a return. The next major step in the tax formula involves the subtraction of deductions.

Deductions

Deductions in U.S. tax law are a matter of legislative grace. In other words, **nothing is deductible in the absence of specific statutory authority permitting it**. Note that this conclusion is directly contrary to the general rule suggested earlier for income. Income taxation is definitely a heads-we-win, tails-you-lose proposition. This dour observation notwithstanding, the tax process is really not grossly unfair because of a few deduction provisions of very broad scope. Secs. 161 through 196 (i.e., Part VI of Subchapter B) contain most of the deduction provisions that are equally applicable to all taxpayers; Secs. 211 through 220 (or Part VII of Subchapter B) harbor a few additional deduction provisions for individual taxpayers only. We will cover the former set here and the latter in Chapter 6. The section titles in the former group read as follows:

Sec. 165.	Losses
Sec. 166.	Bad debts
Sec. 167.	Depreciation
Sec. 168.	Accelerated cost recovery system
Sec. 169.	Amortization of pollution control facilities
Sec. 170.	Charitable, etc., contributions and gifts
Sec. 171.	Amortizable bond premium
Sec. 172.	Net operating loss deduction

Calculating the Tax Liability

Sec. 173.	Circulation expenditures
Sec. 174.	Research and experimental expenditures
Sec. 175.	Soil and water conservation expenditures
Sec. 176.	Payments with respect to employees of certain foreign corporations
Sec. 178.	Amortization of cost of acquiring a lease
Sec. 179.	Election to expense certain depreciable assets
Sec. 180.	Expenditures by farmers for fertilizer, etc.
Sec. 183.	Activities not engaged in for profit
Sec. 184.	Amortization of certain railroad rolling stock
Sec. 186.	Recoveries of damages for antitrust violations, etc.
Sec. 188.	Amortization of certain expenditures for child care facilities
Sec. 190.	Expenditures to remove architectural and transportation barriers to the handicapped and elderly
Sec. 192.	Contributions to black lung benefit trusts
Sec. 193.	Tertiary injectants
Sec. 194.	Amortization of reforestation expenditures
Sec. 194A.	Contributions to employer liability trusts
Sec. 195.	Start-up expenditures
Sec. 196.	Deduction for certain unused business credits

Although these 30-plus sections cover most of the garden-variety deduction provisions, the Code is replete with additional sections that sometimes contract, and otherwise often modify, these basic rules.

Sec. 162 is almost certainly the statutory deduction provision of most general interest. Subsection 162(a) reads in part as follows:

> There shall be allowed as a deduction all of the ordinary and necessary expenses paid or incurred during the taxable year in carrying on any trade or business, including
>
> 1. a reasonable allowance for salaries or other compensation for personal services actually rendered;
> 2. traveling expenses (including amounts expended for meals and lodging other than amounts which are lavish or extravagant under the circumstances) while away from home in the pursuit of a trade or business; and
> 3. rentals or other payments required to be made as a condition to the continued use or possession, for purpose of the trade or business, of property to which the taxpayer has not taken or is not taking title or in which he has no equity.

The variety of expenditures that can qualify as a tax deduction under the authority of this one subsection alone is obviously very broad. On the other hand, the courts and administrative interpretations that limit the outer boundaries of this provision in the more egregious tax schemes are legion. Observe that expenses are not deductible under the authority of Sec. 162(a) unless they are

1. ordinary,
2. necessary, and
3. incurred in a trade or business.

Furthermore, salaries must be "reasonable in amount" and travel expenses *cannot* be "lavish or extravagant." These highly subjective, limiting, statutory words and phrases provide ample opportunity for administrative and judicial authorities to disallow a taxpayer's questionable deductions. For individual taxpayers the trade-or-business requirement is a major hurdle. Attempts to disguise expensive hobbies as trades or businesses are usually futile. Many part-time, profitable activities also fail this requirement when tested in the courts. In general, an intent to profit and some entrepreneurial effort are required; the involvement of a reasonable number of external parties is also helpful. The actuality of profit is not mandatory. Facts and circumstances in each particular case govern the results. Although corporations are generally presumed to be engaged in a trade or business, that conclusion is not guaranteed.

The effect of the numerous official interpretations of the Code is sometimes to give common words an uncommon meaning. For example, "ordinary" (as used in Sec. 162(a)) does not mean frequent or commonplace. Rather, it is interpreted to mean that other taxpayers in similar circumstances—even if only in once-in-a-lifetime occurrences—would behave similarly. And "home" (in Sec. 162(a)(2)) generally has been interpreted to mean a taxpayer's primary place of business; not one's castle for sleeping and eating.

In addition to numerous definitional nuances, some deduction sections are replete with explicit internal limitations. Sec. 163 is an excellent example. The one-sentence general rule of Sec. 163(a) appears to authorize the deduction of virtually all interest expense. It reads as follows:

> There shall be allowed as a deduction all interest paid or accrued within the taxable year on indebtedness.

Subsequent subdivisions of this authorizing section then proceed to limit severely the deduction of interest expense in a variety of circumstances. The following partial list is exemplary:

Calculating the Tax Liability

- Sec. 163(b)(2) limits interest deductions in certain installment purchases.
- Sec. 163(d) limits interest on debts incurred to purchase or carry properties held for investment purposes.
- Sec. 163(e) limits interest deriving from "original issue discount" on certain securities.
- Sec. 163(f) limits interest on certain obligations not in registered form.
- Sec. 163(g) limits interest on debt with respect to which a mortgage credit certificate was issued under section 25.
- Sec. 163(h) separately limits the deduction of "personal interest" and "qualified residence interest."

To make matters even worse, other sections proceed to place even further restrictions on the deduction of interest expense. For example:

- Sec. 263(f) limits interest on debt incurred to produce certain inventory items.
- Sec. 265(a)(2) limits interest on debt incurred or continued to purchase or carry investments which produce tax-exempt income.
- Sec. 279 limits interest on debt incurred by one corporation to acquire the stock or assets of another corporation.
- Sec. 312(n)(1)(B) limits "construction period" interest.

And, unfortunately, this list goes on and on. We *cannot*, obviously, define in this "essentials" book even the relatively few critical words and phrases in this one paragraph pertinent to interest expense only. That task must be left for numerous other volumes to be found in a professional tax library. We can only note that the statutory general rules that authorize deductions must be read with a great deal of care, even by tax experts.

As a general observation you should observe that all of the costs incurred by any taxpayer during a year must be analyzed for their federal income tax effect. The various possible results are illustrated in the decision tree of Exhibit 3.1. Taxpayers prefer to move to the lower branches of this decision tree as quickly as possible, *other things being equal*. Although the concept is simple, application of this cost-classification system for tax purposes is complex because of the diversity of primary authorities needed to classify real-world events correctly in this purely legal taxonomy. Those persons who attempt to apply the concept should always keep uppermost in mind the adage

ESSENTIALS OF U.S. TAXATION / 3.09

Calculating the Tax Liability

that nothing is deductible in the absence of valid authority to the contrary.

The arithmetic difference between a taxpayer's "gross income" and "deductions" is technically known as "taxable income." This quantity is of major importance because it represents the ultimate tax-rate base, which, when multiplied by the tax rate, yields the taxpayer's gross tax liability for the year.

Tax Rates

The federal income **tax rates** in the United States have at least three fundamentally important characteristics. They are:

1. The tax rates are applied in a unitary rather than a schedular manner.
2. There are six different statutory tax rate structures; four for individual taxpayers and one each for corporate and fiduciary taxpayers.
3. The tax rates are, in general, progressive for taxpayers reporting lesser amounts of taxable income and proportional for taxpayers reporting greater amounts of taxable income.

These particular characteristics of U.S. income tax rates are designated as ones of fundamental importance because they are motivating factors in many tax-planning models.

Income tax systems can be classified as unitary or schedular. Unitary systems purport to tax all income, from various sources, in the same way. In other words, in a pure unitary system, income is income is income. In a schedular system, on the other hand, income is deliberately classified by "sources" or "kinds" of income, and each separately identified "kind" of income is subject to a different set of tax rates (or tax schedules). In general, the English- and Germanic-language countries tend to utilize a unitary system; Romance-language countries, a schedular system. The number of schedules varies greatly among nations. Separate tax rate schedules have been created in some jurisdictions for income from wages, salaries and other personal compensation; interest, dividends and rents; mining and manufacturing; farming; etc.

Although the United States purports to have a unitary system, it is not a pure one. For example, we previously noted that interest from certain state and local bonds is tax-exempt. Hence that exclusion could be deemed to constitute a schedule separate from all other

Calculating the Tax Liability

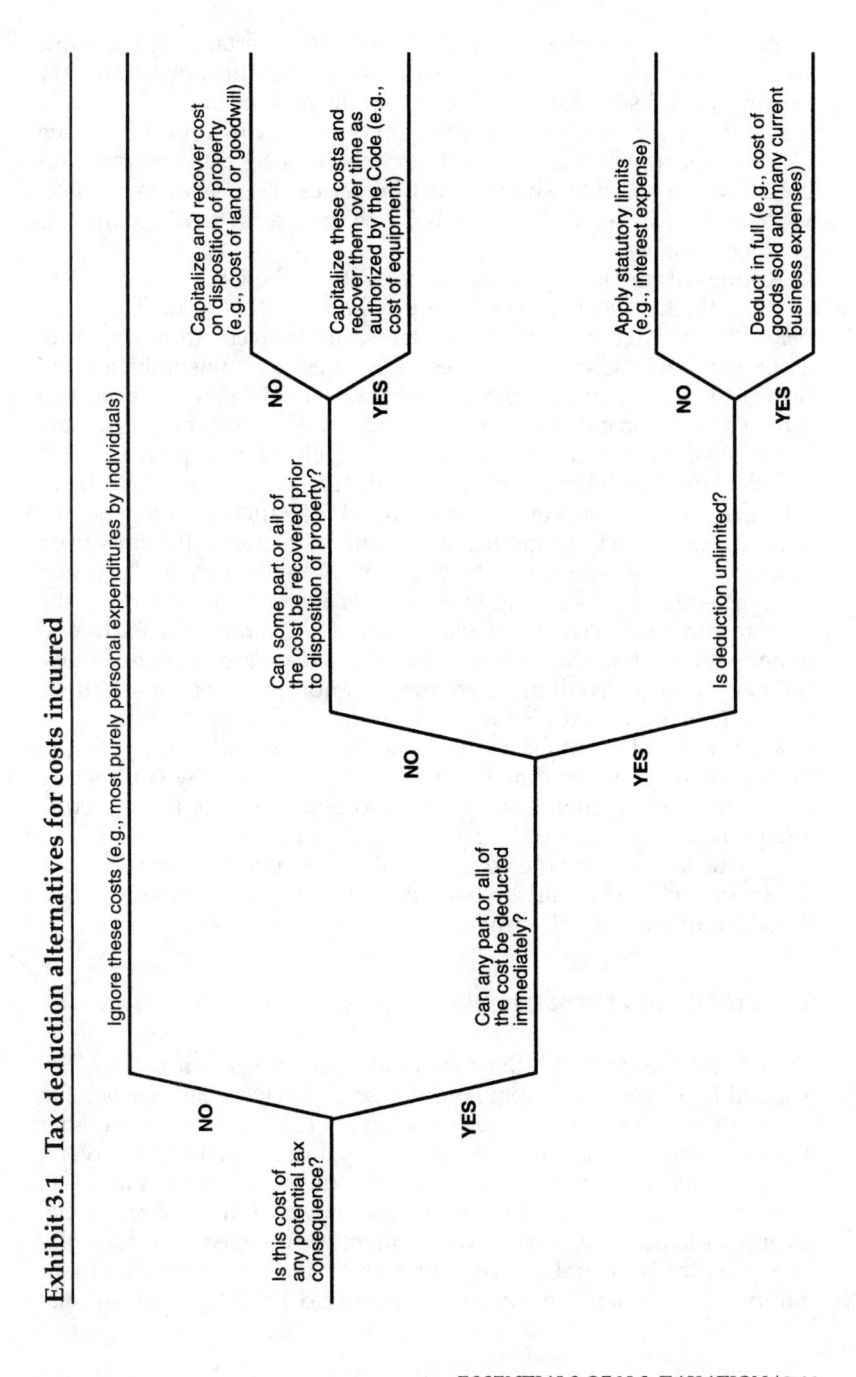

Exhibit 3.1 Tax deduction alternatives for costs incurred

Is this cost of any potential tax consequence?
- **NO** → Ignore these costs (e.g., most purely personal expenditures by individuals)
- **YES** → Can any part or all of the cost be deducted immediately?
  - **NO** → Can some part or all of the cost be recovered prior to disposition of property?
    - **NO** → Capitalize and recover cost on disposition of property (e.g., cost of land or goodwill)
    - **YES** → Capitalize these costs and recover them over time as authorized by the Code (e.g., cost of equipment)
  - **YES** → Is deduction unlimited?
    - **NO** → Apply statutory limits (e.g., interest expense)
    - **YES** → Deduct in full (e.g., cost of goods sold and many current business expenses)

ESSENTIALS OF U.S. TAXATION / **3.11**

Calculating the Tax Liability

income. In the years between 1922 and 1986, certain capital gains were also given very special treatment in our purported unitary system. That distinction could return in the near future.

Although U.S. tax law generally ignores any differences between kinds or sources of income, it deliberately imposes different tax rates on corporations, individuals, and fiduciaries. The tax rates on individuals are further differentiated by marital and family status, as explained in Chapter 4.

At present, the lowest marginal tax rate in the United States is 15 percent; the highest (effective) marginal rate is 39 percent. The number of "steps" in the progressive rates varies between three and four, as explained in Chapter 4. These tax rates are unusually low, in historical perspective, for the United States. In 1985 the top marginal rate was 50 percent; in 1980, 70 percent. The current rates were instituted as part of the Tax Reform Act of 1986. That major revision in U.S. tax law is well known for (1) a major broadening of the tax base, (2) a general reduction in tax rates, and (3) a reduction in the income tax collected from individuals, offset with increased collections from corporations. Although the 1986 act was intended to be "revenue neutral"—i.e., it was intended to neither increase nor decrease the total revenue collected from the income tax overall—the early evidence suggests that the real net result was a decrease in tax revenues. Because of the shortfall in federal tax revenues, many people believe that an increase in taxes is inevitable after the 1992 elections.

Regardless of what happens in future years, all taxpayers can determine their net income tax liability for any year by subtracting credits and prepayments from their gross tax liability. If the credits and prepayments exceed the gross tax liability, a refund check will be sent to the taxpayer by the government. In the reverse circumstances, the taxpayer must remit the balance due to the government. Additional compliance details are noted in Chapter 9.

Tax Credits and Prepayments

Tax credits are direct (dollar-for-dollar) reductions in a tax liability granted by Congress to taxpayers for some very special reason. Tax deductions, on the other hand, reduce a tax liability by some smaller amount—the precise amount being dependent on the taxpayer's marginal tax rate; i.e., the deduction *multiplied* by the marginal rate *equals* the tax reduction. Tax credits are usually intended as special incentives to cause taxpayers to do something deemed either socially or economically desirable. **Prepayments**, on the other hand, are mandatory advance deposits against a current tax liability. Conventional wisdom holds that many taxpayers would be unable to meet their annual income tax obligations in the absence of the pay-as-you-earn provisions that mandate tax prepayments.

Tax Credits

For several years prior to 1986, the Code authorized an **investment tax credit** (ITC). The ITC was an inducement for taxpayers to purchase certain productive equipment deemed essential to an increase in national output and employment. It was by far the largest and most important tax credit in recent years. Although the ITC provisions were repealed in 1986, some taxpayers still have investment tax credit carryforwards from years prior to 1986. These excess credits arose because of maximum annual credit limitations in earlier years.

The provisions governing current tax credits are generally found in Part IV of Subchapter A of the Code (i.e., in Secs. 21 through 53). That part includes the following seven subparts:

Subpart A. Nonrefundable personal credits
- Sec. 21. Expenses for household and dependent care services necessary for gainful employment
- Sec. 22. Credit for the elderly and the permanently and totally disabled
- Sec. 23. Residential energy credit
- Sec. 26. Limitation based on tax liability; definition of tax liability

Subpart B. Foreign tax credit, etc.
- Sec. 27. Taxes of foreign countries and possessions of the United States; possession tax credit
- Sec. 28. Clinical testing expenses for certain drugs for rare diseases or conditions
- Sec. 29. Credit for producing fuel from a nonconventional source

Subpart C. Refundable credits
- Sec. 31. Tax withheld on wages
- Sec. 32. Earned income
- Sec. 33. Tax withheld of source on nonresident aliens and foreign corporations
- Sec. 34. Certain uses of gasoline and special fuels
- Sec. 35. Overpayments of tax

Calculating the Tax Liability

    Subpart D. Business related credits

        Sec. 38. General business credit
        Sec. 39. Carryback and carryforward of unused credits
        Sec. 40. Alcohol used as fuel
        Sec. 41. Credit for increasing research activities
        Sec. 42. Low-cost housing credit

    Subpart E. Rules for computing credit for investment in certain depreciable property

        Sec. 46. Amount of credit
        Sec. 47. Certain dispositions, etc., of section 38 property
        Sec. 48. Definitions; special rules
        Sec. 49. Termination of regular percentage

    Subpart F. Rules for computing targeted job credit

        Sec. 51. Amount of credit
        Sec. 52. Special rules

    Subpart G. Credit against regular tax for prior year minimum tax liability

        Sec. 53. Credit for prior year minimum tax liability

Once again, even a cursory reading of subpart and section titles can be instructive. Observe, for example, that (in Sec. 31) the Code treats at least some prepayments as credits. Although the mechanical effect of these two tax adjustments is virtually identical, in concept they are different; hence they are discussed separately in this text. Observe also that some credits (e.g., those in Subpart C) are refundable—that is, they will actually be paid to the taxpayer if these tax credits exceed the taxpayer's gross tax liability; some (e.g., those in Subpart A) apply only to individual taxpayers; some (e.g., those in Subpart B) are of interest only to those engaged in multinational commerce; some (e.g., Secs. 21, 22, 28, 42, and 51) are of largely social concern; and some (e.g., Secs. 23, 41, and 46) are of largely economic orientation.

The details of the various credits are best left to longer volumes written for very different purposes. The general outline of the more important credits can be summarized as follows:

- Sec. 21 authorizes a tax credit of up to $1440 per year for taxpayers who incur expenses for the care of either children under 15 or an incapacitated dependent of any age, so that the parent(s) might either work or attend school full time.

Calculating the Tax Liability

- Sec. 27 permits a taxpayer to claim a credit for any foreign income tax paid in an amount not to exceed the U.S. income tax on the taxpayer's foreign-source income.
- Sec. 32 allows taxpayers who earn relatively low incomes, while supporting a child, to claim a credit of approximately $900 or less each year. This refundable credit is intended both to encourage employment and to reduce the effect of substantial social security taxes on low-income earners.
- Sec. 38 does not authorize any unique tax credit by itself. Rather, it provides a set of rules that apply commonly to five other business-related credits determined under Secs. 40, 41, 42, 46, and 51.
- Sec. 41 and 51 have several times in the past been allowed to expire and then been retroactively reenacted or extended with relatively minor alterations. Their original purpose was (1) to increase business investment in research and (2) to encourage the employment of the hard-core unemployed, respectively. Both causes are of current political interest, and it is unlikely that they will be allowed to permanently expire in the near future.
- Sec. 42 authorizes a credit of varying amounts for taxpayers who construct or rehabilitate housing units leased to low-income families. The requirements that qualify a taxpayer to claim this credit are both numerous and cumbersome.
- Sec. 46 includes a provision authorizing a tax credit of up to 20 percent of the amount expended to rehabilitate specified older buildings and certified historical structures. It is, obviously, intended to arrest urban decay.
- Sec. 53 is a unique credit of concern only to those taxpayers who are required to pay the alternative minimum tax—a subject explained briefly in Chapter 10.

Except for the foreign tax credit—which is required to avoid the multiple taxation of a single income stream earned by certain U.S. taxpayers outside the United States—most tax credits are of dubious value. There is no clear evidence to support the conclusion that tax credits achieve their intended objectives in a more efficient manner than alternative options, such as direct government support of the intended results. The credits appear, however, to be politically popular. The future of some tax credits, therefore, seems reasonably secure in spite of the unnecessary complexity that they add to an already difficult Code.

ESSENTIALS OF U.S. TAXATION / 3.15

Tax Prepayments

Individual taxpayers who earn nearly all of their annual income in the form of wages and salaries achieve their **tax prepayments** through a withholding system. This system requires an employer to withhold from an employee's wages an amount that will, at the end of the year, closely approximate the employee's gross tax liability. A series of IRS forms and tables have been developed to facilitate the implementation of the withholding system. In general, employers are required to immediately transfer to the government any amounts withheld as taxes. This both reduces any incentive to over-withhold and minimizes the risk of an employer's misappropriation of funds.

Self-employed individuals, corporations, and fiduciaries achieve their prepayments through a system of quarterly prepayments. These taxpayers must estimate their gross tax liability for each year and make four advance deposits throughout the year to reflect their estimated gross tax liability. Because of the interest and penalties assessed for significant underestimation, there is no incentive for noncompliance. And, because the government does not pay interest for advance deposits in excess of the actual liability, there is no incentive for overestimation either.

Critics of the income tax frequently argue that the prepayment system is socially undesirable because it tends to mask the real size of a taxpayer's annual gross tax liability by substituting a series of small payments each payday for one large payment at the end of each year. These critics argue that voters would not be so tolerant of government spending if they were more aware of how much income tax they really pay. Whether or not the conclusion is correct, there is little doubt but that the average employee thinks and acts in terms of take-home pay, rather than in terms of gross salary. Those taxpayers who make quarterly estimated payments are generally more aware of their actual tax liability.

Income tax prepayments can also be generated from excess social security tax payments made by the employee. Employees who work for more than one employer during a year, and who earn in total an amount in excess of the maximum social security tax base, can claim their excess social security tax payments as an income-tax credit. The excess payments attributable to the *employers'* matching payments are, however, not creditable to either the employee or the employer.

This concludes our overview of the general tax calculation procedure for all taxpayers. The next chapter will explain how various business and legal entities are integrated into the income tax system.

Calculating the Tax Liability

Key Points to Remember

- ❏ Income in general less exclusions equals gross income.
- ❏ Gross income less deductions equals taxable income.
- ❏ Taxable income times the tax rate(s) equals the gross tax liability.
- ❏ The gross tax liability less prepayments and tax credits equals the net tax liability.
- ❏ Exclusions are those items of income that Congress has specifically exempted from income taxation.
- ❏ Nothing is deductible in the absence of statutory authority permitting it.
- ❏ In general all ordinary and necessary expenses incurred in a trade or business are deductible.
- ❏ Not every activity undertaken with an intent to profit is deemed to constitute a trade or business for tax purposes.
- ❏ The United States income tax rates are progressive at least for those taxpayers reporting relatively modest amounts of taxable income.
- ❏ The United States income tax is, in general, a unitary tax. This means that all kinds of income are generally subject to the same tax rate(s).

TAXPAYERS AND TAX RATES

In Chapter 3 we noted that the United States imposes one federal income tax on three different taxable entities. In this chapter we will both (1) investigate additional details concerning the taxation of the three taxable entities and (2) learn how the income earned by other entities is taxed.

Before we investigate any entity-level detail, we should observe that the U.S. income tax is a **global** tax. This means that, in general, U.S. taxpayers are subject to tax on their worldwide income. Many other countries impose only a **territorial** income tax. In these countries taxpayers pay the local income tax only on that portion of their income that is derived from local sources. In the absence of some relief provision, it would appear that U.S. taxpayers would be taxed on foreign income twice; once by the government in whose territory the income was earned and again by the U.S. government. The foreign tax credit, a credit against the U.S. income tax allowed for foreign taxes paid on income taxable by the U.S., eliminates the double taxation that would otherwise occur.

Both global and territorial systems require the specification of source rules. The need for source rules is obvious for the territorial tax since the source determines what jurisdiction will tax the income. But the source rules are also of great importance to a global tax system like that of the U.S. for two reasons. First, income taxable by the U.S. is eligible for the foreign tax credit only if it is, under U.S. rules, *foreign-source* income. Second, the foreign tax credit available to a taxpayer is limited to the amount of domestic tax that would be payable on an amount equivalent to the foreign-source income. The net result of these conditions is to cause foreign-source income to be taxed at the higher of the U.S. income tax rate or the foreign income tax rate and to preclude the use of foreign taxes to offset the U.S. tax due on domestic source income. That is, if the foreign tax paid is $20 and the U.S. tax on the same amount of income would be $35, the taxpayer will pay $15 to the U.S. But if the foreign tax paid is $40 and the U.S. tax on that income would be $35, no further tax is paid to the U.S. and the additional amount of tax paid to the foreign government cannot be used to offset U.S. taxes due on domestic sources of income. The primary U.S. source rules are found in Sec. 861 and the related

Treasury regulations, particularly Reg. Sec. 1.861-8 (popularly known as the "dash-eight" regulations). Because this is an "essentials" text, we must once again forego an investigation of these interesting provisions and concentrate our attention on other details of more general interest.

The details considered in this chapter are organized in five major parts. The first three parts are concerned with the three taxable entities: individual, corporate, and fiduciary taxpayers. Part four is a discussion of the taxation of income initially earned by other business entities. Chapter 4 ends with a brief examination of two major entity-related problems: one involves definitional questions; the other concerns the correct identification of the taxpayer in more complex circumstances.

Individual Taxpayers

The wording of Sec. 1 is important for at least two reasons. First, it imposes the income tax on **every individual**. Second, it establishes different tax rates for each of four separately defined classes of individual taxpayers, namely, (1) married persons filing joint returns, (2) heads of households, (3) unmarried individuals, and (4) married individuals filing separate returns.

The fact that Sec. 1 imposes a tax on *every individual* is significant because that terminology totally negates such potentially important social factors as age, mental capacity, and citizenship. Although the U.S. law generally does ignore all three of these (and other) factors to the maximum extent possible, a number of special provisions have been enacted to address social factors in the more extreme cases. Legal guardians are responsible for filing the tax returns of individuals incapable of self-compliance, but the taxpaying entity remains the individual, not some other combination of individuals such as the family unit. This means, obviously, that any income earned by either an infant or a mentally incompetent individual must be reported on the tax return filed on behalf of that person and must include only the income, deduction, and credit items properly attributed to him or her. In some instances it is easier to identify the existence of income than it is to identify the correct taxpayers. These issues will be examined in greater detail at the end of Chapter 4.

Questions of citizenship pose a fundamentally different set of problems. Although it is easy for the U.S. government to declare that every individual is subject to the U.S. income tax, gaining legal jurisdiction and enforcing that declaration on nonresident aliens (in particular) is virtually impossible. U.S. citizens (regardless of where they live) and resident aliens are more easily taxed. To put it simply, one cost inevitably associated with both U.S. citizenship and U.S. residence is the cost of the U.S. income tax on an individual's worldwide income. Since the United States cannot obtain jurisdiction over nonresident aliens not engaged in a U.S. trade or business, it must satisfy itself with a more crude form of income taxation on that set of individuals. In general, they pay the U.S. income tax only on the passive income that they derive from U.S. sources. Jurisdiction is achieved by making the person who pays the passive income to the nonresident alien a withholding agent of the U.S. government. If the U.S. payor of passive income fails to withhold, the payor becomes liable for any tax due from the nonresident. In general, this tax is imposed at a flat 30 percent rate on gross income to further facilitate collection. This statutory rate is stated in Sec. 871(a); it is frequently overridden by tax treaty provisions and/or other statutory provisions. For example, Sec. 871(b) imposes a progressive tax rate on the taxable income of any nonresident alien that is "effectively connected with the conduct of a trade or business within the United States." The several critical words and phrases in this section present major definitional questions that must remain outside the scope of this book. In general, however, the reader should observe that the U.S. taxation of multinational income is substantially modified by the provisions of Subchapter N.

Individual citizens and resident aliens are generally subject to the tax rates provided in Subsections 1(a) through 1(d). Originally the U.S. tax law provided only one set of tax rates for all individual taxpayers, excluding nonresident aliens. Because of the effect of the community property laws on the tax liabilities of residents of certain states, however, Congress created two tax rate schedules for individuals in 1948. For several years thereafter the tax rate brackets for married individuals—i.e., the predecessor of those now found in Sec. 1(a)—were exactly twice as wide as those for single individuals. This design in tax rates negated the income-splitting tax benefits associated with community-property laws. That innovative solution to a tax-equity problem proved to be politically unacceptable, however, because of major differences in the gross tax liability of married versus single persons earning the same amount of income. Individuals who lost a spouse due to death or divorce, but who were left with other family responsibilities, were particularly hard hit by this arrangement. To resolve that problem, Congress created the head-of-household tax rates in 1951. Those rates are now found in Sec. 1(b). In response to the continuing concerns of other single individuals, Congress again adjusted the rate brackets in 1969 and, since then, the United States has continuously had four different tax rate schedules for individual taxpayers.

Taxpayers and Tax Rates

Each of these four schedules, however, follows a common pattern. Each taxes some relatively small amount of taxable income at a 15 percent rate, a second higher segment of income at 28 percent, and taxes all additional income at 31 percent. The only difference between the four schedules is the precise dollar amount of taxable income at which the tax rates increase from 15 to 28 to 31 percent. The general pattern is illustrated in Exhibit 4.1. The point at which the marginal rate increases from 15 to 28 percent and from 28 to 31 percent varies slightly from year to year because of tax rate adjustments necessitated by changes in the consumer price index (CPI). The *approximate* points can be summarized currently as follows:

Levels at Which Higher Rates First Apply to Income

	Married Filing Jointly	Heads of Households	Unmarried Persons	Married Filing Separately
For 1992:				
28% of income over	$35,800	$28,750	$21,450	$17,900
31% of income over	86,500	74,150	51,900	43,250
For 1991:				
28% of income over	$34,000	$27,300	$20,350	$17,000
31% of income over	82,150	70,450	49,300	41,075

Exhibit 4.1 General pattern of individual tax rates.

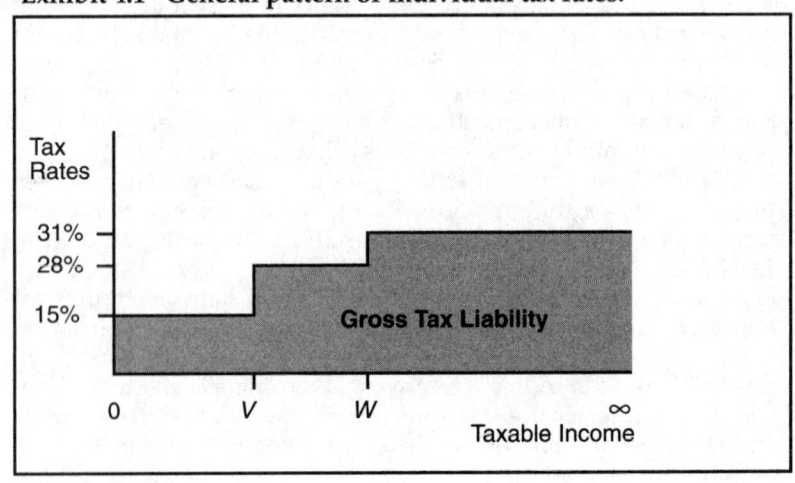

4.04 / *ESSENTIALS OF U.S. TAXATION*

In other words, the distance OV in Exhibit 4.1 is $35,800 for married individuals who file joint returns; approximately $28,750 for heads of households, etc. Readers who are interested in either (1) the precise points at which this change in tax rates occurs for other years or (2) the definition of such statutory terms as "married persons" or "heads of households" should consult other reference works. Those constantly changing details are not essential to understanding the U.S. income tax.

One additional point with respect to tax rates. The maximum rate of tax on *net capital gains* is 28 percent. Thus, a taxpayer with sufficient income to be taxed at 31 percent could save 3 percent to the extent that taxable income includes net capital gains. The details of property transactions and capital gains are discussed in some depth in Chapter 7.

The tax due from any taxpayer is, of course, calculated by taking the rate times the base for the tax. And, although the rates set out above are complete, some taxpayers will be taxed at marginal tax rates higher than 31 percent. Congress, apparently unwilling to be identified with explicit increases in tax rates, has managed to increase the effective tax rate by altering the definition of the tax base for certain higher income taxpayers. The two provisions that accomplish this feat do so by cutting back on the amount of otherwise allowable itemized deductions that can be claimed and by phasing out deductions for exemptions.

Deductible itemized expenses are reduced for high income taxpayers by 3 percent of AGI in excess of point X in Exhibit 4.2. As with many of the provisions in this segment, the exact point at which the provision becomes operative varies slightly from year to year due to adjustments to match changes in the CPI. Point X was originally set at $100,000 (and half of that, or $50,000, for married taxpayers filing separately) but has been increased to $105,250 for 1992. To illustrate the provision, assume that a taxpayer has AGI of $205,250 and itemized deductions of $20,000 prior to application of the cutback provision. Allowable itemized deductions will be reduced by $3,000 (3% x [$205,250 less $105,250]) to $17,000. Since the taxpayer will in all likelihood be in the 31 percent nominal marginal tax rate bracket, this represents an increase in the effective tax rate of just under 1 percent (31% x 3% = .93%).

The cutback in itemized deductions applies to many but not all itemized deductions. It does not apply to medical expenses, investment interest, casualty and theft losses, and deductible (to the extent of winnings) gambling losses. It does apply to taxes, other forms of deductible interest, moving expenses, charitable contributions, and some other miscellaneous items. In addition, the cutback will not reduce the itemized deductions to which it applies by more than 80

Taxpayers and Tax Rates

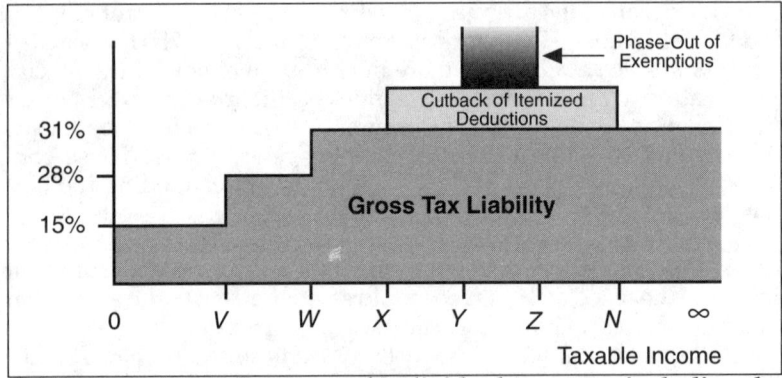

Exhibit 4.2   General pattern of individual tax rates, including the itemized deduction and exemption cutbacks

percent. Thus, although Exhibit 4.2 suggests that the phase-out of itemized deductions will end at point N, the rightmost boundary point is uncertain and specific to each taxpayer depending on the relationship of total covered itemized deductions, AGI, and filing status. That is, since the phase-out is a specific amount for each dollar of excess AGI, the phase-out could extend to very high income levels if covered itemized deductions are very large.

Taxpayers are allowed to deduct $2,300 per exemption, both personal and dependent, for 1992. But taxpayers in excess of threshold AGI amounts lose 2 percent of otherwise allowable exemption deductions for each $2,500 (or fraction thereof) by which AGI exceeds that threshold. That is, there is a point (Y) at which the provision goes into effect and a point (Z) at which deductions for exemptions are completely lost. Since the taxpayer will lose 2 percent per $2,500 of excess AGI, the spread between point Y and point Z should be 50 x $2,500 or $125,000 (the spread is actually $122,501, given the fractional part rule). The points at which the itemized deduction cutback and exemption disallowance rules kick in for 1992 can be summarized as:

	Itemized Deduction Cutback Threshold	Exemption Phase-out Threshold Amount
Married filing jointly	$105,250	$157,900
Heads of households	$105,250	$131,500
Single	$105,250	$105,250
Married filing separately	$52,625	$78,950

4.06 / ESSENTIALS OF U.S. TAXATION

The cutback in itemized deductions resulted in an increase in marginal tax rates of just under 1 percent over the relevant range. But the effect on marginal tax rates of the phase-out of exemptions is .57 of one percent for each exemption. That is, a single taxpayer with $10,000 of excess AGI will lose 8 percent if his or her single $2,300 deduction resulting in an increase in tax of $57 ($10,000/$2,500 = 4 x 2% = 8%; 8% x $2,300 = $184; $184 x 31% = $57). But a married couple filing jointly with two dependents and AGI of $167,900 would lose 8 percent of their larger exemption deduction, or $736, because of the $10,000 excess AGI ($10,000/$2,500 = 4 x 2% = 8%; 8% x 4 x $2,300 = $736). At 31 percent, the couple's taxes will increase by $228; a 2.28 percent increase in their marginal tax rate. A similarly situated large family with ten exemptions would experience an increase in their marginal tax rate of 5.7 percent. Thus, the phase-out of the deduction for exemptions must be diagrammed in Exhibit 4.2 with set leftmost and rightmost points but no upward bounds.

Putting these details together, we are now prepared to approximate the four tax rate schedules currently applicable to individual taxpayers (see Exhibit 4.3).

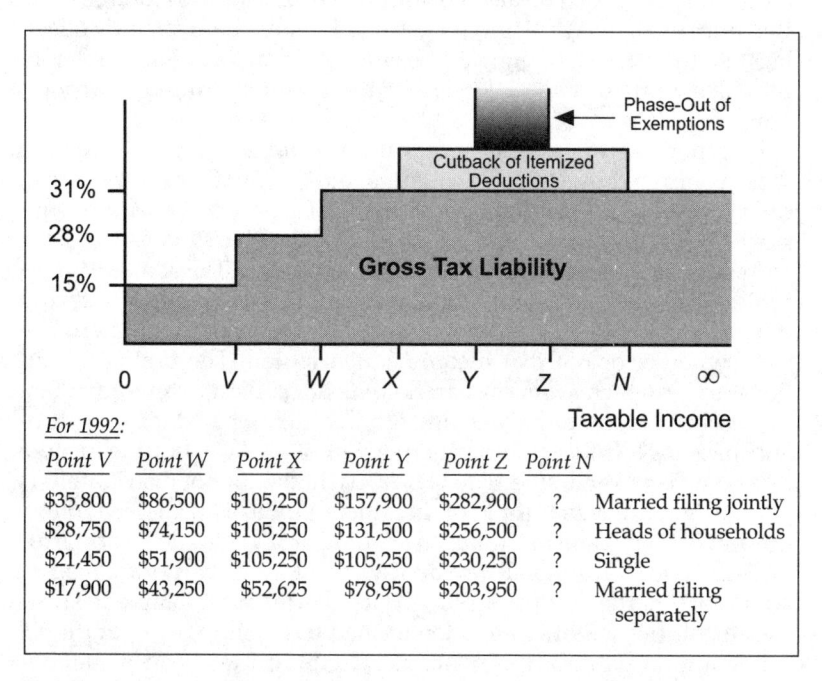

For 1992:

Point V	Point W	Point X	Point Y	Point Z	Point N	
$35,800	$86,500	$105,250	$157,900	$282,900	?	Married filing jointly
$28,750	$74,150	$105,250	$131,500	$256,500	?	Heads of households
$21,450	$51,900	$105,250	$105,250	$230,250	?	Single
$17,900	$43,250	$52,625	$78,950	$203,950	?	Married filing separately

Exhibit 4.3 Approximate individual tax rates

Additional details concerning the calculation of an individual taxpayer's tax liability are deferred to subsequent chapters, especially Chapter 6. Fortunately there is only one tax rate schedule for corporate taxpayers. Consequently the next several pages of this chapter are less confusing than the pages just completed.

Corporate Taxpayers

The wording of Sec. 11—the statutory provision that imposes the income tax on corporations—is similar to that of Sec. 1. It stipulates that one tax rate be applied to the taxable income of *every* corporation to determine the corporation's federal income tax liability. Because corporations hold no citizenship, they can be classified only as domestic or foreign. Domestic corporations are those with charters issued by a U.S. government, usually one of the 50 states. Foreign corporations are, in general, those with charters issued by a non-U.S. government. Although the wording of Sec. 11 implies that U.S. tax laws will be imposed on all corporations—domestic and foreign—the U.S. once again has difficulty in gaining jurisdiction over and collecting tax from most foreign corporations. Therefore, Subchapter N provides numerous special rules for the taxation of foreign corporations.

In general terms, foreign corporations are divided between (1) those controlled by U.S. shareholders and (2) all others. The former, called controlled foreign corporations (CFCs), are more readily subject to U.S. taxation because a majority of the shareholders of those corporations are (by definition) U.S. taxpayers. The United States achieves at least partial jurisdiction over CFCs by sometimes taxing the U.S. shareholders on some part or all of the income earned by the CFC, whether or not that income is distributed. The precise conditions under which a CFC's shareholders are subject to an immediate taxation of corporate income are detailed in Subpart F of Part III of Subchapter N. Consequently the portion of a CFC's taxable income that is subject to an immediate U.S. tax (whether or not distributed) is popularly known as **Subpart F income**. Ordinarily a CFC will have no Subpart F income in the absence of major tax-avoidance opportunities, a condition generally evidenced by a foreign corporation operating outside the country in which its charter was obtained. These extraterritorial activities are often termed **base-company operations**.

Foreign corporations that are not CFCs are taxed in a manner similar to the taxation of nonresident aliens. In other words, those foreign corporations are (per Sec. 881) subject to the U.S. income tax only if, and to the extent that, they earn income from U.S. sources. Income they earn from passive investments in the U.S. will generally be taxed at a flat (30 percent) rate based on gross income. Income of noncontrolled foreign corporations effectively connected with a U.S. trade or business are (per Sec. 882) subject to the more ordinary U.S. income tax.

Domestic corporations as well as foreign corporations carrying on a U.S. trade or business are subject to the tax rates stipulated in Sec. 11(b). That subsection generally provides the following three-step, progressive tax-rate structure:

First $50,000 of taxable income	15%
Next $25,000 of taxable income	25%
All additional taxable income	34%

These apparent rates can be illustrated as in Exhibit 4.4. With one major exception, explained later, one set of tax rates is generally applicable to all corporations. Therefore, there is no need to begin with undefined quantities as was required for individual taxpayers. Otherwise Exhibit 4.4 is very similar to Exhibit 4.1.

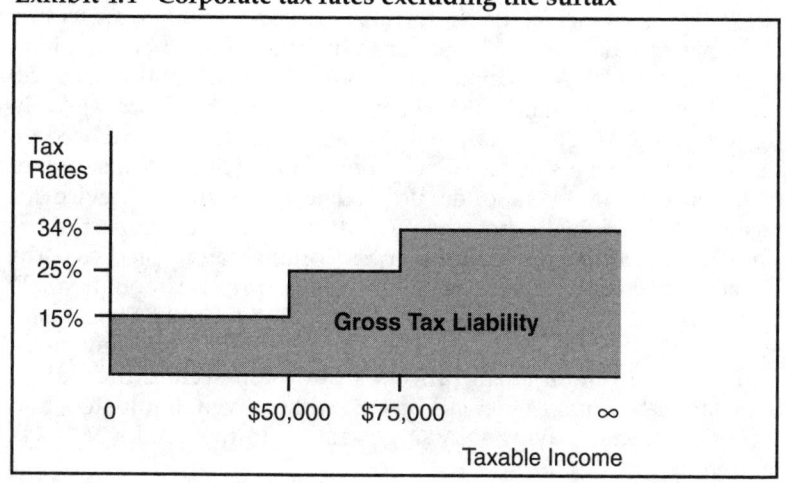

Exhibit 4.4 Corporate tax rates excluding the surtax

In addition to the three-step progression in corporate income tax rates, Sec. 11(b) imposes an additional 5 percent surtax on all corporations earning over $100,000 of taxable income. The intent of this surtax is to recapture the tax benefit associated with the 15 and 25 percent marginal tax rates from corporations earning in excess of $100,000 per year. There is in effect, therefore, a temporary fourth marginal tax rate of 39 percent applicable to corporations earning between $100,000 and $335,000. This surtax bracket ends at $335,000 of taxable income because, at that point, the tax benefit of the lower marginal brackets has been fully recaptured. In arithmetic terms, 5 percent of $235,000 equals 19 percent of $50,000 plus 9 percent of $25,000. The real effective corporate tax rates can, therefore, be simply depicted as in Exhibit 4.5. Observe that in this diagram the two cross-hatched areas are exactly equal. This means of course, that all corporations reporting a taxable income in excess of $335,000 per year really pay a flat (or proportional) tax rate of 34 percent on their entire taxable income.

The one major exception to the three-or four-step corporate progressive tax rates concerns certain **personal service corporations** (PSCs). They are taxed at a flat 34 percent rate on their entire taxable income per Sec.11(b)(2). PSCs are defined in Sec. 448(d)(2) to encompass most corporations (1) engaged in such professional service activities as medicine, law, engineering, accounting, etc., and (2) whose employee-stockholders actually perform those professional services.

Observe, by comparing Exhibits 4.5 and 4.3, that the marginal tax rate applicable to a corporation's taxable income is generally greater than that applicable to any individual for all taxable income in excess of $75,000. This means that in the absence of some other overriding objective, it makes no tax sense for individuals to earn and retain in excess of $75,000 per year in any closely-held corporation. For all years between 1913 and 1986, the opposite conditions prevailed. In those years the highest marginal tax rates were always imposed on individual taxpayers rather than corporate taxpayers. Because of that fact, corporations were often utilized as a tax-shelter device for wealthy individuals. When these conditions reversed as part of the 1986 Tax Reform Act, many business commentators predicted the disincorporation of American business enterprise. Although small, closely-held corporations are still common in the United States, their economic behavior has changed significantly in the past few years. Many closely-held corporations opted for something called Subchapter-S status at the end of 1986, others were liquidated, and still others began paying very large salaries to the employee-stockholders.

Taxpayers and Tax Rates

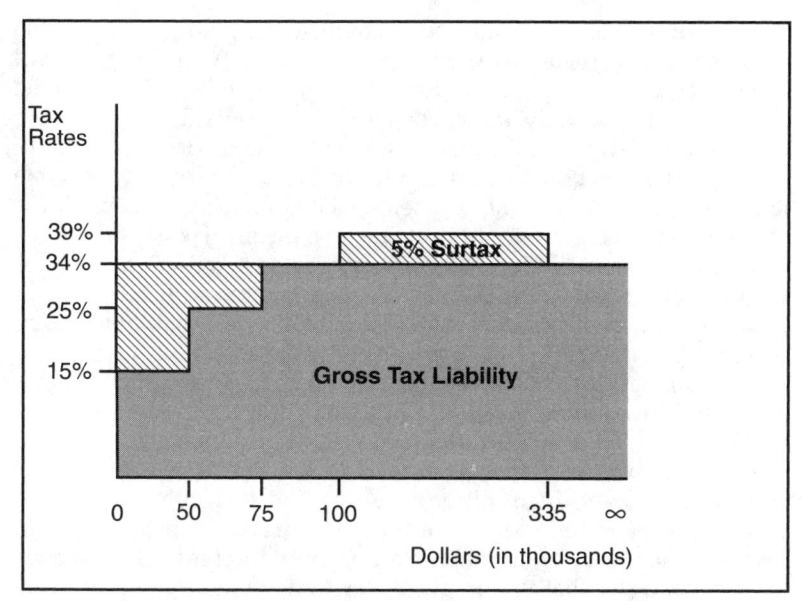

Exhibit 4.5 Corporate tax rates including the 5% surtax

Subchapter S permits certain corporations to retain their *legal* status as corporations but to be taxed in a manner more comparable to partnerships than to corporations. They are technically known as **S-corporations** to distinguish them from taxable corporations, called **C-corporations**. This elective alternative is explained in greater detail later in this chapter.

Corporations that elected to neither liquidate nor be taxed under the provisions of Subchapter S after 1986 frequently modified their behavior to accommodate the 1986 tax revisions by paying larger salaries, rents, royalties, etc., to employee/owner/shareholders. To the extent that the salaries and/or rents paid to the owners are reasonable in amount, they can be deducted by the corporation under the authority of Sec. 162, a provision explained in Chapter 3. The effect of these increased payments is to decrease the amount of taxable income that is subject to the highest marginal tax bracket of financially successful corporations and to increase the amount subject to the lower marginal tax bracket of the corporation's individual shareholder/employee/owners.

The Code does not authorize a C-corporation to deduct any portion of its current or retained income distributed to shareholders as dividends. As a consequence, many closely-held C-corporations never pay any dividends to their shareholders. Those C-corporations that

ESSENTIALS OF U.S. TAXATION / **4.11**

do pay dividends may subject a single income stream to double income taxation. Income earned by, and taxed to, a C-corporation will be subject to a second round of income taxation when, if, and to the extent that the already taxed corporate income is distributed as a dividend to a shareholder who is subject to the income tax on individuals. This phenomenon is commonly referred to as the double taxation of corporate profits. There is no double tax except to the extent that already taxed corporate taxable income is distributed as a dividend to a shareholder who is also subject to tax. Because many C-corporations retain most of their taxable income to fund business expansion internally, and because many corporate shareholders are tax-exempt entities (such as employee trust funds and other charitable organizations), not all income earned by C-corporations is actually subject to double taxation. These and other tax-planning ideas will be examined in somewhat greater depth in Chapter 10.

The U.S. taxation of income earned by a fiduciary is concurrently similar to but yet distinct from the taxation of income earned by corporations and individuals. In the next part of Chapter 4 you will discover the most important similarities and differences in fiduciary taxation in order that you might better understand the essentials of the U.S. income tax.

Fiduciary Taxpayers

Subsection 1(e) imposes the income tax on *every* estate and *every* trust. This wording is similar to that found in Subsections 1(a) through (d) (for individuals) and Subsection 11(a) (for corporations). The interpretation of those same words and phrases differs significantly, however, for estates and trusts. Although every estate (with a sufficiently large taxable income) pays the income tax, many trusts are not treated as taxable entities. Wholly legal trusts that are not taxable entities are called **grantor trusts**. Estates and trusts, other than grantor trusts, are collectively referred to as **fiduciary taxpayers**.

Taxable trusts, like corporations, can be classified as either domestic trusts or foreign trusts. Unfortunately the domestic or foreign classification of a trust is not a simple matter. That classification depends on numerous facts and circumstances including the geographical situs of (1) significant trust assets, (2) the trust administrator, (3) the trust's beneficiaries, (4) the law under which the trust was created, and (5) the citizenship and/or residency of the grantor, i.e., the person who created the trust. In general, domestic trusts are subject to the U.S. income tax on their worldwide income; foreign trusts pay the U.S. income tax only on income earned from U.S. sources. The passive, U.S.-source income earned by a foreign trust is taxed at a flat 30 percent rate on gross income; active income from a U.S. trade or business is taxed at normal rates on a net (taxable income) base. In other words, foreign trusts are generally taxed in the same manner as nonresident aliens and foreign corporations (other than controlled foreign corporations).

Domestic trusts and estates are subject to the tax rates stipulated in Sec. 1(e). That subsection generally provides the following three-step, progressive tax rate structure:

	1991	1992
15% of the first	$3,450	$3,600
28% of additional amounts up to	$10,350	$10,900
31% of all additional taxable income		

The points at which the marginal tax rate increases from 15 to 28 and again to 31 percent are adjusted annually for changes in the consumer price index. Therefore these points must also be considered as approximations, not precise quantities. The approximate fiduciary tax rates can be depicted as in Exhibit 4.6

Estates are created by the death of an individual taxpayer. In general, an estate exists from the moment of the decedent's death

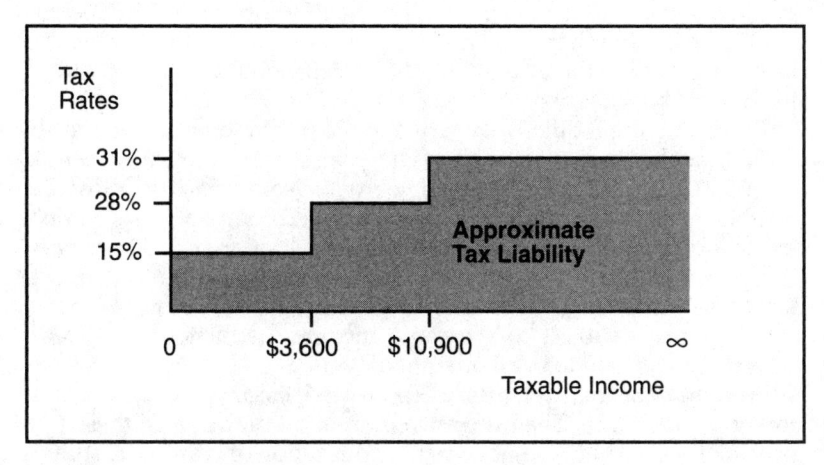

Exhibit 4.6 Approximate fiduciary tax rates

until the final distribution of the last estate asset. This period will vary from a few months, for small estates, to many years, for large estates. If the law did not create a taxable estate following the death of an individual, there would be no viable taxpayer to pay tax on the income earned after a decedent's death and before distribution of the estate's assets.

Trusts are created by the transfer of property from a grantor to a trust to be administered by a trustee. Individuals designated to receive the income earned by the trust are called income beneficiaries; those who receive any assets remaining at the end of the trust's life are called remaindermen. Trusts created while the grantor is alive are called inter-vivos (i.e., among the living) trusts; trusts created at death, by operation of a provision in the last will and testament of a deceased individual, are called testamentary trusts. The grantor (or settlor) sets the conditions of the trust in a legal document called a trust indenture. If the conditions stipulated in a trust indenture provide a 5 percent or greater probability that some trust assets might eventually return to the grantor, the trust will today be classified as a grantor trust. Trusts created before March 1, 1986, were classified as grantor trusts on an entirely different basis. The old rules are best left to a current tax handbook. Classification as a grantor trust means that all of the taxable income earned by that trust will be taxed to the grantor, without regard for how it may actually be retained by the trust or distributed to a beneficiary.

A trust that is subject to tax—that is, a trust other than a grantor trust—is generally allowed to deduct any amount of current income distributed to its beneficiaries. The important effect of this provision is to make taxable trusts something of a half-entity for federal income tax purposes. In other words taxable trusts are subject to the income tax only if, and to the extent that, they retain some amount of taxable income within the trust.

Trusts that are required, by terms of the trust indenture, to distribute all taxable income earned in the year earned, are called simple trusts. Trusts that are permitted to retain some part of all of the taxable income earned during a year are called complex trusts. Simple trusts are allowed a personal exemption deduction of $300 per year; complex trusts, a $100 deduction. Estates are authorized to deduct a $600 personal exemption deduction. Otherwise, fiduciary taxpayers are in general subject to the same income, deduction, and credit provisions applicable to all other taxpayers.

Prior to 1986 many trusts were created largely for tax reasons; today very few are. The difference in motivation between these two periods is largely attributable to the redefinition of grantor trusts and other revisions in the tax rate schedule applicable to fiduciary taxpayers in the 1986 Tax Reform Act. An additional explanation is something called the kiddie tax, a subject explained in Chapter 6.

There is little remaining tax advantage to be gained by a grantor transferring an income-producing property into trust today because most of that income will now be subject to a marginal tax rate of 28 (or 31) percent, the same marginal tax rate that generally applies to any taxable income received by wealthy individuals. Certain domestic trusts created before March 1, 1986, as well as certain foreign trusts created before 1969, retain some tax vitality for reasons too complex to explain here. Suffice it to note that even though certain old trusts may retain some prior tax advantages, no additional assets can be transferred to those trusts today without the incurrence of a significant tax penalty.

The taxation of income earned by legal entities other than corporations, estates, and trusts differs dramatically from the rules explained earlier in this chapter. Those rules are explained in the next few pages.

Other Business Entities

Because the Code imposes the income tax only on individuals, C-corporations, and certain fiduciaries, it might intuitively appear that other business entities—such as sole proprietorships, partnerships, S-corporations, and joint ventures—are a veritable U.S. tax haven. If so, that intuition is definitely incorrect because **the taxable income earned by all other business entities simply passes through those entities and is immediately taxed to the business owners, whether or not any assets are distributed to them**. These other entities are essentially tax-number conduits. This means that the taxpaying owners of other business entities may end up having to report a substantial amount of taxable income earned in and retained by a tax-conduit entity, without receiving sufficient assets from that entity to pay the added income tax liability attributable to the extra taxable income that must be currently reported on the owners' tax returns. Under other circumstances it may also mean that the business owner's personal income tax liability may be reduced because of deductible income tax losses generated in one of these other business entities. As explained in Chapter 9, the right of owners to deduct losses is sometimes restricted.

Although these other business entities do not pay the income tax, most are required to file information (tax) returns with the IRS. Those information returns detail the individual items of gross income, deduction, and credit that must be picked up by (or reported on) the

Taxpayers and Tax Rates

various taxpaying owners' own tax returns. The specific IRS form differs from one entity to another. The most common **information returns** are:

IRS Form	Reporting Business Entity	Tax Paid By
1065	Partnership	Partners
1120-S	S-corporation	Stockholders
Schedule C (Form 1040)	Sole proprietorship	Proprietor

The dual reporting procedure makes it relatively easy for the IRS to be certain that business owners report their share of any taxable income or loss initially earned by a tax-conduit entity. Government computers match the information documents received from nontaxable entities with the tax returns filed by the entity's taxable owners to be sure that the tax numbers are correctly reported and that the income tax is paid currently.

To illustrate this essential tax concept, assume that the XYZ Partnership earns a $400,000 taxable income but distributes none of it to its four equal partners, namely, individual I, corporation C, trust T, and partnership AB. Assume further that the AB Partnership is, in turn, equally owned by individual A and the estate of B. The several information returns, tax returns, and tax payments generated by this one business partnership can be summarized as follows:

Business Entity	IRS Form Filed	Tax Paid	Taxable Income Reported
Partnership XYZ	1065 (Information only)	no	$400,000
Individual I	1040 Tax Return	yes	$100,000
Corporation C	1120 Tax Return	yes	$100,000
Trust T	1041 Tax Return	yes	$100,000
Partnership AB	1065 (Information only)	no	$100,000
Individual A	1040 Tax Return	yes	$50,000
Estate B	1041 Tax Return	yes	$50,000

Those same factors can also be depicted graphically, as in Exhibit 4.7.

The decision to retain or distribute the assets earned by a tax-conduit entity is a financial decision made by management after considering the needs of both the business entity and its owners.

Taxpayers and Tax Rates

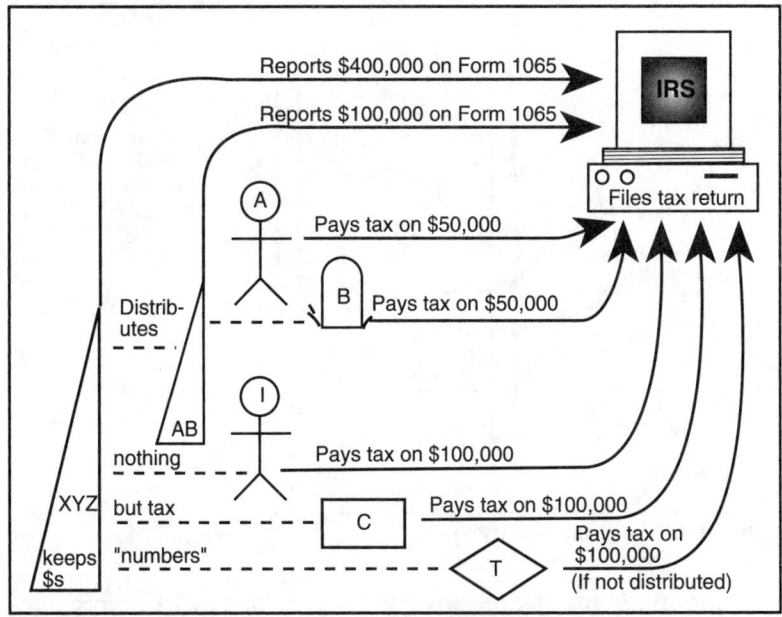

Exhibit 4.7   Entities, information, and taxes

Since business managers are ultimately responsible to owners, there is generally some pressure on managers to distribute at least enough business assets to permit owners to pay their increased income tax liabilities. However, because the distribution of at least some business assets generally does not coincide with the distribution of income tax numbers generated by a tax-conduit entity, the Code has had to create a method by which owners can track their tax rights vis-à-vis both the entity and the government. This tracking system is captured in something called **tax basis**.

The concept of tax basis is relatively complex and cannot be completely explained at this early juncture in the text. In general terms, tax basis represents the taxpayer's unrecovered tax cost in an asset or property. The fundamental idea is illustrated in Exhibit 4.8. The concept is essential to understanding various transactions between owners and tax-conduit business entities. The fundamental idea will be explained here; additional details are deferred to later chapters, most importantly to Chapters 7 and 8.

Property owners can acquire or increase their tax basis in an asset by (1) paying cash, (2) assuming a liability, (3) paying income taxes on a related asset, and (4) exchanging properties. For example:

ESSENTIALS OF U.S. TAXATION / **4.17**

Taxpayers and Tax Rates

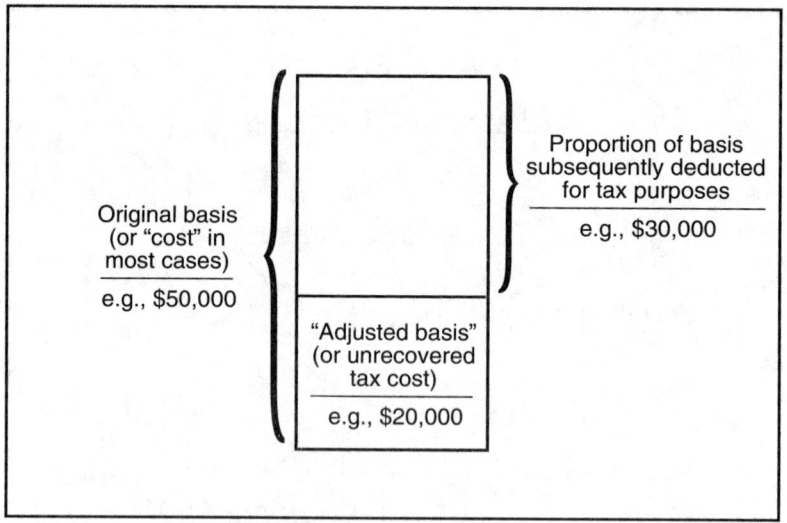

```
┌─────────────────────────────────────────────────────────────┐
│                                                             │
│                      ⎧         ⎫                            │
│                      ⎪         ⎪   Proportion of basis      │
│                      ⎪         ⎪   subsequently deducted    │
│                      ⎪         ⎪      for tax purposes      │
│    Original basis    ⎨         ⎬   ─────────────────────    │
│    (or "cost" in     ⎪         ⎪         e.g., $30,000      │
│    most cases)       ⎪         ⎪                            │
│   ─────────────────  ⎪         ⎪                            │
│       e.g., $50,000  ⎪         ⎪                            │
│                      ⎪         ⎪                            │
│                      ⎪         ⎪   "Adjusted basis"         │
│                      ⎪         ⎪   (or unrecovered          │
│                      ⎪         ⎪      tax cost)             │
│                      ⎪         ⎪   ─────────────────        │
│                      ⎪         ⎪       e.g., $20,000        │
│                      ⎩         ⎭                            │
│                                                             │
└─────────────────────────────────────────────────────────────┘
```

Exhibit 4.8 Tax basis concept

1. If Individual J purchases 100 shares of CNB Corporation's common stock for $2300 cash, J will acquire a tax basis of $2300 in the 100 shares of CNB stock.
2. If Corporation C purchases a 40-acre tract of land for $100,000 cash plus a $400,000 note payable, C will acquire a tax basis of $500,000 in the 40-acre tract of land.
3. If the Trust T acquires a one-fourth interest in the ABC Partnership for $200,000 and pays the income tax on its one-fourth of the $400,000 in taxable income earned and retained by ABC, the T Trust will increase its tax basis in its ABC partnership interest from $200,000 to $300,000 (i.e., $200,000 + 1/4 × $400,000).
4. If Individual X steals a $4000 used car from his employer, and X properly reports the value of the stolen car as taxable income, X will have acquired a basis of $4000 in this automobile.
5. If the NM Partnership exchanges property #1 (P_1) for property #2 (P_2) in a nontaxable exchange, NM will acquire a tax basis in P_2 equal to whatever basis it had in P_1 prior to the exchange.
6. If the R Corporation exchanges property #1 (P_1) for property #2 (P_2) in a *taxable* exchange, and if R correctly paid an income tax on a $5000 gain realized in this exchange, R Corporation will have a tax basis in P_2 equal to whatever basis it had in P_1 prior to the exchange plus $5000.

A property owner can lose tax basis in an asset by (1) deducting a portion of the asset's prior basis, (2) claiming a tax deductible loss on a related asset, and (3) by selling or exchanging one asset for another. For example:

1. If B Corporation acquires a delivery truck for $20,000 cash and claims a (tax) depreciation deduction of $4000 on this truck, B's original basis in the truck is reduced from $20,000 to an adjusted basis of $16,000.
2. If individual D acquires 100 percent of the outstanding stock of D Coy, Inc. (an S-corporation) for $100,000, and if D deducts on her own return the entire $40,000 net operating loss experienced by D Coy, Inc., during the next year, then D's original basis in her D Coy stock will be reduced from $100,000 to an adjusted basis of $60,000.
3. If individual J buys 100 shares of XYZ common stock for $14,000 cash and subsequently sells that same stock for $13,500 and deducts a $500 capital loss realized on that sale, J will have no remaining basis in any stock but will now have basis of $13,500 in the cash received at the time of the sale.
4. If the F Trust exchanges property #1 (P_1) for property #2 (P_2) in a taxable exchange and F deducts a $1000 loss realized in this exchange, F's basis in P_2 will be whatever basis it had in P_1 less $1000.

As illustrated in the preceding ten examples, the tax basis of an asset generally serves to measure the unrecovered tax cost of an asset at any point in time.

An owner's tax basis in any business conducted in a tax-conduit form is subject to frequent modification. In general, an owner's tax basis in such an entity is:

- Increased by
  —an original investment,
  —additional capital contributions,
  —loans to the business, and
  —the taxation of undistributed income;
- Decreased by
  —a partial withdrawal of capital,
  —a distribution of previously taxed income,
  —a liquidation of the business, and
  —a reduction of debt owed to the owner by the business.

By contrast, an owner's tax basis in a separately taxable business entity is only rarely changed. That owner's tax basis is neither (1) increased by the taxation of undistributed income nor (2) decreased by the distribution of previously taxed income. For example, if K owns 100 percent of the stock of a C-corporation, K will not reduce his tax basis in C's stock because of a dividend distribution. This result is in direct contrast with the result that would be obtained if his corporation had made a Subchapter S election because that election would convert the corporation from a separate taxable entity to a tax-conduit entity.

Although there are many additional nuances associated with both the basis concept and tax-conduit entities, details can be deferred to later chapters and other books with minimal pedagogical cost. Before concluding this chapter on taxpayers and tax rates, we must examine at least two special problem areas that are closely associated with the income taxation of certain entities.

Two Major Problem Areas

In some circumstances it is easier to measure the amount of taxable income present in a situation than to identify the real or true taxpayer. In other circumstances it is more difficult to classify a taxpayer correctly than it is to identify who actually earned the income. In the final pages of Chapter 4 we will briefly examine both of these entity-related problem areas.

Identifying the Taxpayer Correctly

Because the Code imposes a potentially progressive income tax on at least three distinct entities, there is a built-in statutory incentive for taxpayers in the higher marginal tax brackets to redirect some amount of taxable income to related or controlled taxpayers in a lower marginal tax bracket. For example, a wealthy taxpayer might try to divert some of his taxable income to one of his children and/or to a wholly owned C-corporation. This general tax objective is commonly referred to as **income splitting**. Perhaps the most interesting aspect of income splitting is that it may be given complete legal recognition in some circumstances and be totally denied recognition in others.

To illustrate, assume that a physician engaged in a general medical practice were to instruct one in every ten patients to make her payments to one or another of the physician's children or parents. Would this simple diversion of cash receipts also divert taxable income from the physician (who is almost certainly in a high tax bracket) to children or parents (who might be in a low tax bracket)? Certainly not. That simple tax plan would be destined to fail under such judicial law as *Lucas v. Earl*, 281 US 111 (1930). In this and other cases the courts have consistently held that income from services will generally be taxed to the person who renders the service, with minimal regard for the person who happens to receive the cash. No **assignment of income** will be tolerated for tax purposes.

At the same time, the Code and other authorities permit a physician or other professional or business person to create a corporation—an artificial, legal person—and have that legal entity recognize the income derived from services rendered to clients by the corporation's sole shareholder-employee. If the corporation distributes anything less than its entire income to the employee-shareholder, some degree of income splitting has been achieved. Recall that there is no remaining tax advantage in this arrangement by **professional service corporations** (PSCs) because PSCs are taxed at a flat rate of 34 percent. The opportunity to gain a tax advantage by splitting income between a small corporation and its owner-employee is still possible, however, for all corporations that can avoid the PSC definition.

The opportunity to assign income derived from property transactions is equally elusive. In general the law provides that income from property must be reported by the taxpayer who owns the property. (See *Helvering v. Horst*, 311 US 112 (1940).) Accordingly, the owner of a coupon bond cannot clip or otherwise separate the interest coupons from the bond prior to their maturity, give them to another individual, and thereby escape income taxation on the interest. That interest income would be taxed to the bondholder with no regard for who actually received the cash on the various interest payment dates.

On the other hand, however, a person can give her child an appreciated property—for example, a common stock originally purchased for $5000 but currently valued at $12,000—and have the child sell the property (and retain the entire $12,000 proceeds) and thereby transfer the $7000 taxable gain realized on the sale of the stock from the parent to the child. Income streams from on-going business ventures can also be transferred in part or in full by transfers of corporate stock, partnership interests, etc. Parents who own a business that is operated as an S-corporation or as a partnership can effectively transfer a portion of the taxable income derived from that business to their children, grandparents, or others, by giving them some of their own corporate stock in the S-corporation, or some fraction of their original partnership interest. If the transfer of their property interest is complete—i.e., if the parents do not retain any control over the property transferred—the child, grandparent, or other individual donee will recognize his or her ratable share of any taxable income earned by the business entity in all future years. Because a degree of income splitting is possible in this arrangement, the IRS will carefully examine the information returns filed by family-owned S-corporations and partnerships to be certain that an appropriate (i.e., sufficiently large) salary has been paid to the parents who actually operate the business. The children, grandparents, or others are supposed to share only the taxable income derived from their capital interest in the business entity, not from the taxable income derived within the business from the parents' services.

In summary, there are at least three major problems commonly encountered in income taxation. They are:

1. determining whether or not any income has been realized (a question of definition),
2. determining how much income was realized (a question of measurement), and
3. determining who must recognize that income (a question of identification).

The first of these three issues was at least partially resolved in Chapter 2, the second in Chapter 3, and the third in Chapter 4. We have not yet, however, adequately defined the various legal entities for federal income tax purposes.

Defining Business Entities Correctly

To state that a corporation or trust is a taxable entity whereas a partnership is not, begs a potentially critical question: namely, What exactly is a corporation, trust, or partnership for income tax purposes? In the vast majority of all cases the answer to this question is obvious. In most instances state law will control. Entities organized and classified as a corporation under state law will ordinarily also be treated as corporations for federal income tax purposes; those organized and classified as partnerships will usually be treated as partnerships. In rare circumstances, however, that general conclusion is invalid.

The Code purports to define a corporation in Sec. 7701(a) as follows:

> The term corporation includes associations, joint-stock companies, and insurance companies.

Although this statutory definition lacks precision, it clearly suggests that for tax purposes the word corporation is sufficiently broad to include unincorporated "associations," whatever that may mean. Fortunately, the Supreme Court, in *Morrissey et al. v. Comm'r.* (296 US 344 (1935)) and Treas. Regs. Sec. 301.7701-2, gives additional guidance in questionable circumstances. These and other primary authorities may be particularly helpful in determining how foreign business entities—with no direct U.S. counterpart—should be classified.

The general approach of both the judicial and administrative authorities is to require that uncertain taxpayers examine all facts and circumstances and, based on that review, identify the presence or absence of six corporate characteristics. In the most succinct of terms, these six characteristics can be described as follows:

	Characteristics	Partnership	Corporation	Trust
1.	What is the primary objective?	Profit	Profit	Protect assets
2.	Are "associates" present?	Yes	Yes	No
3.	Is the entity's life independent of owners?	No	Yes	Yes
4.	Are the owners' interests freely transferable?	No	Yes	Yes
5.	Is each owner's liability limited?	No	Yes	Yes
6.	Is management centralized?	No	Yes	Yes

These six characteristics were first identified by the Supreme Court in *Morrissey*; their relative importance today is determined by Treasury regulations. The regulations provide that an entity that might be classified as either a corporation or a partnership will be treated for tax purposes as a corporation if it has a *majority* of corporate characteristics. Note that characteristics 1 and 2 are commonly shared by both partnerships and corporations, whereas characteristics 3 through 6 differ. Therefore, the administrative majority requirement can be interpreted as requiring either (a) 4 of 6, or (b) 3 of 4, corporate characteristics. The courts (in *Larson*, 65 TC 159 (1975)) held that the two common characteristics should be disregarded; hence the 3-of-4 alternative controls the definitional answer when the question is partnership or corporation.

Observe also that characteristics 3 through 6 are commonly shared by corporations and trusts but that characteristics 1 and 2 differ. When trying to decide whether a specific entity is a corporation or a trust, the courts generally rely on criterion 1 alone. Entities created primarily for the protection of property interests are held to be trusts; those created to carry on business for gain are held to be associations and taxed as corporations.

In summary, although the Code provides in Secs. 1(e) and 11, respectively, that every trust and every corporation are subject to the income tax, other authorities substantially modify a literal interpretation of those two sections. Business ventures organized in corporate form can frequently escape the corporate income tax by electing to be taxed under the provisions of Subchapter S; in more rare instances, the courts will pierce the corporate veil and tax a corporation's owners as if no corporation existed; and in still other circumstances the courts will tax an unincorporated association as if it were a corporation. Similarly, some wholly legal trusts—called grantor trusts—will be ignored for federal income tax purposes; other trusts will be taxed as a separate entity, to the extent that taxable income is retained; while still other trusts may be taxed as an association (or corporation) because they were created primarily to carry on a business for gain.

As demonstrated in this chapter, the words of the Code must be interpreted with great care. A literal interpretation is particularly suspect in circumstances permeated by tax avoidance possibilities. Justice Learned Hand stated this important conclusion very clearly many years ago when he wrote:

> ... as the articulation of a statute increases, the room for interpretation must contract; but the meaning of a sentence may be more than that of the separate words, as a melody is more than the notes, and no degree of particularity can ever obviate recourse to the setting in which all appear, and which all collectively create. (*Helvering v. Gregory*, 69 F.2d 809 (CCA-2, 1934))

Key Points to Remember

- The United States imposes a global income tax. This means that income of most taxpayers will be taxed without regard to where it is earned.
- The three taxable entities in the United States are
  1. Every individual;
  2. Every corporation; and
  3. Certain trusts and estates.

- Nonresident aliens, foreign corporations, and foreign estates and trusts are subject to special tax treatment under United States law.
- Individual taxpayers may be subject to any one of four different tax rate schedules. This means that individual may be taxed as
  1. Married persons filing joint returns;
  2. Heads of households;
  3. Unmarried persons;
  4. Married persons filing separate returns.
- At higher levels of taxable income the marginal tax rate on the taxable income earned by a corporation will exceed the marginal tax rate on an equivalent income earned by an individual.
- Business entities that incorporate may be subject to very different tax treatment depending upon their classification as
  1. A C-corporation;
  2. An S-corporation; or
  3. A personal service corporation (PSC).
- Taxable income that is initially earned by a C-corporation and subsequently distributed as a dividend may be subject to double taxation.
- Neither an S-corporation nor a partnership are ordinarily taxed on the income that they earn. Their income is immediately taxed to their owners whether or not it is distributed to them.
- Taxable trusts are taxed on only that portion of their taxable income that is not distributed.
- All taxable income recognized by a grantor trust is taxed to the person who created the trust regardless of what is done with the income.
- Nontaxable business entities must ordinarily file information returns with the IRS even though they pay no income tax.
- Tax basis generally represents a taxpayer's unrecovered tax cost in an asset or property.

ACCOUNTING PERIODS AND METHODS

The concept of income implicitly assumes both a time constraint and an entity constraint. It is theoretically possible to measure income for a period as brief as one day or less and as long as a decade or more. In general, however, a period of one year is the norm for both financial accounting and federal income tax purposes. Income can also be measured separately for each income-generating unit or in the aggregate for numerous units, concurrently. The statutory rules that govern the time and entity constraints for income tax purposes are commonly known as the accounting period and method provisions. The discussion in Chapter 4 focused on the distinction between taxable and nontaxable business entities. This chapter integrates the accounting period and method rules with those entity concepts.

Chapter 5 is divided into three major parts. The first part explains the fundamental accounting-period rules. The second part discusses the most important accounting-method provisions. The third part introduces two relatively complex tax laws that sometimes permit and at other times demand the aggregation of separate legal entities for income tax measurements.

Accounting Periods

Subchapter E of the Code, entitled accounting periods and methods of accounting, is subdivided into three parts. Part I, entitled accounting periods, includes Secs. 441 through 444. Section 441(a) generally requires that taxable income be computed for a period called a taxable year, a legal term subsequently defined as including (among others) (a) the calendar year, (b) a fiscal year, or (c) a short year (i.e., a period of less than 12 months). Although these three options appear to be almost boundless, other statutory provisions serve to limit their general application. For example, Sec. 441(e) restricts a fiscal year to either (1) any period of 12 months that ends on the last day of a month (other than December 31) or (2) something called a 52–53 week year. The latter term includes as an acceptable taxable year a period that may vary from 52 to 53 weeks a year but only one that always ends on either (1) the same day of the week that last occurs in any calendar month (for example, the last Saturday in January) or (2) on whatever date that same day falls nearest to the last day of any calendar month (for example, the Saturday occurring nearest to January 31). And Sec. 441(g) requires that the calendar year be used if a taxpayer (1) keeps no books, (2) has no annual period, or (3) has an annual period that does not qualify as a fiscal year, as defined above. Finally, Sec. 443 severely limits the circumstances under which a taxpayer may file a return for a period of less than 12 months. Short years (or years of less than 12 months duration) are generally allowed only if the taxpayer is in existence for less than an entire year, or if a change in the accounting period has been approved and the taxpayer is switching from one taxable year to another.

More importantly, Sec. 444 generally restricts (1) partnerships, (2) S-corporations, and (3) personal service corporations to a required taxable year. A required year is one that conforms the taxable year of these entities to the tax years of their owners. This restriction was imposed to close a loophole that existed under prior law.

In Chapter 4 we simply observed that the tax numbers (i.e., the individual items of gross income, deduction, and tax credit) flowed immediately through certain tax-conduit entities, such as partnerships and S-corporations, to their owners. We did not discuss precisely when those numbers passed through the entity to be reported by their owners. Because income must ordinarily be determined by each separate business entity for a full 12-month period, owners of partnerships and S-corporations in the past very often put their tax-conduit entities on a fiscal year ending on (or near) January 31st. The individual owners of these businesses were largely calendar-year taxpayers. As a result of this careful selection of differing year-ends and carefully timed distributions of income, the owners of these partnerships and S-corporations were effectively able to defer the taxation of income earned by the entity for nearly one full year. This opportunity for tax deferral is illustrated in Exhibit 5.1. Note that the individual partners (P) would not report the income earned by the partnership (PS) in fiscal year one (FY-1) until the partner filed his personal tax return for calendar year two, assuming that none of that income was distributed before the end of the first fiscal year.

To end this unintended opportunity for tax deferral, Sec. 444 was added to the Code. That section requires that either (1) the owners and their tax-number-conduit entities utilize the same tax year or (2) the entities make a non-interest bearing, advance-payment deposit equal to the tax advantage achieved by deferral. Furthermore, deferral is generally restricted to a period of three months or less. Personal service corporations, taxed as C-corporations, are handled in a differ-

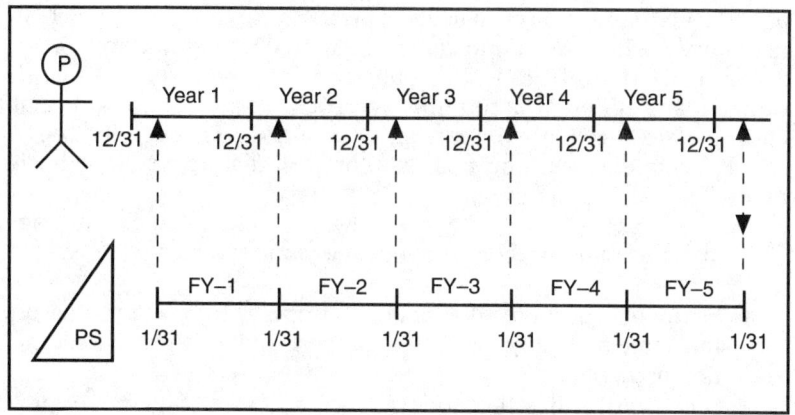

Exhibit 5.1 Tax years of partners and partnerships—deferral possibilities

ent manner. They are denied current deductions if they postpone payments to their employee-owners that are earned in one year but paid in a later year.

C-corporations, other than PSCs, are generally free to elect any (acceptable) taxable year that they wish. They do this by filing a return on a date appropriate for the year selected. A corporation's first year begins on the date of incorporation. If a period of dormancy ensues, it must be included as part of its first year. The first and last years of a C-corporation very often involve a short year.

Short years attributable to a change in the accounting period, unlike the first- and last-year circumstances, require the taxpayer to compute the tax on an annualized basis. This requirement eliminates any tax benefit that might otherwise occur because of the lower marginal tax rate that applies to taxable incomes of less than $100,000 per year, as explained in Chapter 4. For example, if a taxpayer reports a $60,000 taxable income for a three-month short year due to an approved change in the tax year, the tax liability will in general be equal to one-fourth of the tax on a $240,000 taxable income, not the tax on a $60,000 one. It can be important, therefore, to report the initial year correctly so that no later change in tax year need be requested and no annualization need be computed.

Accounting Method

The term **accounting method** is frequently used in the tax literature to refer to both general methods of accounting (such as the cash and accrual methods) and more specific accounting procedures (such as inventory costing and depreciation methods). Although any single tax-recognized entity can have only one accounting period, it can utilize many different accounting methods. In fact, one entity that encompasses several distinct trades or businesses is generally free to select separate accounting methods for each distinct trade or business.

Section 446 provides the general rules for methods of accounting. The most important of those rules can be paraphrased as follows:

- Sec. 446(a) provides that taxable income is to be computed on the same accounting method as the taxpayer uses in keeping her or his books.
- Sec. 446(b) states that the Secretary of the Treasury may prescribe the method of accounting if either (1) a taxpayer maintains no books or (2) those books fail to clearly reflect income.
- Sec. 446(c) identifies certain accounting methods as permissible methods, including
    — the cash receipt and disbursement method,
    — the accrual method,
    — a regulations-approved "hybrid" method, and
    — other methods specifically permitted by Chapter 1 of the Code.
- Sec. 446(e) requires a taxpayer to obtain approval of the Secretary of the Treasury before changing methods, unless automatic approval is otherwise provided.

The general rules are, as always, subject to various statutory exceptions as well as numerous administrative and judicial interpretations.

The Accrual Method

Most important is the limitation on the use of the cash method of accounting found in Sec. 448. That section generally requires the following entities to use the **accrual method** of accounting:

- C-corporations,
- partnerships having one or more corporate partners, and
- tax shelters.

Sec. 448(b) excepts the following entities (other than those defined as tax shelters) from this rule:

- farming and timber businesses,
- qualified personal service corporations, and
- entities with gross receipts not in excess of $5 million.

The Code further provides definitions for the several critical words and phrases in Sec. 448. Sec. 447 provides additional accounting-method rules for corporations engaged in farming.

The accrual method of accounting for financial accounting purposes generally requires that revenues be recognized in the year that they are earned and that all costs incurred in the production of those revenues be matched against the revenue in that same year. Although the rules for the accrual method in taxation are similar to those followed in financial accounting, there are a number of significant differences between the two.

Financial accounting generally defers the recognition of revenue received in advance until the year that it is earned; for tax purposes those same revenue items will usually be taxed in the year received under the claim-of-right doctrine. In limited circumstances, an accrual basis taxpayer can defer the recognition of advance receipts for future services if those services will be performed in the next tax year, but those same taxpayers generally cannot defer the recognition of advance receipts for interest, rents, guarantees, etc. Additional details concerning these tax anomalies in accrual accounting and revenue recognition can be found in such primary authorities as Secs. 455 and 456; Rev. Proc. 71-21 (1971-2 C.B. 549); Reg. Secs. 1.451-1 through -7; and *North American Oil Consolidated v. Burnet* (286 U.S. 417 (1932)).

The general attitude in taxation often seems to be that the government will extract the income tax in the year that the taxpayer has the funds, rather than in the year the income is technically earned. This observation seems to be particularly true as applied to individual taxpayers in nonbusiness circumstances.

The matching concept of financial accounting is also frequently ignored in accrual-income measurements for income tax purposes. The general attitude of the tax authorities relative to deductions seems to be that all estimated expenses must be deferred.

To be deductible, even using the accrual method, an expense must satisfy at least three unique tax tests, namely:

1. an all events test,
2. a reasonable estimate test, and
3. an economic performance test.

The first of these three tests suggests that nothing is deductible until all of the events that determine the fact of the liability have occurred. The second denies a deduction if any substantial contingency remains. The third requires that a taxpayer receive the full performance of services and the receipt or use of property before recognizing a related liability. The details of these tax anomalies to accrual accounting and expense recognition can be located in such primary authorities as Sec. 461, Reg. Secs. 1.461-1 through -4, and *General Dynamics v. U.S.*, 107 S.Ct. 1732 (1987).

The single most important consequence of the authorities noted above is to create frequent and major differences between income numbers as reported by financial accountants following generally accepted accounting principles, and those reported by tax accountants following primary legal authorities, even when both groups of accountants are using the accrual method of accounting. In many other nations of the world, particularly the United Kingdom, accounting rules established by financial authorities are given substantially greater weight in income tax measurements than they are in the United States. These financial and tax accounting differences have also generated a great deal of possibly unnecessary complexity in U.S. tax law. Because many U.S. corporations were frequently able to report large amounts of financial income to both the Securities and Exchange Commission and their stockholders during the same years that they reported little or no income to the Internal Revenue Service, Congress enacted specific provisions intended to minimize the recurrence of this possibility in future years. The most important single provision of this genre is Sec. 55, which imposes an alternative minimum (income) tax (AMT) on certain taxpayers. One unfortunate result of the AMT is that it creates a need for many taxpayers to keep a third and even a fourth set of accounting records. Taxpayers were previously accustomed to keeping at least two sets of accounting records—one for financial accounting purposes and another for income tax purposes—prior to the enactment of the AMT. A third set occasionally had to be reconstructed from tax records for earnings and profits (E&P) purposes—a measure that is important to the definition of a dividend for tax purposes. Today, a fourth set is required for the AMT. Additional details are included in Chapter 10.

The Cash Method

Although the Code authorizes some taxpayers to report their taxable incomes using a cash receipt and disbursement method of accounting, that authority must be interpreted with caution. The **cash method** of accounting generally presumes that all income items will be recognized in the year that they are received (in cash) and that all deduction items will be recognized in the year that they are paid. If this general rule were applied literally, income tax laws would effectively turn the U.S. economy into a barter economy overnight. To negate this unintended result, various legal authorities modify the literal law and apply a cash-equivalence standard. This means that a cash-basis taxpayer must immediately recognize as taxable income not only those income items received in cash, but also the fair market value of many noncash income items received during a year.

To illustrate, assume that Joe Blow exchanges his 100 shares of ABC common stock ($3000 fair market value; $2000 cost basis) for 250 shares of XYZ common stock, also valued at $3000. Unless Joe can identify a special nonrecognition provision that will permit him to defer recognition of the $1000 gain realized when he makes the exchange, he must immediately recognize the entire gain even though he never received any cash. On the other hand, Jane Doe can defer until next year the recognition of income for the salary that she earned by working during the month of December this year, if her regular payday is January 1 or 2 next year, assuming that she is a cash-basis taxpayer. But if Jane also has a savings account at her bank and they credit her account with $310 interest on December 31, Jane must recognize this interest income on her current year's tax return even if she does not withdraw that interest from her savings account. Jane is said to have constructive receipt over the $310 in interest and is taxed accordingly. In short, the cash method applies literally only to the routine wage under these three somewhat similar circumstances.

The Hybrid Method

Treas. Reg. Sec. 1.446-1 authorizes certain taxpayers to use a combination of the cash and accrual methods of accounting in limited circumstances. This accounting method, known as the **hybrid method**, requires the taxpayer to use the accrual method in accounting for both (1) sales and (2) the cost of goods sold. Other expenses—in particular, the selling and administrative expense deductions—can be reported using a cash method of accounting. Either a full accrual method or this hybrid method is required of any unincorporated business venture in which inventories are a material income-producing item. It is commonly utilized by the owners of small businesses because it minimizes the complexity of the accounting records that must be maintained solely for income tax reasons.

Other Accounting Methods

In somewhat more unusual circumstances certain taxpayers may use an installment-sales accounting method (authorized in Secs. 453 and 453A) or a percentage-of-completion accounting method (authorized in Sec. 460(b)). The installment-sale method is generally applicable to deferred payment sales of both real and personal properties by taxpayers who are not dealers in the property sold. This method automatically defers a pro-rata portion of any gain realized, until cash is received, unless the taxpayers elect not to have the rule apply. To illustrate, assume that an individual taxpayer sold for $15,000 an antique that he had purchased many years ago for $5000. If this taxpayer is not an antique dealer and he receives $3000 in year #1, $9000 in year #2, and $3000 in year #3, he will report $2000 of gross income in years 1 and 3 and $6000 in year #2 (i.e., $10,000 profit divided by $15,000 sales price times cash received equals gross income in any year).

The percentage-of-completion and percentage-of-completion/capitalized-cost accounting methods can be used only by taxpayers engaged in long-term construction contracts. (The latter method largely replaces the completed-contract method, which was available to certain long-term contractors prior to 1987.) In general, these two methods require contractors to report a pro-rata share of their anticipated profits on a long-term contract as costs are incurred. The revisions made in the 1986 Code were deliberately aimed at a small number of very large corporations, generally engaged in government defense contracts, that had not reported any taxable income for a number of years prior to 1987 because of the availability of the completed-contract method. Some contracts were alleged to provide that the contract would not be complete until the articles produced were tested under wartime conditions. This contractual provision was capable, under prior law, of deferring the recognition of any gross income until the U.S. declared war on another country. These same companies were typically reporting a substantial financial income to their stockholders during those same years.

The Code authorizes a few other accounting methods in very limited circumstances. Sec. 455 provides special rules for the reporting of prepaid subscription income; Sec. 456 provides special rules to report prepaid dues of certain membership organizations; Sec. 457 provides special rules for deferred compensation plans of certain state and local government employees; etc. Because these special accounting rules are of such limited interest, they are not discussed further in this book.

Accounting Procedures

Specific accounting procedures for varied income-measurement problems are scattered throughout the Code and other primary authorities. Sec. 471 provides that inventories be taken on such basis as reflects the best accounting practice in a trade or business. This requirement is interpreted to include a lower-of-cost-or-market rule if cost flows can be calculated on an average, FIFO (first-in, first-out) basis. Taxpayers electing to use the LIFO (last-in, first-out) basis cannot use the lower-of-cost-or-market rule. Furthermore, the Code stipulates in Sec. 472 that if a LIFO method is used for income tax purposes, it must also be used for financial accounting purposes.

Sec. 167 authorizes various depreciation methods—including the straight-line method, a declining-balance method, and a sum-of-the-years-digits method—while Sec. 168 authorizes an accelerated cost recovery system (ACRS) in lieu of depreciation for properties acquired after a certain date.

Sec. 611 authorizes a cost-depletion deduction for some taxpayers engaged in the extraction of natural resources; Sec. 613 authorizes an alternative, percentage-depletion deduction for other taxpayers engaged in that same industry. Section 616(a) authorizes taxpayers to deduct certain costs incurred in the development of a mine or other natural resource; Sec. 616(b) authorizes a taxpayer to capitalize many of those same expenses under slightly different conditions.

Start-up costs must be capitalized and amortized over a period of 60 months or longer under Sec. 195, and organizational costs are given similar treatment under Sec. 248. Costs incurred in raising capital, selling stocks, and printing securities, on the other hand, are never deductible.

Section 263A, a provision of recent origin, requires taxpayers to capitalize as inventory and/or fixed asset costs many items previously charged off as period expenses. These uniform capitalization requirements generally apply to all taxpayers reporting annual average gross receipts in excess of $10 million for the three prior tax years.

The details of these and many other accounting method provisions are best left for other texts. The only two essential conclusions related to the accounting period and method provisions can be stated as follows:

1. Accounting methods that are entirely acceptable for other purposes—including generally accepted accounting methods that may be mandated by the Financial Accounting Standards Board (FASB), the Securities and Exchange Commission (SEC),

or any other regulatory authority—may be wholly unacceptable for income tax purposes.
2. The accounting methods required by the Code vary substantially from one industry to another and from one circumstance to another. Consequently, every taxpayer engaged in a trade or business of any magnitude should obtain the services of a tax expert to ensure compliance with the various accounting provisions contained in the income tax law.

Although taxable income is ordinarily computed on an entity-by-entity basis for each taxable year, the tax law sometimes mandates and at other times permits the taxable income of two of more legally separate entities to be combined or otherwise adjusted to more clearly reflect the taxable income of closely related business ventures. The most specific authority for a partial reallocation of income and deduction items is found in Sec. 482. That provision gives the Secretary of the Treasury authority to reallocate any items among "two or more organizations, trades, or businesses (whether or not incorporated, whether or not organized in the United States, and whether or not affiliated) owned or controlled directly or indirectly by the same interests... if he determines that such distribution, apportionment, or allocation is necessary in order to prevent evasion of taxes or clearly to reflect the income of any of such organizations, trades, or businesses." The regulations issued under Sec. 482 apply an arm's-length standard to all transactions between potentially related parties. The implementation of this standard is a difficult exercise in the extension of normal accounting method provisions. Other provisions that achieve similar results are less subjective in their application.

Aggregating the Income of Separate Legal Entities

Section 1561 requires, while Section 1504 permits, the taxable incomes of two or more corporations to be combined in the determination of the separate tax liability of each corporation. The former section is intended to limit tax avoidance possibilities otherwise available through the use of controlled corporations. The latter section permits a group of affiliated corporations to file one consolidated income tax return for the entire group.

As explained in Chapter 4, every C-corporation that earns a taxable income of less than $335,000 a year is subject to a progressive tax rate structure. Recall that this rate structure imposes a marginal tax rate of only 15 percent on the first $50,000 of taxable income earned in a year and a top marginal rate of 39 percent on all taxable income of between $100,000 and $335,000 each year. The tax rate applicable to corporations earning $335,000 or more each year is a flat 34 percent. This tax rate structure obviously creates a possibility for tax minimization through the use of numerous small corporations rather than one larger one. Observe that the annual tax liability of one corporation earning $335,000 per year is $113,900 (i.e., $335,000 x 34%) while the aggregate annual tax on ten corporations that each earns $33,500 is only $50,250 (i.e., $33,500 x 15% x 10). This represents an annual tax saving of $63,650—an effective cost reduction that is significant in both absolute and relative terms for an income stream of only $335,000 per year. Were it not for such punitive provisions as Secs. 482 and 1561, taxpayers operating relatively small business ventures would almost certainly take advantage of the tax saving opportunities available through multiple corporations.

Section 1561 requires any group of controlled corporations (as defined in Sec. 1563) to add together the (positive) taxable income of all members of the group; determine the income tax liability that would obtain on that total, as if it had all been earned by only one corporation; and then reallocate that total income tax liability back to the several members of the controlled group as their own separate tax liability for the year. If the ten corporations in the example above were members of a controlled group of corporations, their separate tax liabilities would be $11,390 each (i.e., 1/10 of $113,900), rather than $5025 (i.e., 15% of $33,500), and the apparent $63,650 annual tax saving would completely disappear.

The definition of a controlled group of corporations is sufficiently broad to catch most closely held corporate business ventures that do not plan very carefully to avoid this tax trap. The definition includes (1) parent–subsidiary groups, (2) brother–sister groups, and (3) combined groups, i.e., single groups that encompass both parent–subsidiary and brother-sister groups. Although the precise details of the statutory definitions common to each group are too complex to permit their inclusion in an essentials text, the general outline of the differences can be readily depicted as in Exhibits 5.2, 5.3, and 5.4.

Reallocations of income and deduction items under Sec. 482 are common among controlled groups of corporations because there is some reduction in the tax benefit associated with these multiple corporate entities any time that one or more of the corporations has either (1) a loss or (2) taxable income of more than $50,000 in a year. To illustrate, consider the owners of two almost-but-not-quite brother–sister corporations. If the almost-brother corporation recognizes a $50,000 net operating loss for the year and the almost-sister corporation reports a $150,000 taxable income, Sec. 1561 does not authorize

Accounting Periods and Methods

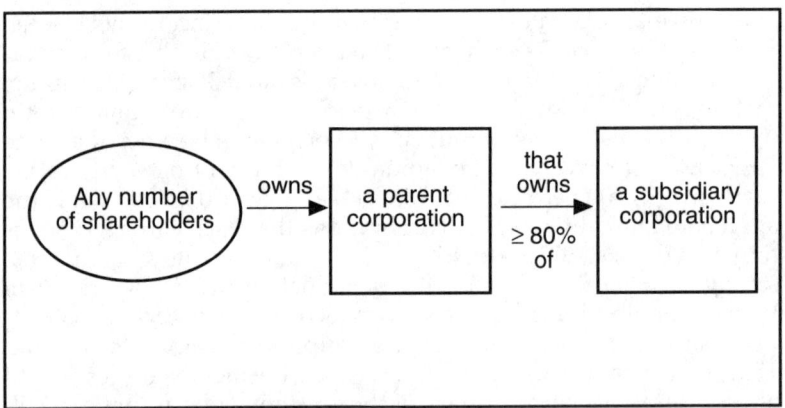

```
            owns                that owns
[Any number] ----> [a parent] ---------->  [a subsidiary
of shareholders]   corporation    ≥ 80%      corporation]
                                   of
```

Exhibit 5.2 A parent–subsidiary group

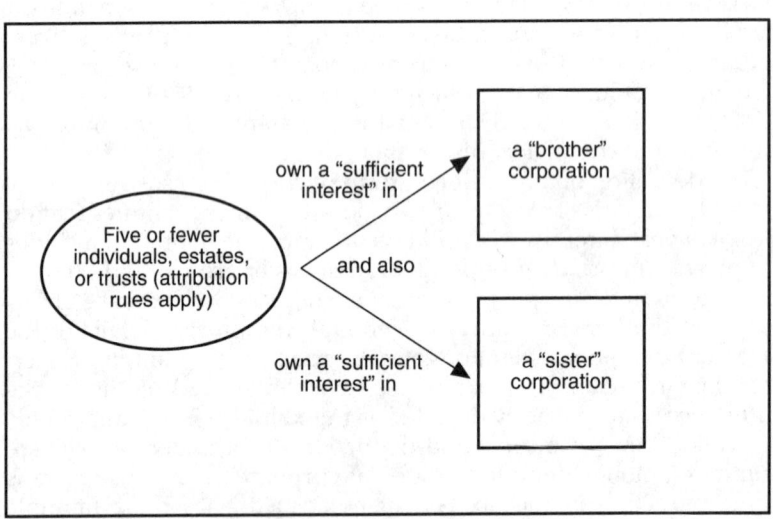

```
                        own a "sufficient
                         interest" in        [a "brother"
                       ------------------>    corporation]
[Five or fewer
individuals, estates,     and also
or trusts (attribution
rules apply)]
                        own a "sufficient
                         interest" in        [a "sister"
                       ------------------>    corporation]
```

Exhibit 5.3 A brother–sister group

Note: The "sufficient interest" definition can be found in Sec. 1563(a)(2); it includes a general 80% ownership test and an "identical" 50% ownership test—tests too complex to detail in an essentials text.

Accounting Periods and Methods

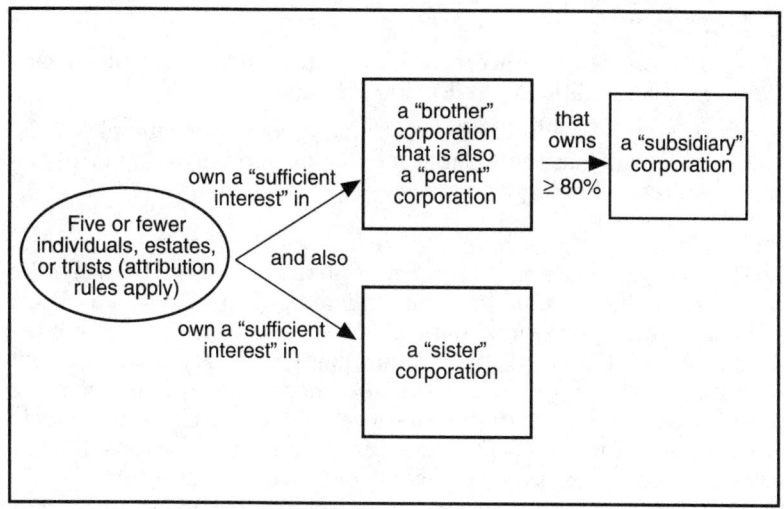

Exhibit 5.4   A combined group

the offsetting of the loss in a brother corporation against the taxable income of a sister corporation. Because these two illustrative corporations are not quite brother–sister corporations (i.e., they fail the definitional requirements of Sec. 1563(a)(2) for some unexplained reason), the owners of the two corporations will be tempted to move income of $100,000 out of the almost-sister corporation and into the almost-brother corporation so that each corporation can report a $50,000 taxable income and the two will pay the minimum aggregate tax of $15,000 (i.e., 2 × $50,000 × 15%). Similarly, if one almost-brother corporation recognized a $10,000 taxable income in a year during which an almost-sister corporation recognized a $90,000 taxable income, there would be good tax reasons for the owners trying to move $40,000 of taxable income from the almost-sister to the almost-brother corporation. This might be attempted by having the favored corporation dispose of an appreciated asset, by intercompany lease arrangements, by intercompany debt and interest payments, etc. The ability of the Secretary of the Treasury to reallocate individual items of gross income and deduction under these circumstances is a major deterrent to many tax-motivated transactions.

The provisions of Sec. 1504 (the consolidated return rules) differ from those of Sec. 1561 (the controlled group rules) in three important ways, namely,

Accounting Periods and Methods

1. Section 1504 is elective, not mandatory;
2. Section 1504 is concerned solely with chains of parent–subsidiary corporations (see Exhibit 5.2); and
3. Section 1504 allows the net operating loss of one member to be offset against the taxable income of another member of the same affiliated group.

Although there are fine-line definitional distinctions between the parent–subsidiary members of an affiliated group (as defined in Sec. 1504) and the parent–subsidiary members of a controlled group (as defined in Sec. 1563(a)(1)), both definitions share a general 80 percent ownership requirement. Consequently, most chains of two or more corporations organized in the parent–subsidiary format must decide whether or not it is advantageous for them to make a consolidated return election. The primary benefits of doing that are ordinarily (1) the right to offset losses of one member against the income of another and (2) the right to ignore any income realized on intergroup transactions until a property has passed outside the affiliated group. Among the costs associated with that election are (1) the need for all members to share common accounting elections and periods (although separate accounting methods are allowed) and (2) the need for the entire group to apply the unusually complex regulations of Sec. 1502 to the transactions of each member. Although the details of these 90 regulations must remain beyond the confines of this book, their existence should be known to anyone who even considers operating multiple corporations in a parent–subsidiary relationship.

In summary, the accounting period for income taxation is generally a period of 12 months, most frequently a calendar year. Although most entities are free to select either a calendar or a fiscal year, conduit entities generally must either (1) be on the same accounting period as their owners or (2) pay in advance for any tax deferral achieved through different years. Affiliated corporations filing a consolidated tax return must also share a common tax year.

Most entities can select freely among various accounting method options. Large C-corporations, tax shelter ventures, and partnerships with corporate partners may, however, be required to use the accrual method of accounting. In addition, any business with substantial inventories must use an accrual method to calculate both net sales and the cost of goods sold. The accrual method of accounting for tax purposes is not the equivalent of that used for financial accounting purposes. And the cash method of accounting cannot be interpreted literally, even for individual taxpayers.

Finally, although most entities compute their tax liability considering only their own accounting periods and methods, a few entities are subject to certain aggregation rules. These special aggregation rules include both (1) those applicable to controlled groups of corporations and (2) those applicable to the consolidated tax return of affiliated groups of corporations.

Key Points to Remember

- Taxable income is computed for a period called a tax year which, in appropriate circumstances, can be
    1. A calendar year,
    2. A fiscal year, or
    3. A short year.
- Short years are permitted only if a taxpayer is in existence for less than a year or the IRS has approved a change in the taxpayer's accounting period.
- Nontaxable entities generally must utilize the same tax year as that used by their primary owners.
- C-corporations, partnerships having a corporate partner, and tax shelters must ordinarily use the accrual method of accounting.
- If the amount of an expense can only be estimated in amount, no deduction generally will be allowed.
- The cash method of accounting includes a cash equivalence standard that turns many noncash transactions into immediately taxable events.
- If inventories are a material income-producing factor, taxpayers must calculate sales and cost of goods sold on an accrual basis even if other items of income and deduction are computed on a cash basis. This possibility is called the hybrid method of accounting.
- Accounting methods that may be mandated by financial accounting authorities are sometimes wholly unacceptable for federal income tax purposes.
- Corporations that are members of a controlled group of corporations—including parent–subsidiary corporations, brother–sister corporations, and combined groups of corporations—are generally not eligible to utilize the low marginal tax rates for separate corporations earning a taxable income of less than $100,000.

Accounting Periods and Methods

- ❏ Corporations that are members of an affiliated group of corporations—defined to include only certain parent-subsidiary groups of corporations—can generally file consolidated tax returns and offset the losses of one or more members of the group against the gains of other members.

SPECIAL RULES FOR INDIVIDUAL TAXPAYERS

Individual taxpayers are generally subject to the same gross income, deduction, and tax-credit provisions as all other taxpayers. There are, however, a sufficient number of provisions that are uniquely applicable to individuals to justify their discussion in a separate chapter. The uniquely human provisions of the Code are generally motivated by a desire for equity or fair play. These equity concerns are often attuned to opposite ends of the same spectrum. Some of the provisions are primarily concerned with the overtaxation of individuals earning a small income, while others are concerned with the undertaxation of individuals earning a large income.

This chapter is organized into four major parts. The first part is substantially more detailed than the other three; it concerns the tax treatment of deductions for individual taxpayers. Part two provides additional detail concerning the personal and dependent exemption deduction provisions; part three explains an interesting tax-rate aberration commonly called the kiddie tax; and part four describes how individual taxpayers report their income and loss from various business interests. The last part of this chapter in particular must be read in the context of all other chapters because nonemployee business income earned by an individual is in general subject to the same tax provisions as all other income.

Deduction Options

Individual taxpayers are subject to at least three major deduction provisions that have no counterpart for other taxpayers. The three major differences in the deductions provisions can be summarized as follows:

1. Individuals must distinguish between items that are deductible for adjusted gross income (AGI) and those deductible from AGI.
2. Individuals may claim a standard deduction if it is larger than their (itemized) deductions from AGI for any year.

3. Most individuals can claim a personal exemption deduction in addition to claiming the larger of the standard deduction or itemized deductions each year. Some individuals may also claim one or more dependent exemption deductions.

These three distinctions can be integrated into the tax formula, introduced in Chapter 4, by expanding it for individual taxpayers (only) as follows:

Gross income
Less deductions for AGI
Equals AGI
    Less: 1. the larger of—
                  a) Deductions from AGI or
                  b) The standard deduction; and
          2. personal and dependent exemption deductions
Equals taxable income

To begin, let us examine the notion of deductions for AGI.

Deductions for AGI

Section 62 defines adjusted gross income for individual taxpayers as the arithmetic difference between gross income and 12 specified deductions. Note that **Sec. 62 does not authorize the deduction of anything**; it provides only that individual taxpayers will treat 12 deductions in a special way if (and to the extent that) they are otherwise entitled to claim any of those 12 deductions. The deductions singled out for this special treatment are:

1. trade and business deductions (**other than** those incurred in the trade or business of being an employee);
2. certain trade or business deductions of employees, specifically (a) reimbursed expenses **to the extent of reimbursement** and (b) certain expenses of performing artists, as defined in Sec. 62(b);
3. losses from the sale or exchange of property;
4. deductions attributable to income from rents and royalties;

5. certain deductions of life tenants and income beneficiaries of property;
6. contributions to pension, profit-sharing, and annuity plans for self-employed taxpayers;
7. certain retirement savings contributions;
8. a portion of any lump-sum distribution from specified pension plans;
9. penalties imposed because of an early withdrawal of funds from time-savings accounts or deposits;
10. alimony;
11. certain reforestation expenses; and
12. certain required repayments of supplemental unemployment compensation benefits.

For individual taxpayers in general, the deductions for AGI of most significance are those numbered 1, 2, 3, 4, 6, 7, 9, and 10. Although the basic concept is apparent in this brief description, a few additional words concerning these eight deductions may be appropriate.

- Item 1. Before any taxpayer can deduct anything as a Sec. 162 (trade or business) expense, the taxpayer must first establish that he or she is engaged in a venture that qualifies as a **trade or business** for income tax purposes. (This requirement was discussed in Chapter 3.)
- Item 2. The effect of this provision is generally a wash for most employees. That is, an employee must first report the reimbursement as income and then deduct it (to the extent of the reimbursement) for AGI. Any deductible amount in excess of reimbursement is thereby relegated to the from AGI classification.
- Item 3. Losses from the sale or exchange of property are frequently subject to limits that are explained in more detail in Chapter 8.
- Item 4. This item assures an individual taxpayer the right to deduct expenses related to rents and royalties even if those activities are insufficient to be classified as a (full-fledged) trade or business.
- Item 6. The maximum contribution to a self-employed taxpayer's qualified retirement plan is generally equal to the maximum deduction available through a corporate plan.
- Item 7. This item generally involves contributions made to an IRA (individual retirement account).

Special Rules for Individual Taxpayers

- Item 9. This effectively assures a taxpayer the right to deduct any penalty paid on the early retirement of a CD (certificate of deposit) or other time-savings account, even if they claim a standard deduction.
- Item 10. Because the recipient must report alimony as income, fairness demands that it be deductible by the payor.

The other four deductions mentioned in Sec. 62(a) are of limited general interest; hence they are dismissed with no additional comment.

Itemized Deductions from AGI

By default, Sec. 62(a) also defines deductions from AGI. Since Sec. 62 merely identifies 12 specific deductions as deductions for AGI, anything else that an individual taxpayer can legally deduct must be a deduction from AGI. Many of the items that can be deducted by individual taxpayers were previously noted on page 39 of Chapter 3. That list includes the deduction provisions that are equally applicable to all taxpayers, i.e., the deductions authorized by Secs. 161 through 196, or Part VI of Subchapter B of the Code. In addition, Part VII—currently Secs. 211 through 219—authorizes six additional deductions for individual taxpayers only. That list includes:

- Sec. 212. Expenses for the production of income
- Sec. 213. Medical, dental, etc., expenses
- Sec. 215. Alimony, etc., payments
- Sec. 216. Deduction of taxes, interest, and business depreciation by cooperative housing corporation tenant-stockholder
- Sec. 217. Moving expenses
- Sec. 219. Retirement savings

The details of these six deduction provisions are numerous; hence we will note in passing only a few of the more important ones.

- Sec. 212 is an important section because it authorizes an individual taxpayer to deduct three very specific, yet generic types of expenditures, even when those items are incurred in something less than a (full-fledged) trade or business. The three deductible expenses under Sec. 212 are those paid or incurred—

Special Rules for Individual Taxpayers

1. for the production or collection of income;
2. for the management, conservation, or maintenance of property held for the production of income; or
3. in connection with the determination, collection, or refund of any tax.

This section, therefore, authorizes an individual to deduct expenses incurred in conjunction with rent and royalty income, even if those activities are *not* considered a trade or business. (Sec. 62(a)(4) goes on to make these same items deductions for AGI rather than deductions from AGI.) Sec. 212 (3) also authorizes an individual to deduct the expense incurred in filing his or her annual income tax return. (Because this item is not included in the list of 12 noted in Sec. 62(a), it is a deduction from AGI that may be claimed only if the taxpayer does not claim a standard deduction.)

- Sec. 213 requires a taxpayer to reduce her or his actual medical and dental expense costs by both (1) any insurance reimbursements and (2) 7 1/2 percent of his or her AGI, in the calculation of the deductible amount. Accordingly, very few individuals are entitled to any medical/dental expense deduction under current law.
- Sec. 215 authorizes the deduction of alimony only. Neither child-support payments nor property settlements are considered alimony. Additional definitional details are best left to other volumes.
- Sec. 217 authorizes the deduction of certain job-related moving expenses if certain time and distance requirements are satisfied. The details of definition and limitation must also remain outside the confines of this essentials text.

For a vast majority of all individual taxpayers, their itemized deductions from AGI will not exceed the standard deduction before the year in which they purchase a home. Once they make that purchase the deduction of home-mortgage interest (authorized by Sec. 163) and real property taxes (authorized by Sec. 164) are generally sufficient to make their itemized deductions larger than the standard deduction.

In aggregate terms, the deduction of interest is the largest single itemized deduction; that of taxes is the second largest. Charitable contribution deductions are the third largest. All of the other itemized

Special Rules for Individual Taxpayers

deductions combined account for approximately 15 percent of the total.

Section 67, added to the Code in 1986, reduced the significance of the miscellaneous or other itemized deductions by requiring the reduction of these expenses (in total) by a floor amount equal to 2 percent of the taxpayer's AGI. Miscellaneous itemized deductions can be claimed today only if, and to the extent that, they collectively exceed 2 percent of the taxpayer's AGI. Miscellaneous itemized deductions are defined in Sec. 67(b) as all deductions from AGI other than 13 specifically identified deductions. The six most important deductions in this list of 13 *not* subject to the 2 percent floor are:

Deduction	Authorized in
Interest	Sec. 163
Taxes	Sec. 164
Losses	Sec. 165(c)(3) or (d)
Charitable contributions	Sec. 170
Medical expenses	Sec. 213
Moving expenses	Sec. 217

The other seven deductions not subject to the 2-percent-of-AGI floor are only rarely encountered by most individuals.

Certain travel and transportation expense deductions claimed by individual taxpayers may be subject to both a 2-percent-of-AGI floor and a separate 20-percent-of-AGI limitation. The 20 percent limit, stipulated in Sec. 274(n), restricts any deduction for (1) meal and (2) entertainment expenses to 80 percent of the cost incurred. The disallowed 20 percent is intended as a crude measure of the purely personal part of any meal and entertainment deduction. If an employee is fully reimbursed for these costs, it is the employer, not the employee, who loses 20 percent of the expense as a deduction. To the extent that an employee is not reimbursed for deductible meal and entertainment expenses, however, the employee must first reduce those expenses by 20 percent of the unreimbursed expenses and then by an additional 2 percent of his AGI, when the remainder of those expenses is combined with all other miscellaneous itemized deductions.

The Code contains many other limitations on the various expenses that may sometimes be deducted by individual taxpayers. Those rules are of limited significance in the overall scheme of income taxation. Therefore, they too are left for other volumes with different objectives.

The Standard Deduction

The Code authorizes individual taxpayers to claim the larger of (1) a standard deduction or (2) other itemized deductions. The amount of the basic standard deduction may vary from one taxpayer to another and from one year to another. The basic standard deductions for 1991 and 1992 can be summarized as follows:

Tax Classification	1991 Amount	1992 Amount
Single persons	$3400	$3600
Heads of households	5000	5250
Married persons filing jointly	5700	6000
Married persons filing separately	2850	3000

In addition to the basic standard deduction, additional amounts may be claimed by certain taxpayers. The additional standard deductions for both 1991 and 1992 can be summarized as follows:

Tax Classification	1991 Amount	1992 Amount
Blind married taxpayers	$650	$700
Married taxpayers 65 or older	$650	$700
Single blind taxpayers	$850	$900
Single taxpayers 65 or older	$850	$900

To illustrate a few of the many possible combinations, note the varying amount of the standard deduction for each of the following taxpayers:

- Single person, age 25, with normal vision: $3400 for 1991 or $3600 for 1992
- Single person, age 66, with normal vision: $4250 for 1991 or $4500 for 1992
- Single person, age 70, and blind: $5100 for 1991 or $5400 for 1992
- Married taxpayers both under age 65, with normal vision: $5700 for 1991 or $6000 for 1992
- Married taxpayers, age 65 and 61; both with normal vision: $6350 for 1991 or $6700 for 1992

Special Rules for Individual Taxpayers

- Married taxpayers, both over age 64; one has normal vision and the other is blind: $7650 for 1991 or $8100 for 1992

All of the standard deduction amounts may be readjusted annually for changes in the CPI. Because inflationary increases are rounded down, to the nearest $50, there may be no adjustment in some years.

Claiming a standard deduction significantly simplifies the annual tax return filing process for most individual taxpayers, especially for those with little or no income from any source other than wages or salary. Taxpayers electing to claim a standard deduction should be certain that they are not sacrificing a significantly larger itemized deduction total simply to gain the ease of compliance associated with a standard deduction.

Personal and Dependent Exemption Deductions

All individual taxpayers, at least initially, may claim some amount as a personal (and, possibly, a dependent) exemption deduction in addition to claiming the larger of (a) the standard deduction or (b) itemized deductions from AGI. One personal exemption deduction is ordinarily claimed for each taxpayer on a return. On the joint return of a married couple, there are ordinarily two personal exemption deductions claimed—one each for the wife and the husband, both of whom are taxpayers on that return. On nearly all other returns from individual taxpayers, only one personal exemption deduction can be claimed.

In addition many individual taxpayers are allowed to claim exemption deductions for dependents. To be claimed as a dependent by another taxpayer, five tests must be satisfied. Those five tests can be summarized as follows:

1. *Relationship.* The dependent must either (a) be a relative of the taxpayer (as defined in Sec. 152) or (b) live with the taxpayer for the entire year.
2. *Gross income.* The dependent must recognize a gross income of less than the amount of one exemption deduction. Exceptions are permitted for (a) the taxpayer's child under 19 years of age and (b) full-time students under age 24. No maximum gross income limit applies to these two special cases.
3. *Support.* The taxpayer claiming a dependent must pay more than half of the total amount spent by the dependent during

the year for support (or basic living costs). Special rules apply to students, children of divorced parents, and individuals supported by two or more persons.
4. *Citizenship/residency.* The person claimed as a dependent must be either a citizen of the United States or a resident of the United States, Canada, or Mexico.
5. *Filing status.* The person claimed as a dependent generally cannot file a joint return with another taxpayer.

A few of the words and phrases used in the brief description of these five tests are given a somewhat uncommon definition for tax purposes. Anyone who attempts to apply the five tests to an actual situation should do so with appropriate caution.

The amount of each exemption deduction is $2150 for 1991 and $2300 for 1992. The amount of the exemption deduction is adjusted each year for changes in the CPI in the same manner as adjustments are made in the standard deduction amounts.

Although nearly all individual taxpayers can initially claim at least one personal exemption deduction, and many taxpayers can also claim additional dependent exemption deductions, they are both effectively taken away from individuals earning a sufficiently large taxable income. The details of this exemption phase-out, including the points at which it becomes operative, were explained in Chapter 4.

The "Kiddie Tax"

The mere existence of three tax factors— (1) a progressive tax rate, (2) a standard deduction, and (3) a personal exemption deduction—created a natural tax avoidance opportunity for wealthy individuals with unemployed (or minimally employed) children. These wealthy individuals had the opportunity to transfer income-producing properties to their children and thereby divert some part of their own taxable income stream to their children. To the extent that the children were otherwise unable to utilize their own standard deduction, personal exemption deduction, and/or low marginal tax rate(s)—because of insufficient income—this diversion made good tax sense.

To illustrate, assume that (1) a married couple earned a sufficiently large taxable income to put them in a 33 percent marginal tax bracket, (2) part of their income derived from two $50,000 certificates of deposit, each earning 8 percent interest per year, and (3) this couple also had two young children who earned no income of their own.

Special Rules for Individual Taxpayers

Given these facts, these parents paid an annual income tax of $2640 on their $8000 interest income from the two CDs. Were there no special tax provisions to modify the usual rules, these parents could transfer one $50,000 CD to each of their two children; the children could both file their own tax returns, claiming a ($2300) personal exemption deduction and a ($3600) standard deduction; and the ($2640) annual income tax liability would completely disappear.

The scenario described in the preceding paragraph was entirely possible, and frequently achieved, in most years prior to 1987. Because of recent changes in the Code, however, that happy tax result is no longer possible. The recent statutory modifications that most directly effect this situation can be summarized as follows:

1. Persons properly claimed as a dependent by someone else *cannot* claim a personal exemption deduction on their own tax return (Sec. 151(d)(2)).

2. The standard deduction for any person properly claimed as a dependent by someone else cannot exceed the greater of (a) $550 or (b) that person's earned income (Sec. 63(c)(5)). The term *earned income* includes only the income derived from a taxpayer's own efforts; it excludes such passive income as interest, rents, and royalties.

3. Any net unearned income recognized by children under 14 years of age is taxed at their parents' marginal rate if that results in a larger tax liability (Sec. 1(i)). Unfortunately, the statutory definition of the term net unearned income is too complex to justify a complete explanation of it here. The general idea, however, is explained below.

The popular press has come to identify the possible taxation of a child's unearned income at their parents' marginal rate (item #3, above) as the kiddie tax. To determine the amount of income subject to this special tax rate, you first determine the child's taxable income considering the special rules for the personal exemption and standard deduction, above. (That is, considering items #1 and #2, above.) The next step is the determination of the child's net unearned income. In general this amount is equal to the **lesser** of (a) the child's taxable income or (b) the child's gross unearned (or passive) income less $1100. (The prior sentence ignores special complexities that arise if the child's deductions from AGI exceed the standard deduction—a rare phenomenon. Those complexities are ignored in this text.)

To illustrate these three new provisions, reconsider the example suggested earlier in which parents transfer an 8-percent, $50,000-face CD to each of two young children. The children would each report a taxable income of $3450 (i.e., a $4000 gross income less only a $550 standard deduction). Each child would also have net unearned income of $2900 (i.e., the lesser of $3450 or $2900). Given these facts, each child would pay an income tax of $1040, determined as follows:

Net unearned income ($2900) taxed at the parents' (33 percent) marginal rate:	$ 957
Plus all remaining taxable income ($550) taxed at the child's (15 percent) marginal rate:	83
Total tax liability per child:	$1040

Today these parents would save only $560 per year (i.e., $2640 less 2 x $1040) by giving the CDs to their children, so long as the children are under age 14. The statutory changes have substantially reduced the incentive for parents to transfer income producing properties to young children. On the other hand, the same statutory changes have greatly increased the incentive for parents (and grandparents) to give young children Series E savings bonds and other selected assets that permit a taxpayer to defer the recognition of any income until the maturity of the bond—a date carefully timed to fall sometime after the child's 14th birthday!

The correct computation of the tax liability for a child under 14 who has both earned and unearned income can become inordinately complicated, especially in large families of divorced parents. To facilitate compliance, if the child's gross income is under $5000 and is derived entirely from interest and/or dividends, the parents may simply include the child's income on their return for years after 1988. Anyone interested in the nuances of the income tax law for children under 14 must consult other books or visit a qualified tax adviser.

Business Income

The income that a taxpayer earns by operating a trade or business as a sole proprietorship is reported on Schedule C, Form 1040. A separate schedule should be filed for each separate trade or business. The net income from each schedule is simply carried over to the first page of

Special Rules for Individual Taxpayers

the proprietor's personal (or individual) Form 1040 where it is added to his or her income from all other sources. The tax provisions that govern the reporting of this business income are the same rules as are explained in other chapters of this text.

Individuals earning interest and/or dividend income report that income in a similar manner using Schedule B. Capital gains and losses are reported on Schedule D; income from rents and royalties, on Schedule E; income from farming, on Schedule F; etc. An individual partner's share of any partnership income or loss items is reported on Schedule K-1 (Form 1065); a stockholder's share of any income or loss items from an S-corporation is reported on Schedule K-1 (Form 1120-S) as well as on Schedule E.

In addition to the various business income schedules, an individual taxpayer's complete tax return may include many other schedules and documents. For example, wages and salaries (as well as the income tax withheld on those items) is reported on Form W-2. Itemized deductions (from AGI) are reported on Schedule A. An individual subject to the passive activity loss limitation—a provision explained in Chapter 8—will also file a Form 8582. Those persons claiming a child care credit file Form 2441; those required to pay the social security tax on self-employment income file Schedule SE. And the list of forms goes on and on. A few additional details concerning the compliance process are included in Chapter 9.

In summary, the complete tax return of an individual taxpayer can be a very complex report that encompasses both some very special rules that are unique to individual taxpayers and many general rules applicable to all taxpayers. The manner in which these diverse rules come together in one Form 1040 is depicted in Exhibit 6.1. The essential conclusion is that individual taxpayers are responsible for currently reporting not only the income that they earn in the form of wages and salaries, but also much of the business income generated within the United States as well as some portion of that generated in other countries.

Key Points to Remember

- ❏ Deductions claimed by individual taxpayers must be divided between deductions for adjusted gross income (AGI) and deductions from AGI by applying the rules provided in Sec. 62.
- ❏ Individual taxpayers generally can claim the larger of their itemized deductions from AGI or a standard deduction. In

Special Rules for Individual Taxpayers

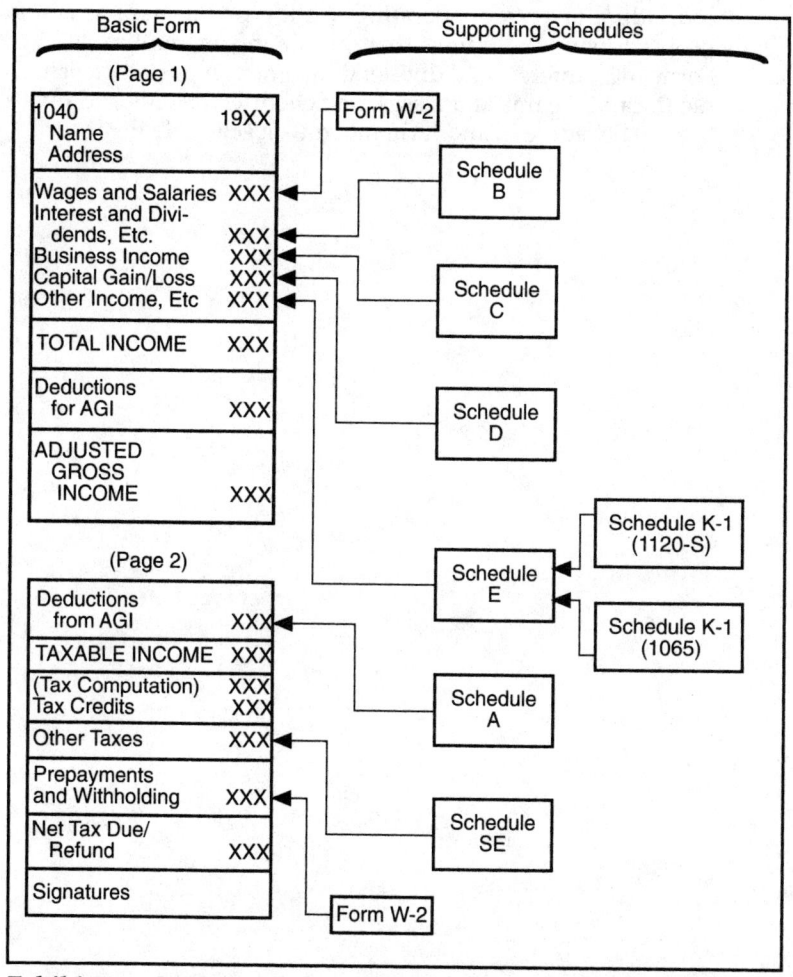

```
          Basic Form                    Supporting Schedules
           (Page 1)

  1040                 19XX       Form W-2
    Name
    Address
                                       Schedule
  Wages and Salaries   XXX            B
  Interest and Divi-
    dends, Etc.        XXX
  Business Income      XXX
  Capital Gain/Loss    XXX
  Other Income, Etc    XXX             Schedule
                                          C
  TOTAL INCOME         XXX

  Deductions
    for AGI            XXX             Schedule
                                          D
  ADJUSTED
   GROSS
    INCOME             XXX
                                                     Schedule K-1
                                                       (1120-S)
          (Page 2)                     Schedule
                                          E
  Deductions                                         Schedule K-1
    from AGI           XXX                             (1065)
  TAXABLE INCOME       XXX
  (Tax Computation)    XXX             Schedule
  Tax Credits          XXX                A
  Other Taxes          XXX

  Prepayments
  and Withholding      XXX
  Net Tax Due/                          Schedule
    Refund             XXX                SE

  Signatures
                                   Form W-2
```

Exhibit 6.1 Overview of an individual's tax return

addition, most individual taxpayers can also claim some amount as a personal and dependent exemption deduction.

❑ Children under 14 years of age reporting unearned income in excess of $1100 per year must determine their tax liability on any additional amount of unearned income using the parents' (if higher) marginal tax brackets(s). Under some conditions the parents may include this child's taxable income on their own tax return.

ESSENTIALS OF U.S. TAXATION / **6.13**

Special Rules for Individual Taxpayers

- ❏ Individual taxpayers operating a trade or business as a sole proprietorship will report that taxable income on Schedule C, Form 1040. Interest and dividend income is reported on Schedule B; capital gains and losses, on Schedule D; rents and royalties, on Schedule E; and farm income on schedule F.

PROPERTY TRANSACTIONS

The definition of income provided in Sec. 61 leaves no doubt concerning the taxation of **gains** from property transactions. It reads, in part, as follows:

> Except as otherwise provided in this subtitle, gross income means all income...including...gains derived from dealings in property.

Sec. 61 says nothing, however, about the right to deduct losses from property transactions. This void suggests that the income concept used in taxation does not automatically include negative as well as positive results derived from dealings in property.

As explained in Chapter 3, deductions are a matter of legislative grace. In the absence of specific authority, nothing is deductible. Fortunately, the Code does include several provisions that authorize the deduction of losses in various circumstances. The rules concerning loss deductions are sufficiently complex that they are best examined separately. A detailed discussion of the loss provisions is deferred to the next chapter.

This chapter is divided into three major parts. The first explains how both gains and losses from property transactions are measured. The second part discusses the capital asset provisions briefly. Although not every property transaction involves a capital asset, many do, and—because those transactions may be subject to special rules—they must be considered separately for tax purposes. The final part introduces a few of the more important nontaxable exchange provisions. Recall that gains from property dealings are taxable **except as otherwise provided** in the Code. The nontaxable exchange provisions are the exceptions obliquely referred to in this familiar statutory phrase.

Measuring Gains and Losses

The primary authority governing both (1) the measurement of and (2) the need to recognize gains and losses from property transactions is

Sec. 1001. The basic measurement rules are found in Sec. 1001(a); the recognition rules, in Sec. 1001(c). They read as follows:

- Sec. 1001(a): "Computation of gain or loss.—The gain from the sale or other disposition of property shall be the excess of the amount realized therefrom over the adjusted basis provided in section 1011 for determining gain, and the loss shall be the excess of the adjusted basis provided in such section for determining loss over the amount realized."
- Sec. 1001(c): "Recognition of gain or loss.—Except as otherwise provided in this subtitle, the entire amount of the gain or loss, determined under this section, on the sale or exchange of property shall be recognized."

Even a cursory reading of Sec. 1001(a) suggests that the definition of two terms is critical to the measurement of gains and losses. Those two terms, *amount realized* and *adjusted basis*, are defined below.

Section 1001(c) is more difficult to comprehend quickly. First, note that subsection (c) appears to authorize the deduction of all losses derived from property transactions. Unfortunately, this initially sweeping conclusion is tempered with that common qualification, "except as otherwise provided in this subtitle." Because the word *subtitle* refers to all six chapters of the income tax, there is ample opportunity for modification elsewhere. As you will discover in Chapter 8, the Code does so otherwise provide in a number of places; consequently, many property losses are not deductible. An even more subtle distinction is buried later in the deceptively simple, one-sentence subsection 1001(a). The Code provides that gain or loss is to be measured on "...the sale **or other disposition of property**"; whereas subsection (c) requires a "sale **or exchange**" (emphasis added). This subtle distinction was noted by the courts many years ago and as a result some taxpayers were denied the right to deduct a loss for want of a **sale or exchange**. For example, stock or securities held until they are worthless cannot be sold to anyone or exchanged for anything of value in a free market. To accommodate the administration of tax law, the sale-or-exchange requirement of Sec. 1001(c) has generally been modified by other statutory provisions that create an artificial or assumed sale in appropriate circumstances. For example, Sec. 165(g) provides that losses from worthless securities shall "...be treated as loss from the sale or exchange, on the last day of the taxable year, of a capital asset." Today the most common problem inherent in the taxation of property transactions is one of measurement.

Amount Realized

The term **amount realized** is defined in Sec. 1001(b) as "...the sum of any money received plus the fair market value of the property (other than money) received." The courts have added a third component to the meaning of amount realized. The judicial addition is, oversimplified, debt relief. (See *Crane v. Com'mr.*, 331 U.S. 1 (1947).) If a taxpayer makes a property disposition and in the process is also relieved of some amount of debt associated with that property, the taxpayer making the property disposition is deemed to have received something of value equal in amount to the debt relief achieved. Incidentally, it makes no difference whether or not the taxpayer remains secondarily liable on the debt after the disposition. If the party acquiring the property either assumes the debt or takes the property subject to the debt, the transferor is deemed to have received something of value in addition to any cash and any other property received. This conclusion is equally applicable to relief from ordinary debt as it is to relief from nonrecourse debt. (See *Com'mr. v. Tufts*, 461 U.S. 300 (1983).)

The practical problems associated with the valuation of noncash properties are legion. The law generally requires the immediate valuation of all properties involved in a transaction, major practical problems notwithstanding. If the IRS refuses to accept the value determined by a taxpayer engaged in a property transaction, that dispute may have to be resolved in court. The judicial issue is a question of fact; hence the decision reached by the trial court is of particular importance because appellate courts only rarely overturn lower courts on questions of fact. Professional valuation experts are frequently engaged to help taxpayers estimate a reasonable value that the IRS will likely accept. In many cases the major problem is not the aggregate valuation of a collection of properties—because that total value is frequently established in an arm's-length, contractual arrangement—but is, rather, a question of the allocation of the total purchase price among the various properties acquired. The taxpayer typically wants to allocate most of the total purchase price to items that can be deducted in the immediate future, or at least in the near term. The IRS, on the other hand, seems prone to allocate as much of the total to goodwill and other assets (such as land) that provide no tax deduction in the short run. For some purposes, regulations have been issued to clarify the IRS's interpretation of the correct allocation procedure. The most important of these are the regulations under Sec. 1060 dealing with the acquisition of a business.

Regardless of how any valuation question may be resolved, the amount realized in a property transaction is equal to the arithmetic sum of:

Property Transactions

1. any cash received plus
2. the fair market value of any noncash property received plus
3. the amount of debt transferred to, or assumed by, another taxpayer.

To illustrate, assume that taxpayer X transferred a tract of undeveloped land to Y in exchange for $80,000 cash plus a secondhand airplane (valued at $150,000) and that taxpayer Y assumed an outstanding mortgage of $195,000 on this land. Given these facts, taxpayer X will have an amount realized equal to $425,000 (i.e., $80,000 cash plus a $150,000 airplane plus $195,000 in debt relief). If taxpayer X's adjusted basis in the land given up is $300,000, X must recognize a gain of $125,000 (i.e., $425,000 amount realized less $300,000 adjusted basis). But if taxpayer X's adjusted basis were $500,000, X may or may not be able to recognize a loss of $75,000 (i.e., $500,000 adjusted basis less $425,000 amount realized.) The conclusions concerning both the $125,000 gain and the possible $75,000 loss are subject to the presumption that no special Code section provides some other result.

Adjusted Basis

The simple cross reference from Sec. 1001(a) to Sec. 1011, to determine the adjusted basis of property, is grossly misleading. Section 1011 directly cross references two sections and indirectly refers to an uncertain number of unidentified ones (sections that may be found in any of four subchapters of the Code) for the determination of basis. It reads, in critical part, as follows:

> Sec. 1011(a): "General rule.—The adjusted basis for determining the gain or loss from the sale or other disposition of property whenever acquired, shall be the basis (determined under section 1012 or other applicable sections of this subchapter and subchapters C (relating to corporate distributions and adjustments), K (relating to partners and partnerships), and P (relating to capital gains and losses)), adjusted as provided in section 1016."

A complete investigation of each of the several basis provisions in Subchapters C, K, O, and P, plus the details of Secs. 1012 and 1016, is impossible in an essentials text. What follows in lieu thereof is a cursory summary of the more commonly encountered basis provisions. The reader must understand that the actual result in a specific situation may be subject to additional rules not summarized here. The general rules provided below should not be used, without additional investigation, in the calculation of the gain or loss in an actual property transaction.

Purchased Property. The original basis of property acquired in a taxable transaction is ordinarily equal to its cost, per Sec. 1012. The original basis of any property may change over time; as it does, its basis will be referred to as an adjusted basis. The **adjusted basis** of a purchased asset is generally equal to its original basis (or cost) **plus** capital improvements **less** depreciation (as measured for income tax purposes). This is a tax equivalent of book value for financial accounting purposes. It is a concept that is specifically applicable to most fixed assets such as plant and equipment.

The original basis of a purchased stock or security in a C-corporation, on the other hand, will be equal to its initial cost plus any broker's commission incurred to acquire the stock or the security. In many instances this original basis in stock will not change between the date of acquisition and the date of disposition. It may change, however, because of subsequent events. For example, the receipt of a tax-free stock dividend by a shareholder would necessitate a reallocation of the original basis over a larger number of shares, whereas the receipt of a cash dividend would require no basis adjustment. To illustrate, if taxpayer Z purchased 100 shares of ABC common stock for $10,000 cash plus a broker's commission of $200, Z's original basis would be $102 per share (or $10,200 divided by 100). If Z were to receive a $1000 cash dividend on these 100 shares, there would be no change in Z's tax basis in the 100 shares owned. Rather, the extra basis acquired via the payment of an income tax on the $1000 dividend received would logically "lodge" in the $1000 cash. On the other hand, if Z received a **nontaxable stock dividend** consisting of 20 additional shares of ABC common stock, Z would adjust the original basis downward from $102 to $85 per share (i.e., the $10,200 original basis divided now by 120 shares). Taxpayers who purchase securities (i.e., the long-term debt of corporations) may similarly be permitted to increase their basis in the securities that they own if they are required to amortize and report for income tax purposes any discount associated with that corporate security.

Shareholders in S-corporations and partners in partnerships, on the other hand, must constantly adjust their original basis in these investments to reflect the tax consequences that transpire relative to their property interest. To illustrate, if taxpayer A paid $500,000 cash for 50 percent of the outstanding stock of XYZ Corporation—a subchapter-S corporation for federal income tax purposes—A's original basis in the XYZ common stock would be $500,000. If XYZ thereafter reported a $400,000 taxable income for the next year, A would be required to report and pay tax on $200,000 (or 50 percent) of that same income, and A would thereby be entitled to increase the basis in the XYZ stock from $500,000 to $700,000. If, sometime during the second year, XYZ were to distribute $100,000 cash to its shareholders, A would not have to report the receipt of half that cash (or $50,000) as a dividend (because XYZ is an S-corporation), but A would have to decrease the basis in the XYZ stock from $700,000 to $650,000 following the receipt of the $50,000 cash.

Shareholders in S-corporations and partners in partnerships must also decrease their tax basis in an S-corporation's stock or a partnership interest whenever tax losses are reported by these conduit entities. In summary, both the original tax basis and an adjusted tax basis can be critical to the measurement of any gain or loss on the disposition of a purchased property.

Inherited Property. The original basis of an inherited property is usually equal to its fair market value on the date of the decedent's death, per Sec. 1014. The most important exception to this general rule arises when the executor of a decedent's estate elects to value the property for estate tax purposes on the alternate valuation date which is, in general, exactly six months after the day of death. If the executor elects this alternate valuation date, the basis of a property inherited from such an estate will ordinarily be equal to its value on that same (alternate) date. This basis rule is a very important one for tax planning purposes. Although it is commonly referred to as the step-up-in-basis rule—because the value of most property tends to increase over time, due to the effects of inflation—this same rule also triggers a step-down in basis for any property in a decedent's estate that has an adjusted basis in excess of its value. To appreciate the significance of the basis rule for inherited property, consider what happens tax-wise on the death of many successful entrepreneurs. Their estates are often characterized by a large block of corporate stock with very little basis. Had the decedent sold this stock prior to death, he or she would have had to pay a large amount of income tax, frequently measured in millions of dollars. At the moment after their death, however, their heirs can (theoretically at least) sell that same stock and recognize no gain or loss because the amount realized on the sale will equal the adjusted basis in the stock sold. Note also that an estate tax will have to be paid whether or not an income tax was paid on the disposition of any stock prior to the decedent's death. The estate tax is based on the net value of all property owned by the decedent at death, plus the value of taxable gifts the decedent made during life. Therefore, the estate tax will not be reduced by pre-death income tax liabilities except to the extent that those income tax liabilities have directly decreased the value of the decedent's remaining estate. Because of this basis rule for inherited properties, many elderly individuals are said to be "locked-in" to highly appreciated investments.

Gift Property. The original basis of property acquired by gift is usually equal to the adjusted basis of the gifted property in the hands of the donor prior to the gift, per Sec. 1015. To illustrate, assume that taxpayer A gives taxpayer B 1000 shares of common stock in XYZ Corporation. If taxpayer A's basis in those 1000 shares was $5300 prior to the gift, that will also be taxpayer B's basis in those same shares unless an exception to the general rule applies. The two most important exceptions concern (1) depreciated properties and (2) gifts that trigger a gift tax liability. As used in the preceding sentence, the term **depreciated property** means a property with a basis greater than its value. To illustrate, consider again the gift of 1000 shares of XYZ common stock by A to B. If the value of those 1000 shares was less than A's basis of $5300 on the date A gave them to B, then the shares would be a depreciated property and a special exception to the general rule (suggested above) would apply. That exception provides that B's basis for measuring loss (only!) is equal to the fair market value of the shares on the date of the gift. To continue the prior illustration, if the value of the 1000 shares was $4000 on the date of the gift, then B would have a $4000 basis for the measurement of loss and a $5300 basis for the measurement of gain. Therefore, if B were sometime later to sell these 1000 shares for $3500, B would recognize a loss of only $500. And if B were to sell the shares for $5000, B would recognize neither gain nor loss because the selling price falls between the basis for loss and the basis for gain. As a practical result of this provision, people who know the basis rules rarely give away a depreciated property, at least in those circumstances where the donor could sell the property and recognize the entire loss implicit in the decline in value.

The second exception to the general basis rule for property received by gift allows a donee to increase the donor's basis in those cases where a gift tax was triggered by the making of the gift. The exact amount of the increase in basis depends upon the date of the gift. Because those rules are relatively complex, and because so few gifts are subject to a gift tax of any large amount, they are not explained in this text. Those readers who have received gifts in excess of $10,000 in one year, from any one donor, should look elsewhere for the details of this second exception.

Bartered Property. The basis of property acquired in a partially or completely nontaxable exchange usually involves something known as either **substituted basis** or **carryover basis**. The statutory authority for the exact basis rule in these circumstances depends largely on the statutory provision that makes the transaction either partially or wholly nontaxable. The most frequently encountered nontaxable exchange provisions are explained in the final part of this chapter. Accordingly, the discussion of the basis rules that apply to these nontaxable property transactions is also deferred to that portion of this chapter.

The Capital Gains Provisions

The capital gain provisions were of major importance to U.S. income taxation in all years from 1922 through 1986. The Tax Reform Act of 1986 eliminated the preferential treatment of capital gains while retaining the unfavorable treatment of capital losses. However, the complete elimination of preferential treatment for capital gains turned out to be short-lived. As a result of the Revenue Reconciliation Act of 1990, capital gains now receive modestly favorable treatment as compared to ordinary income. The maximum tax rate applied to capital gains income is 28 percent. Since the maximum rate of tax applied to ordinary income is 31 percent, a taxpayer may save up to 3 percent. Although such savings are of little importance, the relative significance of the capital gains provisions is likely to increase greatly if either of two things happen. First, a significant number of legislators have backed a cut in the tax rates applied to capital gains on the grounds that such a cut would stimulate investment and economic growth. Second, the continuing large deficits suggest that, sooner or later, substantial increases in tax rates on ordinary income will occur. Even in the absence of such changes, the identification of and treatment of capital losses are of significant interest; a discussion that is deferred to Chapter 8.

For the years immediately prior to 1987, the benefit of recognizing a net long-term capital gain, rather than ordinary income, differed between corporate and non-corporate taxpayers. (The classification of capital gains and losses as short-term or long-term depends on how long the taxpayer holds the property. Today long-term status is achieved after holding a property for more than one year. In the past, that holding period was often as short as six months.) Corporations had the option of paying a 28 percent (maximum) alternative tax rate on net capital gains; noncorporate taxpayers could claim a special deduction equal to 60 percent of the net capital gain realized in any year. Both of these provisions were a major incentive for taxpayers to convert ordinary income into capital gain. Individuals were anxious to recognize only $400,000 rather than $1,000,000 in taxable income (because of the long-term capital gain deduction) and corporations were equally anxious to pay 28 percent, rather than 46 percent, of their income in taxes when realizing a million dollar gain.

Given the generosity of these two tax incentives, it is easy to understand why the definition of capital assets was so important prior to 1987 and why it could become important again in the near future. The critical definition begins with Sec. 1221 and extends through some 25 to 30 additional provisions in Part IV of Subchapter O (i.e., in Secs. 1231 through 1257). The latter sections modify, extend, and/or contract the initial statutory definition. We will not review these definitional complications here because (1) they are of limited significance today and (2) they are inordinately complex, even for the Code. If the capital gain provisions regain their pre-1987 importance, a detailed investigation of those same rules would be appropriate for any reader of this book.

Section 1221 provides that **all assets are capital assets unless they are included in one of the five categories detailed below**. The five categories of property excluded from the definition of capital asset are:

1. Inventory or other "...property held by the taxpayer primarily for sale to customers in the ordinary course of his trade or business";
2. Real or depreciable property, if used in a trade or business;
3. Created properties in the hands of the creator (or one who has the creator's basis) plus "a letter, memorandum, or similar property" in the hands of the person for whom it was prepared or produced;
4. Receivables acquired from the sale of inventory in the ordinary course of a trade or business; and
5. Government publications acquired in some manner other than by purchase.

The reasons for some of the exceptions are obvious; others require explanation. Inventories and receivables from the sale of inventory must be excluded from any definition of capital assets to avoid the classification of normal business profits as capital gain, rather than as ordinary income. The reason for excluding other assets is less apparent.

ESSENTIALS OF U.S. TAXATION / **7.09**

Property Transactions

The exclusion of fixed assets, or plant and equipment (as those terms are used by financial accountants), clearly requires further explanation. Fixed assets were capital assets in all years prior to the Great Depression of the 1930s. Because of some limitations on the deduction of capital losses—explained in Chapter 8—they were first excluded from the definition of capital assets in 1938. This politically expedient solution to a loss problem proved to be unacceptable to many taxpayers who sold their fixed assets at large gains during the high-tax years following World War II. To rectify that dilemma, Congress enacted the predecessor of what is now known as Sec. 1231. That provision gives the taxpayer the best of both worlds relative to fixed assets and selected other properties by holding the definition of capital assets in abeyance until the end of each tax year: If the net losses on Sec. 1231 properties exceed the gains on those same properties for the year, they are all classified as ordinary assets; but if overall gains exceed losses, they are classified as capital assets. This political solution eventually proved to be unacceptable to the Treasury because it created too great an opportunity to convert ordinary income (via depreciation deductions, claimed during the years in which fixed assets were used) into capital gains (via Sec. 1231 classification at the time fixed assets were sold). Therefore, numerous recapture sections —such as Secs. 1245 and 1250 which recapture depreciation—were added to the Code, to limit these tax-avoidance opportunities. To summarize, Sec. 1221(2) first provides that fixed assets are *not* capital assets; Sec. 1231 goes on, however, to provide that those same assets *may* be treated as capital assets under some conditions (if gains exceed losses for the year); then still other sections—such as Secs. 1245 and 1250—provide that the exception of Sec. 1231 might not apply, at least to the extent that a deduction has been claimed in prior years, under varying circumstances for different assets and different taxpayers. As noted before, the details of these and other definitional complexities can largely be ignored only so long as the capital asset provisions play a minor role in U.S. income taxation.

The exception of "created properties" from the capital asset definition is noteworthy for at least two reasons:

1. This exception generally causes the income earned by artists, writers, composers and others to be treated for tax purposes like the income earned by mechanics, physicians, farmers, and other business persons. (The one notable exception to this conclusion involves the right of U.S. patent holders to get capital gain treatment, under certain circumstances, per Sec. 1235.)

Property Transactions

2. This exception also minimizes the opportunity for former presidents and other political and creative leaders to achieve private gain from public service through the donation of their private papers to a public library upon retirement or death. This limitation is achieved by the interaction of two apparently separate Code provisions: Sec. 1221(3), which makes these properties ordinary (or noncapital) assets, and Sec. 170(e), which limits the amount of the charitable contribution deduction for most ordinary-income properties to their basis (rather than to their fair market value).

Finally, observe that Sec. 1221(1) excludes from the capital asset classification both (a) inventory and (b) "other assets" held primarily for resale. Various courts have held that these two statutory terms, joined by the conjunction *or*, cannot be interpreted synonymously. These judicial holdings have created a substantial amount of ambiguity as to the correct classification of any properties sold by a taxpayer, with some degree of frequency over a prolonged period, even though the taxpayer is not *primarily* engaged in that specific trade or business. Actors, executives, physicians, attorneys, and many other professionals have frequently engaged in real estate transactions in the same years that they engaged in their other primary occupations. In most instances, any gains realized on the real estate transactions have been reported as capital gains from investments. In some cases, however, the IRS has contended that the taxpayer's activities justify the conclusion that the taxpayer is concurrently engaged in two or more trades or businesses, and that all gains from the real estate transactions must be reported as ordinary income, rather than capital gain, per the "other-property" exception of Sec. 1221(1). The traditional taxpayer and IRS roles may be reversed in those years in which net losses occur from the disposition of real estate properties. In loss years taxpayers often argue the "other-property"/ordinary-loss result, whereas the IRS will argue for investment asset/capital loss treatment.

In summary, the one essential conclusion is that the capital-asset status of many properties may be difficult to determine because of either (a) numerous statutory exceptions to the initial definition of Sec. 1221 or (b) numerous judicial decisions interpreting the various words and phrases used in Sec. 1221. International taxpayers in particular must understand that the concepts of capital gain and loss utilized for income tax purposes vary significantly from one national jurisdiction to another. The assumption that the term *capital gain* means the same thing in different countries is exceedingly dangerous.

Property Transactions

Some Nontaxable Exchange Provisions

Although there are numerous nontaxable exchange provisions scattered throughout the Code, most of these apparently disparate provisions have several things in common. In addition to a uniquely defined property requirement in each section, the four most important commonalties can be summarized as follows:

1. Either
   a) a direct-exchange requirement or
   b) a time-for-completion requirement,
2. a carryover basis rule,
3. a "boot" provision, and
4. very specific, definitional requirements.

The two common patterns for the nontaxable exchange transaction can be illustrated as in Exhibits 7.1 and 7.2. Exhibit 7.1 illustrates a **direct exchange**; Exhibit 7.2, an **indirect exchange** (with a time-for-completion requirement). In these and all subsequent illustrations in this chapter a set of common abbreviations will be used. They are:

P = a property, other than cash (P_1 = property #1, P_2 = property #2 etc.),
$\$$ = cash,
B = adjusted basis on the date of the sale or exchange, and
V = fair market value on the date of the sale or exchange.

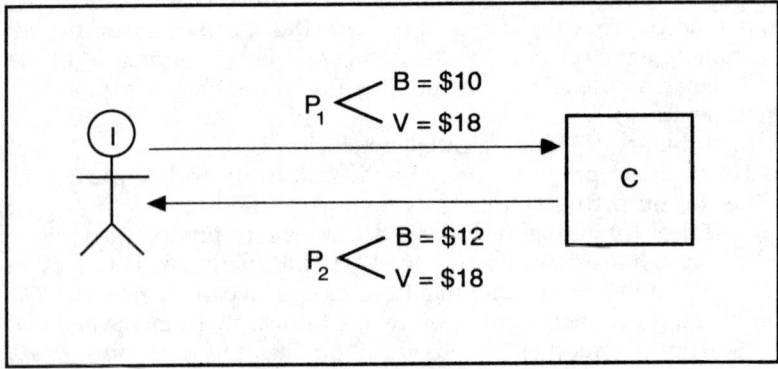

Exhibit 7.1 A direct property exchange

7.12 / ESSENTIALS OF U.S. TAXATION

Property Transactions

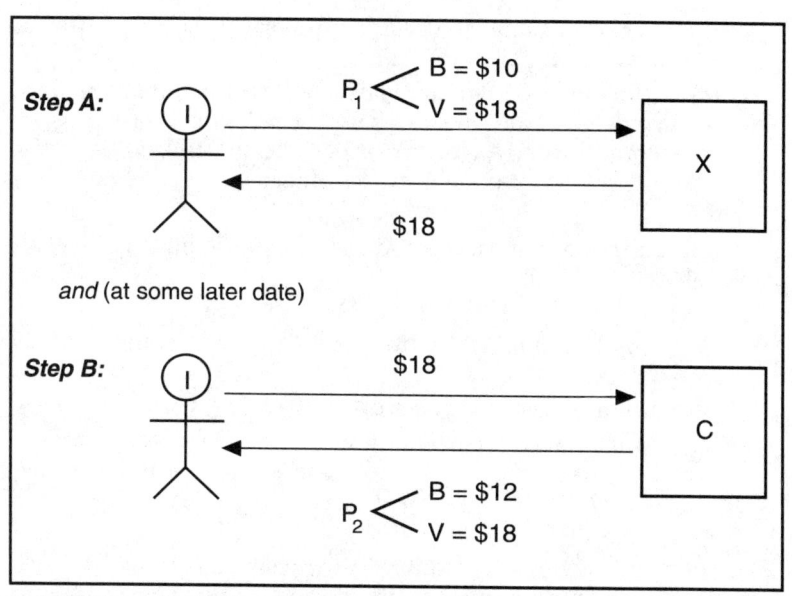

```
Step A:   (I)      P₁ < B = $10
                       V = $18
          ———————————————————————→  [X]
          ←———————————————————————
                    $18
```

and (at some later date)

```
Step B:   (I)           $18
          ———————————————————————→  [C]
          ←———————————————————————
                     P₂ < B = $12
                          V = $18
```

Exhibit 7.2 An indirect property exchange

Given these symbols and the tax provisions discussed earlier in this part, the essential tax questions should be reasonably apparent. Observe that in the transaction illustrated in Exhibit 7.1 an individual taxpayer (person I) is directly exchanging property #1 for property #2, and that a corporate taxpayer (corporation C) is doing just the reverse; i.e., C is exchanging property #2 for property #1. The two most important tax questions can be summarized as follows:

1. Must I recognize $8 of income?
2. Must C recognize $6 of income?

(If the small numbers used in this example make the transaction appear either unrealistic or trivial, simply add as many zeros as reality or significance demands. The tax principle will be the same if question #1 concerns either $8 or $8,000,000 of income.) To translate the illustration of Exhibit 7.1 into statutory terms, question #1 could be rephrased as three questions as follows:

   a) What is I's "amount realized?" (*Answer*: $18, the fair market value of property #2.)

ESSENTIALS OF U.S. TAXATION / **7.13**

Property Transactions

      b) What is I's adjusted basis in property #1? (*Answer*: $10, as given in the illustration.)

      c) Must the $8 difference between the ($18) amount realized and the ($10) adjusted basis be recognized as gross income by I? (*Answer*: Yes, per Sec. 1001(c), *unless* some other Code section provides otherwise.)

The most important questions and answers pertinent to taxpayer C are equally obvious: That is,

      a) What amount did C realize? (*Answer*: $18, the value of property #1.)
      b) What basis did C give up? (*Answer*: $12, per Exhibit 7.1.)
      c) Must C recognize $6 of gross income? (*Answer*: Yes, per Sec. 1001(c), *unless* some Code section provides otherwise.)

The two transactions in Exhibit 7.2 appear at first blush to be nothing more than an indirect route to the same end result as that depicted in Exhibit 7.1. In other words, in Step A of Exhibit 7.2, individual taxpayer I appears to be selling P_1 to corporation X for $18, cash, and then (sometime later) I appears to be acquiring P_2 from corporation C for $18. In Exhibit 7.1, I moves *directly* from P_1 to P_2; in Exhibit 7.2, I moves indirectly from P_1 to P_2, with an undefined but temporary cash-holding period being inserted between the disposition of P_1 and the acquisition of P_2. One critical tax question remains the same as before; i.e., must I recognize the $8 of gain realized in Step A of Exhibit 7.2? The answer of Sec. 1001(c) is still pertinent; i.e., yes, unless some special nontaxable exchange rule provides otherwise.

Before explaining some of the nontaxable exchange provisions that might apply to the transactions of Exhibits 7.1 and 7.2, three additional areas of caution must be considered.

1. In general, nontaxable exchanges are intended to provide only temporary relief from the need to recognize gain. To implement this temporary deferral, a carryover basis rule is commonly applied.
2. If a taxpayer receives any property other than that uniquely authorized in a given nontaxable exchange section, the additional property is called **boot** and the mere presence of boot ordinarily triggers the recognition of at least some of the gain realized in an otherwise nontaxable transaction.

3. Each nontaxable exchange section contains unique words and phrases that must be interpreted with appropriate caution before applying the general rule to an actual situation.

To understand carryover basis, return once more to Exhibit 7.1 and assume that individual I can locate a Code provision that authorizes nontaxable exchange treatment for this exchange. Given the existence of a nontaxable exchange rule, there almost certainly is another statutory rule that requires I to carryover the $10 basis that he originally had in P_1 to the newly acquired P_2. Thus, if I later sells P_2 for $18 (or more), I will have to recognize both (1) the $8 of income realized but deferred when I exchanged P_1 for P_2 and (2) any subsequent increase in the value of P_2 after it was acquired by I.

To illustrate the boot rule, return once more to Exhibit 7.1, but now assume that P_2 has a fair market value of only $16. Under these revised assumptions, I would not be willing to exchange P_1 (with a value of $18) for P_2 (with a value of $16) unless the corporation (C) also gave I "something to boot" worth $2. The most common form of boot is cash. If C gives P_2 plus $2 to I, I will still have an amount realized of $18 and a realized gain of $8. Because of the presence of the $2 boot any nontaxable exchange rule that I might locate in the Code to protect him from the need to recognize the $8 gain almost certainly would require him to recognize gain to the lesser of (a) the gain realized ($8) or (b) the boot received ($2). As revised, the nontaxable exchange would really be only a partially nontaxable exchange: I would recognize $2 of gain and defer $6. I's carryover basis in P_2 would still be $10—so that I will recognize the remaining $6 of gain if and when he sells P_2 for its fair market value of $16.

The special definitions of each nontaxable exchange section are best studied in the context of a particular statutory provision. No commonalties, other than unique tax definitions, are apparent in these rules.

Section 1031 (Like-Kind Exchanges)

One of the nontaxable exchange provisions that might apply to either I or C in the transaction illustrated in Exhibit 7.1 is Sec. 1031. The special definitional provisions applicable to Sec. 1031, in that context, can be summarized for individual I as follows:

1. P_1 must be either a "productive use" or an "investment property" per Sec. 1031(a)(1);

2. P_2 must be property of a "like kind" per Sec. 1031(a)(1); and
3. Neither P_1 nor P_2 can be an excluded property per Sec. 1031(a)(2).

If these three conditions are satisfied, I will not recognize gain but I's basis in P_2 will be $10 per Sec. 1031(d). If I received any boot, I must recognize some amount of gain per Sec. 1031(b). The meaning of some, but not all, of the words and phrases found in Sec. 1031 are unusual. The term *productive property* generally means a fixed asset used in a trade or business—a reasonable definition. The term *investment property*, on the other hand, does *not* include any of the following, which are specifically excluded in Sec. 1031(a)(2),

a) stock in trade or other property held primarily for sale;
b) stocks, bonds, or notes;
c) other securities or evidences of indebtedness or interest;
d) interests in a partnership;
e) certificates of trust or beneficial interests; or
f) choses in action.

Several of the excluded properties can be thought of as investment property.

Even more surprising is the definition of the phrase "like kind." Numerous administrative and judicial authorities support the general notion that (subject to the statutory exceptions noted above) most any realty is of like kind when exchanged for other realty. And, until recently, we would have said that any personalty (i.e., property other than realty) is of like kind when exchanged for other personalty. But in 1991 regulations were issued that require a greater degree of similarity for *depreciable* personalty that is exchanged to be considered of like kind. In general, non-taxable exchanges of depreciable personalty will have to be for properties of the same *general business asset* class. In Exhibit 7.1, P_1 might be undeveloped land in west Texas and P_2 might be a Chicago skyscraper, and yet both would be of like kind. P_1 could be, alternatively, an oil transport ship and P_2 a computer. Prior to the issuance of the 1991 regulations the exchange would be of like kind. If P_1 were a leased office building and P_2 were a leased airplane, however, these two would not (under most circumstances) qualify as properties of like kind because one is realty and the other is personalty.

In summary, whether individual I (or corporation C) in Exhibit 7.1 can or cannot qualify for tax deferral under Sec. 1031 depends on many facts and circumstances. Each situation must be investigated in light of specific statutory requirements and reported accordingly. Incidentally, Sec. 1031 is a mandatory section; if the stipulated conditions are satisfied, the tax result is automatic whether or not the taxpayer prefers that result. It also applies to losses as well as gain. The words of Sec. 1031(a) begin as follows: "No gain or loss shall be recognized if...." If a taxpayer desires to recognize either a gain or a loss realized on the direct exchange of productive use or investment properties, it is incumbent on that taxpayer to somehow avoid one or more of the conditions stipulated in Sec. 1031; if she or he does not avoid them, the tax consequences will automatically follow from her or his actions.

Section 351 (Transfer of Property to a Controlled Corporation)

A second nontaxable exchange provision that could apply to taxpayer I (but *not* to taxpayer C) in the transaction diagrammed in Exhibit 7.1 is Sec. 351. The special definitional provisions applicable to Sec. 351 can be summarized for individual I as follows:

1. P_1 can be property of any kind, but it cannot be services;
2. P_2 must be either stock or securities issued by C (the corporation in Exhibit 7.1); and
3. taxpayer I (along with any other transferors of property) must own 80 percent or more of the outstanding stock of C immediately after the transfer.

If these three conditions are satisfied, I's basis in the C stock or securities received will be $10 per Sec. 358. If I receives anything other than C's stock or securities—i.e., if I receives any boot, as that term is defined for purposes of Sec. 351—I must recognize some amount of gain per Sec. 351(b). Sec. 351 is *not* an elective section, and it applies to both gains and losses. If taxpayer I in Exhibit 7.1 wants to avoid the automatic tax results associated with Sec. 351, I must avoid one or more of the stipulated conditions. There are many words and phrases in Sec. 351 that need to be examined with care before any conclusions are drawn concerning the tax results in an actual case.

Section 354 (Stock-for-Stock Exchanges in a Corporate Reorganization)

A third nontaxable exchange provision that could apply to taxpayer I (and to taxpayer C) in the transaction diagrammed in Exhibit 7.1 is

Property Transactions

Sec. 354. The special definitional provisions applicable to Sec. 354, in the context of the original Exhibit 7.1, can be summarized for individual I as follows:

1. P_1 must be stock or securities in a corporation that is party to a reorganization as defined in Sec. 368(b); and
2. P_2 must also be stock or securities in a corporation that is party to a reorganization.

If these two conditions are satisfied, I's basis in the stock or securities received will be $10 per Sec. 358. If I receives anything other than stock or securities in a corporation that is party to the reorganization—i.e., if I receives any boot as that term is defined for purposes of Sec. 354—I must recognize some amount of gain per Sec. 356. In fact, I may also have to treat some securities as boot per Sec. 354(b) if I gives up less in principal amount of securities surrendered than that received. Whether or not a transaction can qualify as a reorganization for tax purposes—as defined in Sec. 368(a)(1)—is a major definitional problem; without a reorganization there can be no party to a reorganization and, therefore, no nontaxable exchange under Sec. 354.

The direct exchange of one property for another may or may not cause income or loss to be recognized for income tax purposes. The general statutory rule—located in Sec. 1001(c)—is that gain or loss must be recognized whenever property is exchanged unless some other provision provides to the contrary. Three specific provisions that provide otherwise are Secs. 1031, 351, and 354. There are many other nontaxable exchange provisions in the Code. A taxpayer should generally assume that gain or loss must be recognized whenever property is exchanged, but the taxpayer must also know that a contrary rule might apply in special circumstances. The need for professional help in identifying special circumstances should be obvious.

The presumption of the need to recognize gain or loss on the exchange of property for money is even greater than the presumption that exists in a direct exchange. The likelihood of a nontaxable exchange provision applying to the two transactions of Exhibit 7.2 is somewhat less than the likelihood of such a rule applying to the single transaction of Exhibit 7.1. There are, however, a limited number of nontaxable exchange rules that do apply in the circumstances of Exhibit 7.2. We will consider two such provisions here.

Section 1033 (Involuntary Conversions)

One nontaxable exchange provision that could apply to taxpayer I in the two transactions diagrammed in Exhibit 7.2 is Sec. 1033. The special definitional provisions applicable to Sec. 1033, in the context of Exhibit 7.2, can be summarized for individual I as follows:

1. P_1 must have been "compulsorily or involuntarily converted" per Sec. 1033(a);
2. P_2 must be property that is "similar or related in service or use to the property so converted" per Sec. 1033(a)(1); and
3. the acquisition of P_2 must be made within (in general) two years after the end of the year in which P_1 was compulsorily or involuntarily converted per Sec. 1032(a)(2).

In general, Sec. 1033 applies to the destruction of a taxpayer's property by theft, condemnation, or an act of God. If the conditions are satisfied, I's basis in P_2 will be $10 per Sec. 1033(b). If I spends less cash for P_2 (in step B) than I received for P_1 (in step A), then that excess cash will be considered to be boot per Sec. 1033(a)(2), and I will be taxed accordingly. On the other hand, if I spends more cash (in step B) to acquire P_2 than I received (in step A) on the disposition of P_1, the added cash will increase I's basis in P_2. To illustrate, assume that I paid $21 for P_2 (rather than $18) in Exhibit 7.2, step B. In that event, I's basis in P_2 will be $13 consisting of (1) the $10 carryover basis plus (2) the extra $3 cash invested in step B.

The most surprising aspect of Sec. 1033 is the narrow way the administrative and judicial authorities define property that is similar or related in service or use. To qualify as a nontaxable exchange under Sec. 1033, P_1 and P_2 must be nearly identical properties. If P_1 is a moving van used to transport household goods that is destroyed in a wreck, P_2 must also be a household moving van if Sec. 1033 is to apply. If P_2 were a truck used to transport raw milk rather than household goods, Sec. 1033 would probably *not* apply. The lack of empathy by tax authorities under conditions of stress for the taxpayer is unfortunately obvious in both the administrative and judicial interpretations generally.

Incidentally, Sec. 1033 is elective, and it applies only to gains. Losses are always recognized immediately—unless barred for reasons explained in Chapter 8—and gains may be recognized, at the option of the taxpayer, in the event of theft, condemnation, or an act of God.

Section 1034 (Sale of a Principal Residence)

A second nontaxable exchange provision that could apply to taxpayer I in the two transactions diagrammed in Exhibit 7.2 is Sec. 1034.

The special definitional provisions applicable to Sec. 1034 can be summarized for individual I as follows:

1. P_1 must have been I's principal residence in the past, per Sec. 1034(a);
2. P_2 must be I's principal residence now (and for a reasonable future period) per Sec. 1034(a); and
3. the acquisition of P_2 must occur sometime within the period beginning 24 months before I sold P_1 and ending 24 months after that sale.

If the conditions of Sec. 1034 are satisfied, I's basis in P_2 will be $10 per Sec. 1034(e). If I spends less cash for P_2 (in step B) than I received for P_1 (in step A) that excess cash will be considered to be boot and taxed accordingly. To illustrate, assume that I paid only $15 for P_2 (rather than $18) in Exhibit 7.2, step B. In that event, I must recognize gain of $3 (an amount equal to the excess cash retained by I), and I's basis in P_2 will remain $10. On the hand, if I spends more than $18 for P_2 (in step B) the added cash (or increased liability) can also be added to I's basis in P_2.

The application of Sec. 1034 is automatic if the conditions are satisfied; it is not elective. Sec. 1034 applies only to gain. Losses on the sale of a primary residence are considered personal losses and are nondeductible. These and other loss limitation rules will be further explained in Chapter 8.

In summary, the Code contains several nontaxable exchange provisions that may override general rules otherwise applicable to most property transactions. The difficulties encountered in property transactions are most frequently one of three general types. First, many problems are encountered in the measurement of gain and loss because of difficulties in quantifying the amount realized and/or the adjusted basis. Second, a taxpayer without special expertise may encounter trouble in trying to determine which special rules apply to any given property transaction. Third, even after a taxpayer locates the statutory rule that is applicable to a specific situation, the interpretation of the various words and phrases used in the law may be nearly impossible to uncover without the assistance of a qualified tax advisor.

Key Points to Remember

❏ The gain or loss recognized on the sale or exchange of a property is equal to the difference between (a) the amount realized and (b) the adjusted basis of the property sold or exchanged.

- ❑ The amount realized in a sale or exchange can be defined as the sum of
    1. Any cash received;
    2. The fair market value of any property received; and
    3. The amount of any debt that is transferred to or assumed by another taxpayer in the sale or exchange transaction.
- ❑ A taxpayer's adjusted basis in a property will vary depending on how the taxpayer acquired the property.
- ❑ The term capital asset is defined to mean any asset other than one specifically excluded by Sec. 1221(1)–(5).
- ❑ The definition of a capital gain varies from one country to another.
- ❑ The nontaxable exchange provisions generally operate in a way that serves only to defer the recognition of a gain or loss, not to exclude it forever.
- ❑ The details of the definitional requirements unique to each nontaxable exchange provision vary significantly from one section to another.

LOSSES

Questions concerning a taxpayer's right to deduct losses can arise from either one of two fundamentally different circumstances. On the one hand, a taxpayer may experience a year in which aggregate deductions exceed gross income. On the other hand, a taxpayer may experience one or more isolated transactions in which the adjusted basis of a property exceeds the amount realized on disposition. In both circumstances, the taxpayer must (1) determine if any portion (or all) of the loss is deductible, (2) measure the amount of any deductible loss, and (3) report the loss correctly for income tax purposes.

The correct tax treatment of losses is complicated because there are at least four or five distinctly different, yet interrelated and major, rules that may limit the right of a taxpayer to claim a loss deduction either immediately or at some future date. The more important of the general loss limitation rules are Sec. 172, which authorizes a net operating loss (NOL) deduction; Sec. 469, which limits the right of certain taxpayers to claim passive activity losses (PALs), at least initially; Sec. 1211, which limits the amount of net capital loss that taxpayers may deduct against ordinary income in any one year; and Sec. 165(c)(3), which limits personal loss deductions for individual taxpayers. In addition to these four provisions of general application, there are many other sections that restrict the right of a taxpayer to claim a loss deduction in more limited circumstances. Among the latter provisions are Sec. 267, which limits loss deductions realized on transactions between related parties; Sec. 166, which limits the manner in which a taxpayer may deduct both "business" and "nonbusiness" bad debts; Sec. 1091, which limits the rights of taxpayers to deduct losses incurred in certain "wash sales"; Sec. 465, which limits the amount of a loss deduction to the amount that the taxpayer has "at risk" in an activity; Sec. 183, that limits hobby-loss deductions; and various other sections that limit loss deductions in special circumstances.

The details of every possible loss provision cannot be investigated in an essentials text. What we will do is consider the four most commonly encountered loss provisions in some detail and simply note the need for a more detailed examination of the Code in other

Losses

circumstances. The four provisions to be covered here apply to NOLs, PALs, capital losses, and personal losses.

NOLs or Net Operating Losses

An NOL—commonly pronounced as a series of three separate letters, N, O, L—arises when the aggregate tax deductions exceed the gross income recognized by a taxpayer in one year. It is a tax approximation of what is described in the financial press as an operating loss. Sec. 172 permits taxpayers to carry an NOL back and treat it as a newly discovered deduction on the tax return filed for the third prior year. A corporation experiencing an NOL for calendar year 1993 will carry that NOL back and claim it as a deduction on the tax return it filed approximately three years earlier, for the year 1990. Based on this added deduction, the corporation will be entitled to a current refund of some part or all of the income tax that it originally paid for 1990. If the NOL is greater than the taxable income reported in the third prior year, any excess is carried next to the second prior year and, if need be, to the immediately preceding year. To return to the earlier illustration, an NOL experienced in 1993 would be carried back and offset against the taxable incomes reported in 1990, 1991, and 1992, in that sequence. If the taxpayer is unable to deduct the entire NOL in the three-year carryback period, or if the taxpayer exercises an election to forego the carryback, any excess is carried forward and offset against the taxable income earned in each of the next 15 years, until it is either fully deducted or time expires. To summarize, an NOL can be deducted in a three-year carryback and a 15-year carryforward period.

The effect of Sec. 172 is to expand the accounting period for NOL years from a minimum period of 12 months to a maximum period of 19 years; i.e., the loss year plus the three-year carryback and the 15-year carryforward period. NOLs accumulated over two or more years are claimed on a FIFO (first-in, first-out) basis. Short tax years count as full years for NOL purposes.

The general intent of Sec. 172 is to restrict any NOL deduction to the real economic loss incurred in a genuine trade or business for the year. Accordingly, some taxpayers must add back specified deductions when converting the excess of their deductions over gross income for the year into an NOL deduction. Individual taxpayers must add back personal and dependent exemption deductions, any capital loss deduction, and certain nonbusiness deductions in excess of nonbusiness income. Other special rules may also apply to certain taxpayers (including regulated transportation corporations; REITs, or real estate investment trusts; and bank cooperatives) as well as to certain losses (including foreign expropriation losses, product liability losses, tort liability losses, and bad debt losses of commercial banks). Although the many special rules found in the various subsections of Sec. 172 may complicate the calculation of a specific taxpayer's NOL, the general concept is not difficult to comprehend. And it is the concept, not the detail, that is essential to understanding the U.S. income tax.

The mere existence of a corporate NOL deduction has created an interesting problem in tax policy. The fundamental question involves the right of certain new owners to utilize the NOL deduction largely attributable to the efforts of other (old) owners of a single corporate shell. To illustrate the problem in an extreme example, assume that individual X owned 100 percent of the outstanding stock of A Corporation, which engaged in the manufacture of horseshoes for ten years. Assume also that A Corporation was never a financial success and that it accumulated a $1 million NOL before closing its doors forever on December 31, 1989. The question is: Can taxpayer Y purchase all of individual X's stock in A Corporation, begin an entirely new business within A Corporation (say, for example, the manufacture of tennis shoes, rather than horseshoes), and claim the old NOL deduction against the income subsequently earned in this same corporation?

To the extent that a transplanting of NOLs is allowed, the tax law has effectively made the most worthless corporation (i.e., the one characterized by the largest NOL) into the most valuable one. The maximum market value of an NOL shell-corporation will equal the amount of the NOL deduction times the highest marginal corporate tax rate.

Because there were relatively few constraints on the acquisition of corporate NOL deductions in the United States during the decade of the 1950s, there was a brisk business in the acquisition of loss corporations (i.e., corporations characterized by a large NOL). Congress eventually decided that this was not a reasonable result and imposed limitations on the right of successor owners to use NOL deductions created within a corporate entity by prior owners. Having made the decision to stop the trafficking in loss corporations, however, Congress discovered that it was not easy to determine exactly how large the change in ownership and/or how major the change in business should be before the NOL deduction should be denied to the same or some successor corporate entity. (Successor entities usually involve the acquisition of one corporation by another in a corporate reorganization.)

Today the single most important provision limiting the right of any corporation to claim an NOL deduction is that of Sec. 382. In very general terms, it limits the amount of income that can be offset in any year by an NOL deduction if there has been an ownership change of 50 percentage points or greater in the three prior years. If such a major ownership change has occurred, the amount of income that can subsequently be offset by an existing NOL deduction is equal to the fair market value of the loss corporation, immediately prior to the ownership change, times the applicable long-term tax-exempt interest rate. (This interest rate is determined and published monthly by the Treasury Department.) To claim even this limited NOL deduction the corporation (or its successor) must also satisfy a continuity-of-business-enterprise test for a two-year period. That test requires the corporation either to (a) continue the old business that created the loss or (b) use a significant portion of the old (loss) corporation's assets in a new business.

The limitations of Sec. 382 on the rights of taxpayers to claim a corporate NOL deduction under Sec. 172 are of relatively recent origin; hence it is difficult to ascertain their eventual effect. It is believed that the new rules will act as a strong deterrent to the purchase and sale of loss corporations.

PALs or Passive Activity Losses

A PAL—commonly read as one word, pal—generally arises when certain taxpayers try to reduce their total tax liability for a year by offsetting losses, incurred through carefully selected passive investments, against income earned in more active ways. The adjectives *passive* and *active* are defined later in this chapter. Suffice it to note here that these two words refer to the extent of the taxpayer's involvement in any activity in which he or she has invested. To understand the PAL provisions of Sec. 469, it is helpful to understand the tax milieu that existed in the United States prior to 1986. One significant aspect of that milieu concerned individuals who earned relatively large incomes but who legally paid little or no income tax. Among their favorite devices for reducing high tax bills was the opportunity to make a tax-shelter investment. The opportunities were so great that an entirely new industry was created in the years between (approximately) 1960 and 1985. This industry was characterized by a subtle blend of aggressive salesmanship plus technical knowledge that spanned the more traditional areas of taxation and finance. Investment counselors and personal financial planners frequently collected both professional fees and sales commissions on carefully selected investments recommended to (and purchased by) clients who sought investment advice, tax relief, and personal economic security, all from the same source.

Tax-shelter investments came in many forms including shopping centers; office buildings; apartment complexes; cattle breeding and feeding operations; video tapes and phonograph records; and oil and gas wells, to name a few. Most of these investments included some combination of four basic ingredients, namely, (1) a mismatching of gross income and deductions, at least in the classic accounting sense; (2) the utilization of one or more preferential income tax provisions; (3) the use of a tax-conduit business entity; and (4) the chance to borrow some part of the investment being made.

The basic idea that generally sold these investments can be illustrated simply as in Exhibit 8.1. It depicts a 12-year investment that will produce losses in years 1 through 5 and incomes in years 6 through 12. Although a more traditional investment might return the same total income at a constant rate over the 12-year period, the special advantage sought in the tax-shelter investment was timing: the recognition of the loss in years 1 through 5. So long as a taxpayer could offset the operating losses in years 1 through 5 against income earned from other sources, tax-shelter investments were preferred over other investments. Under ideal conditions, taxpayers could invest enough to eliminate their tax liability totally on income from other sources such as salary, dividends, and interest.

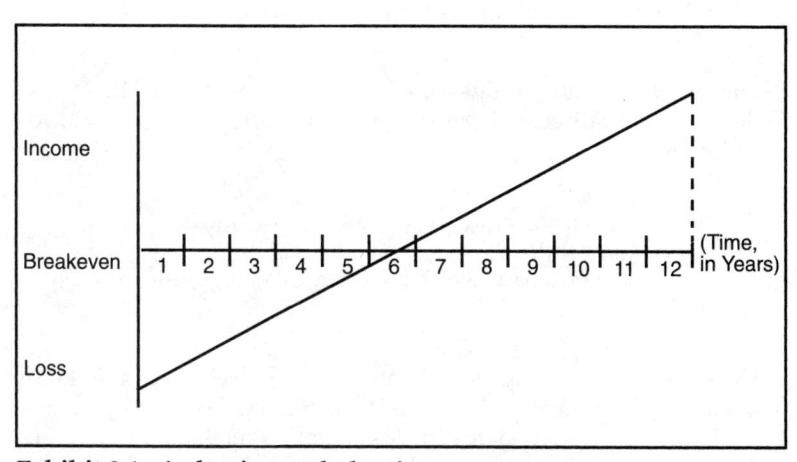

Exhibit 8.1 A classic tax-shelter investment

The more observant investors fully realized that, to be successful in the long run, they would have to put increasingly larger and larger investments into more and more ventures, but they hoped that the inevitable consequence of those investments would be a greater and greater accumulation of assets and, eventually, a larger estate to be left to family and friends. Not all investments worked out so well. Many failed because of faulty economic assumptions; others, because of outright fraud. Nevertheless their popularity continued to grow until the PAL provisions were enacted in 1986—the same year that many of the preferential tax provisions (which made tax-shelter investments possible) were repealed. Because of these changes, the tax-shelter investment industry in the United States all but disappeared. The changes in the tax law, however, remain very much alive, to the detriment of taxpayers who hold investments acquired before these changes were enacted.

The most important change was the enactment of Sec. 469. It fundamentally provides that most taxpayers (other than C-corporations that are not personal service corporations) can no longer offset losses from passive activities against income from either active or portfolio sources. Given only this paraphrasing of the Code, the significance of definitions should be immediately obvious; however, the only one of the three critical terms used in the preceding sentence that is defined in the Code is passive activity which, in Sec. 469(c)(1), is defined as follows:

> the term "passive activity" means any activity—(A) which involves the conduct of any trade or business, and (B) in which the taxpayer does not materially participate.

This provision clearly links the concept of passive to the lack of material participation, which is subsequently defined in Sec. 469(h)(1) as follows:

> A taxpayer shall be treated as materially participating in an activity only if the taxpayer is involved in the operations of the activity on a basis which is—(A) regular, (B) continuous, and (C) substantial.

The Code goes on to specifically include and exclude certain kinds of income from the passive activity category. For example, Sec. 469(c)(2) provides that income or loss from a rental activity must be included as a passive activity while Sec. 469(c)(3) provides that income or loss derived from a working interest in an oil or gas property should be excluded from the passive activity category. In anticipation of the many problems that would arise under this section, Congress gave the Treasury Department specific authority to issue regulations to interpret the new provision further.

The Treasury Department soon came to realize the difficulty of this assignment. More than five years after the enactment of Sec. 469, over 100 pages of Temporary Regulations have been issued. These regulations do not resolve all the difficulties and are, in many respects, still controversial. Suffice it to observe that the meanings of many words and phrases used in Sec. 469 remain uncertain in application. It will take years of litigation before the outer boundaries of Sec. 469 are generally understood, even by tax professionals. For purposes of this text, only a general description of the intent of the Code can even be attempted.

The prohibition against offsetting passive activity losses against active income prevents executives, doctors, lawyers, dentists, and accountants from reducing or eliminating the tax on their earned income through the use of tax shelters. But if Congress thought the use of tax shelters to escape the tax on earned income was worth stopping, using passive activity losses to escape the tax on certain passive "unearned income" (i.e., income from capital investments, such as dividends and interest, which almost always produce income rather than losses) could not be allowed to continue. Hence, the inclusion of portfolio income as a class of income that cannot be offset by passive activity losses. This provision is made clear in Sec. 469(e)(1)(A). It provides that the net income from interest, dividends, annuities, and royalties is *not* to be combined with income from passive activities despite the fact that they typically cannot be classified as *active* income. The need for a three-way division of taxable income is further supported by Sec. 469(e)(2)(b), which states that net active income must exclude both (1) income and loss from passive activities and (2) any items "described in paragraph (1)(A)"—i.e., any portfolio items, such as interest, dividends, annuities, etc.

Incidentally, Sec. 469(e)(2)(A) makes it clear that C-corporations, other than personal service corporations, can offset income from passive losses against income from active sources, but not against income from portfolio sources. Consequently, some individuals who owned both (1) old tax-shelter investments and (2) a controlling interest in a C-corporation that was engaged in a mercantile business were able to continue their use of the tax-shelter loss by transferring the investment to the corporation in years after 1986. As explained in Chapter 7, this property transfer can generally be made on a nontaxable exchange basis by operation of Sec. 351.

Losses

Most tax-shelter investments originally involved either (1) a partnership interest or (2) stock in an S-corporation because the investor wanted the losses generated in the business to flow through and be offset against his or her personal income. The partnership and/or S-corporation frequently engaged in an active trade or business but many of the owners did not *personally* participate in that business on a regular, continuous, and substantial basis. Consequently, their pro-rata share of most gross income and deduction items, generated within the tax-conduit entity, are passive activity items for them. Limited partners are automatically treated as nonmaterial participants per Sec. 469(h)(2). The partners and/or shareholders who do participate on a material basis, on the other hand, report active rather than passive income and deductions.

The initial reaction of the marketplace following the enactment of Sec. 469 was the creation of a new industry engaged in the sale of PIGs, passive income generators. The belief was that PIGs could be sold to the same individuals who had previously purchased PALs to allow them to make use of the losses still being generated by the investments acquired before 1987. That initial reaction was short-lived for two reasons. First, Congress included certain transition rules that allowed taxpayers to deduct some part of any loss currently incurred on pre-1987 investments. The specific portion allowed was 65 percent in 1987; 40 percent in 1988; 20 percent in 1989; and 10 percent in 1990. Second, the regulations issued by Treasury closed the door on many PIGs by reclassifying certain kinds of income. Income generated from many limited partnership interests was effectively reclassified as portfolio income rather than passive-activity income. (A limited partnership interest is one in which an investor cannot, by law, lose more than the amount invested. Hence a limited partner does not share the liability of a general partner for all partnership debts.) And income from certain rental-type operations was reclassified as active income rather than passive-activity income. Because the administrative law under Sec. 469 appears to be very aggressive in defining various statutory words and phrases to minimize opportunities for the PIG salesperson, any reader who has a personal interest in these provisions simply must consult with a qualified tax advisor to determine the latest word in this rapidly changing area of tax law.

Many individuals wanted to sell or exchange tax-shelter investments because of their inability to provide significant tax savings after 1986. These transactions should be monitored closely by a competent tax advisor. The general intent of Sec. 469 is simply to prevent the offsetting of losses from overall passive activities against income from other sources. Passive activity losses from one source can al-

Losses

ways be offset against passive activity income from other sources. Any passive activity loss disallowed in one year can be carried forward (indefinitely) and offset against passive activity income in future years. Tax-shelter investments that were economically sound may still be good investments once the early loss years have passed. A taxpayer may eventually deduct any losses denied in prior years because those losses merely go into suspension until the taxpayer makes a complete disposition of the entire activity in a taxable transaction.

Because of tax complexities, very few taxpayers will want to dispose of a tax-shelter investment in a nontaxable exchange. Partial dispositions and gifts sometimes create equally cumbersome results; therefore, they should be undertaken only after consultation with an expert. Dispositions at death are less complex, but they do create new and special tax problems for the executor of a decedent's estate, the individual left with the responsibility of filing the last tax return.

Dispositions can also create unexpected results. On many occasions a disposition of a tax shelter will create an amount of income well in excess of any cash proceeds realized on the sale or exchange. This phantom income typically derives from a reduction in the taxpayer's debt. As explained in Chapters 2 and 7, a decrease in debt alone, even nonrecourse debt, can cause the realization of gross income.

Furthermore, even before the application of the PAL rules, a taxpayer generally cannot claim a loss deduction that is greater in amount than the amount the taxpayer is at risk. The amount at risk is equal to the sum of the cash paid, the fair market value of property exchanged, and the debt assumed in the acquisition of a tax shelter. Further details concerning the at-risk limitation on loss deductions can be found in Sec. 465. These limits may apply during the years that a taxpayer holds a tax-shelter investment as well as in the year of disposition.

The one essential aspect of Sec. 469 can be understood easily with a simple example. Suppose that an individual taxpayer or a personal service corporation were directly or indirectly engaged in three different activities with the following tax results:

Activity #1 $300,000   income
Activity #2 $150,000   loss
Activity #3 $100,000   loss

Depending upon the correct classification of activities 2 and 3, this taxpayer would currently have to pay tax on one of four different amounts of taxable income, namely, $50,000 ($300,000 − $150,000 − $100,000), $150,000 ($300,000 − $150,000), $200,000 ($300,000 − $100,000), or $300,000 ($300,000 − $0). Obviously, other things being equal, this taxpayer would prefer that neither activity 2 nor activity 3 be deemed to constitute a PAL for income tax purposes because that conclusion would minimize the tax liability for the year.

Before leaving the world of PALs and PIGs, one final subsection should be noted. Section 469(i) provides a special rule for certain passive activity losses generated by real estate activities. It allows a taxpayer to deduct up to $25,000 per year from real estate losses if the taxpayer "actively participates" in the real estate activity and reports an AGI of $100,000 or less. The $25,000 maximum is reduced by $.50 on the dollar for AGIs in excess of $100,000; hence no amount can be deducted under this special rule for individuals earning more than $150,000. (Special limits apply to married taxpayers filing separate returns.) The relatively low income limit supports the idea that this provision was put into the Code to accommodate the many mom-and-pop real estate activities that were strongly encouraged by the pre-1987 tax laws. This conclusion is also supported by the relatively loose definition required for active participation, in direct contrast with that required for material participation. In summary, this special provision concerning losses from rental activities is of interest only to taxpayers reporting a relatively small income.

Capital Losses

Statutory restrictions on the right of taxpayers to deduct net capital losses were enacted long before the PAL limitations. Because those limits (stipulated in Sec. 1211) were not repealed with the enactment of Sec. 469, both sets of limitations must be applied simultaneously. Because the Code does not explicitly resolve potential statutory overlap problems, the final resolution of some issues remains uncertain. The first set of regulations issued under Sec. 469, however, gives some indication of exactly how the two sections are to be applied. (See Treas. Reg. 1.469-1T(D)(2).)

Section 1211(a) denies a corporate taxpayer the right to offset any amount of net capital loss against ordinary income; Sec. 1211(b) limits most other taxpayers to a maximum deduction of $3000 per year. Both corporate and noncorporate taxpayers can offset capital losses against capital gains with no limit; the limitation arises only when a taxpayer tries to offset *net* capital losses (i.e., *all* capital losses less *all* capital gains) against ordinary income. For this reason, the capital asset definition included in Chapter 7 is still of substantial importance for certain taxpayers today.

Corporations recognizing net capital losses in any year can, per Sec. 1212(a), carry them back and offset them against any net capital gain recognized in the three prior years, beginning with the third prior year. If the net capital loss exceeds the aggregate net capital gains reported in those three years, any remaining excess can be carried forward and offset against net capital gains recognized in the five subsequent years until either (1) the entire capital loss has been deducted or (2) the maximum five-year carry forward period has expired. In other words, net capital losses recognized by a corporation in 1993 will be offset against net capital gains recognized in 1990, 1991, 1992, 1994, 1995, 1996, 1997, and 1998, in that order. Net capital losses incurred in two or more years are claimed on a FIFO basis; short tax years count as a full year. Special rules may apply to certain corporations (e.g., to regulated investment companies) and to certain capital losses (e.g., to foreign expropriation capital losses). Individual and fiduciary taxpayers are not entitled to any net capital loss *carrybacks*. They generally can, however, carry net capital losses forward for an indefinite period, per Sec. 1212(b).

The potential for overlap between the limitations imposed by Secs. 469 and 1211 are most frequently encountered by individual taxpayers. To illustrate, assume that an individual taxpayer recognized a $10,000 capital gain and a $12,000 ordinary loss, both from a passive activity. If this taxpayer recognized no additional capital gains or losses from regular sources, the net $2000 passive activity loss would be subject to suspension in the manner described earlier in this chapter.

If a second individual experienced a $10,000 ordinary income and a $12,000 capital loss, both from a passive activity, however, that taxpayer would be subject to both loss limits. In other words, this second taxpayer would have to suspend $2000 because of the net passive activity loss and, in the same year, could claim only $3000 of the $12,000 capital loss (assuming no other capital gains and losses were realized.) In still other words, this second taxpayer would have to defer the deduction of $9000 of the $12,000 net loss currently realized, $2000 because of both Sec. 469 and Sec. 1211, and another $7000 because of Sec. 1211 alone—all of it being a capital loss.

Personal Losses of Individual Taxpayers

Section 165(a) begins with an exceedingly generous general rule that reads as follows:

Losses

> There shall be allowed as a deduction any loss sustained during the taxable year and not compensated for by insurance or otherwise.

Unfortunately for individual taxpayers, this generous provision is subsequently proscribed in various ways, most importantly in Sec. 165(c) which reads as follows:

> In the case of an individual, the deduction under subsection(a) shall be limited to—
>
> 1. losses incurred in a trade or business;
> 2. losses incurred in any transaction entered into for profit, though not connected with a trade or business; and
> 3. except as provided in subsection(h), losses of property not connected with a trade or business or a transaction entered into for profit, if such losses arise from fire, storm, shipwreck, or other casualty, or from theft.

Section 165(c)(1) authorizes individuals to deduct losses incurred in a trade or business and Sec. 165(c)(2) authorizes individuals to deduct all losses from investments, subject to such limiting provisions as Secs. 469 and 1211. However, Sec. 165(c)(3) limits the right of individual taxpayers to deduct losses from any other property (i.e., purely personal property) to those sustained in a fire, storm, shipwreck, other casualty, or theft.

This means that any loss sustained by an individual taxpayer on the sale or exchange of his or her personal residence, private car or airplane, and clothing or furniture *cannot* be deducted even though any gain realized on the sale or exchange of those same properties would be taxable. Although this provision appears to be inequitable, it is consistent with the general rule of Sec. 262 that personal, living, and family expenses are not deductible. The fact that Sec. 165(c)(3) allows a deduction for personal loss in the face of tragedy is an attempt to provide some degree of social conscience in tax law. As a practical matter, however, very few individuals ever obtain much tax relief from Sec. 165(c)(3) because of further limitations imposed in Sec. 165(h). The latter subsection sets forth a series of special rules that determine the amount of a personal casualty deduction. In general, no deduction is allowed (in these circumstances) for:

1. any decrease in value that occurred prior to the casualty, plus
2. any loss covered by insurance or recovered through salvage value, plus
3. a $100 per-casualty *de minimis* amount, plus
4. an amount equal to 10 percent of the individual taxpayer's AGI, considering all casualty losses for the year.

To illustrate just how small the casualty loss deduction usually is, consider the plight of an individual who reports an AGI of $25,000 and "totals" her personal automobile in an accident. If this car originally cost $18,000 and had a fair market value of $10,000 immediately before the accident, and if $6000 is collected from insurance and salvage combined, then the taxpayer will have a remaining personal casualty deduction of only $1400 determined as follows:

Original basis	$18,000
Decline in value before wreck	(8,000)
Insurance and salvage	(6,000)
De minimis amount	(100)
AGI limitation	(2,500)
Remainder	$ 1,400

This taxpayer will be entitled to the $1400 casualty loss deduction only if she does not claim the standard deduction. The $6000 from the insurance/salvage plus the $392 tax savings (i.e., 28% x $1400) will not replace the car destroyed.

Other Losses

As noted in the introductory paragraphs of this chapter, there are many other Code sections that limit the right of a taxpayer to claim a deduction for losses incurred in other, less common circumstances. To illustrate just a few of the many possibilities, consider the following loss limitation rules:

- Losses from wagering transactions are limited to gains from such transactions unless the taxpayer is engaged in the trade or business of gambling. (See Sec. 165(d).)
- Losses from nonbusiness bad debt losses are automatically treated as (short-term) capital losses. (See Sec. 166(d).)

- Losses realized on the sale of stock or securities will be disallowed if substantially identical stock or securities are acquired within a period beginning 30 days before and ending 30 days after the sale or exchange. (See Sec. 1091.)

In some instances disallowed losses are permanently lost; in other circumstances an adjustment can be made to the basis of property to allow the taxpayer (or a successor taxpayer) the right to claim the disallowed loss at some later date when the acquired property is disposed of in a taxable transaction. These and many other rules applicable to somewhat unusual loss situations are best deferred to other books written for other purposes. The critical point to remember is that the Code is replete with special provisions limiting the right of taxpayers to deduct losses in various circumstances.

Key Points to Remember

- A net operating loss (NOL) is equal to the excess of deductions (after possible adjustment) over gross income for a year.
- An NOL can generally be carried back and deducted from income recognized in the prior three years and, thereafter, be carried forward and deducted from income recognized in the next 15 years.
- The amount of an NOL deduction that may be claimed by a corporation will be limited if there has been a 50 percentage point or greater change in the ownership of that corporation during the prior three years.
- A passive activity loss (PAL) is any loss incurred in an activity in which the taxpayer does not participate on a regular, continuous, and substantial basis.
- Taxpayers—other than C-corporations that are not personal service corporations—cannot currently deduct a PAL against income generated from either an active activity or from a portfolio source. PALs may be deducted against
  1. Income currently generated by another passive activity;
  2. Income generated in a subsequent year either by the same or by another passive activity; and
  3. Income from active and portfolio sources but only in the year in which an entire passive activity is sold or exchanged in a taxable transaction.
- Capital losses are those losses incurred on the sale or exchange of capital assets.

❏ If deductible capital losses exceed capital gains realized in a year the right of the taxpayer to deduct the loss may be subject to restriction.
   1. Individual and fiduciary taxpayers may deduct a maximum of $3000 in net capital losses against ordinary income in any year; any excess capital loss is carried forward indefinitely to future years.
   2. Corporate taxpayers cannot deduct any amount of a net capital loss against ordinary income. Corporations may, however, carry capital net losses back and offset them against any net capital gains recognized in the prior three years and, if additional capital losses remain, carry those losses forward and offset them against any net capital gains recognized in the next five years.
❏ Individual taxpayers generally can not deduct any loss recognized on the sale, exchange, or other disposition of a property unless
   1. The property is used in a trade or business;
   2. The property is held for production of income; or
   3. The disposition is due to a casualty or a theft.

THE COMPLIANCE PROCESS

The U.S. income tax is a self-assessed tax. This means that every taxpayer has the responsibility of independently complying with the law. The government does, of course, design and distribute forms and other instructional aids that assist the taxpayer in performing this obligation. Many taxpayers also engage professional tax advisors to help them structure business transactions in the most tax advantageous manner, to comply with the tax law, and to represent the taxpayer in any dispute that may arise with the IRS. Regardless of how much help a taxpayer may receive, however, the ultimate responsibility for compliance remains with the taxpayer.

This short chapter is an overview of four important aspects of the compliance process, namely, (1) the filing of returns, (2) the audit procedure, (3) the possible imposition of interest and penalties, and (4) assessing the quality of expert assistance. The final chapter will explain in somewhat greater detail the services that the tax experts render in the area of tax planning.

Filing Returns

The initial due date for the annual income tax return varies by the type of taxpayer. In general, corporate returns are due by the fifteenth day of the third month following the end of the year. For calendar year returns the initial corporate due date is March 15. Individual, fiduciary, and partnership returns are initially due by the fifteenth day of the fourth month, e.g., by April 15 for calendar-year taxpayers. If the fifteenth day of the month falls on a Saturday, Sunday, or legal holiday, the due date is automatically extended to the next business day. Tax returns filed by mail are deemed to be timely filed if they bear a U.S. postmark dated on or before the due date.

All taxpayers are entitled to an automatic extension of the due date if they file the proper form on or before the due date. Corporate taxpayers are generally entitled to a six-month extension if they file a Form 7004, individual taxpayers to a four-month extension if they file a Form 4868. Fiduciary taxpayers and partnerships can get a three-

The Compliance Process

month extension by filing Form 8736. Taxpayers can also request an additional extension for good cause, but approval of such a request is entirely within the discretion of the IRS. Ordinarily no extensions are granted beyond six months. Special due dates apply to individuals who are outside the United States on the normal filing date, to foreign corporations, to nonresident aliens, to tax-exempt organizations, etc. The general due dates can be summarized as follows:

		For Calendar-Year Taxpayers	
Taxpayer	General Rule	Initial Date	With Extension
Corporation	15th day/3rd month	March 15	Sept. 15
Individual	15th day/4th month	April 15	Aug. 15
Fiduciary	15th day/4th month	April 15	July 15

The tendency of taxpayers to take advantage of an automatic extension has increased greatly in recent years. Because of numerous extensions, the tax-preparation business has expanded from a three- or four-month busy season to one of eight or nine months each year. Because of both the increasing frequency of change and added complexity in tax law, the community of tax practitioners has badly needed this extended time for compliance work, even with the advances made in computer-prepared returns.

Although taxpayers can get an extension for the tax return due date, they cannot postpone the payment of the tax liability. In general, a taxpayer must have paid at least 90 percent of the eventual tax liability at the time an extension is requested. Interest is charged on any underpayment; penalties will also apply if the unpaid tax exceeds a 10 percent maximum.

The tax return form to be filed also varies by each type of taxpayer and, in some instances, within types of taxpayers, depending upon the complexity of the return. The most common tax return forms can be summarized as follows:

- Actual tax returns
    —Corporate taxpayers, either
       –Form 1120-A (the easier, "short" form) or
       –Form 1120 (for more complex returns)
    —Individual taxpayers
       –Form 1040EZ (the easiest form),
       –Form 1040A (the "short" form), or
       –Form 1040 (the "long" form, for more complex returns)

—Fiduciary taxpayers
  –Form 1041
- Information (only) returns
  —S-corporations
  –Form 1120S
  —Partnerships
  –Form 1065

The requirements that determine whether or not any particular taxpayer can use a particular form are best left for other books. Other, special forms are also available for less routine situations. Foreign corporations file Form 1120-F; nonresident aliens, Form 1040-NF; exempt organizations reporting unrelated business income, Form 990-T; exempt farm cooperatives, Form 990-C; etc.

Income tax returns can ordinarily be filed at either a designated district director's office or a service center. The designated location is determined by the residence or domicile of the taxpayer. By far the largest number of tax returns are filed at one of ten Internal Revenue Service Centers in the United States. International returns can be filed at specified local offices; with the District Director at Baltimore, Maryland; with the Philadelphia Service Center; or with the Director of International Operations in Washington, D.C., depending on the circumstances.

In addition to the annual income tax return, many other tax forms must be filed with the IRS throughout the year. Information forms (Form 1099) for interest, dividends, miscellaneous business payments, etc., must generally be filed by February 28. Estimated tax returns, with appropriate tax prepayments, are due on April 15, June 15, September 15, and January 15 for calendar-year individual and fiduciary taxpayers and on April 15, June 15, September 15, and December 15 for calendar-year corporate taxpayers. Annual returns—in the Form 5500 series—from employers or plan administrators of qualified pension, profit-sharing, and stock bonus plans are due by the last day of the seventh month following the end of the taxpayer's year, or July 31 for calendar-year taxpayers. And amended returns—Form 1120X for corporations and Form 1040X for individuals—can be filed at any time to correct errors in previously filed returns.

Most of the returns filed with the IRS are accessed by a taxpayer identification number or TIN. For individual taxpayers, the TIN is usually the taxpayer's social security number. All permanent information is stored at the IRS computer center in Martinsburg, West Virginia; temporary storage of forms is maintained at local sites throughout the United States.

The Audit Procedure

Upon the receipt of a tax return, an IRS employee performs various clerical checks to be certain that correct numbers were carried from supporting schedules to the face of a tax return, to determine arithmetic accuracy, to verify that required signatures were made, to deposit checks and process refunds, etc. The discovery of an error at this level will generate an IRS notice with a bill for any additional tax due, if that is appropriate. This preliminary examination is not, however, an actual audit.

Returns are selected for a formal audit in a variety of ways. Some are selected randomly in a Taxpayer Compliance and Measurement Program (TCMP) to help the IRS identify the types and numbers of errors being made so that corrections in the system can be accomplished. Other returns are selected for audit because of their high DIF (discriminant function) score. A DIF score is given to each individual taxpayer's return by a secret and closely guarded computer program that attempts to assess the return's examination potential. Still other returns are selected for audit simply because of the large income reported, an abnormally low gross profit margin, unusually large deductions, or some other special characteristic deemed important by the IRS.

During recent years the IRS has audited no more than 1 percent of all returns filed. The probability of audit is substantially higher for high-income taxpayers; most Fortune 500 corporations are continuously subject to audit. Low-income taxpayers, on the other hand, are only rarely subject to a detailed audit unless their return reflects some definite abnormality such as an unusually large number of exemption deductions or an unusually large charitable contribution deduction.

Audits are conducted by personnel assigned to an IRS district office. The audit may take place at the IRS office (called an office audit) or at the taxpayer's office (called a field audit). Large audits, involving many records, are virtually always conducted in the field-audit format.

To audit a return and assess a deficiency, the IRS normally has three years from the later of (1) the initial due date or (2) the date a return is actually filed. The normal statute of limitations will be extended, however, under two circumstances. First, if a taxpayer understates gross income by more than 25 percent in any year, Sec. 6501(e) extends the statute from three to six years. Second, Sec. 6501(c) provides an indefinite statute of limitations if any part of a tax deficiency is due to fraud. Most routine audits are made by employees classified as revenue agents; audits involving fraud, by those classified as special agents. Taxpayers under investigation by a special agent should seek advice from competent legal counsel, rather than a certified public accountant (CPA) or an enrolled agent, because only an attorney can exercise the right of privileged communication.

In general, a taxpayer has the burden of proof in contesting a tax deficiency. Although this sometimes makes it appear as if a taxpayer is guilty until proven innocent, any rule to the contrary would almost certainly encourage taxpayers to minimize (and even to destroy) valuable records. The major exception to the general rule involves cases of fraud; in that instance the government must prove its case beyond a reasonable doubt, just as it must in other criminal proceedings. The degree of proof required in an audit may vary greatly from one auditor to another. In most instances, however, the better the records, the easier it is to resolve any dispute.

The administrative procedures available to resolve disputes within the IRS before resorting to a court are numerous. Two of the more important opportunities are (1) an Appeals Division conference and (2) a request for technical advice from the National Office. An appeals office conference is conducted by an officer (a "conferee") assigned to the regional office without the field agent who made the original examination being present. This procedure generally assures the taxpayer a reasonably unprejudiced review of any dispute. A request for technical advice is most appropriate in relatively unusual or complex cases; it can also be effective when there is no uniform interpretation of the law in various courts.

The formal statutory notice of deficiency, or ninety-day letter, is the document that must be filed before a tax deficiency can be assessed and collected. It gives the taxpayer 90 days to decide how to proceed. The available options include (a) the filing of a petition with the Tax Court; (b) payment of the deficiency, filing a claim for refund, and suing in either a federal district court or the Claims Court—two options further explained in Chapter 1.

Interest and Penalties

Chapters 67 and 68 of the Code provide numerous sections that establish a taxpayer's liability for interest and penalties in addition to the basic liability for the income tax itself. Section 6601 imposes an interest charge for the underpayment, nonpayment, or extension of time for payment of the tax. Section 6611 provides for an interest payment to a taxpayer on certain overpayments of tax. And Sec. 6621 establishes the interest rate that will be applicable to both overpayments and underpayments. In general, the rate for overpayments is

The Compliance Process

the federal short-term rate plus two percentage points; the rate for underpayments, the federal short-term rate plus three percentage points. The one-percentage-point differential suggests that the government has a slightly better credit rating than the average tax debtor. The federal short-term rate is adjusted once every three months to reflect changes in the interest rates.

The interest charges imposed on corporate taxpayers can ordinarily be deducted as a business expense. Those same charges on individual taxpayers are generally not deductible on the theory that they represent a purely personal expense. As noted in Chapter 3, purely personal interest is generally not deductible. Penalties, on the other hand, are generally not deductible by any taxpayer.

The wide diversity in additional taxes and penalties that can apply is apparent from even a cursory review of the section titles of Chapter 68. The additions are contained in Subchapter A (Secs. 6651-6665); the penalties, in Subchapter B (Secs. 6671–6724). A partial list reads as follows:

- Sec. 6651. Failure to file tax return or pay tax
- Sec. 6652. Failure to file certain information returns, registration statements, etc.
- Sec. 6654. Failure by individual to pay estimated income tax
- Sec. 6655. Failure by corporation to pay estimated income tax
- Sec. 6656. Failure to make deposit of taxes
- Sec. 6657. Bad checks
- Sec. 6662. Imposition of accuracy related penalties
- Sec. 6663. Imposition of fraud penalty
- Sec. 6672. Failure to collect and pay over tax or attempt to evade or defeat tax
- Sec. 6673. Sanctions and costs awarded by courts
- Sec. 6677. Failure to file information returns with respect to certain foreign trusts
- Sec. 6683. Failure of foreign corporation to file return of personal holding company tax
- Sec. 6689. Failure to file notice of redetermination of foreign tax
- Sec. 6694. Understatement of taxpayer's liability by income tax return preparer
- Sec. 6698. Failure to file partnership return
- Sec. 6701. Penalties for aiding and abetting understatement of tax liability
- Sec. 6702. Frivolous income tax return

- Sec. 6713. Disclosure or use of information by preparers of returns

We cannot examine the details of these many sections. Suffice it to observe that the penalties include one that amounts to 5 percent a month, up to a maximum of 25 percent of the tax, for filing a late return (Sec. 6651). An additional penalty equal to 20 percent of the underpayment may also apply if the taxpayer was negligent; a term which is defined as encompassing certain misstatements of valuation (including transfer price violations), pension liabilities, or income tax. If the misstatement is very large, the penalty is doubled to 40 percent of the underpayment. Fraud penalties are even larger, and will amount to 75 percent of the underpayment in addition to the possibility of prison terms for the offending individuals.

Finally, observe that some of the penalties are imposed on tax return preparers rather than on taxpayers. Among the former group are Secs. 6694, 6695, 6701, and 6713. Most of these penalties will not apply, however, if the tax return preparer has done a conscientious job and can cite reasonable authority for any advice given to a client. In extreme cases an unethical tax return preparer can be barred by court injunction from doing further tax work.

Assessing a Tax Expert

Because of the brevity of this book and the complexity of our income tax law, numerous subjects were merely introduced and then dismissed with a warning that no attempt should be made to apply this part of the law without additional investigation and/or assistance. For most readers, the likely option is seeking the aid of a tax expert rather than undertaking a research assignment in a strange library. Even that effort may prove to be more difficult than was anticipated because true tax experts are surprisingly difficult to identify.

The average person believes that most lawyers and CPAs are reasonably well trained in matters of income taxation and are, therefore, more or less automatic tax experts. This belief is given nearly official sanction by virtue of the fact that attorneys and CPAs are automatically granted the right to practice before the IRS based on professional qualifications. As a matter of fact, it is entirely possible to earn a well-recognized law degree, pass a state bar exam, and be admitted to practice law before the various courts without ever having completed even one academic or professional course in income taxation. CPAs are in very similar circumstances in that one can complete an accounting degree at many well-recognized schools without taking a single course in income taxation. To pass the nationally administered CPA exam and receive a license to practice, however, a candidate must successfully complete a four-part exam including a one-day part devoted to accounting practice. This portion of the CPA exam has for many years allocated between 20 and 30 percent of the total points possible to tax questions. Because of this requirement, virtually all CPAs will complete one tax course simply to pass this exam. The level of tax knowledge required to pass the CPA exam is not particularly high. Consequently the assumption that all CPAs are tax experts is patently incorrect.

Although not all attorneys and CPAs are tax experts, most real tax experts are either an attorney or a CPA. A few other individuals have also achieved that status through their work experience, typically by working for the IRS. These experts may also be permitted to practice before the IRS as enrolled agents, a status achieved either by work experience or by passing a special examination. In summary, the world of tax experts might be illustrated as in Exhibit 9.1. That representation attempts to capture the one confusing but essential idea that most tax experts will be either an attorney or a CPA even though most attorneys and CPAs are not tax experts. Many of the younger attorneys and CPAs who are true tax experts hold an advanced degree in law or accounting with a specialization in taxation. The older professionals will have acquired equivalent knowledge from the school of hard knocks.

In general, CPAs do most of the tax compliance work in the United States. The more sophisticated tax planning work is divided between the best of both professional camps. Litigation of tax disputes before the courts is almost exclusively in the domain of the attorney although a very few CPAs have been admitted to practice before the Tax Court.

Anyone looking for expert tax assistance will be well advised to seek recommendations from other taxpayers who have engaged one or more tax experts in the past. After engaging an individual or a firm to perform these tasks, the service received should be monitored rather closely. In the author's opinion, routine compliance services—even those of high quality—are *not* adequate tax services for an ongoing business venture. There are many aspects of everyday business management that conceal major tax consequences. Therefore professional tax advice should be made a routine aspect of most management decisions rather than a once-or-twice-a-year exercise in compliance. For large corporations, this prescription usually leads to in-house tax counsel. For smaller businesses, an ongoing relationship

The Compliance Process

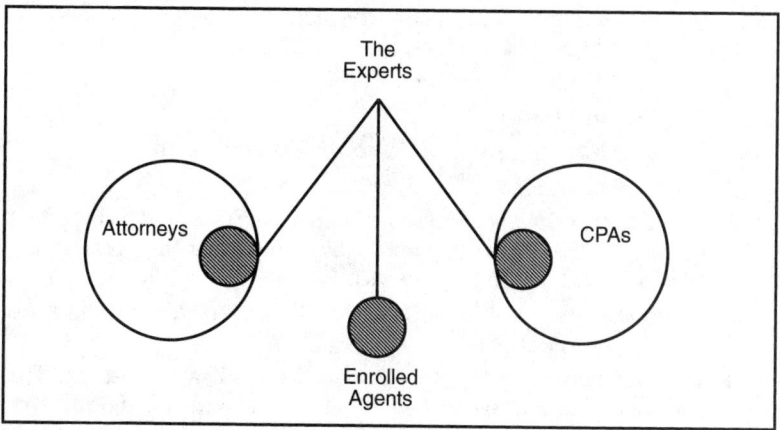

Exhibit 9.1 Tax experts identified

with a professional organization staffed with a reasonable number of true tax experts will suffice. The world of taxation has become so complex that no one person can be a tax expert on all topics. Consequently some critical mass is essential for any real degree of tax expertise. Tax advisors who merely respond to calls from clients are not doing the job that needs to be done. Real experts contribute importantly to the continuing dialogue that leads to good tax results. They must monitor the constantly changing tax laws and bring recommendation for change to clients on a timely basis. To be fair, clients must also learn to alert their tax advisors to any business plans sufficiently far in advance to permit the experts to investigate all of the tax consequences of the proposed plans and to make recommendations accordingly.

The final chapter of this text will explain in somewhat greater detail what it is that tax experts do when they undertake a tax planning engagement. That chapter includes a few examples to illustrate the potential for good tax advice on an ongoing basis.

Key Points to Remember

- ❏ The United States' income tax is a self-assessed tax. This means that every taxpayer has the sole responsibility of complying with the tax law.

The Compliance Process

- ❑ Professional tax advisors are frequently engaged by taxpayers to assist them with
    1. Filing returns;
    2. IRS audits;
    3. Planning transactions to control tax costs; and
    4. Tax litigation.
- ❑ The IRS provides various forms and instructional aids to help taxpayers comply with the tax law. These aids are available at IRS locations around the world.
- ❑ Approximately 1 1/2 percent of all the tax returns filed are audited by the IRS.
- ❑ The IRS generally has three years to audit a tax return. This statute of limitations will be extended indefinitely if a return is fraudulently prepared.
- ❑ A taxpayer generally has the burden of proof in tax litigation.
- ❑ The IRS may assess both interest and penalties for the underpayment of any tax. Criminal penalties, providing jail sentences for errant taxpayers, may also be imposed.
- ❑ Most real tax experts are either CPAs or attorneys or both. At the same time, many CPAs and many attorneys have minimal competence in tax matters.

TAX PLANNING

A successful manager will learn to treat taxes very much like any other cost of doing business. The end objective is not to minimize taxes but to control them in a manner that is consistent with an organization's overall objectives. A business can totally eliminate both income taxes and labor costs by closing up the shop. That drastic action, however, is entirely inconsistent with the general objective of profit maximization for the ordinary trade or business. The important task facing the manager is the need to insure that tax factors are given adequate consideration whenever business decisions are made. As noted in Chapter 9, this task can be accomplished either through the employment of in-house tax counsel or through the engagement of external tax professionals on a permanent basis. Because of the complexity of tax law, managers of any business should not attempt to do their own tax planning, the term that is generally used to describe most of the work that tax professionals do to control tax costs.

This chapter is divided into three major parts. The first part is an overview of tax planning in general; it explains why tax costs can sometimes be manipulated in a wholly legal way. Part two contains two specific but common examples of tax planning. The first example is concerned with alternative executive compensation techniques; the second, with methods of avoiding double taxation. The last part of this chapter explains why some tax plans occasionally do not succeed as well as was originally hoped. It introduces a few of the statutory provisions and judicial doctrines that limit tax planning opportunities in the more extreme circumstances.

Fundamentals of Tax Planning

Every taxpayer's tax costs are determined by three fundamental factors, namely, (1) the law, (2) the facts, and (3) an administrative and/or judicial process. For purposes of this text, we will assume that there is nothing that a taxpayer can legally do to intervene in either the administrative or the judicial process. Given that assumption, there are two fundamentally different ways in which a taxpayer can minimize tax costs; that is, the taxpayer can either change the law or change the facts and thereby achieve tax savings.

Relatively few taxpayers attempt to change the tax law in a way that will benefit themselves, personally, because the chances for success are so low and the apparent cost for success is so great. Nevertheless, it is one way to achieve legal tax savings that is available to a relatively few taxpayers, generally under somewhat unusual circumstances. The one recurrent occasion on which this opportunity receives greater than normal attention is the consideration of new tax legislation by the Joint (House and Senate) Conference Committee, immediately after a tax bill has been approved by both legislative chambers and immediately before a final version of a tax bill is resubmitted to the two Congressional bodies for ratification. At that very special point in time, it is not unusual to discover that an apparently minor and innocuous provision has been inserted into the Code for some obscure reason. Those who routinely work with tax law recognize these provisions as "private law," sometimes called **transition rules**, usually inserted to help gain the support of legislators whose votes are deemed critical to passage of a tax bill. The only effect of these unique provisions is to benefit certain taxpayers by granting them a special immunity from general provisions otherwise applicable to other taxpayers in similar circumstances. In a well-documented series of articles (published by the *Philadelphia Inquirer* from April 10 to April 16, 1988), Donald L. Bartlett and James B. Steele detail how some 650 taxpayers received personal tax savings of more than $10 billion, in precisely this manner, when the 1986 tax law ended its tortuous path through the legislative process. Because so few are able to utilize this entirely legal—though morally reprehensible—method of tax avoidance, the remainder of this discussion considers the alternative route to tax savings; that is, it considers how a modification of the facts can also change a tax liability.

The precise manner in which a person achieves a business objective will often have a major impact on both the costs incurred and the success attained. To illustrate, consider the many options available to transmit a message from, say, New York to London. The list of available options includes surface mail, airmail, telephone conversation at various hours of the day, telegraph, thermofax, and personal courier, to name only a few. The cost of even these few options may range from a few dollars to several thousand dollars. The chance of the message achieving its desired objective may vary directly with the cost incurred. Even though it frequently is difficult to identify and measure the causal factors of success, management should at least consider each of the primary options available. This conclusion is as true in taxation as it is in communication. A primary aspect of the tax advisor's task is, therefore, to identify the available options and to estimate the tax costs associated with each alternative, leaving the final choice to the business managers.

To be truly effective, a tax advisor must be directly involved in nearly every business decision at the earliest possible moment. This involvement gives the tax advisor an opportunity to investigate the tax implications of every option suggested and make recommendations that additional alternatives be considered, primarily for tax reasons. The tax advisor should be given an opportunity to modify plans so that the events that actually transpire are those that are consistent with the preferred tax result.

Two Examples of Tax Planning

Successful tax planning includes both (1) avoiding detrimental results and (2) achieving favorable results. Some tax plans are situation-specific—i.e., they involve only one isolated transaction—while others are ongoing programs that require periodic review. Two examples will be considered briefly. One involves the complete disposition of a closely held business, an example of a situation-specific opportunity. The other involves executive compensation in a publicly owned corporation, an example of an ongoing tax challenge. We will consider the latter example first.

Executive Compensation

The compensation of corporate employees for services rendered can take many forms. The most common form is cash payments as salaries and/or bonuses. The major problem related to the salary paid to executives concerns determining the amount to be paid—a task typically assumed by some subset of the board of directors. In the publicly owned corporation, unlike the closely held firm, the salary payments present relatively few tax problems because there is minimal opportunity for corporate managers to set their own salaries. There is little chance that the IRS will contend that any salary is unreasonably large and treat it as a disguised dividend. There are, however, many additional ways in which corporate executives can be compensated, and most of these alternatives involve critical tax consequences.

Corporate executives may be provided with various "perks" (or perquisites) that can be either taxable or nontaxable to them personally. The reason that some perks are not taxable is because an exclusion provision exempts that item from taxation. The list of executive perks that can, under the right circumstances, be at least partially nontaxable includes:

- Health and accident insurance (Sec. 106),
- Group term life insurance (Sec. 79(a)),
- Meals and lodging (Sec. 119),
- Certain death benefits (Sec. 101),
- Employee discounts (Sec. 132(a)(2)), and
- Working condition fringes (Sec. 132(a)(3)).

Even though these (and other) executive perks may be received partially or fully tax free by an executive, the cost of providing the perk can generally be deducted by the corporate employer. This combination appears to provide the best of all possible worlds from a tax point of view because it generates real personal income with no tax cost.

Because Congress and the IRS are well aware of the opportunity created by these exclusion provisions, they attach many requirements that must be met before the tax-free result can be achieved. Most importantly, the employee exclusion sections generally include a nondiscrimination provision that makes them taxable unless the rank-and-file employee also receives a benefit that is equal, or at least proportionate, to the benefit received by the executive. (The exclusion of lodging, under Sec. 119, is a notable exception to this general rule.) The added cost associated with nondiscriminatory coverage of all employees makes the decision to provide tax-free perquisites to executives vastly more difficult than it would otherwise be in a large corporation.

Qualified pension, profit-sharing, and stock-bonus plans can also be used to provide a tax-favored form of compensation to an executive. The tax advantage of these plans differs significantly from the advantage associated with other perks in that benefits derived from these plans will, at some time, be taxed to the recipient employee. Although the corporate employer is entitled immediately to deduct the contributions that it makes to an employee trust fund under a qualified plan, the employee need not report those same contributions as personal income until some later date. The employee trust fund is a tax-exempt entity; hence the contributions can accumulate and grow much more rapidly than would be possible with a nonqualified plan. Finally, the executive may be entitled to an advantageous tax treatment when funds are withdrawn, particularly if they are withdrawn in a lump sum.

Because of the major tax advantages associated with qualified pension and profit-sharing plans—i.e., because of the right to an immediate deduction by the employer, the right to tax deferral by the employee, the right to tax-free growth in the interim, and the right to possible preferential treatment on withdrawal—Congress once again imposes many requirements on plans that achieve a tax-preferred treatment. Those requirements include (among others) nondiscrimination provisions, funding and reporting requirements, and certain vesting rules. (Vesting means the employee's right cannot be terminated, after some period of employment, even if the employee resigns, dies, or is fired.) The decision to provide executives with qualified pension or profit-sharing plans becomes a very difficult one because the costs associated with instituting and maintaining a qualified plan are substantial. The decision to implement a plan must be considered carefully.

Executives can also be compensated through stock-option plans. Many managers believe that these stock option plans are preferable because they tie an executive's compensation directly to the price of the stock, the most tangible benefit received by the shareholders from the executive's services. For many years stock-option plans harbored primary tax benefits because, under the right conditions, income from the disposition of stock acquired through an executive stock option could be reported as a long-term capital gain. As explained in Chapter 7, the tax advantages long associated with capital gains were almost entirely eliminated after 1986. Today, therefore, there are no tax reasons to prefer compensating executives with stock options rather than cash. There still are some tax factors associated with stock compensation plans. Plans that provide the executive with the opportunity to purchase stock at a preferential price can trigger both (a) the recognition of income for the executive and (b) the right to deduct compensation for the corporation at the time an option is granted, assuming the value of the option is ascertainable and the option price is set below the market price. In addition, there are various financial accounting and legal factors that must be considered with any executive stock option. Financial accounting standards currently provide that no expense will be reported for stock options exercised by executives. Hence a corporation can get a tax deduction, and even a cash receipt, while reporting no amount of income or expense to the shareholders for executive compensation paid in stock options.

Finally, executives can be given a deferred compensation arrangement. This alternative basically promises to defer the pay for work done now until sometime in the future. The tax consequences of these plans can be significant. So long as the executive has received nothing other than the corporation's general unsecured obligation to pay, both the executive's income and the corporation's deduction will ordinarily be deferred until payment is made. If the executive receives something more than the rights of a general creditor, the recognition of taxable income will likely be accelerated. The right of the employer to deduct compensation expense whenever the executive recognizes taxable income, however, may not be available in this latter case.

Because of the many considerations associated with executive compensation techniques, a well managed business will institute a procedure to insure that this entire subject is periodically reviewed for necessary changes and improvements. Major changes in the tax law frequently mandate major changes in compensation arrangements. A qualified tax advisor will monitor proposed legislation as well as actual statutory changes and alert business mangers to the need for modification at the most desirable time. Tax planning for executive compensation is a never-ending task. The decision to dispose of an entire business is more often a nonrecurring problem in tax planning.

Business Disposition

Although large corporations may acquire and sell entire businesses with some frequency, the tax planning associated with that dramatic event is usually situation-specific. That same conclusion is even more likely in the context of a closely held business. The tax rules that apply to a business disposition vary greatly depending upon the organizational or legal form in which the business has been conducted. In other words, the tax consequences associated with the disposition of a sole proprietorship may differ greatly from those associated with the disposition of a partnership or a corporation. In this example, we will examine only the tax consequences generally associated with the disposition of a wholly owned C-corporation.

Once the owner of a corporation decides that the time has come to dispose of a business being conducted in a wholly owned corporation, the services of a tax consultant should immediately be acquired. There are at least four relatively obvious and distinctly different ways to proceed, namely,

1. simply have the owner sell all of the stock of the corporation;
2. have the corporation sell all of its business assets and pay off all remaining liabilities—the owner can then either liquidate

the corporation or continue to operate a new business within the old corporate shell;
3. have the corporation distribute all of its assets to the owner in liquidation after paying off all corporate liabilities, and allow the owner to personally sell the old business assets and retain the proceeds; or
4. have the owner exchange the corporate stock for stock in another corporation and/or other assets.

Although these four alternatives may be the more obvious options, there are others, and there are several subtle variations contained within each alternative. As a complete alternative to any of the four choices suggested above, the owner might give away all of the stock. That additional option contains such variations as giving all of the stock to family members or to faithful employees, giving all the stock to a favorite charity, or giving some stock to each group. Another option is the sale of stock to an ESOP, an employee stock ownership plan. The tax consequences vary significantly, depending on exactly how the disposition is made.

To illustrate the diversity of the tax consequences associated with the disposition of a business, let us consider only the broad outline of the four alternatives listed above, using one common example. The critical but common assumptions are detailed in Exhibit 10.1. Given these facts, one might conclude that I's stock has a fair market value of $8.2 million, i.e., the net worth of C Corporation (or $12.5 million in assets less $4.3 million in liabilities).

I — Owns 100% of → C Corp.

I's basis in the C stock is only $200,000.

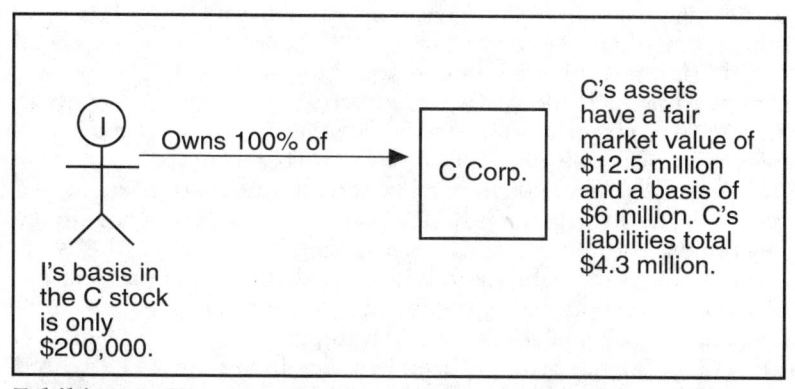

C's assets have a fair market value of $12.5 million and a basis of $6 million. C's liabilities total $4.3 million.

Exhibit 10.1 Facts assumed in subsequent examples (Exhibits 10.2 through 10.4)

Tax Planning

If I's stock is actually worth $8.2 million, a sale of that stock will cause I to recognize a capital gain of $8 million (i.e., $8.2 million amount realized less $200,000 adjusted basis in the C stock). Tax on an $8 million long-term capital gain would be $2.24 million, leaving I with approximately $6 million to reinvest. As a practical matter, a buyer would probably not be willing to pay I $8.2 million for the stock of C because that buyer would have indirectly acquired the assets of C for $8.2 million but would have acquired tax basis of only $6 million in those assets. The $2.2 million lower basis in the assets could mean substantially higher income taxes for the buyer in future years; therefore, the buyer may very well reduce the price offered for all of C's stock to something less than $8.2 million. There is a special provision in the Code (Sec. 338) that gives a **corporate purchaser** of stock the right to make an election to step up the basis of the assets acquired in a qualifying stock purchase to the amount paid for the stock plus the liabilities assumed. If the corporate buyer makes the Sec. 338 election, however, the acquired corporation (or C, in our example) will have to pay the income tax on the $6.5 million difference between the $12.5 million value of the assets held and their $6 million basis, just as if C has sold those same assets to an outside party. That tax would reduce the net assets left in C by the amount of the tax liability, or by approximately $2.21 million in our example. This added income tax would also reduce the value of C's net worth from $8.2 million to approximately $6 million. In short, because of tax consequences, 100 percent of C's stock may well be worth something less than $8.2 million, even if the facts assumed in Exhibit 10.1 are otherwise entirely complete and correct.

To summarize, individual I should be able to sell all of the C stock, probably for some amount less than $8.2 million, assuming that both parties understand the tax consequences of that method of disposition. If individual I can find a buyer willing to pay $7.5 million for all of C's stock, the first method of disposition can be summarized and illustrated as in Exhibit 10.2. This alternative requires I to pay an income tax of more than $2 million (i.e., $7.3 million x 28%) and leaves I with approximately $5.5 million to reinvest or spend.

If I elects to pursue the second of the four alternatives suggested earlier, the results will differ somewhat from those experienced in the first option. The tax consequences of C Corporation selling the assets and paying off the liabilities are illustrated and summarized in Exhibit 10.3. Note that this leaves the after-tax assets inside C corporation, not in I's own pocket. C would recognize income of $6.5 million (i.e., $12.5 million amount realized less $6 million adjusted basis) and pay a tax of $2.21 million (i.e., 34% x $6.5 million). Therefore, after paying off its original creditors, C would be left with nearly $6 million

Tax Planning

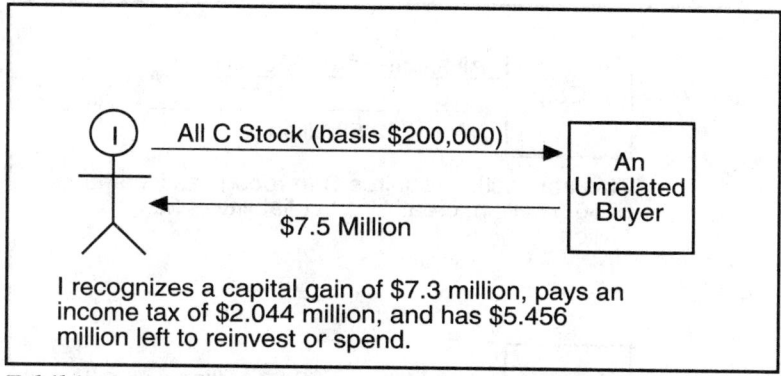

```
   ( I )    All C Stock (basis $200,000)       ┌──────────┐
    |    ─────────────────────────────────►   │    An    │
   /|\                                         │ Unrelated│
   / \         $7.5 Million                    │  Buyer   │
         ◄─────────────────────────────        └──────────┘

I recognizes a capital gain of $7.3 million, pays an
income tax of $2.044 million, and has $5.456
million left to reinvest or spend.
```

Exhibit 10.2 I's sale of all of C's stock for $7.5 million

(i.e., $12.5 million received less $2.21 million in taxes and less $4.3 million in liabilities) either to distribute to I or to reinvest in a new business. If C distributes the $5.99 million to I, I must recognize income of $5.79 million (i.e., $5.99 million amount realized less $200,000 adjusted basis) and pay a tax of approximately $1.621 million (i.e., 28% x $5.79 million). This leaves I with approximately $4.37 million after taxes to reinvest or spend.

If C does not proceed with step 3 in Exhibit 10.3 and does not distribute the nearly $6 million to I, C would have to reinvest it in another active business. If C attempts simply to invest the $6 million in secondary investments, the corporation will be a personal holding company. That status will subject C in future years to both the corporate income tax and the personal holding company tax—a very undesirable tax result. C is also precluded (by Sec. 1362(d)) from electing status as an S-corporation if it reinvests the proceeds in secondary investments. In summary, C has few good choices after it sells its operating assets other than either liquidating or pursuing a second active business. And the second active business option is generally not what the owner (I, in our example) had in mind when he or she decided to dispose of the original business in the first place.

If I decides to pursue the third of the four alternatives suggested earlier, she or he will discover that the tax consequences are essentially identical to those described in the second alternative, with the liquidation option. These results can be illustrated and summarized as in Exhibit 10.4. For tax purposes, the distribution of the assets by C to I in liquidation will trigger the recognition of income just as if C's assets had been sold to an unrelated third party. C must recognize income of $6.5 million (i.e., $12.5 million value less $6 million basis)

ESSENTIALS OF U.S. TAXATION / **10.09**

Tax Planning

Step 1

C Corp. → All assets (basis $6 Million) → Unrelated Buyers

← $12.5 Million

This transaction requires C to recognize income of $6.5 Million, creating a tax liability of $2.21 Million.

Step 2

C Corp. → $4.3 Million + $2.21 Million → Original Creditors and IRS

← Liabilities Paid

This leaves C with $5.99 Million and further tax problems (see text for details). If C distributes cash to I, note what happens:

Step 3

C Corp. → $5.99 Million → I

← All of C's Stock (basis $200,000)

I recognizes a copital gain of $5.79 Million and pays a tax of approximately $1.621 Million; this leaves I with only $4.379 Million.

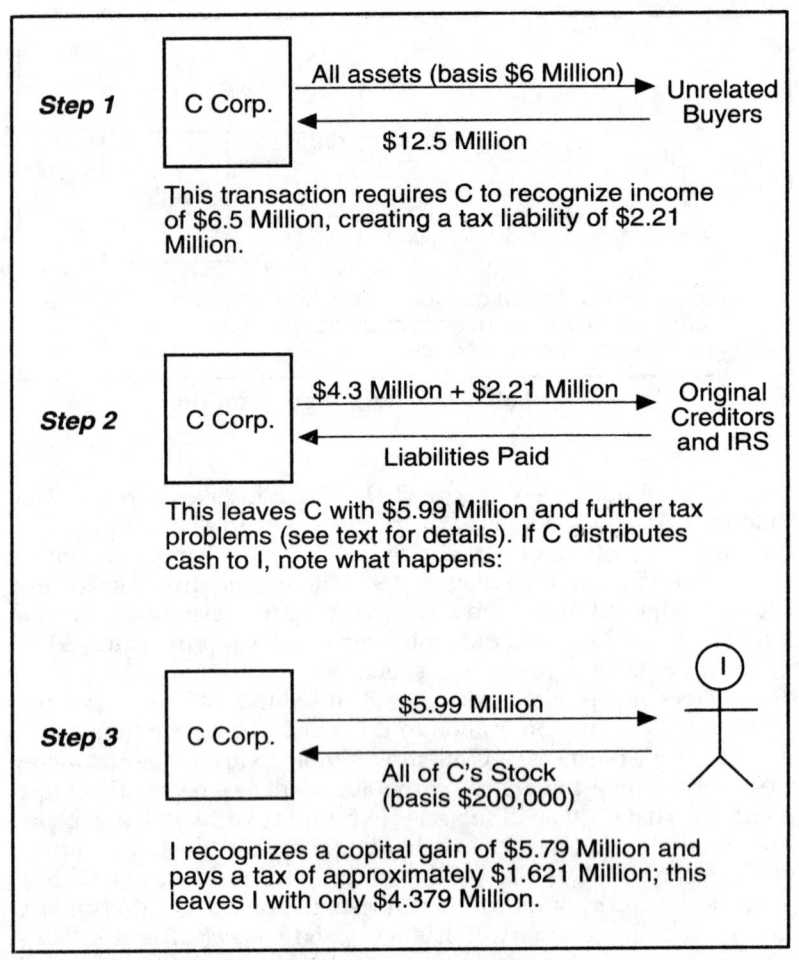

Exhibit 10.3 Sale of assets by C for $12.5 Million and payment of all C's liabilities

when it distributes its assets to I in liquidation. This creates a new income tax liability of $2.21 million for C (i.e., $6.5 million x 34%). Because of this added income tax liability, I will actually receive net assets of only $5.99 million (i.e., $12.5 million less $4.3 million original debts and less $2.21 million in additional taxes). Individual I must also recognize a capital gain of $5.79 million (i.e., $5.99 million amount realized less I's $200,000 adjusted basis in C's stock). This causes I's

Tax Planning

Step 1

C Corp. —— All Assets (basis $6 Million) ——▶ I

I —— All of C's Stock (basis $200,000) ——▶ C Corp.

This distribution requires C to recognize income of $6.5 Million and I to recognize capital gain of $5.9 Million.

Step 2

I —— $4.3 Million + $2.21 Million + $1.621 Million ——▶ C's Original Creditors and the IRS

◀—— Liabilities Paid ——

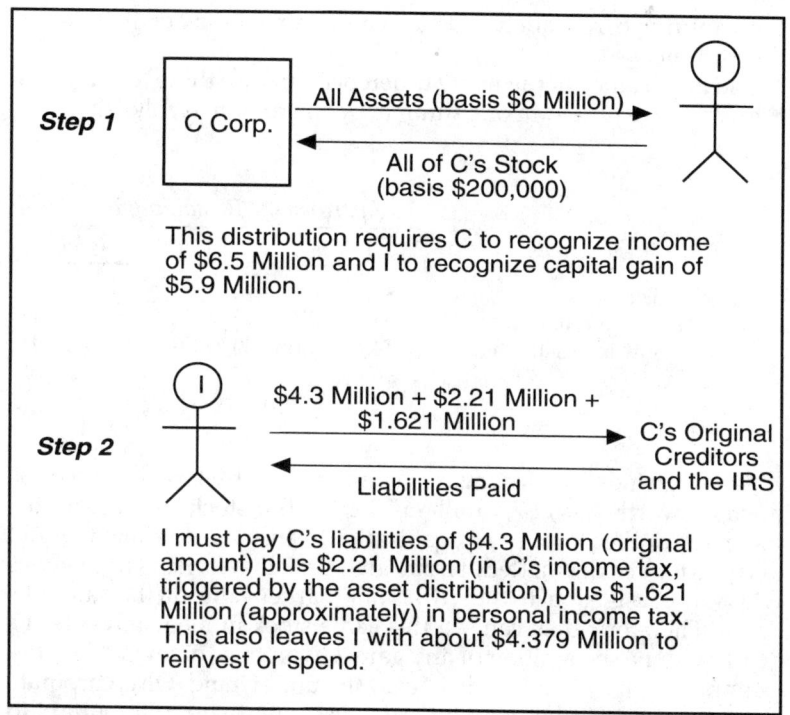

I must pay C's liabilities of $4.3 Million (original amount) plus $2.21 Million (in C's income tax, triggered by the asset distribution) plus $1.621 Million (approximately) in personal income tax. This also leaves I with about $4.379 Million to reinvest or spend.

Exhibit 10.4 Distribution of assets by C to I and liquidation of C

---

personal income tax to increase by approximately $1.621 million (i.e., $5.79 million x 28%). In the end individual I is left with only $4.379 million to reinvest. This is exactly the same result as would be achieved by the second option, with the liquidation.

The fourth and final alternative to be considered here can, under the proper circumstances, put I in a very different situation. As explained in Chapter 7, if individual I can exchange his or her stock in C Corporation solely for stock in another corporation that is also party to a reorganization as defined in Sec. 368(a)(1), that exchange will be a tax-free transaction. This means that individual I will have disposed of the entire business (conducted by C) without any diminution in values because of income taxes. The value of the shares received by I will likely be something less than $8.2 million for exactly the same reasons as were explained in option 1; a value of $7.5 million is a reasonable estimate. If I finds need for some amount of cash after the exchange, she or he can sell the necessary number of shares of stock in the acquiring corporation and pay a much smaller tax on that limited disposition.

The importance of the many differences among these four alternatives can be captured in one summary comparison as follows:

	I's Approximate Remaining Net Worth	
Alternative	In Cash	In Other Assets
1. Sell stock	$5.5 million	$0
2. Sell assets and liquidate	$4.4 million	$0
3. Distribute assets and liquidate	$4.4 million	$0 (if the assets are sold)
4. Merge C	$0	$7.5

Although individual I would have a carryover basis of only $200,000 in stock worth (say) $7.5 million—i.e., in the stock received in the merger (or other form of reorganization)—that tax detriment would disappear at I's death. Recall from Chapter 7 that I's heirs or devisees will take a basis equal to the stock's fair market value on the date of I's death. Therefore, they can sell this same stock immediately after I's death with no recognition of any gain. Given this somewhat lengthy example of tax planning, it is easy to understand why corporate reorganizations and other nontaxable exchanges are so important to successful tax planning and why good tax advisors are so important to successful business management.

Limitations to Tax Planning

Not every tax plan succeeds as well as the one explained in the last few pages. Some plans fail because of statutory provisions that were enacted specifically to counteract what Congress deems to be unduly generous tax results; others fail because of judicial doctrines that courts may apply to defeat what they deem to be unduly aggressive tax positions. Some of the antiplanning statutory provisions are situation-specific; others are very general in application. Virtually all judicial doctrines are, almost by definition, of general application. In the remaining pages of this text we will consider very briefly two antiplanning examples of statutory origin —one situation-specific and the other very general—as well as the broad outline of a few judicial doctrines that may limit tax planning in other circumstances.

The Double Tax Provisions

As explained in Chapter 6, income that is initially earned in a C-corporation can be taxed twice; that is, first to the corporation, when it is originally earned, and second to the shareholder, if and when it is distributed as a dividend. Many large, publicly owned corporations minimize this potential for double taxation by reinvesting most of their incomes in the business. Shareholders of these corporations may be satisfied with the low dividend payout so long as the retained and reinvested incomes are reflected in higher stock prices, especially in those years when capital gains (which would be triggered by the sale of stock) are treated much more favorably for tax purposes than is ordinary income (which is defined to include dividends).

Smaller, closely held corporations were faced with a similar problem in the past. As long as the top marginal tax rate on income earned by a corporation was substantially lower than the top marginal tax rate on income earned by individuals, there was a powerful incentive to earn and retain income within a corporate entity. The eventual extraction of that income, however, would usually trigger a second tax on a single income stream, and taxpayers and their advisors expended a great deal of attention in mitigating this double tax. For each tax plan attempted, Congress proved equal to the challenge by enacting corrective legislation.

To illustrate the extraction of income from a corporation in the most obvious way, consider the extreme circumstance diagrammed in Exhibit 10.5. It depicts a situation in which individual I owns 100 percent of the outstanding stock of two financially successful C-corporations (C and D). Given these facts, any distribution by C to I of $10 million or less in (1) cash, (2) other property, and/or (3) C's own securities (i.e., C's long-term debt) will be taxed as a dividend to individual I. And any distribution by D to I of $15 million or less will also be taxed as a dividend. This results in that dreaded double tax on a single income stream. To minimize this result, individual I may be tempted to sell some of his or her C shares to C Corporation, as diagrammed in Exhibit 10.6. Because C is acquiring its own outstanding stock, that transaction would generally be labelled a stock redemption in the financial press. The critical tax problem for individual I can be stated simply: Should this stock redemption be treated as a sale of stock or as a dividend? If it is a sale of stock, I must report a capital gain of $600,000; if it is a dividend, I must report ordinary income of $1 million.

Given the assumption (in Exhibit 10.5) that I owns 100 percent of C Corporation, it is fairly obvious that I's surrender of some of his or her

Tax Planning

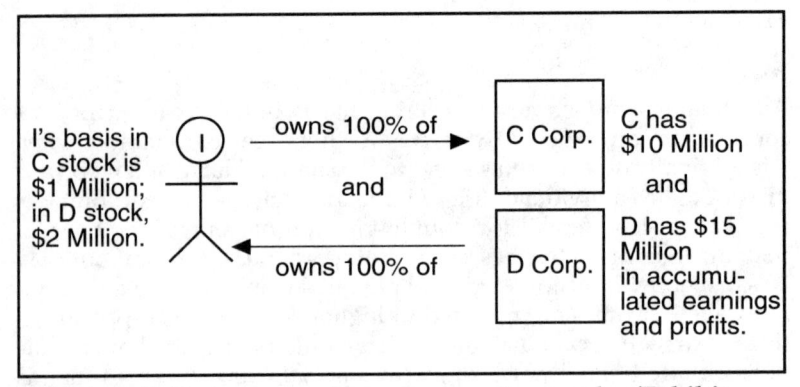

Exhibit 10.5 Facts assumed in subsequent examples (Exhibits 10.6 and 10.7)

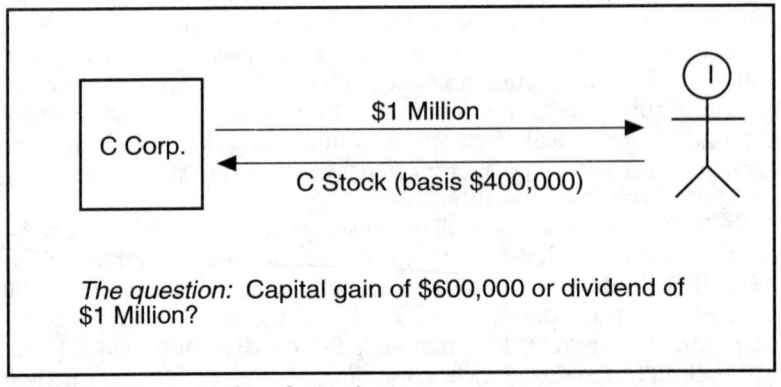

[Diagram: Individual I (basis in C stock is $1 Million; in D stock, $2 Million) owns 100% of C Corp. (C has $10 Million) and owns 100% of D Corp. (D has $15 Million in accumulated earnings and profits.)]

[Diagram: C Corp. transfers $1 Million to I; I transfers C Stock (basis $400,000) to C Corp. *The question:* Capital gain of $600,000 or dividend of $1 Million?]

Exhibit 10.6 A stock redemption

shares of stock back to C is totally meaningless. Individual I owns all of C both before and after the transaction. Accordingly, the result of a simple distribution of $1 million in cash would be exactly the same—at least in real economic terms—as is the stock redemption alternative. Sec. 302 was inserted into the Code to achieve precisely that tax result.

In drafting Sec. 302 Congress realized that not every stock redemption will have this same tax consequence. In some instances—where one shareholder gives up a substantially disproportionate number of shares compared to other (unrelated) shareholders—that shareholder's stock redemption should be treated as a sale rather

10.14 / *ESSENTIALS OF U.S. TAXATION*

than as a dividend. Sec. 302 was carefully drafted to distinguish between those stock redemptions that are to be treated as sales and those to be treated as dividends. To make this antiplanning section apply as it was intended, it incorporates the stock attribution rules of Sec. 318. The latter provision treats shareholders as owning not only those shares owned directly (in their own names), but also those owned indirectly through other related parties, including those owned by certain family members and by related corporations, partnerships, estates, trusts, etc.

Given Sec. 302, individual I in Exhibit 10.5 might be tempted to rearrange the facts ever so slightly. Instead of I surrendering some of his or her shares in C back to C, I might attempt to sell some of his or her shares in D to C. This rearrangement of facts can be diagrammed as in Exhibit 10.7. The tax question really has not changed; i.e., Should I treat this as a sale of stock or as a dividend? Given the fact that I owns 100 percent of both C and D corporations, the answer should be obvious. For tax purposes, this transaction is nothing more than a disguised dividend, and Sec. 304 treats it as such for income tax purposes. Sec. 304 was enacted specifically to insure that taxpayers could not easily convert a larger dividend into a smaller capital gain simply by rearranging the facts in a manner that made a dividend look like a sale of stock. Both Secs. 302 and 304 are good examples of situation-specific Code provisions that limit tax planning opportunities under specific circumstances. A much more general antitax planning net was cast when Congress enacted the alternative minimum tax (AMT) provisions.

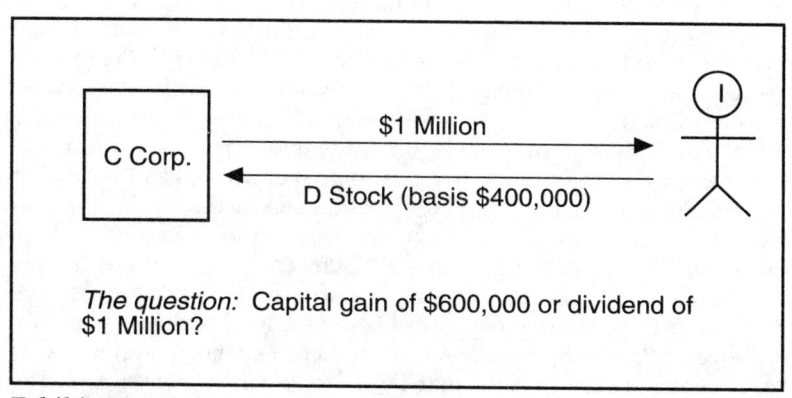

The question: Capital gain of $600,000 or dividend of $1 Million?

Exhibit 10.7 Sale to a related party

Tax Planning

The AMT

Over the years, many provisions were put into the Code to encourage a preferred economic behavior by taxpayers in general. One tax credit was enacted to stimulate greater business investment; another to stimulate hiring of the hard-core unemployed; another to increase expenditures on research and development; another to encourage the rehabilitation of historic structures; etc. Because of the many and varied preferential tax provisions, some taxpayers were able to significantly reduce their federal income tax liabilities to little or nothing. These tax stories were constantly reported and aggrandized by the media until a public outcry of unfairness caused Congress to react in a most unusual way. Instead of repealing the preferential provisions, Congress elected to impose an *alternative* income tax on those taxpayers who had, in their opinion, been too successful in their own tax planning efforts. This alternative tax is the AMT.

The primary provisions of the AMT are currently those of Secs. 55 through 59. Unfortunately, the details of these five sections are so complex that they cannot be even generally described in a text restricted to the essentials of income taxation. In lieu thereof, we will consider only the concept of the AMT and leave all details to other volumes. The concept is fairly simple. It provides two entirely different ways for taxpayers to compute their income tax every year and then requires taxpayers pay the larger of the two tax liabilities.

The procedure begins with taxable income calculated in the normal way. To that dollar amount, taxpayers must add back any tax preferences, as defined in Sec. 57. Taxpayers must also add back or subtract out certain adjustments, as defined in Secs. 56 and 58. This adjusted dollar figure can, under certain circumstances, be further reduced by an exemption deduction to determine the adjusted minimum taxable income (AMTI). Finally, AMTI is multiplied by the AMT tax rate (20 percent for corporate taxpayers and 24 percent for all other taxpayers) to determine the alternative income tax.

The exemption deduction is just large enough ($40,000) to effectively excuse the average individual taxpayer as well as the smaller corporate taxpayer from having to worry about the AMT; it is also just small enough to cause a big surprise for those who have done even a little tax planning in many instances. The effects of the tax preference and adjustment items are often sufficient to cause the AMT to be larger than the income tax determined in the regular way for those who have done even a modicum of tax planning. This conclusion does not imply that tax planning is a useless exercise. Rather, it suggests that successful tax planning must consider not only the general rules described earlier in this text, but also the special AMT rules that can apply in surprisingly common circumstances.

Judicial Doctrines

Tax plans that avoid all of the many and varied statutory provisions that have been put into the law to limit their effectiveness must still clear one last hurdle. That hurdle is the right of any court to deny a taxpayer a carefully contrived tax result simply because, at least in the opinion of the court, it is somehow inconsistent with the apparent intent of the law. The colorful names commonly given to these judicial doctrines include

- substance over form,
- step transaction,
- business purposes,
- fruit and tree,

and several others. Although each judicial doctrine can be carefully distinguished from every other doctrine, the doctrines collectively suggest that a court need not be bound by either (1) the actual events that transpired or (2) the literal words of the Code if the court finds that the tax result is in some way absurd. Every good tax advisor will consider these highly subjective judicial doctrines when recommending a tax plan to a client; and every client-taxpayer will give equally serious consideration to his or her own "smell-test" before trying to implement any recommended plan. Tax plans that smack of undue chicanery are best left untested by the courts.

Key Points to Remember

- ❑ Effective tax planning can substantially reduce a taxpayer's federal income tax cost in many situations.
- ❑ Most tax planning is achieved by the timely rearrangement of details associated with common business transactions.
- ❑ Large businesses can best control tax costs by employing in-house tax experts; smaller businesses can best achieve the same objective by the retention of external tax experts on a permanent basis.

Tax Planning

- ❏ Executive compensation packages are frequently modified in response to changes in the federal income tax law.
- ❏ A tax advisor should always be consulted before a taxpayer engages in any nonroutine transaction involving a significant amount of assets or liabilities.
- ❏ Otherwise viable tax plans sometimes fail because of either
    1. Specific statutory provisions that have been put into the Code to minimize the tax plan's effect; or
    2. General judicial doctrines that courts may apply to mitigate unintended, favorable tax results.

Glossary

1. The explanations presented are intended as an introduction to the meaning of the terms. They do not encompass all the nuances or qualifications.
2. If a page number or chapter number is given in parenthesis, a more complete description of the term will be found beginning at that reference.

A

Accelerated cost recovery system: A tax-accounting procedure used to determine the annual tax deduction associated with the use of a fixed asset acquired after 1980. **(5.09)**

Accounting method: Any one of several alternative general ways of measuring income. **(2.07; see also Chapter 5)**

Accounting period: The period of time for which income has been measured, usually a year. **(5.01)**

Accounting procedures: Special rules that are applied to various income measurement problems within the context of a more general accounting method. **(5.09)**

Accrual method: A general method of accounting that requires income to be recognized in the year in which it is earned regardless of when it may be received in the form of cash or other property. **(5.04)**

ACRS: *See* Accelerated cost recovery system.

Active income: Income that is neither passive income nor portfolio income as defined in the Code. **(8.07)**

Active participant: An owner who participates in the trade or business of a tax-conduit entity on a regular, continuous, and substantial basis.

Additional standard deduction: A statutorily determined amount that may be added to the (basic) standard deduction by individual taxpayers who are (1) blind and/or (2) over 64 years of age. (The amount of the additional standard deduction may vary from $700 to $1800 for any individual in 1992.) **(6.07)**

Adjusted basis: In general, adjusted basis represents a taxpayer's unrecovered tax cost in a property. In more technical terms, adjusted basis is a taxpayer's original basis in a property plus any subsequent increases in basis and less any subsequent recoveries of basis. A taxpayer's original basis in a property will vary depending on how the taxpayer acquired the property. **(4.18; 7.04)**

Adjusted gross income: The arithmetic difference between an individual's gross income and the sum of any amounts claimed for 12 deductions specifically identified in Sec. 62. **(6.01)**

Administrative interpretations: *See* Administrative tax law.

Administrative tax law: Interpretations of the Code rendered by officials in the

ESSENTIALS OF U.S. TAXATION / **11.01**

Glossary

administrative branch of the government. **(1.11)**

Affiliated group: A chain of two or more corporations organized in parent-subsidiary format, in which the parent corporation owns 80% or more of the outstanding stock of the subsidiary corporation(s), and which corporations have elected to file one consolidated tax return for all members of the affiliated group. **(5.14)**

AFTR 2d: Common abbreviation for the *American Federal Tax Reporter*, second series, published by Prentice-Hall, Inc./ Research Institute of America. **(1.23)**

AGI: *See* Adjusted gross income.

Alien: A citizen of a country other than the United States. **(4.02)**

Alternative minimum tax: The statutory provisions which effectively create a second and parallel income tax system to insure that all U.S. taxpayers earning an income pay some minimal amount of income tax. **(10.16)**

Alternative minimum taxable income: An adjusted amount of taxable income that constitutes the tax base for the alternative minimum tax. **(10.16)**

Amount realized: The sum of (1) any cash received, (2) the fair market value of any property received, and (3) the amount of debt transferred to (or assumed by) another taxpayer at the time of a property disposition. **(7.03)**

AMT: *See* Alternative minimum tax.

AMTI: *See* Alternative minimum taxable income.

Appreciate: To increase in value. **(7.07)**

Appreciated property: Any property that has a fair market value in excess of its tax basis. **(7.07)**

Assignment of income: Any attempt to redirect income from the taxpayer who earned it to another for the purpose of decreasing the income tax payable on that income. **(4.21)**

Attorney: An individual who has earned a law degree. A licensed attorney is an attorney who has been licensed by a state or other government to practice law before certain courts. **(9.07)**

Audit: The examination of a tax return to determine its accuracy. **(9.04)**

Average tax rate: The tax rate determined by dividing a taxpayer's gross tax liability for a year by the taxpayer's taxable income for that same year.

B

Base-company operations: The commercial activities of a multinational corporation outside the geographical boundaries of the country which granted the corporation its charter. **(4.08)**

Basic standard deduction: *See* Standard deduction.

Basis: The amount that a taxpayer may recover as a tax-free return of the capital when disposing of a property. *See also* Adjusted basis.   **(4.17; 7.04)**

BNA: *See* Bureau of National Affairs.

Boot: Any property other than that which can be exchanged tax-free in a "nontaxable exchange." **(7.14)**

Brother–sister group: Two or more legally separate corporations in which

Glossary

five or fewer individuals, estates, or trusts own a sufficient shareholder interest (as defined by Sec. 1563(a)(2)). **(5.11)**

Bureau of National Affairs: The commercial publisher of a widely used tax service, *Tax Management*. **(1.20)**

Business purpose: A judicial doctrine that is sometimes cited as authority to tax a transaction in a way that is inconsistent with the literal terms of the Code because the transaction has no apparent business purpose other than saving taxes. **(10.17)**

C

Capital asset: Any property other than those specifically identified in Sec. 1221 (1)–(5). **(7.09)**

Capital gain: The gain realized on the sale or exchange of a capital asset. **(7.08)**

Capital improvement: Any expenditure that will benefit future accounting periods and that should, therefore, be added (at least in part) to an asset account rather than being expensed in its entirety in the current period. **(7.05)**

Capital loss: The loss realized on the sale or exchange of a capital asset. **(7.08; 8.10)**

Carryover basis: Any tax basis that implicitly reflects some amount of previously realized but not-yet-recognized gain or loss. **(7.12)**

Cash equivalent: The fair market value of any noncash items received by a taxpayer. **(2.08)**

Cash method: A general method of accounting that requires income to be recognized in the year in which it is received in cash (or a cash equivalent), regardless of when it may have been earned, and in which deductions are recognized in the year that they are paid. **(5.06)**

CB: *See* Cumulative Bulletin.

CCH: *See* Commerce Clearing House.

C-corporation: Any corporation subject to the usual or ordinary tax rules applicable to corporate taxpayers. (Used to distinguish ordinary corporations from S-corporations.) **(4.11)**

Certified Public Accountant: A person who has successfully completed a national examination in accounting and who has been licensed by a state to perform certain accounting tasks. **(9.07)**

CFC: *See* Controlled foreign corporation.

Circuit courts of appeal: Twelve geographically bounded federal courts of appellate jurisdiction. These courts hear appeals from both the Tax Court and federal district courts. **(1.17)**

Citation: A reference to a primary or secondary tax authority made in a standard format. **(1.21; 1.22)**

Claims court: One of three courts of original jurisdiction in federal income tax litigation. A federal court with jurisdiction limited to claims against the United States. **(1.17)**

Cl. Ct.: Common abbreviation for the Claims Court reporter series published by the Government Printing Office. **(1.23)**

Closely-held corporation: A loosely defined and nontechnical term that is generally used to refer to any corpora-

Glossary

tion if a significant portion of that corporation's stock is owned or controlled by one or a few shareholders. **(4.11)**

Code: An integrated compilation of the numerous federal income tax laws enacted by Congress during various time periods. The current Code is The Internal Revenue Code of 1986, as amended. **(1.01; 1.04)**

Code section: A reference to statutory law designated by an Arabic number and sometimes an English capital letter immediately after the number. The most common and appropriate reference to a subdivision of the Code. **(1.08)**

Combined group: Three or more corporations that include both (1) a brother-sister group and (2) a parent-subsidiary group of controlled corporations. **(5.11)**

Commerce Clearing House: The commercial publisher of a widely used tax service, *Standard Federal Tax Reports*. **(1.20)**

Complex trust: Any trust that can, by terms of the trust indenture, retain some part or all of the income that it currently earns. **(4.14)**

Conduit: *See* Tax conduit.

Conferee: An IRS employee assigned the responsibility of reviewing audit decisions reached at lower levels of the administrative procedure to resolve disputes be-tween taxpayers and the IRS. **(9.05)**

Consolidated tax return: A single tax return filed on behalf of two or more legally separate corporations that are members of an affiliated group. **(5.10)**

Controlled corporation: In general, any corporation in which an individual, or some designated group of individuals, own 80% or more of the corporation's outstanding stock. (*Note*: For some tax purposes, an ownership of 50% or more may suffice.) **(7.17)**

Controlled foreign corporation: A corporation, chartered by a non- U.S. government, if more than 50% of that corporation's stock is owned or controlled by U.S. stockholders. **(4.08)**

Controlled group: Two or more legally separate corporations whose gross tax liabilities must be calculated as if their separate taxable incomes had been earned by a single corporate entity, but only if the ownership of the separate corporations is held in a way uniquely described in Sec. 1563. **(5.11)**

Corporate reorganization: The restructuring of a corporation's equity interests in a manner that satisfies one of the definitional alternatives of Sec. 368(a)(1)(A)–(G). **(7.17)**

Corporate taxpayers: The Code, in Sec. 11, designates "every corporation" as a person responsible to report and pay the income tax. Other sections provide special rules for foreign corporations, S-corporations, and other special corporations. **(4.08)**

Corporation: A legal entity whose rights and obligations are determined by the laws of the state which granted the entity the privilege to exist. **(4.08; 4.22)**

Court of Appeals for the Federal Circuit: A federal court of appellate jurisdiction that hears cases on appeal from the Claims Court. **(1.18)**

CPA: *See* Certified Public Accountant.

Credits: *See* Tax credit.

Cumulative Bulletin: A semi-annual bound volume of IRS publications previously issued in more temporary form. **(1.22)**

D

Dash-eight regulations: The treasury regulations that source items of gross income and deductions as domestic or foreign. Specifically, Treas. Reg. Sec. 1.861-8. **(4.02)**

Deduction: An item that may be subtracted from gross income in the calculation of taxable income. **(3.06)**

Deductions for AGI: Any of 12 deductions specifically identified in Sec. 62. **(6.02)**

Deductions from AGI: Any deduction claimed by an individual taxpayer other than the 12 deductions specifically identified in Sec. 62. **(6.04)**

Deferred compensation: The promise to pay an employee for current services at some date in the future. **(10.04)**

Dependent: An individual who satisfies each of five tests specified in Sec. 152. The five tests concern (1) relationship, (2) gross income, (3) support, (4) citizenship or residency, and (5) filing status. **(6.08)**

Dependent exemption: A statutorily determined amount that an individual taxpayer may claim for each person that qualifies as the taxpayer's dependent. (The dependent exemption for 1992 is $2300.) **(6.09)**

Depletion: A tax-accounting procedure used to determine the annual tax deduction associated with the production and sale of a natural resource. **(5.09)**

Depreciate: To decrease in value. **(7.07)**

Depreciated property: Any property that has a tax basis in excess of its fair market value. **(7.07)**

Depreciation method: Alternative accounting procedures that allocate the cost of a fixed asset over some period of time longer than one year. **(5.09)**

DIF (or DIF score): *See* Discriminant function.

Discriminant function: A secret computerized formula used by the IRS to aid in the selection of tax returns to be audited. **(9.04)**

District court: One of three courts of original jurisdiction in federal income tax litigation. A federal court with general authority and the only court that may involve a jury trial in tax disputes. **(1.16)**

District office: Any one of the 63 IRS facilities located throughout the United States to conduct audits of tax returns, to assist taxpayers in their compliance efforts, and to collect overdue tax liabilities. **(9.04)**

Dividend: Any nonliquidating distribution of a corporation's assets or securities to its shareholders, in their role as shareholders, if the corporation has either current or accumulated earnings and profits equal to or greater than the amount distributed. **(4.11; 10.13)**

Domestic corporation: A corporation whose charter was granted by a governmental body organized within the United States, usually one of the 50 states. **(4.08)**

Domestic trust: A legal trust that is generally subject to U.S. income taxation on its worldwide income. **(4.12)**

Donee: The person who receives a gift. **(7.07)**

Glossary

Donor: The person who makes a gift. **(7.07)**

E

Earned income: The income that is attributable to the personal efforts of the individual taxpayer. **(6.10)**

Employee benefits: *See* Employee perquisites. **(3.03)**

Employee perquisites: Valuable items in addition to routine compensation payments, given to executives and other employees in exchange for their services. **(10.03)**

Employee stock ownership plan: A contractual arrangement which transfers control over some portion of the corporation's stock to its employees in exchange for a preferential tax treatment. **(10.07)**

Enrolled agent: An individual who is not an attorney or a CPA but who is authorized to practice before the IRS by virtue of his or her work experience or by successful completion of a national examination. **(9.08)**

ESOP: *See* Employee stock ownership plan.

Estate: A fiduciary entity that exists from the moment of death of an individual taxpayer until the final distribution of the last estate asset. **(4.12)**

Exclusion: An item of income that Congress has deliberately elected not to tax. **(2.07;** *see also* **3.02)**

Executive compensation: The value of all benefits given to business managers in exchange for their services to an employer. **(10.03)**

F

Fair market value: The price that would be paid in an arm's length transaction between two parties having complete knowledge.

FASB: *See* Financial Accounting Standards Board.

Fiduciary taxpayer: The Code, in Sec. 1(e), designates "every estate" and "every trust" as a legal or jural person responsible to report and pay the income tax. Estates and taxable trusts are collectively referred to as fiduciary taxpayers. Special rules are provided for foreign trusts, grantor trusts, etc. **(4.12)**

Field audit: An IRS audit of a tax return that is carried out at the taxpayer's place of business. *See also* Office audit. **(9.04)**

FIFO (first-in, first-out): An inventory costing procedure that assigns the oldest costs (first-in) to the first units sold (first-out). **(5.09)**

52–53 week year: An acceptable tax year that may vary from 52 to 53 weeks in any year. **(5.01)**

Financial Accounting Standards Board: A private-sector organization that determines generally accepted accounting standards for financial accounting purposes in the United States. **(5.09)**

Fiscal year: A period of one year ending on a day other than December 31. **(5.01)**

Foreign corporation: A corporation whose charter was granted by a non-U.S. government. **(4.08)**

Foreign trust: A legal trust that is generally not subject to U.S. income taxation except to the extent that it has income from U.S. sources. **(4.12)**

11.06 / *ESSENTIALS OF U.S. TAXATION*

Glossary

Form 1040: The (long-form) income tax return filed by individual taxpayers.

Form 1041: The income tax return filed by a trust or an estate. **(4.16)**

Form 1065: The information-only income tax return filed by a partnership. **(4.16)**

Form 1120: The income tax return filed by C-corporations. **(4.16)**

Form 1120-S: The information-only income tax return filed by an S-corporation. **(4.16)**

Fruit and tree: A popular legal analogy often used to distinguish income (fruit) from capital (the tree) and to tax income to the source which created it. **(10.17)**

F. Supp.: Common abbreviation for the *Federal Supplement Reporter* published by West Publishing Co. **(1.23)**

F.2d: Common abbreviation for the *Federal Reporter*, second series, published by West Publishing Co. **(1.23)**

G

Gain realized: The excess of the amount realized over the adjusted basis of a property at the time of disposition. **(7.01)**

General partner: A partner whose liability for the debts and obligations of the partnership are unlimited. **(8.08)**

Gift tax: A tax on the right to transfer property paid by the donor (or person making a gift); a part of the donative transfer tax in the United States. (The other part is an estate tax.) **(7.07)**

Global tax: An income tax system that taxes a taxpayer's income without regard for where it its earned. **(4.01)**

Golsen rule: A judicial rule that generally requires the Tax Court to honor prior decisions of a specific circuit court of appeal when rendering decisions for taxpayers who reside in the jurisdiction of that court. **(1.16)**

Grantor: The person who transfers property to a trust. Also known as a "settlor." **(4.12)**

Grantor trust: A legal trust that is not recognized as a separate taxable entity for federal income tax purposes. **(4.12)**

Gross income: All income less exclusions equals gross income (a technical term). **(3.01)**

Gross tax liability: The product of any tax base (like taxable income) multiplied by the tax rate(s); alternatively, the taxpayer's tax liability before subtraction of prepayments and tax credits. **(3.01)**

H

Head of household: One of four tax rate schedules that may be applied to the income earned by individual taxpayers. In general, this rate schedule applies to individuals who are not married, but who claim one or more dependent-exemption deductions. **(4.02)**

Hybrid method: A general method of accounting that is accepted for tax purposes, in limited circumstances, which combines aspects of both the accrual method and the cash method of accounting. **(5.07)**

ESSENTIALS OF U.S. TAXATION /**11.07**

Glossary

I

Income: "All income from whatever source derived." Operationally, any increase in net worth between two moments in time plus the fair market value of items consumed during that same time period. **(2.02)**

Income beneficiaries: Individuals designated as potential recipients of income earned by a trust. **(4.03)**

Income-splitting: A colloquial term used to describe the various techniques used by taxpayers to divide a single income stream into two or more parts to achieve a tax advantage. **(4.20)**

Indenture: *See* Trust indenture.

Individual taxpayer: The Code, in Sec.1, designates "every individual" as a person responsible to report and pay the income tax. Other sections provide special rules for nonresident aliens. **(4.02)**

Information return: A tax form that does not involve the computation of a tax liability but does convey data that are useful in determining the tax liability of others. **(4.15)**

Installment sales method: A method of accounting that is limited in its application to deferred-payment sales of property by taxpayers who are not dealers in the propery sold. **(5.08)**

Intent of Congress: The explanation of why Congress enacted any particular provision in the Code. **(1.02)**

Internal Revenue Bulletin: A weekly publication of the Internal Revenue Service containing among other things, Temporary, Proposed, and (final) Regulations, Revenue Rulings, TIRs, TAMs, etc. **(1.22)**

The Internal Revenue Code of 1986: The compilation of all statutory tax law enacted since October 1986 and the law that generally determines the tax consequence of transactions today. **(1.01)**

Internal Revenue Code: *See* Code.

Inter-vivos trust: A trust created during the life of the grantor. **(4.14)**

Involuntary conversion: Any change in a taxpayer's property due to theft, condemnation, or an act of God. **(7.18)**

IRB: *See* Internal Revenue Bulletin.

Itemized deductions: The nonbusiness deductions of an individual taxpayer other than (1) deductions for AGI and (2) the personal and dependent exemption deductions. An individual can claim the larger of (1) itemized deductions or (2) a standard deduction. **(6.01)**

J

Joint return: A single tax return that concurrently reports the items of gross income and deduction attributable to two taxpayers who are married to each other. **(4.02)**

Judicial doctrines: General rules of law that derive from the decisions rendered by various courts. **(10.12; 10.17)**

Judicial interpretations: *See* Judicial tax law.

Judicial tax law: Interpretations of the Code rendered by the various courts in the United States. **(1.14)**

11.08 / *ESSENTIALS OF U.S. TAXATION*

Glossary

K

Kiddie tax: The special tax rules that apply to unearned income recognized by children under 14 years of age if it exceeds $1100 in any year. **(6.09)**

L

Letter ruling: *See* Private letter ruling.

Lexis: The trade name of a computerized data base of tax information maintained by Mead Data, Inc. **(1.20)**

LIFO (last-in, first-out): An inventory-costing procedure that assigns the most recent costs (last-in) to the first units sold (first-out). **(5.09)**

Like-kind exchange: A property exchange that is fully or partially nontaxable because it satisfies the specific requirements of Sec. 1031. **(7.15)**

Limited partner: A partner who by agreement and by law does not share the liability of a general partner for all of the obligations incurred by a partnership. **(8.08)**

Limited partnership: A partnership having one or more limited partners. **(8.08)**

Liquidation: The distribution of a corporation's net assets to its shareholders and the cessation of doing business by the corporation being liquidated. **(10.06)**

Loss realized: The excess of the adjusted basis of a property over the amount realized at the time of the disposition. **(7.01)**

M

Marginal tax rate: The tax rate(s) that will apply to any incremental amount of taxable income. **(4.04)**

Material participation: The personal involvement of a taxpayer in an activity on a regular, continuous, and substantial basis. **(8.08)**

Memo decision: *See* Memorandum decision.

Memorandum decision: A decision of the Tax Court that is not deemed to be of sufficient general importance to justify its publication in the Tax Court reporter series. The decision is, however, published by private (commercial) sources. **(1.16)**

Method of accounting: *See* Accounting method.

Merten's: A widely used tax service, *Merten's Law of Federal Taxation*, published by Callagahan & Co. **(1.20)**

Miscellaneous itemized deductions: All of the deductions from AGI, which may be claimed by an individual taxpayer, other than the 12 deductions specifically identified in Sec. 67(b). **(6.04)**

N

Net operating loss (NOL): The excess of a taxpayer's deductions (after possible adjustment) over gross income for a year. **(8.02)**

Net operating loss deduction: The amount that a taxpayer may deduct in a carryback or carryforward year because of an NOL. **(8.02)**

ESSENTIALS OF U.S. TAXATION / **11.09**

Glossary

Net tax liability: Gross tax liability less prepayments and tax credits; alternatively, the liability remaining to be paid at the time a tax return is filed. (*Note*: If negative, the net tax liability is generally called a refund.) **(3.01)**

90-day letter: The formal statutory notice of a tax deficiency which gives the taxpayer 90 days in which to decide how to proceed with a tax dispute prior to assessment and collection procedures. **(9.05)**

NOL: *See* Net operating loss.

Nondiscrimination rules: Tax provisions that forbid preferential treatment among employees for certain tax-favored compensation techniques. **(10.04)**

Nonrecognition rules: Statutory provisions that allow a taxpayer to defer temporarily the recognition of a gain or loss that has been realized. **(2.09;** *see also* **7.12 et seq.)**

Nonrecourse debt: A debt that precludes a creditor from taking any of the debtor's property beyond the property that is mortaged as security for a debt. **(7.03)**

Nonresident alien: A citizen of a foreign country who permanently resides outside the United States. *See also* Resident alien. **(4.02)**

Nontaxable exchange: A direct or indirect exchange of one property for another that results in a complete or partial deferral of the realized gain or loss because of a special provision in the Code. **(7.12)**

O

Office audit: An IRS audit of a tax return that is carried out at an IRS facility rather than the taxpayer's home or office. *See also* Field audit. **(9.04)**

Original basis: A taxpayer's basis in a property at the moment of aquisition. The taxpayer's original basis in a property will vary if it is purchased, self-constructed, inherited, received as a gift, or acquired in a fully or partially nontaxable exchange. **(7.05; 7.12)**

P

PAL: *See* Passive activity loss.

Parent–subsidiary group: A chain of two or more corporations in which a parent corporation owns 80% or more of the outstanding stock of the subsidiary corporation(s). **(5.11)**

Partnership: An unincorporated business with two or more owners. **(4.15; 4.23)**

Passive activity: Any activity (a) which involves the conduct of a trade or business (b) in which the taxpayer does not materially participate. **(8.06)**

Passive activity loss: The loss incurred by a taxpayer in an activity in which the taxpayer does not personally participate on a regular, continuous, and substantial basis. **(8.04)**

Passive income generators (PIGs): Investments that create income that the investor can classify as passive income. **(8.08)**

Penalty: *See* Tax penalty.

Pension plan: A contractual agreement between an employer and an employee intended to provide income to the employee at the time of retirement. **(10.04)**

Glossary

Percentage-of-completion method: A general method of accounting that may be used only by taxpayers engaged in long-term construction projects. **(5.08)**

Percentage-of-completion/capitalized-cost method: An accounting method that may be used by certain taxpayers engaged in long-term construction contracts which requires 90% of the income from the contract to be reported using the percentage-of-completion method and the other 10% using the taxpayer's normal method, usually the completed contract method. **(5.08)**

Perks: *See* Employee perquisites.

Perquisites: *See* Employee perquisites.

Personal exemption: A statutorily determined amount that may be claimed by most individual taxpayers, on their own tax return, in addition to the amounts that they may claim as (1) a standard deduction or (2) itemized deductions from AGI. (The personal exemption deduction for 1992 is $2300.) **(6.09)**

Personal loss: The excess of the adjusted basis over the amount realized on the disposition of any property that is neither a property used in a trade or business nor an investment property. **(8.11)**

Personal service corporation: A corporation engaged in a professional service (such as medicine, law, engineering, or accounting) whose employee-stockholders actually perform most of the professional services technically rendered by the corporation. **(4.10)**

P-H: *See* Prentice-Hall.

Phantom income: A colloquial term for income that is attributable to the fact that any reduction in a taxpayer's debt (even nonrecourse debt) must be included as part of the amount realized on a disposition of property. **(8.09)**

Phinet: The trade name of a computerized data base of tax information maintained by Prentice-Hall, Inc./Research Institute of America **(1.20)**

PIG: *See* Passive income generators.

Portfolio income: In general, income from interest, dividends, annuities, and royalties. **(8.07)**

Prentice-Hall: The commercial publisher of a widely used tax service, *Federal Taxes*. **(1.20)**

Prepayments: Mandatory advance deposits made by a taxpayer against a current tax liability. **(3.12)**

Primary authority: Statutory law (Code) and interpretations thereof made by designated administrative and judicial officials.

Principal residence: A taxpayer's primary home. If a taxpayer has more than one home, only one—determined by all the facts and circumstances—can constitute the taxpayer's principal residence. **(7.19)**

Private law: *See* Transition rules.

Private letter ruling: The IRS response to a taxpayer's inquiry concerning the correct interpretation of tax law in a specific circumstance. Although this response is not published by the government, it can be obtained from private (commercial) sources after modification to delete the taxpayer's identity. **(1.13)**

Profit-sharing plan: An agreement between an employer and an employee intended to permit the employee to

Glossary

share in the profits realized by the employer. **(10.04)**

Progressive tax rate: Any tax rate schedule that imposes a higher tax rate(s) for incrementally larger amounts of a tax base. **(3.10)**

Proportional tax rate: Any tax rate schedule that imposes the same tax rate for all possible amounts of a tax base; alternatively, a flat tax rate. **(3.10)**

Proposed regulations: The initial and tentative administrative interpretations of statutory tax law prepared by the Treasury Department and circulated for public comment prior to the release of final regulations. **(1.12)**

PSC: *See* Personal service corporation.

Published ruling: The IRS response to a taxpayer's inquiry, concerning the correct interpretation of tax law in a specific circumstance, published by the government in a form that does not reveal the taxpayer's identity. **(1.13)**

Q

Qualified pension plan: A pension plan that achieves preferential tax treatment in exchange for satisfying various legal requirements. **(10.04)**

Qualified profit-sharing plan: A profit-sharing plan that achieves preferential treatment in exchange for satisfying various legal requirements. **(10.04)**

R

Realization: For federal income tax purposes, realization generally occurs when there has been (1) a significant change in the form or the substance of a taxpayer's property or property right and (2) the involvement of a second taxpayer. **(2.05)**

Realized: An adjective used to describe income; income will not be taxed until it has been realized. *See* Realization.

Recognition: For federal income tax purposes, a taxpayer generally must recognize income in the same year that it is realized. Major exceptions to this general rule may apply because of (1) the exclusion provisions, (2) accounting method options, or (3) a nontaxable exchange provision. **(2.06)**

Regular decision: A decision of the Tax Court deemed of sufficient importance to be published by the Government Printing Office in the *Tax Court Reporter* series. **(1.16)**

Regulations: The most general administrative interpretations of statutory tax law issued by the Treasury Department. **(1.11)**

Remainderman: Individuals designated as potential recipients of any assets that remain upon the termination of a trust. **(4.14)**

Reporter series: Published volumes of judicial decisions. **(1.23)**

Research Institute of America: The commercial publisher of a widely used tax service, *Federal Tax Coordinator, 2d*. **(1.20)**

Resident alien: A citizen of a foreign country who lives in the United States for a significant period of time. Residency is technically defined in Sec. 7701(b). **(4.02)**

Revenue agent: An IRS employee who audits tax returns. **(9.04)**

Revenue procedure: Interpretations of the more procedural aspects of tax law isssued by the Treasury Department to aid taxpayers in compliance. **(1.14)**

Revenue ruling: An administrative interpretation of tax law issued by the IRS relative to specific circumstances. **(1.13)**

Rev. Proc.: *See* Revenue procedure.

RIA: *See* Research Institute of America.

S

Schedular income tax: Income tax systems that deliberately impose different tax rates on different kinds of income. **(3.10)**

Schedule A: The attachment to Form 1040 used to itemize deductions from AGI. **(6.12)**

Schedule B: The attachment to Form 1040 used to report income from interest and dividends. **(6.12)**

Schedule C: The attachment to Form 1040 used to report income and deductions from a sole proprietorship. **(6.11)**

Schedule D: The attachment to either Form 1040 or Form 1120 used to report capital gains and losses. **(6.12)**

Schedule E: The attachment to Form 1040 used to report income and deductions from rents and royalties. **(6.12)**

Schedule F: The attachment to Form 1040 used to report income and deductions from farming. **(6.12)**

S-corporation: Any corporation that has elected to be taxed under the provisions of Subchapter S of the Code. **(4.11)**

S. Ct.: Common abbreviation for the *Supreme Court Reporter* published by West Publishing Co. **(1.23)**

SEC: *See* Securities and Exchange Commission.

Secondary authority: Any unofficial interpretation of federal tax law. **(1.19)**

Section: *See* Code section.

Securities and Exchange Commision: A government unit that has authority over the financial affairs of public companies in the United States. **(5.09)**

Self-compliance tax: Any tax which places the responsibility for the determination of the amount of tax payable on the taxpayer. **(9.01)**

Service Center: Any one of ten IRS facilities located throughout the United States to receive and process income tax returns and related documents. **(9.03)**

Settlor: *See* Grantor.

Short year: A tax year of less than 12 full months' duration. **(5.01; 5.03)**

Simple trust: Any trust that must, by terms of the trust indenture, distribute currently any income earned by the trust. **(4.14)**

Small claim division: A less formal part of the Tax Court created to hear disputes involving $10,000 or less. **(1.16)**

Sole proprietorship: An unincorporated business with a single owner. **(4.15)**

Source rules: The tax provisions that assign items of gross income and deduction to specific countries or territorial areas. **(4.01)**

Glossary

Special agent: An IRS employee who investigates cases of alleged taxpayer fraud. **(9.04)**

Standard deduction: A statutorily determined amount that an individual taxpayer may deduct in lieu of itemized deductions from AGI. (The amount of the (basic) standard deduction for 1992 varies from $3000 to $6000.) **(6.07)**

Statutory regulations: Treasury regulations issued under the specific authority of a particular Code section rather than under a more general authority. **(1.12)**

Statutory tax law: The body of tax provisions as specifically worded in the various Congressional acts that are subsequently integrated into the Internal Revenue Code. **(1.02)**

Step transaction: A judicial doctrine that is sometimes cited as authority to tax a complex series of transactions in a way that the same economic result would have been taxed had the taxpayer taken a more direct route to the same final result. **(10.17)**

Stock option: The right to acquire additional shares of a corporation's stock at a fixed price for a stipulated period of time. **(10.05)**

Stock redemption: A corporation's purchase of its own outstanding stock from a shareholder. **(10.13)**

Subpart F income: The part of a controlled foreign corporation's taxable income that may be taxed immediately to a U.S. shareholder. **(4.08)**

Substance over form: A judicial doctrine that is sometimes cited as authority to tax a transaction based on the economic consequence of what has transpired rather than on the technical form in which it was achieved. **(10.17)**

Substituted basis: *See* Carryover basis.

Supreme Court: The final appellate authority in federal litigation. **(1.19)**

T

Taxable entity: A fundamental unit designated by law as one responsible for the reporting of income and for the payment of the income tax thereon. In the United States, individuals, corporations, and certain fiduciaries are designated as taxable entities. **(4.01)**

Taxable income: The statutorily defined quantity that is the tax base for the U. S. income tax. Technically, taxable income is the excess of gross income over deductions. **(2.01;** *see also* **3.01)**

Taxable year: The period of time for which a taxpayer's tax liability is determined. Taxable years include calendar years, fiscal years, and short years. **(5.01)**

Tax audit: *See* Audit.

Tax basis: *See* Basis; Adjusted basis.

Tax conduit: Any business or legal entity that is itself not subject to taxation but whose items of gross income and deductions are attributed to its owners without regard for any actual distribution of assets. **(4.15)**

Tax Court: One of three courts of original jurisdiction in federal income tax litigation. A federal court whose authority is restricted to tax issues. **(1.15)**

Tax credit: Direct (dollar-for-dollar) reductions in a taxpayer's tax liability specifically authorized by Congress. **(3.13)**

Glossary

Tax deficiency: The difference between the "correct" tax liability, as determined by the IRS, and the tax liability as determined by the taxpayer, plus interest and penalties on the difference. **(9.05)**

Tax experts: Individuals who, by education and/or experience, are most capable of assisting a taxpayer in solving a tax problem. **(9.07)**

Tax liability: Taxable income times the tax rate equals gross tax liability; the gross tax liability less tax credits and prepayments equals net tax liability. **(3.01)**

Taxpayer compliance and measurement program: An ongoing audit research effort undertaken by the IRS on randomly selected tax returns for the purpose of determining the types and frequency of errors being made by taxpayers in general. **(9.04)**

Taxpayer identification number: The number used to identify, file, and retrieve tax returns. For most individual taxpayers the TIN is their Social Security number; for others it is a number assigned by the IRS. **(9.03)**

Tax penalty: Any one of several increases in a tax assessment, in addition to interest, that may be imposed on a taxpayer failing to determine and pay the correct tax liability on a timely basis. **(9.05)**

Tax planning: Efforts undertaken for the purpose of reducing a tax liability in a manner that is consistent with the taxpayer's ordinary business objectives. **(10.01)**

Tax prepayments: *See* Prepayments. **(3.16)**

Tax rate: The fractional part of a taxpayer's taxable income that is paid as a tax. *See also* Average tax rate; Marginal tax rate. **(4.02)**

Tax rate schedule: A tabulation used to determine a taxpayer's gross tax liability for varying amounts of taxable income. **(4.03)**

Tax return preparer: Any individual who, for a fee, assists a taxpayer in the preparation of a tax return. **(9.07)**

Tax schedule forms: *See* Schedule A–Schedule F; Form 1040–1120–S.

Tax service: A privately published compilation of primary and secondary authority used by professionals in resolving tax questions. **(1.19)**

Tax-shelter investments: Investments that (for one reason or other) tend to decrease the investor's income tax liability, at least in the short run. **(8.04)**

TC: Common abbreviation for the Tax Court reporter published by the Government Printing Office. **(1.23)**

TCMP: *See* Taxpayer compliance and measurement program.

Technical information release: A Treasury Department interpretation of a more technical aspect of tax law. **(1.14)**

Temporary regulations: Tentative administrative interpretations of statutory law issued by the Treasury Department, without the normal external input, because of the taxpayer's need for immediate guidance. **(1.12)**

Territorial tax: An income tax system that taxes a taxpayer's income only if it is earned in a specified territory or country. **(4.01)**

Testamentary trust: A trust created at death by a provision in the last will and

ESSENTIALS OF U.S. TAXATION / 11.15

Glossary

testament of a deceased individual. **(4.14)**

TIN: *See* Taxpayer identification number.

TIR: *See* Technical information release.

Transition rules: Unique provisions in statutory tax law enacted primarily as a method of gaining the political support of key legislators; tax provisions that usually benefit only one or a small group of taxpayers. **(10.02)**

Treasury regulations: *See* Regulations.

Trust: A legal arrangement involving property rights that creates a separate legal entity which may be recognized as a taxpayer for U.S. income tax purposes. **(4.12; 4.23)**

Trustee: The person designated to administer property that has been placed in trust. **(4.14)**

Trust indenture: The legal document that determines the rights and obligations of various parties to property that has been placed in trust. **(4.14)**

U

Unearned income: Income recognized by an individual taxpayer that cannot be attributed to the personal efforts of that individual. **(6.10)**

Unitary income taxes: Income tax systems that tax all income in the same way, regardless of how the income is earned. **(3.10)**

U.S.: Common abbreviation for the *U.S. Supreme Court Reporter* published by the Government Printing Office. **(1.23)**

USTC: Common abbreviation for the *United States Tax Cases Reporter* published by Commerce Clearing House. **(1.23)**

V

Vesting: A contractual agreement which fixes an employee's rights to certain future benefits even if the employment relationship is terminated. **(10.05)**

W

Westlaw: The trade name of a computerized data base of tax and legal information published by West Publishing Company. **(1.20)**

Writ of certiorari: A formal legal document prepared to request a review by the United States Supreme Court of the legal proceedings in lower courts. **(1.15)**

Notes

Notes

NOTES

Notes

NOTES

Notes

344471

INDEX

Video/Copyright Seminar, 162–163
Videolog, 67
Viewing skills, 218–219
Vlcek, Charles, 163

Weeding, 24–35
  at Ames Public Library, 49
  at Baltimore County Public Library, 73–75
  criteria for, 30–35
  goals of, 26–28
  at Grant Wood Area Education Agency, 86–90
  at Grant Wood Area Education Media Center, 107
  at Lake County Public Library, 43
  methods of, 28–30
  in model selection policy, 81–82
  at Skokie Public Library, 41
Weeding Library Collections—II, 30
What Educators Should Know about Copyright, 162
Whittle Communications, 146–147, 227
Withdrawals. *See* Weeding
Workbook copying, 197
Written policies, 5–10

Young adult videos, 79–80

Selection policies *(continued)*
  Los Angeles County Office of
    Education on, 94–95
  of Manchester Community
    School District, 94
  model, 75–82
  of Phoenix Public Library, 60–68
  of public libraries, 44–68
  responsibility for, 46, 76, 98, 109
  of school library media centers,
    90–115
  of Thousand Oaks Public
    Library, 51–55
  types of, 20–22
Selection tools. *See* Reviewing
  sources
Separated collections, 49–50, 155
Service philosophy statements,
  3–5, 45, 92, 225
Services, acquisition, 67
Sex education, 171–172, 205
*Sheck vs. Baileyville School
  Committee*, 93
Shelf time, 27, 28
Shoreham-Wading River Public
  Library, 23
*Sight & Sound International Film
  Quarterly*, 66
Sightlines, 66
16mm films, 32, 97–99
Skokie (IL) Public Library, 17, 36–41
Slides, audiovisual, 199
Slote, Stanley J., 27–28, 30
Social content standards, 104–105,
  111, 213
Software, computer, 174, 175–176,
  181–182
Songs, 198
Sony Betamax case, 184
Specialty videos, 1–2, 53, 54, 79.
  See also Instructional videos
Sponsored films, 86, 113
Statement on Labeling, 120
Storage, 25
Student copyright privileges,
  185–186

Study library collections, 38–39
Subject collections. *See* Separated
  collections
Subject indexes, 96
Subscription television services.
  See Pay-TV channels
Subtitled films, 65
Supreme Court, U.S., 184
Suspense videos, 29

Teachers, 147–148, 206, 227–228,
  230
Television broadcasts, 156, 161,
  165, 172–173.
  See also Off-air taping; Public
  broadcast systems
Temporary videotaping, 156
Theatrical exhibition. *See* Public
  performances
Thousand Oaks (CA) Public
  Library, 51–55
Training, in-service, 216
Transparencies, 196
Turnover rates, 27, 29, 73, 81
Two-tiered pricing, 154

U.S. Supreme Court, 184
University of Utah Media Services
  Department, 157
Use patterns and policies. *See*
  Collection use; Patrons

Van Orden, Phyllis, 6, 19
*Variety's Complete Home Video
  Directory*, 96
Video industry, 1
The Video Librarian, 217
Video Magazine, 66
Video Movie Guide, 68
Video players, 120, 122–123, 131,
  133
Video Rating Guide for Libraries,
  96
Video Review, 67
Video Sig, 155
The Video Source Book, 96

INDEX

Reconsidered materials
  forms for, 222–224, 230–231, 234–237, 239
  at Grant Wood Area Education Media Center, 108
  at Lake County Public Library, 44
  policies on, 220–221
  procedures for, 221–224, 227–228
Recreational reading, 47
Reed, Mary Hutchings, 161
Regional topic videos, 63, 84
Reissued materials, 78
Rental outlets. See Retail outlets
Replacement, 43–44, 81, 89
Research level library collections, 39–40
Research Library Group (RLG), 16
Reserves, 118, 123–124, 132, 196–197
Responsibility, administrative
  for collection development, 43
  for off-air taping, 206
  for selection, 46, 76, 98, 109
Retail outlets, 1–2, 61, 69, 75
Reviewing sources
  of Ames Public Library, 49
  of Baltimore County Public Library, 71, 72
  of Birmingham Public Library, 60
  of Burlington County Audio-Visual Aids Commission, 98–99
  of Phoenix Public Library, 60, 65–68
  of school libraries, 91
  selection criteria and, 78
  of Skokie Public Library, 40
  subject access in, 96
Revised Copyright Act of 1976, 151, 180–181, 189–191, 203–204
Rewinding of videotapes, 130, 132
RLG (Research Library Group), 16

Rockefeller Foundation, 19, 20
Roger Ebert's Movie Home Companion, 67

St. Louis (MO) Public Library, 155
San Diego County Office of Education, 170–171, 201–213
Santa Monica (CA) Public Library, 129–132
Satellite taping, 157–159, 171, 183, 208
Schaumburg Township (IL) Public Library, 132–133
Scheuer, Steven H., 67
School Library Association, 229
School Library Journal, 66
School library media centers
  circulation policies of, 144–148
  intellectual freedom policies of, 148, 225–240
  selection policies of, 90–115
Seattle (WA) Public Library, 75
Secondary school libraries, 92–93
Selection policies, 18–24
  of Alabama Public Library Service, 83–86
  of Ames Public Library, 44–51
  of Baltimore County Public Library, 70–73
  of Birmingham Public Library, 57–60
  of Burlington County Audio-Visual Aids Commission, 97–99
  copyright and, 157
  criteria in, 77–80, 98, 100–105, 110–113
  of Delaware-Chenango Board of Cooperative Educational Services, 109–115
  elements of, 22–24
  of Frankfort Community Public Library, 55–56
  of Grant Wood Area Education Media Center, 106–107
  of Lake County Public Library, 43

Pacific Arts Video, 2
Pacific Northwest Conspectus Worksheets, 39
Palmer, Joseph W., 219
Parental consent/restriction
 ALA on, 218, 251, 252
 ethics of, 119, 146
 policies on, 220–221, 226–227, 228–239
Pascarelli, Anne M., 14
Patrons, 76, 120, 123, 161.
 See also Collection use
Pattie, Kenton, 184
Pay-TV channels
 Grossmont Union High School District policy on, 170, 171
 off-air taping and, 158, 166
 San Diego public school policy on, 207
PBS Video, 2
Performances, public, 59, 154, 156–157, 196
Periodicals, 65–67, 91, 191–192, 196–197
Permission slips. *See* Parental consent/restriction
Philosophy/purpose statements, 3–5, 45, 92, 225
Phoenix (AZ) Public Library, 60–68, 133–145
Pitman, Randy, 217
Pluralism, cultural, 104–105, 111, 213
Policy Questions for Audiovisual Services in Public Libraries, 4
Policy statements, 5–10
Porter, Marsha, 68
Preview/evaluation, 33
 by Birmingham Public Library, 59–60
 by Burlington County Audio-Visual Aids Commission, 99
 forms for, 33, 34–35, 99–105, 113–115

Pricing, 154
Print materials copying, 191–192, 196–197
Privately taped videos
 in Grossmont Union High School District, 170
 in San Diego public schools, 207
 school media centers and, 146, 158, 168, 239–240
Prize-winning films, 65, 78, 80
Procedure statements, 6, 19
Producers, television, 172–173
Public broadcast systems, 78, 194
Public domain videos, 154–155
Public libraries
 circulation policies of, 124–145
 collection development policies of, 36–86
 intellectual freedom policies of, 220–224
 philosophy/purpose statements of, 4–5
 selection policies of, 44–68
The Public Library: Democracy's Resource: A Statement of Principles, 124–125
Public Library Association, 124
Public performance videos, 80, 152–153, 164
Public performances, 59, 154, 156–157, 196
Public relations, 33, 51, 216, 226
 See also Flyers
Purchase orders, 156
Purchase requests, 51
Purging. *See* Weeding
Purpose/philosophy statements, 3–5, 45, 92, 225

Quality Educational Data, 96

Ranganathan, Shiyali R., 219
Ratings, MPAA. *See* Motion Picture Association of America (MPAA) ratings

INDEX

Media centers. *See* School library media centers
Media station policies, 127
Memphis Schools, 158–159
Microcomputer software
   copyright of, 174, 175–176, 181–182
Miller, Jerome K., 160–161, 162–163
Minors' access, 119, 132, 217–219, 251–253
Mission statements, 3–5, 45, 92, 225
Model forms
   for complaints, 238, 239
   for damage assessment, 31, 121, 143–145
   for media loans, 125–126
   for off-air program taping, 168, 210–212
   for permission to copy, 187–188
   for preview/evaluation, 34–35, 99–105, 113–115
   for reconsideration of materials, 222–224, 234–237, 239
Monroe County (MI) Library System, 2
Motion Picture Association of America (MPAA) ratings
   ALA on, 219–220, 252
   Baltimore County Public Library and, 71
   fees and, 120
   minors' access and, 217
   in model selection policy, 76
Movie Home Companion, 67
Movies on TV and Videocassette, 67
MPAA ratings. *See* Motion Picture Association of America (MPAA) ratings
Multiple copies, 31, 41, 53
Murphy, B., 40
Music, 185, 195–196, 198
Musical production videos, 63

National Geographic Specials, 161
Networks, television, 172–173
The New York Academy of Medicine Library Collection Development Policy, 14
New York Times, 66
New York Times Co. v. Roxbury Data Interface, Inc., 190
Newhouse, G., 41
Nippersink (IL) Public Library, 8–10
Nonfiction videos. *See* Instructional videos; Specialty videos
Nonverbal films, 84
Northern Illinois Library System, 217

Off-air taping
   by California Instructional Video Clearinghouse, 199–200
   by Carmel Clay Schools, 182–184
   copyright and, 157–159, 199–200, 207
   by Grossmont Union High School District, 170–172
   by Los Angeles County Office of Education, 177–178
   program alteration and, 172, 184
   request forms for, 168, 210–212
   responsibility for, 206
   San Diego County Office of Education on, 201–213
   in school policies, 166–167
   in selection policies, 80, 161
   See also Privately taped videos
Off-Air Video Recording Issues and Answers, 201–213
Opaque projectors, 185
Opera videos. *See* Musical production videos
Osburn, Charles B., 14

Home-use-only videos *(continued)*
  policies on, 164–166, 184–185, 194, 200, 207
How-to videos. *See* Instructional videos

Iconographic films, 64
Informal weeding, 88
Informational reading, 47
"Infotainment" videos. *See* Instructional videos
Ingram's Video, 67
In-house preview/evaluation. *See* Preview/evaluation
In-house viewing, 123–124
In-service training, 216
Instructional television, 170–171, 208, 227
Instructional videos, 63, 71, 85, 132
Intellectual Freedom Manual, 5–6, 215
Intellectual freedom policies, 215–253
  of Ames Public Library, 48
  of Birmingham Public Library, 59
  of Lake County Public Library, 42, 44
  of public libraries, 220–224
  of school media centers, 148, 225–240
  selection policies and, 22, 75–76
  See also Censorship; Challenged materials; Reconsidered materials
Interlibrary loan, 118, 186
Iowa City Public Library, 24

Jacob, M., 40
Jobbers, 67
Juvenile access, 119, 132, 217–219, 251–253
Juvenile videos, 63–64, 71, 79–80, 85

Kastenmeier, Robert W., 193, 203
Kemp, Betty, 91
Kidvid: A Parent's Guide to Children's Video, 67

Labeling, 252–253.
  See also Motion Picture Association of America (MPAA) ratings
Lake County (IN) Public Library, 42–44
Landers Film Reviews, 66
Languages, foreign, 24, 80, 250
Laramie County (WY) Library System, 127–129
The Last Temptation of Christ, 148
Latch-key children, 76
Leonard Maltin's TV Movies and Video Guide, 67
Liability limitations, 120, 123
Librarian's Video Service, 67
Library Bill of Rights, 147, 245–253
Library Journal, 66
Local topic videos, 63, 84
Lora, Pat, 118
Los Angeles County Office of Education, 94–95, 174–178
Los Angeles Unified School District, 144, 148, 239
Lyrics, 196, 198

Magrill, Rose Mary, 13–14
Mahon, Carol, 27
Maintenance of collections. *See* Collection maintenance
Maltin, Leonard, 67
Manchester Community School District, 94
Maps, 185–186
Martin, Mick, 68
Materials reconsideration. *See* Reconsidered materials
Materials selection policies. *See* Selection policies

INDEX

current, 28
weeding and, 30, 31, 90
See also Circulation policies and procedures; CLSI circulation system; Turnover rate
Circulation policies and procedures, 117–148
  of Ames Public Library, 124–127
  of Baltimore County Public Library, 73, 74
  of Laramie County Library System, 128–129
  of Nippersink Public Library, 9–10
  of public libraries, 124–144
  of Santa Monica Public Library, 129–131
  of Schaumburg Township Public Library, 132–133
  of school library media centers, 144–148
Classic films, 62, 64.
  See also Film study
Clients, 76, 120, 123, 161.
  See also Collection use
Closed-captioned films, 40, 84
Closed-circuit/broadcast rights.
  See Broadcast rights
CLSI circulation system, 138
  ADDATA field, 139, 140
  ADDITEM field, 136
  CCPATRON process, 140, 142
  ITEM function, 141
  OVERDUE ALERT function, 137
Coles, Ronald R., 93
Collection development, 13–116
  by Baltimore County Public Library, 68–75
  conspectus approach in, 16–17
  functions of, 14–15
  by Grant Wood Area Education Media Center, 106–108
  by Lake County Public Library, 42–44
  levels of, 37–40

  policies for, 17–18, 75–82
  by public libraries, 36–86
  responsibility for, 43
  by Skokie Public Library, 37–41
Collection evaluation, 15, 16, 82
Collection maintenance, 43–44, 81.
  See also Damaged videotapes
Collection separation, 49–50, 155
Collection use, 28, 44, 173–174.
  See also Circulation; Patrons
Commercial messages, 80, 86, 146–147, 227
Communities. *See* Patrons; Public relations
Complaint policies, 221, 228–239
  ALA on, 215–216
  forms for, 238, 239
  at Lake County Public Library, 44
Computer software copyright, 174, 175–176, 181–182
Computerized circulation. *See* Circulation, computerized
Conable, Gordon, 147
Concept films, 85
Concert videos. *See* Musical production videos
Controversial films, 86, 112.
  See also Avant-garde/experimental films
Copyright, 149–213
  of audiovisual materials, 194–195, 198–199
  of computer software, 174
  defined, 150, 180
  expurgation and, 248
  of music, 195–196, 198
  permission requests for, 172–173, 187–188
  of print materials, 191–192, 196–197
  resources on, 162–163
  special privileges in, 185–187
Copyright: What Every School, College, and Public Library Should Know, 162

American Library Association
(ALA) *(continued)*
Freedom To View and, 244
Guide to the Evaluation of Library Collections, 15
Guidelines for the Formulation of Collection Development Policies, 37
Intellectual Freedom Manual, 5–6, 215
Library Bill of Rights, 147, 245–253
Statement on Labeling, 120
on Whittle Communications, 146–147
Ames (IA) Public Library, 44–51, 124–127
Anglo-American Cataloguing Rules, 220
Association for Information Media and Equipment (AIME), 162
Audio recordings, 185
Audiovisual policies
of Ames Public Library, 50
of Birmingham Public Library, 59
of Burlington County Audio-Visual Aids Commission, 97–99
on copyright, 194–195, 198–199
of Phoenix Public Library, 133–144
on selection, 23
See also Media station policies
Avant-garde/experimental films, 65.
See also Controversial films
Award-winning films, 65, 78, 80

Back-up computer programs, 174
Baker & Taylor, 154
Ballet videos. *See* Musical production videos
Baltimore County (MD) Public Library, 28, 68–75

Basic library collections, 38, 75
Bender, Ivan R., 162
Beta format, 40, 41, 127
Biased materials, 113
Birmingham (AL) Public Library, 57–60
Boggs, G., 41
Book copying, 191–192, 196–197
Booklist, 65
Branch libraries, 72–73
Broadcast rights, 156–157, 174, 200.
See also Off-air taping; Television broadcasts
Brussels Satellite Convention, 183
Bruwelheide, Janis H., 159
Burlington County Audio-Visual Aids Commission, 97–99
Business videos, 79, 84

Cable television, 158, 161, 170, 208
California Instructional Video Clearinghouse, 99–105, 189–200
Captioned films, 40, 84
Carmel Clay Schools, 179–188
Catch-22, 148
Censorship, 220–221, 247–248
Challenged materials, 229–234, 245.
See also Censorship; Complaint policies; Parental consent/restriction; Reconsidered materials
Channel One, 146–147
Charges. *See* Fees and fines
Children, latch-key, 76
Children's access, 119, 132, 217–219, 252
Children's Video, 66
Children's videos, 63–64, 71, 79–80, 85
Circulation
client-centered evaluation and, 16
computerized, 29, 120

INDEX

Academic library collection development, 16–17
Access for Children and Young People to Videotapes and Other Nonprint Formats, 119, 218, 219–220, 226, 234, 251–253
Access for minors, 119, 132, 217–219, 251–253
Access to Resources and Services in the School Library Media Program 119, 218, 226, 249–250
Acquisition. *See* Collection development; Selection policies
Acquisition services, 67
Administrative responsibility. *See* Responsibility, administrative
Advanced interest library collections, 38–39
Advertising, 80, 86, 146–147, 227
Aerobic and Fitness Association of America, 79
Afterschool Specials, 80
AFVA (American Film and Video Association), 244
AFVA Evaluations, 65
Age of items, 27, 28
  See also Copyright date

Age restrictions, 119, 132, 217–219, 252
AIME (Association for Information Media and Equipment), 162
ALA. *See* American Library Association
Alabama Public Library Service, 83–86
Alabaster, Carol, 68
American Dietetics Association, 79
American Film and Video Association (AFVA), 244
American Film & Video Festival, 33
American films, 64–65
American Library Association (ALA)
  Access for Children and Young People to Videotapes and Other Nonprint Formats, 119, 218, 219–220, 226, 234, 251–253
  Access to Resources and Services in the School Library Media Program, 119, 218, 226, 249–250
  documents of, 229, 245–253
  Free Access to Libraries for Minors: An Interpretation of the Library Bill of Rights, 251

255

VIDEO
POLICIES
and
PROCEDURES
for
LIBRARIES

VIDEO
POLICIES
and
PROCEDURES
for
LIBRARIES

James C. Scholtz

ABC-CLIO

Copyright © 1991 by James C. Scholtz

All rights reserved. No part of this publication may be reproduced, stored in a retrieval system, or transmitted, in any form or by any means, electronic, mechanical, photocopying, recording, or otherwise, except for the inclusion of brief quotations in a review, without prior permission in writing from the publishers.

Library of Congress Cataloging-in-Publication Data

Scholtz, James C., 1956–
 Video policies and procedures for libraries / James C. Scholtz.
   p. cm.
 Includes index.
 1. Libraries—Special collections—Video recordings. 2. Video tape recorders and recording—Library applications 3. Video recordings—Collectors and collecting. I. Title.
 Z692.V52S37 1991   025.2'87—dc20   91-21350

ISBN 0-87436-582-1 (alk. paper)

98 97 96 95 94 93 92 91   10 9 8 7 6 5 4 3 2 1

ABC-CLIO, Inc.
130 Cremona Drive, P.O. Box 1911
Santa Barbara, California 93116-1911

This book is printed on acid-free paper ∞ .
Manufactured in the United States of America

CONTENTS

List of Figures, xi
Preface, xiii
Acknowledgments, xvii

1 A Policy Rationale, 1

The State of the Union, 1

Developing a Service Philosophy, 3

The Purpose and Definition of Policy and Procedure, 5

Developing Written Policies, 6

Practical Suggestions for Writing Policies, 8

    Model Public Library Videocassette Policy, 9

2 Collection Development and the Selection Policy, 13

Collection Development, 13

    Elements of a Collection Development Policy, 17

The Selection Policy, 18

    Types of Selection Policies, 20

    Elements of a Selection Policy, 22

Video Collection Weeding, 24

    Weeding Goals, 26

    Weeding Methods, 28

    Specific Weeding Criteria, 30

In-House Preview/Evaluation, 33

Summary, 33

Sample Collection Development, General Selection, Video Selection, and Weeding Policies for Public Libraries, 36

    Video Collection Development Policy: Skokie (Illinois) Public Library, 36

        Collection Development Policy: Skokie Public Library (Excerpts), 37

    Collection Development Policy: Lake County Public Library, Merrillville, Indiana, 42

        Lake County Public Library: Collection Development Policy, 42

    Selection Policy: Ames (Iowa) Public Library, 44

        Materials Selection Policy: Ames Public Library, 45

Sample Video Selection Policies, 51

    Thousand Oaks (California) Public Library, 51

        Thousand Oaks Library Video Policy, 52

    Frankfort (Indiana) Community Public Library, 55

        Frankfort Community Public Library: Videotape Acquisitions Policy, 55

    Birmingham (Alabama) Public Library, 57

        Birmingham (Alabama) Public Library: Media Services Department Selection Policy, 58

    Phoenix (Arizona) Public Library, 60

        Phoenix Public Library: Collection Development Policies, 61

CONTENTS

vii

      Baltimore County Public Library, Towson, Maryland, 68

          Baltimore County Public Library: Videocassette Policy, 68

      Model Videocassette Selection Policy, 75

      Alabama Public Library Service, 83

          Alabama Public Library Service Video Selection Policy, 83

      Weeding Policy: Grant Wood Area Education Agency, 86

          Grant Wood Area Education Agency Weeding Rationale, 87

School Library Media Center Selection Policies, 90

    Surveying the Field, 90

    Toward a Service Philosophy, 92

    A Goal Statement for Materials Selection, 92

    The Evaluation Process, 94

    Sample Selection Policies for School Library Media Centers, 96

        Burlington County AVA: Policies and Procedures for 16mm Film Selection, 97

        California Instructional Video Clearinghouse: Evaluation Materials, 99

        Grant Wood AEA, Cedar Rapids, Iowa: Procedure for Materials Selection and Weeding Policy, 106

        Delaware-Chenango Board of Cooperative Educational Services: Instructional Materials Selection Policies and Procedures, 109

3 Circulation and Use Policies and Procedures, 117

Circulation Procedures, 117

Videocassette Circulation Policies, 122

Equipment/VCR Loan, 122

In-House Viewing, 123

Sample Circulation Policies, 124

    Ames Public Library Policy Statement on Fees and Charges, 124

    Laramie County (Wyoming) Library System: VHS Videocassette Information, 127

    Videocassettes and Video Player Regulations: Santa Monica (California) Public Library, 129

    Videocassette Circulation Policy: Schaumburg Township (Illinois) Public Library, 132

    Damaged Nonprint Material: Phoenix Public Library, 133

Video Circulation by School Library Media Centers, 144

4 Copyright Issues and Policies, 149

Copyright Defined, 150

The Copyright Act of 1976, 151

Public Performance and Public Domain, 152

    Copyright, 155

Public Performance and Broadcast Rights, 156

Off-Air and Satellite Taping, 157

    Warning! Guidelines for Video Recording and Classroom Use, 158

Developing a Copyright Policy, 159

Specific Applications of Policy, 160

Sample Copyright Policies, 163

    Model School District Policy, 163

    Reproduction and Use of Copyrighted Materials (Nonprint/Print): Grossmont Union High School District, 169

CONTENTS ix

> Los Angeles County Office of Education: Guidelines on Copyright, 174
>
> Carmel Clay Schools: Copyright Policy, 179
>
> California Instructional Video Clearinghouse: Copyright Guidelines, 188
>
> Off-Air Video Recording Issues and Answers: San Diego County Office of Education, 200

5 Intellectual Freedom Issues and Policies, 215

Principles of Intellectual Freedom, 215

Access for Minors, 217

MPAA Ratings, 219

The Public Library, 220

> Censorship and Materials Reconsideration, 220
>
> Public Library Reconsideration Procedures, 221

School Library Media Centers, 225

> School Library Reconsideration Procedures, 227
>
> Parental Restriction of Materials, 228
>
> Model Challenged-Materials Policy and Procedures for Schools, 229
>
> Use of Nonschool Materials, 239

Summary, 240

Appendix A Freedom To View, 243

Appendix B Challenged Materials: An Interpretation of the *Library Bill of Rights*, 245

Appendix C Expurgation of Library Materials: An Interpretation of the *Library Bill of Rights*, 247

Appendix D Access to Resources and Services in the School
            Library Media Program: An Interpretation of the
            Library Bill of Rights, 249

Appendix E Access for Children and Young People to
            Videotapes and Other Nonprint Formats: An
            Interpretation of the *Library Bill of Rights*, 251

Index, 255

FIGURES

Figure 2.1 Sample Video Circulation Statistics Form, 29
Figure 2.2 Model Patron Damage Evaluation Form, 31
Figure 2.3 Model Library Preview/Evaluation Form, 34
Figure 2.4 Model Media Preview/Evaluation Form for Schools, 35
Figure 2.5 Baltimore County Public Library Partial Videocassette Purchasing Formulas for Branches, 72
Figure 2.6 Towson's Video Weeding Method, 74
Figure 3.1 Model Video Damage Condition Report Form, 121
Figure 3.2 Model Video Damage Log Form, 121
Figure 4.1 Model School District Form A: Request for Off-Air Program Taping, 168
Figure 5.1 Model Public Library Request for Reconsideration Form for Visual Media, 222
Figure 5.2 Model School Library Request for Reconsideration of Materials Form, 234
Figure 5.3 Model Simple Complaint Card, 238
Figure 5.4 Model Response to Complainant, 239

PREFACE

This book is an outgrowth of my previous text, *Developing and Maintaining Video Collections in Libraries* (ABC-CLIO, 1989). Since 1987, while speaking about video at various national and state library conferences, I have received myriad questions concerning videocassette policies and procedures. Three years ago the concept of library video collections was in its infancy, and few libraries had set policies to guide video services. Thus the first book was intended as a start-up and operations primer for librarians seeking broad but relatively in-depth information on beginning a circulating video collection or reconfiguring an existing one. Although the book covered issues and concerns using a multitype library approach, the major emphasis was on public libraries. Only one model collection development policy was provided, and circulation policies and cataloging procedures were only briefly discussed.

Today, much has happened to broaden the scope of video in libraries. During the 1989 conference of the American Library Association (ALA), discussions concerning video in libraries assumed prominent spots on the agenda, even invading the realms of technical services and intellectual freedom. The Video Interest Group questionnaire tallies revealed the topics of selection, censorship, security, and copyright as top choices for future programs. Clearly, video

is not just for AV librarians anymore. Both the ALA/Carnegie VCR project and the MacArthur Foundation Video Classics project for select subject-content videos were a rousing success. The Association for Library Services for Children (ALA's division ALSC) sponsored a preconference on children's video in libraries, and the ALA and Carnegie Foundation are funding a joint venture entitled Quality Video for Youth. Also, the Rockefeller Foundation is currently examining the popularity of various nonmainstream genres such as foreign, experimental, independent, and documentaries in public libraries.

As video collections expand into other library departments and existing collections grow exponentially, policies and procedures regulating those collections and their use will become increasingly important and complex. Although common service denominators exist in all libraries, school and public libraries are widely disparate institutions and, as such, treat and use video differently. To be successful in either type of institution, however, video cannot be viewed as a special, often ephemeral medium; it must be channeled into the mainstream of library service and collections as a valid alternative information source. To accomplish this task, the overall information philosophy of the library must be broadened to include video. The best philosophy is one that interweaves all media formats—forming an integrated collection fabric. Librarians desire specific information with concrete examples; consequently, a more focused, multitype approach concerning collection development, selection, copyright/in-house use, and circulation is needed.

The purpose of this text is to provide public and school librarians with a sampling of video policies and procedures that present alternative methods, operations, and applications for video service. To this end, noted AV librarians throughout the country were asked to recommend libraries possessing exemplary and/or innovative video policies and procedures. Over 100 libraries were identified; of these, 35 submitted vital statistics and policies. The policies reprinted here have been chosen because they reflect varying methods of service, operations, and philosophy; they include both

divergent and common policy elements; and they offer varying degrees of coverage depth. No one policy is more correct than another; each works well within its community, library governance structure, and administration style. What the policies have in common is that they all have been researched, thought-out, written down, approved by a governing body, enforced, and regularly evaluated, revised, and updated. They are living, working documents rather than dust-gathering archival papers.

These policies do not necessarily represent eclectic policy models. They should be viewed only as examples of average library video policies. Many authors of policy books give prefatory precautions concerning the dangers of piecing together a policy from the "good parts" presented within. Usually, a cognitive approach to policy elements allows the policymaker significant latitude as to element inclusion and wording, based on community needs and institutional factors, but sometimes such an approach is not enough. Policies are highly philosophical and theoretical documents and, rather than starting from scratch, many librarians desire models from which they can extract pertinent segments, altering and enlarging them to suit their needs. As long as policymakers realize that policies must be personalized based on an individual library's or district's needs, I feel that the jigsaw method (the piecing together of a policy from many "good parts") of policy-writing is valid. Certainly, it is more desirable than having no policy at all and provides a starting point from which to deviate as philosophies, goals and objectives, and services mature.

☐ ORGANIZATION OF THIS BOOK

This book is topically arranged, with each chapter discussing and presenting a particular type of policy (e.g., selection, copyright, access for minors, etc.). Within the chapters, where appropriate, the policies are divided by public library and school library type. Each policy section begins with an in-depth commentary using a model policy outline or discussion of pertinent concepts. Thereafter, individual policies are

presented in one of three forms: in their entirety, abridged, or excerpted. Brief explanatory/analytical notes have been included where appropriate. The purpose of these notes is not to find fault with or to laud any given policy; rather, it is to reinforce the analytical thought processes used in asking the questions, "Why was it written or structured this way, and what might be included to make it fit the more traditional form?" All sample policies presented in this text have been similarly styled in an attempt to maintain consistent form and element inclusion. In the case of variant spellings and word divisions such as "videocassette" versus "video cassette," one single spelling has been chosen and consistently applied throughout all of the policies. Grammatical corrections have been made where necessary, and inconsistent usage has been modified. However, these changes in no way alter the intent, integrity, or word connotations of any of the documents.

In some instances, sample policies and forms were not available. To this end, I have constructed some model policies and forms, in essence taking the best parts of existing documents and creating model composites. These documents are clearly labeled Model Policy or Model Form. Common documents, such as ALA's Freedom To View and Access for Minors statements, are referred to where applicable in the various policies, but reprinted only once in the appendices.

ACKNOWLEDGMENTS

The author would like to thank all the people who helped make this book a reality. My editor, Heather Cameron, sparked the initial idea, kept my writing focused, and gave me encouragement. Thanks go to the many AV librarians, library directors, and system consultants who provided me with contact names and actual policies for this text; without them, this text would not have been possible. I would also like to recognize Irene Wood, Sally Mason, and the entire staff of ABC-CLIO for their unwavering faith in my subject knowledge of video in libraries and for giving me the chance to express that knowledge in book form. I would like to thank my wife for keeping our two children at bay while I neglected my household and fatherly duties, researched, pondered, wrote, rewrote, and pondered some more. Lastly, I would like to thank my coworkers at NILS, who put up with constant intellectual mutterings and hypothetical situations, and provided feedback to my silly questions. I do not pretend that my work fills any grand literary or scholarly void, but only hope that it provides food for thought concerning alternate methods for enhancing video services as they relate to the entirety of library service.

1 A POLICY RATIONALE

THE STATE OF THE UNION

Today, video has grown up, as shown by the following statistics:

- 72 percent of American homes have at least one VCR, with 1.2 machines being the average per household.[1]
- 43 percent of all VCR households purchased a tape within the last six months. Major motion pictures and children's video accounted for 72 percent of all prerecorded purchases,[2] with the average per-title cost of $17.61 and a mode of $29.95.[3]
- Consumer polls show that 29 percent of VCR households rent 60 percent of the videos.
- In 1988, total retail rental transactions exceeded 1.1 billion, accounting for almost $9 billion in revenue.[4] During that same time period, the sellthrough market topped $2.5 billion.[5]

In the past, libraries targeted the special-interest, how-to, and documentary market because video retail stores did not stock such tapes. In effect, libraries tried to complement, rather than compete with, the retail stores' collections by filling a community need that was unfilled by retail outlets. Today, however, special-interest video has gained a respectable

foothold in the retail market, with 25.3 million Americans (43 percent of all VCR households) either renting or purchasing a special-interest video in 1989.[6] Even small video stores have racks of travel, sports, exercise, and how-to videos. Special interest has also invaded the gift catalog market, and catalogs can be found in places as varied as supermarkets and airplanes.

Many librarians still feel that their original collection philosophy is justified because many special-interest videos, such as those from the MacArthur Grant, Films Incorporated, Annenberg/CPB (distributed by Intellimation), and PBS Video, are not available to the consumer market. This is rapidly changing, however; for example, Pacific Arts Video recently made a deal with PBS Video to market select PBS titles to consumers. Also, a variety of Films Incorporated titles are available to consumers through a subsidiary company named Home Vision. In the near future, there will be little distinction between a library- and a consumer-available title. Prerecorded video prices will stabilize on the low end, and consequently titles will become more available, in multiple formats, to consumers. Libraries will be forced into a competitive market. In order to be successful they will have to target their audience, market their products (emphasizing the unique items), and, above all, define their collection and service roles in relation to other available sources. Therefore, prioritizing services, defining the library's niche within a community need, and developing policies that describe, reinforce, and outline action for delivering focused services will be of great importance.

Today, circulating video collections are present in more than 85 percent of U.S. public libraries serving a population of 25,000 or more,[7] and 62.5 percent of all U.S. public libraries.[8] Indeed, at the Monroe County Library System in Monroe, Michigan, video circulation accounts for more than 43 percent of the total materials circulation, with nationwide figures reporting overall circulation statistics between 15 and 20 percent.[9] Clearly, in 1990, video in libraries has arrived. The video revolution has given way to the video evolution—a slow process whereby mutations or superior

aberrations of video service will be the guideposts to the future of video service in libraries. These mutations will take various forms, but they will have two things in common: they will accurately reflect current community needs and trends, and they will be an intrinsic part of the total library service picture.

DEVELOPING A SERVICE PHILOSOPHY

The formulation of library policies does not establish a total service philosophy; rather, policies are a reflection of that philosophy. Policies establish functional parameters that define long- and short-term goals and measurable objectives. Many librarians separate various services and collections from the library's basic service philosophy in the wording of their philosophy statement. If a philosophy is unfocused or arbitrarily weighted toward one service or collection to the detriment of another, serious service rifts, dissatisfied staff and patrons, and unbalanced funding can result. Services work best when wedded together, complementing and supporting one another.

For example, many librarians view the charging of fees for circulating videocassettes as an excellent way to fund an otherwise underfunded videocassette collection. Such a system, however, is demand driven. Best-sellers must be purchased to keep circulation steady or on the rise. If revenues drop off, the budget is cut. Video has then been successfully separated from the rest of the collection, destined to become a mediocre entertainment format, effectively removed from the funding umbrella. Some librarians rationalize that this funding methodology is better than providing no service at all; however, it provides little investment risk on the library's part, making the service easy to curtail or eliminate in times of lean budgets or falling circulation.

All services and collections should be based on goals and objectives, which in turn are driven by an underlying philosophy. Through the evaluation of present video services and the analysis of other library services and community

parameters, the questions who, what, where, how, and when will provide the basis for a video service philosophy and future policy decisions. The book *Policy Questions for Audiovisual Services in Public Libraries* (ALA, 1985) is an excellent resource that provides a series of questions with insightful comments on starting a service.

A hypothetical example of a combined philosophy/purpose statement for a medium-sized (25,000–150,000 population) public library might read as follows:

> The library exists to acquire, and provide free access to, materials that facilitate informal self-education, limited scholarly and educational research, subject reference, and recreation to all members of the defined community. The library also acts as a vehicle for interlibrary loan and a clearinghouse for various community information endeavors. The library will encourage library use by all factions of the community; promote broad dissemination of ideas; and support educational, civic, and cultural activities within the community.
>
> The library endorses the principles affirmed in the American Library Association–endorsed Library Bill of Rights, Freedom To Read, and Freedom To View statements. The library also supports the ALA philosophy against labeling and access for minors. These principles are as follows:
>
> 1. Censorship in selection will not be practiced. Materials will not be excluded because of the creation entity's views or background.
> 2. Materials will represent all points of view, restricted only by accessibility and budgetary limitations. Materials will not be proscribed or removed because of partisan or doctrinal disapproval or censorship attempts.
> 3. Recognizing the advancing role of technology in information/entertainment dissemination, and in tune with community needs, the library will attempt to acquire diverse media collections, basing selection on prescribed criteria and the overall suitability of the media for imparting information.

A POLICY RATIONALE

4. A person's right to use the library will not be denied or abridged because of origin, age, background, or views.

Many people would argue that the above affirmations are far too specific to be included in a philosophy statement, but it is just such a statement that results in focused goals and measurable objectives. At first, the sentence "the library will attempt to acquire diverse media collections, basing selection on prescribed criteria and the overall suitability of the media for imparting information" may seem out of place in the philosophy statement, belonging instead in the collection development policy as a prefatory remark. However, it is this sentence that sets the tone for active collection integration, regardless of media types. It impacts upon all facets of operation from budgeting, public services, and facilities to technical services, circulation, and collection development. In effect, it provides an equal footing basis for all collections and services whereby funding, at least on some level, must be provided.

THE PURPOSE AND DEFINITION OF POLICY AND PROCEDURE

Before librarians write and compile policy and procedure documents and manuals, it is essential that they understand both terms in an administrative context. Hugh A. Durbin, Media Services Director for the Columbus School System (Ohio), voices the following thoughts on policy:

> Policy statements serve as the basis for planning, budgeting, and providing staff with a guide for day-to-day activities. They inform the public, define expectations, and should enlist support. Policy safeguards against falling prey to fads, but allows for some experimentation. Policy must be flexible, adaptable when necessary, and must recognize the multimedia nature of the library. [Also,] statements should lead to a greater equity between book and nonbook resources.[10]

The ALA's *Intellectual Freedom Manual* states that a written policy:

> ... encourages stability and continuity in the library's operations ... [and] will help assure smooth transitions when organization or staff changes occur. Second, ambiguity and confusion are far less likely to result if a library's procedures are set down in writing.[11]

Elaborating upon Phyllis Van Orden's definition, policies explain *why* services and collections exist, establish the basis for all related activites, and delineate *what* will be the parameters and scope of those activities. Procedures explain *how* policies will be implemented on a practical, day-to-day basis and identify *who* is responsible. "Policies, therefore, need to be developed before procedure statements can be written."[12] Van Orden believes that policy statements should be issued separately from procedure statements; in practice, however, many policy statements include both policies and procedures without differentiating their functions.[13] Policy statements tend toward expressing the ideal, while "procedures direct the implementation of policies and should be concrete and measurable."[14] Policies are usually conceived through administrative activity, and are board approved, while procedures are formulated on the administrative/department-head level. It is strategically important to have governing board/entity approval of policies before they are implemented; otherwise serious conflicts can result.

DEVELOPING WRITTEN POLICIES

Often, librarians resist formulating written policies because of a perception that doing so is an arduous and time consuming task. Also, they feel restricted by rigid guidelines that force standardization and consistent application of rules and methods. Although the initial development stage is indeed arduous and time consuming, the perception of policies as rigid documents is only true when the documents are ill-conceived. Well-formulated policies, based upon goals and objectives that reflect community needs, not only provide a set of dynamic, flexible guidelines from which procedures

A POLICY RATIONALE 7

can be developed, but they also act as protection devices, effectively interpreting board wishes, transferring goals and objectives to personnel, and providing the authority base to perform certain activities within a prescribed scope. Liability is also removed from the staff and placed with the board (governing entity), where it belongs. Policies are dynamic documents that should be reviewed and revised periodically to reflect changes in philosophy, interpretations, laws, and goals. A well-developed policy provides a measure of security along with certain objective/task clarifications and evaluation criteria, and gives the institution a sense of purpose.

On a practical level, policies serve as the basis for planning and budgeting, and provide the staff with a guide for day-to-day activities. They also act as public relations devices, informing the public about service/collection expectations. Hugh Durbin offers this theoretical affirmation of policies as practical instruments:

> We must start with a theory of what our library is and let it determine practice. Theory will always be the foundation on which practice is built. Practice may be static.... It has, however, no principles for dealing with what it doesn't know. Practice cannot adapt readily in a changing environment and may get sidetracked in efforts to cope with constantly changing demands.[15]

Policies, therefore, define the present and prepare for the future.

When thinking of library policies, most librarians envision a cumbersome notebook (or several) comprising several distinct policies, such as: collection development (with various selection policies within that document); acquisitions; circulation (access for minors); copyright/off-air use; shelving and housing/preservation; and cataloging/processing. Any given policy not only reflects the philosophy of that library, but also reveals its organizational structure, however complex or simple, as well. But even the shortest policy, if it is thoughtfully and thoroughly written, will take a great deal of staff time, perspiration, and energy to write.

PRACTICAL SUGGESTIONS FOR WRITING POLICIES

- Keep all policies in a three-ring, loose-leaf notebook. This will facilitate easy revision.
- Number and date all pages.
- Be sure all pages possess headings.
- Stamp draft policies for easy recognition.
- Assemble a table of contents.
- Write goals and objectives on a separate sheet so that revision will be easier without retyping the entire document.
- Format all pages double-spaced with wide margins for writing in revision ideas.
- To facilitate brevity, organize all writing in an expanded outline form with text rather than in straight narrative form.

Following is an example of a policy statement that successfully melds multiple policies into a single document. Adapted from an original document used by the Nippersink Public Library (Richmond, Illinois; population 1,068), the policy merges the videocassette selection, circulation, equipment, and in-house use policies of a small library. It illustrates how, even when merging several policies, a simple, brief document can be just as effective as a long, complex one. The document's organization and wording make it usable as an advertisement flyer for patrons as well.

References to the Library Bill of Rights, the Freedom To View statement, and the Access for Minors Interpretation have been intentionally omitted in the following document. These will be illustrated and discussed in detail in the upcoming chapters. This model library videocassette policy represents a purely functional document, incorporating a measurable collection objective of adding 850-plus videocassettes to the collection over a two-year period, with the eventual acquisition of a 50/50 split of features/nonfiction. Although readers may not agree with all of its principles, the

document nonetheless serves its somewhat limited purpose in this small library setting.

Model Public Library Videocassette Policy

The Collection
The Public Library has built a collection of 150 VHS videocassettes since January 1984. While rental outlets tend to emphasize multiple copies of recent popular theatrical releases, the purpose of our video collection is to emphasize single copies of award-winning, classic titles that will endure the test of time. Efforts are made to include videos representing all genres as well as major performers and directors. Nonfiction videos represent about 40 percent of the collection, and are chosen for their relevance of format to content, community need, and technical quality. In selecting both features and nonfiction videos, favorable reviews from recognized review sources (print and televised) are utilized. All selection is done by the library director.

The collection includes the following genres: children's videos and cartoons; feature film classics, such as *Rear Window, The African Queen, Casablanca, The Sound of Music,* and *West Side Story*, representing the best in film history from the silent era to the present; popular, award-winning movies achieving a measure of longevity; instructional and how-to videos; and subject documentaries.

Circulation
The videos are checked out for three days to Public Library cardholders and system reciprocal borrowers holding a valid, adult card (at least 18 years of age). All users must sign a Responsibility Statement the first time they check out a tape. There is a two title limit per patron, with a one dollar overdue fine per day per title, and no renewals. Videos can be returned in the building book drop or at the circulation desk. A convenience we provide patrons is to allow children to check out videos on the parent's card if the parent calls or sends a note giving him/her permission.

In conjunction with the video collection, the library has two VCRs available for one-day loan. A Loan Form needs to be filled out, and there is a five dollar per day overdue charge.

Reserves for titles on order or currently checked out are taken, with a patron limit of three titles. Reserves are 15 cents each, and patrons will be notified by postcard, with titles being held for one week. VCRs cannot be reserved.

Goals and Selection Formula

The Library Board has determined that we will build the collection to 1,000 videocassettes within the next two years, with a 50/50 split in acquiring movies/nonfiction titles. Our policy in selecting titles is to "give the people what they want," within the limits of good selection criteria as stated in the Materials Selection Policy. Basically, a positive review from a reliable magazine or positive staff preview report is needed for title acquisition. Gifts will be retained as long as they meet the Materials Selection requirements. Weeding is accomplished primarily through damage assessment, occurring at the point of circulation return, based upon patron responses on the Viewing Report Form, which accompanies each title. We do consider suggestions from patrons for specific titles or subjects, and encourage comments and suggestions for improving our service.

☐ NOTES

1. Earl Paige, "AVA Poll Reveals Viewer Sophistication," *Billboard*, 17 September 1988, 48.
2. Jack Schember, "Tales from the Peoplemeter," *Video Software Dealer* 5 (October 1989): 116.
3. Tomm Carroll, "Nontheatrical Videos: Inside and Out," *Video Software Dealer* 5 (February 1990): 32.
4. "Consumer Poll," *Video Software Dealer* 5 (September 1989): 130.
5. Carroll, 34.

6. Ibid.
7. Randy Pitman, "Video in Libraries 1989: A Review," *Video Librarian* 4 (February 1990): 1.
8. Ray Serebrin, "Video: Planning Backwards into the Future," *Library Journal* 120 (15 November 1988): 33.
9. Pitman, 12.
10. Hugh A. Durbin, "Using Policy Statements To Define and Manage the Nonbook Collection," in *Policy and Practice in Bibliographic Control of Nonbook Media,* ed. Sheila S. Inter and Richard P. Smiraglia (Chicago: ALA, 1987), 38–39.
11. Office for Intellectual Freedom of the American Library Association, comp., *Intellectual Freedom Manual,* 2d ed. (Chicago: ALA, 1983), 155.
12. Phyllis J. Van Orden, *The Collection Program in Elementary and Middle Schools: Concepts, Practices and Information Sources* (Littleton, CO: Libraries Unlimited, 1988), 75.
13. Ibid.
14. Ibid.
15. Durbin, 38–39.

2 COLLECTION DEVELOPMENT AND THE SELECTION POLICY

COLLECTION DEVELOPMENT

"Collection development is probably the single most important and difficult library theory to effectively put into practice because it requires so much preplanning and a broad field of vision."[1]

The collection development document translates the library's purpose and mission into long-term goals and short-term measurable objectives, which in turn are reflected in the selection policy. But what is the difference between a collection development and a selection policy? Historically in the library world, the three terms collection development, selection, and acquisitions have been used interchangeably; however, they are radically different. Rose Mary Magrill and John Corbin state that "collection development has come to encompass a broad range of activities related to the policies and procedures of selection, acquisition, and evaluation of library collections."[2] Hendrik Edelman suggests that these terms represent a hierarchy, with the highest level, collection development, being the planning function.[3]

From the established collection development plans of the

> library flow the decisions about inclusion or exclusion of specific items in the collection ... in other words,

selection, the second level of the hierarchy. Acquisitions, the next level, is the process that implements selection decisions. . . . [It is] the process of verifying, ordering, and paying for . . . materials.[4]

Selection and acquisitions can be viewed as single activities, while collection development is neither a single activity nor a group of activities, but a planning and decision-making process. Charles B. Osburn states that collection development "implies that collection response to changing conditions is to be part of a predetermined definable system of relating the collection to the community managed by the librarian."[5]

An excellent example of a collection development policy used by a special library, but applicable to other libraries as well, is *The New York Academy of Medicine Library Collection Development Policy*, prepared by Anne M. Pascarelli (1982). This document clearly illustrates the hierarchical relationships and presents the various selection policies (delineated by format) within the broader collection development document. Essentially, the collection development policy serves to establish a mutually dependent relationship between information formats (i.e., print and nonprint) and disciplines/subject areas. It also links many policies together, including selection, acquisitions, and weeding.

Goals, measurable objectives, community analysis, and evaluation are the four keys to describing collection development. These four items alone distinguish a collection development document from a selection policy. A collection development policy also serves the following functions:

1. It establishes a planning guideline and working tool for selectors.
2. It operates as a communications medium between the library and external administrative bodies.
3. It states the codified rationale for decisions in budgetary matters where materials are concerned.
4. It helps achieve a unified view of what areas of the collection should be developed.

COLLECTION DEVELOPMENT AND THE SELECTION POLICY

5. It helps develop coordination between different individuals' responsibilities for the collection.
6. It helps achieve consistency in materials selection by clarifying specific objectives and reducing the number of ad hoc decisions related to the selection process.
7. It provides for methods of performance evaluation for continuation of the collection-building cycle.[6]

Every library collection should be established for a definite purpose, concurrently housing a wide variety of subjects/genres/formats that provide information and recreation for a wide range of patrons. Goals will determine the formats to be acquired. Within those formats, subjects and genres will vary in depth of coverage related to the library's mission and goals, who uses the collection, and why they use it. The ALA's *Guide to the Evaluation of Library Collections* comments on coverage depth by stating: "The collection may be developed for research, recreation, community service and development, instruction, support of a corporate activity, or a combination of these or other purposes"[7] represented by multiple levels of in-depth coverage.

Librarians practicing collection development should first identify the current levels of service and collection strengths/weaknesses, trying to discover when/how/why they were begun and how they have developed and evolved. The clientele makeup should be analyzed along with the budget picture. Then, the library's goals and objectives should be overlaid, resulting in a prioritization process with simple modification/addition/deletion decisions.

Collection evaluation and analysis methods are essential in making the entire collection development process cyclical. Collection development begins and continues the process, providing dynamic "snapshot photographs" of the collection and specific subgroups in three time phases—past, present, and future. Librarians can ascertain where the collection was, where it is now, and what they want it to look like in the future.

While it is not the intent of this book to describe in detail specific evaluation techniques, some mention of the two basic data sources for obtaining information is imperative to an understanding of collection development concepts. The two data sources are clients and collections.

Client-centered evaluation revolves around patron need/demand analysis. Serving the unserved, discovering what patrons want and need, what material they use and to what degree they use it, and what material they do not use are some of the areas requiring attention. Circulation as a measure of popularity, need, and demand expressed as a turnover rate (number of titles, prints, or volumes divided by circulation) are some of the data examined.

Collection-centered evaluation revolves solely around the library collection. A collection's weaknesses and strengths are gauged against standard subject bibliographies or weighted using specific subgroup percentages of titles or volumes held. Average or modal copyright dates of subject areas are useful in ascertaining out-of-date material. A collection may be examined as a whole, broken down by subject, discipline, floor, or department, or it may be divided by media format.

Both sources have certain advantages and disadvantages in their use. Collection-centered evaluation is very objective and global in perspective. It does not take into consideration any popularity factors or community factors—it looks at collection use, age, and coverage depth in limited scope. Client-centered evaluation, on the other hand, is extremely subjective and local in perspective. It looks at the specific needs and demands of patrons. If care is not taken, however, demand can be misconstrued as need, and the collection will become totally "demand-driven."

An alternative method called the conspectus approach has become a standard tool for coordinating collection development in academic libraries. Developed by the Research Library Group (RLG), this method effectively profiles a collection, subject by subject, systematically evaluating its depth of coverage (often referred to as "level of study"). Six broad, descriptive levels ranging from "out of scope—no

COLLECTION DEVELOPMENT AND THE SELECTION POLICY

holdings and nothing bought" to "comprehensive—exhaustive holdings, buying everything available" are used to describe specific subject areas.[8] Other types of libraries have successfully modified this approach to suit their needs; the Skokie (Illinois) Public Library policy in this text is one example.

A combination of these sources, serving as a reflection of how the collection fits a specific community works the best. From this data, specific collection goals can be gathered and prioritized. Also, narrative statements concerning the scope, coverage depth, limitations, and expectations of specific media formats and/or subject areas can be written.

☐ ELEMENTS OF A COLLECTION DEVELOPMENT POLICY

The elements of a collection development policy include the following:

1. Introduction. Here, the purpose and materials-inclusion scope of the policy are defined. The audience is delineated and the governing body adopting the policy is declared. The date of adoption should also be in this section.
2. The library mission or general philosophy statement and institutional goals for collection management and service are stated. This statement creates a theoretical foundation on which the more practical sections will be built. Other standard and inclusive statements of patron's rights in reading/viewing/listening, access to materials, and censorship (as interpreted and enforced by the library), such as the ALA/American Film and Video Association (AFVA) Freedom To View and Intellectual Freedom documents, are referred to here (actual documents should appear in an appendix).
3. Analysis of the library's objectives. This section describes the external environment and boundaries (limits) of the collection as a whole.
    A. Description of clientele and community to be served.

> B. Description of library programs both currently available and planned within the next two to three years.
> C. Brief overview of the collection, including history, limitations, boundaries, special collections, subjects, formats, genres emphasized/de-emphasized, exclusions, and collection locations. (Narrative statements or the conspectus approach should be used here to delineate levels of collection and levels of users.)

4. Organization of collection management and development program:

   A. Staffing.
   B. Liaison with user groups.

5. Various selection policies, or one all-encompassing, general policy, appear here. Sources and percentages of materials funds might be mentioned as well as materials duplication and multiple copies. Selection methods and departmental or personal selection responsibility should be designated here. Also, specific criteria for selection based on subject/genre/format should be included. Challenged-materials documents, forms, and policy hierarchy should be delineated.
6. Relationships to policies and programs for the management of collections, such as preservation, weeding, and storage.
7. Cooperative collection development agreements (description of programs).
8. Collection evaluation techniques and methods.[9]

THE SELECTION POLICY

In reality, most of the policies presented in this book represent a synthesis of collection development and selection policies. Many policies contain procedures (such as acquisitions) as well. Policies are functions of boards, while procedures are interpretations of policies and come from management. The problem then becomes one of differentiating between policy

and procedure. Van Orden presents six questions that librarians can use to distinguish between policy and procedure:

1. Does the statement address the purpose of the collection: why it exists? (policy)
2. Does the statement identify what types of materials will be included or what authority is responsible for the collection? (policy)
3. Does the statement explain why materials will be added or withdrawn from the collection? (policy)
4. Does the statement explain how the collection will be created? (procedure)
5. Does the statement explain who will be involved in the selection process? (policy)
6. Does the statement explain how [various personnel and departments] will be involved in the selection process? (procedure)[10]

Usually, in collection development, the term collection means the collection as a whole, regardless of formats or subjects/genres. Many times, however, the collection development policy is just a group of selection policies brought together by a common mission and goals. Many collection development documents are actually only selection policies. The Rockefeller Foundation survey revealed that only about one-third of the 17 respondents possessed separate video selection policies, "feeling that the overall materials selection policy was broad enough to cover video collection development."[11] Hugh Durbin writes of the dangers of this practice:

> Many policies have been written with the idea that one need only insert the word *nonbook* in order to give equal status ... but each format has individual characteristics and demands different criteria or basis of selection than the others. Each medium makes its own contribution as a carrier of information, and should be judged accordingly.[12]

The problem is not whether the general policy is broad enough, but rather, whether portions of it are sufficiently

20 COLLECTION DEVELOPMENT AND THE SELECTION POLICY

narrow or specific enough to accurately represent video's special characteristics. The following Rockefeller survey findings illuminate the existing dichotomy between broad theoretical policies and restrictive actual library practices:

1. Concerns about controversial content and access for minors were widespread; approximately 50 percent of U.S. public libraries have age restrictions to part or all of their video collections.
2. Not surprisingly, packaging and price of videos are very important to libraries, with over half of the Rockefeller-surveyed libraries reporting general limits of $100 or less.
3. Collections tend to reflect librarians' selection/acquisition sources. Librarians who use jobber catalogs, flyers, and brochures for ordering are collecting primarily narrower, mainstream items. Librarians who use varied library and other review sources and independent filmmaker catalogs tend to have more depth/breadth in their collections.[13]

Media, and particularly video, are especially appropriate for particular subjects and in particular learning situations. Librarians, however, must recognize that any item has multiple uses depending upon the individuals involved and the learning environment.

☐ TYPES OF SELECTION POLICIES

A library may choose any one of the following selection policy style outlines, or a mix of the three:

1. A generic materials selection policy for the entire collection. Best suited to small libraries, this type of policy eliminates differences in formats, concentrating on the shape and coverage of the entire collection. By its very nature, it will be simplistic and cursory because differences in format selection criteria *do* exist.
2. One materials selection policy with specific sections by media format (i.e., film, video, art prints, books, etc.)

and/or specific subjects/genres or locations. This type of policy works well in small- to medium-sized libraries with coexisting departments. The fracturization of interdepartmental communication is not a problem in this library structure, and selection/acquisitions for each department is not widely disparate. Selection may be done by department heads in a committee atmosphere. This policy is the perfect conduit for outlining the different selection criteria for the various formats/subjects, but also for reinforcing the similarities and interdependency between those different groups.
3. Several selection policies, each being a distinct entity with separate selection criteria regarding media format, subject/genre inclusion, or media location. This type of arrangement works best in highly departmentalized or division/branch libraries where clientele and subject/genre coverage and depth differ widely, and where disparate entities [such as department heads] make selection decisions and house collections within their departments. Selection and acquisitions methods probably differ widely from department to department. Also, the format/subject characteristics may be discussed at length, possibly with multiple levels of collection depth; therefore, separate policies are easier to manipulate, use, and revise than a longer merged document.

To a great degree, the size of library staff, degree of departmentalization, materials budget breakdown by department, departmental lines of communication, and selection authority will determine the overall shape, contents, and depth of the selection policy(ies). Large libraries usually have collection development departments to coordinate all collection development activities. Subject-departmentalized libraries and branches may have different purposes and priorities, and be viewed as composite pieces rather than in totality as a single large library. Department or division heads may hold authority, even over specific branch collections. Selection committees operate with rotating personnel. In medium- and small-sized public libraries,

22 COLLECTION DEVELOPMENT AND THE SELECTION POLICY

librarians are usually involved in the collection development process. However, in these libraries, selection authority is usually departmentalized into adult and children's areas.

□ ELEMENTS OF A SELECTION POLICY

Regardless of the type of library and the resulting reflective selection policy, a general outline should contain the following elements:

1. A statement of objectives, i.e., the purpose and use of the collection (home-use or public performance).
2. A clear statement establishing selection authority and responsibility.
3. A clear statement delineating how selection is performed. This should speak directly to review sources and in-house previewing or other methods, such as on-approval purchases.
4. Specific selection criteria regarding technical, production, aesthetic, artistic, and use-appropriate aspects.
5. Collection maintenance concerns such as branch activities, multiple copy acquisition and distribution, weeding, reassignment, gifts, and damages/replacement.
6. A statement regarding use of the collection, endorsing standard ALA intellectual freedom and objective/balanced acquisitions practices.
7. Reconsideration of material already in the collection statement and forms.

Results from a 1983 public library survey conducted by Elizabeth Futus indicated that more than 82 percent of the 123 libraries responding possessed some type of selection policy, with 24 percent reviewing their policy statements periodically and 19 percent reviewing them annually. Ninety-seven percent of the respondents had intellectual freedom policies in force, with slightly less than half having had materials challenged in the past five years. It is also interesting to note that Futus discovered large discrepancies between "what is written" and "what is practiced."[14]

COLLECTION DEVELOPMENT AND THE SELECTION POLICY

Within the limited scope of the policies researched for this book, I was sometimes confounded by the lack of depth exhibited in the audiovisual (videocassette) policies returned, regardless of library size. Shoreham–Wading River Public Library's policy reduced audiovisual materials selection to a single sentence (specific mention of videocassette or other formats were conspicuously absent): "Audiovisual materials should be selected according to the same standards applied to books, with particular attention paid to technical quality."

Book standards for the library were indicated as follows:

> General factors influencing book and material selection should be community needs, individual merit of each item, the existing collection, and the budget. Selection should be made by a professional librarian, choosing from standard and generally accepted lists, and recognized critical sources. The needs of the community should be evaluated continually and reflected in the acquisition program.

The above statements broadly define selection criteria and its limits, describe who does the selection, and provide for collection evaluation, but give no clues as to the state or makeup of the current collection or as to growth goals. In similar single-phrase fashion, the Findlay–Hancock County Public Library's Audiovisual Collection Selection Guidelines stated:

> Our AV collection reflects the informational needs and entertainment values of the public. Items are chosen in the public interest by professional evaluation. Selection of a work does not constitute or imply agreement with, or approval of, the content. Items represent a diversity of views and expression of artistic taste.

The above statement is quite broad in terms of selection latitude. It does not describe who does the selection, provide a quality selection base or any standard selection methodology, or define the collection and community needs in any way.

Iowa City Public Library's collection development policy presents the following Guidelines for Specific Collections:

> The library's collection of movies on 1/2-inch VHS video cassettes predates local video rental outlets and differs substantially from their collections. While rental outlets tend to emphasize multiple copies of recent popular films, the library's collection represents a broader cross-section of styles, nationalities, and periods. While critical acclaim and demand make a limited number of recent films appropriate, the higher unit cost of best-selling hits precludes emphasizing this aspect of the collection. To aid language instruction, foreign language films are purchased in the original language with subtitles when possible.

Iowa City has a varied non–English-speaking population, and the library recognizes its role in providing book and nonbook materials for this defined population segment, as far as the budget allows. However, the segment outlining this premise, headed "Other Languages & Language Instruction," curiously omits discussion of buying English as a second language or foreign language instruction materials.

These "phrase" policies have severe functional limitations because of gross omissions. It would be correct to assume that these documents do not accurately present the philosophy or selection activities and methods practiced in these institutions, and that those activities are, in reality, infinitely more complex.

VIDEO COLLECTION WEEDING

In my previous book, *Developing and Maintaining Video Collections in Libraries,* I stated that

> video collections are enjoying immense popularity, and libraries have not had to do systematic weeding because the collections are essentially self-weeding. That is, collections are constantly ravaged by significant damages

and losses. Also, the collection sizes, compared to materials budget allotments have not reached a point where "excess" or superficial items are being purchased rapidly.[15]

While for most libraries this precept would still hold true, many libraries have collections that are eight to ten years old, and number as many as 5,000 to 20,000 volumes. For these libraries and the many others that will reach similar collection-size plateaus in the near future, weeding (or deaccession) is an important concern.

A well-developed collection development policy and atunement to patron needs will reduce a library's chances of acquiring slow and nonmoving titles, but mistakes are bound to happen. Popularity shifts will undoubtedly occur, and future advances in technology may diminish the overall popularity of the videocassette in American society. Many librarians have a tendency to treat videocassettes as fragile items to be kept under lock and key. Like other audiovisual items, they may be kept even when they contain outdated information or are in poor condition. Videocassettes should be treated like any other medium: if a title contains outdated information, it should be withdrawn and put in an annual book sale. Weeding is an essential part of collection development and one that will ultimately contribute to building a strong, well-used collection.

Weeding is defined as "the practice of [purging from the collection,] discarding or transferring to storage excess copies, rarely used and non-used materials."[16] The term purging refers to withdrawing the item entirely, while storage refers to maintaining items in a second level of access—usually a warehouse. Warehousing videocassettes for long periods of nonuse poses problems. The magnetic tape and cassette parts must be "exercised" every so often to keep them in proper working order. Also, proper temperature and humidity levels must be maintained for long-term (five- to ten-year) storage. These requirements make long-term storage costly and undesirable for most public and school libraries.

Practically and politically speaking, the development of library collections is a numbers game. While not indicative of quality, title/volume counts are used as positive corollaries reflecting effective service. Many times, increased funding is based solely upon these numbers, using the rationale that increasing the number of volumes will also increase circulation. In the past, theft, vandalism, damage, loss, and unreturned titles have made it largely unnecessary for libraries to perform annual or systematic (continuous) weeding of the videocassette collection. Today, however, the growth of video collections, combined with the lessened novelty of videos, is forcing librarians to consider weeding as a viable collection maintenance function.

Every collection development policy should contain a section that delineates an active, continuous weeding procedure. Unfortunately, there exist two natural weeding "laws" that every experienced librarian knows:

1. No matter how outdated or strange an item may seem, at least one person will find it valuable.
2. No matter how long an item has remained unused, ten minutes after it has been discarded, one person will walk in and ask for it.

Lazy librarians, like lazy gardeners, will find that weeding only gets harder through neglect.

□ WEEDING GOALS

Weeding can encompass one or more of the following goals:

1. Collections should be weeded gingerly, by professional librarians, using good, subjective judgment, not rules.
2. Collections should be weeded so that they are maintained at a predetermined physical size.
3. Library collections should include only those titles likely to provide the maximum circulation (demand versus quality).

COLLECTION DEVELOPMENT AND THE SELECTION POLICY

4. Weeding should increase circulation. The assumption here is that, by getting rid of the noncirculating items, browsing will be positively affected, increasing the likelihood of patrons finding the items they want. Even if circulation stays constant, the decrease in title/volume count will reflect positively on statistical counts such as the turnover rate (circulation divided by volume count).
5. Collections should be weeded so that speed of access is increased and retrieval improved.
6. Those items least likely to be used in the future should be removed. In contrast with the goals of maintaining a collection at a predetermined size, this goal tries to identify a core collection that will satisfy 95 to 99 percent of the present and future use demands.[17]

Carol Mahon identifies five reasons librarians weed:

1. To make the collection more appealing in terms of look and interest
2. To make space for more valuable items
3. To make the collection more current and accurate
4. To encourage patrons to respect the collection by reinforcing items in number 1
5. To assure that full shelves are not just an illusion of a good library[18]

Stanley J. Slote cites five approaches to weeding:

1. Subjective Weeding—using a series of rules, principles, or guides, and a large amount of subjective judgment.
2. Age—items are weeded according to copyright date or date of acquisition. Age data is often combined with subjective weeding and shelf-time periods.
3. Shelf Time—the length of time an item remains unused on the shelf between circulations. In practice, it is not the shelf time that is measured but the last circulation period related to the current date, or the overall circulation frequency measured over a title's shelf life. An arbitrary cutoff point is established and items weeded that fall below that cutoff line.

4. Mathematical Approaches—complex formulas or models based on several variables such as shelf time, turnover rates, age, and historical use patterns.
5. Combined Criteria—the use of shelf time and copyright date, or other combinations.[19]

Today, many libraries possessing video collections have not yet passed the "core collection" or the "collection most likely to be used by patrons" level. They are still building their collections in terms of demand titles, filling in collection gaps, and purchasing for greater subject/genre breadth and depth. The basic assumption of weeding is that the value of an item to patrons can be estimated from its past use in terms of circulation. Most of the controversy over the weeding process surfaces when discussing the most effective way of predicting future use.

Use patterns can be recreated and analyzed in one of two ways. The historical reconstruction approach examines the entire use pattern of an item since its acquisition, while the current-circulation method looks at a recent period of circulation (usually the most recent few days or weeks) and assumes that the present use pattern is a valid sample. The weakness of the latter method is the disregard of seasonal use patterns. Towson's video weeding method, contained within the Baltimore County Public Library's selection policy, is an example of the current-circulation method.

Studies have indicated that shelf time is the most acceptable variable for identifying core collections. The age of items was found to be somewhat predictive of future use, but generally of little consistent value. Past use patterns are highly predictive of future use, but the current-circulation method is also valid in predicting use.[20]

□ WEEDING METHODS

All weeding methods work in a similar manner: they analyze either the entire collection or representative samples for use pattern data, seeking indications of future use. These averages or composite data are used as a standard against which

COLLECTION DEVELOPMENT AND THE SELECTION POLICY 29

to assess all other titles within that respective collection. To a large degree, the amount of work required in weeding depends not only upon the methods used but also on the preparation for using those methods.

For example, at the Decatur (Illinois) Public Library, a continuous weeding process was a logical outgrowth of the collection development process (see Fig. 2.1). A computerized circulation system was used to set up various statistical codes by genre and Dewey subject classes. Accurate counts of titles/volumes held within those respective genres and subjects were kept continuously, along with the acquisition date of every volume. Average turnover rates (genre/subject total circulation during a predetermined time period, such as one year, divided by the total volumes in that genre/subject during that same time period) could be easily calculated. Because different subjects and genres vary in popularity, it would be unfair to compare, for example, a popular feature video with a travel video. Therefore, statistical breakdowns by genre/subject represent a logical approach.

In Fig. 2.1, the suspense genre is represented by 60 volumes. Given a total life-of-circulation suspense genre circulation of 2,900, per volume turnover rate would be 48 (2,900 ÷ 60). The result is divided by the average number of months held in the collection (use 19). The average monthly circulation is 48 divided by 19, or 2.5 circulations. Thus, in this manner, individual titles within the suspense genre can be assessed against the standard of 2.5 circulations per month. Any title with less than this monthly circulation may be a candidate for deaccession if popularity is the only variable. Also, circulation of similar subject/genres should be more valid and representative of the entire collection.

FIG. 2.1 Sample Video Circulation Statistics Form

NO. D.D.C.	NO. OF TITLES	NO. OF VOLS.	MONTHS HELD IN COLLECTION	TOTAL CIRCULATION	AVG. CIRC.
130–139	25	25	12, 15, 2	6, 5, 0	2.8
Suspense	40	60	12, 24, 20	40, 52, 14	15

Weeding methods will depend, to a great extent, on the type of circulation system the library uses. Checkout (book) cards make historical reconstruction implausible, especially for videocassettes, because of the sheer number of circulations during a short time period, and the lack of cards providing complete records for a majority of the collection. Visual identification means, such as spine labeling (colored dots, etc.) would be an excellent alternative. Sampling, rather than measuring the entire collection for average use patterns, is a good method for determining use patterns in noncomputerized circulation situations. Care must be taken that the sample is an accurate indicator of the entire collection. Usually, a random sample of 20 percent is considered an accurate sample; therefore, in a collection of 500 titles, the sample should consist of at least 100 titles. The sampled titles must not reside in similar shelf locations, and should be representative of the genre/subject collection makeup.

Slote recommends that weeding for books be done at the 96 percent keeping level; that is to say that, theoretically, the core collection retained after weeding will represent 96 percent of the collection's former use (circulation). The noncore collection, now weeded, represents 4 percent of that usage.[21] Stanley J. Slote's book *Weeding Library Collections—II*, provides excellent discussion of and examples of weeding techniques that work equally well for videocassettes and books.

☐ SPECIFIC WEEDING CRITERIA

The following weeding criteria should be used only as a guideline, since every library has variables that will affect the criteria. The librarian should establish objectives for weeding, such as:

1. Subject—accurate and up-to-date, suitable for audience.
2. Format—disc, VHS, Beta, etc.
3. Age and Physical Condition—is the tape working properly? Special consideration should be given to videocassettes in the collection more than five years old—these

COLLECTION DEVELOPMENT AND THE SELECTION POLICY

may be candidates for weeding. The patron damage evaluation report (see Fig. 2.2) can be of vital assistance in flagging potential candidates for content weeding.

4. Use—circulation. Special consideration should be given to videocassettes circulated more than 200 times, because they may be candidates for weeding. Weeding of duplicate volumes should also be done based on average circulation.

Videocassettes present problems with categories 1 and 3 because they must be physically viewed to obtain an accurate assessment of their content or condition. If patron damage reports, visual inspection upon circulation return, and damage logs are kept as needed, the process of weeding by damage will largely take care of itself. Practically speaking, shelf life for a prerecorded VHS videocassette is one to five years, with an average of 100 to 250 circulations. Deaccession after this time should be considered, but not before visually examining the tape for wear.

FIG. 2.2 Model Patron Damage Evaluation Form

Please complete this form. It will help us maintain the video collection and provide you with better service.

Title _____ Date _____

Call No. _____ Copy No. _____

Did you experience any trouble with this tape?   YES   NO

Please describe/circle:

visual tracking lines in picture   no sound

fuzzy picture   would not play

lots of dropout   tape torn/crinkled   tape off spool

cracked case   other (please describe)

Describe any content problems/inaccuracies

Would you check this title out again?   YES   NO

Weeding based on content is the hardest to discern in visual media because the librarian must have a thorough knowledge of each title's content, be willing to view the program in its entirety, or rely on patron observations concerning content. Videocassettes pose a particular problem for determining currency. Visual presentation style, costuming, special effects, and language use are the major factors that date visual material. Even though the content may be accurate, today's teens do not want to be taught study skills by a man in bell-bottom slacks and hippie beads. Information may be inaccurate because of new discoveries and theories. Sometimes, however, this information is retained to provide valuable archival information about society during a particular time period.

In the early days of videocassettes, many titles were video transfers from 16mm film. As such, they were already dated, and many of them possessed primitive graphics and titling, and antiquated presentation styles. Because of the diversity and depth of titles available today, these titles, unless historically relevant, should be weeded, and new titles purchased to take their place.

In any method of weeding, it is likely that some items that are removed would have been used had they not been weeded. However, by using combinations of the above techniques and by weeding continuously, rather than once annually, this hazard can be largely avoided. In order to weed effectively, certain objectives, such as use or content currency, must be established. The collection should be broken down into small, workable subject/genre sections that can be easily evaluated. To ensure continuity, one person should be in charge of the weeding program, even though several people may be working on individual sections.

It may be helpful to imagine the library as a profit-making business. It is expensive to keep materials on the shelf, and just as businesses cannot afford to keep unpopular inventory, neither can libraries. Granted, historically and/or locally significant items should be kept, but the entire collection should not be considered historical. Although wise, well-

planned selection can act as an effective counterbalance and prolong the life of a collection, some weeding will eventually be needed. Weeding should thus be considered a positive public relations tool that helps keep a library's inventory current, popular, and responsive to patron demand.

IN-HOUSE PREVIEW/EVALUATION

In-house preview is a viable method of evaluation, although it involves staff time and documentation. However, most home-use-only videos are not available for preview, leaving this method open only for the higher-priced, public performance (producer-sold) titles. It is vitally important that the same standards applying to judging media quality through written review evaluation be applied to previewing as well. Figures 2.3 and 2.4 are sample in-house preview forms adapted from the American Film & Video Festival Evaluation form(s). They cover technical, content, and aesthetic aspects.

SUMMARY

A well-defined collection development and selection policy enables librarians to express the library's clearly defined goals in terms of specific materials that will satisfy those goals. It reflects the library's philosophy, and functions as a tool for standardization and maintenance of consistency. It also presents a dynamic statement useful in daily work as well as in a promotional service document for patrons. It is vitally important that the policy accurately reflect the structure, departmentalization, and dynamics of the library in order to be effective. Finally, the policy provides a means for responding positively to change and to community questions and concerns.

COLLECTION DEVELOPMENT AND THE SELECTION POLICY

FIG. 2.3 Model Library Preview/Evaluation Form

Film/Video Title _____

Distributor _____ Running Time _____

Copyright/Release Date_____ Color_____ B/W _____

Subject/Genre _____

Previewer's Name _____ Date _____

SPECIFIC CRITERIA EVALUATION   (Poor 1–Superior 5 / NA)

A. Programming Possibilities   _____

B. Suitability for Intended Audience   _____

C. Comparison with Others   _____

D. Editing/Camerawork/Special Effects   _____
E. Sound/Music   _____
F. Content-Coverage Thoroughness   _____
G. Animation/Dramatic/Live-Action Style   _____

GENERAL EVALUATION   (Poor 1–Superior 5 / NA)

A. Structure   _____

B. Clarity of Presentation (Content)   _____

C. Script   _____

D. Performance/Narration   _____

E. Originality/Creativity   _____

F. Technical Qualities   _____

G. Accuracy of Content   _____

H. Timeliness   _____

I. Usability for Collection   _____

J. Interest Level for Intended Age Group   _____

K. Fills Collection Gap   _____

L. Aesthetic Qualities   _____

Brief Annotation and Critical Notes: (on verso)

Recommended for Purchase: YES   NO   Possible Reconsideration

COLLECTION DEVELOPMENT AND THE SELECTION POLICY   35

FIG. 2.4   Model Media Preview/Evaluation Form for Schools

Film/Video Title _____

Distributor _____ Running Time _____

Copyright/Release Date _____ Color _____ B/W _____

Subject/Genre _____

Previewer's Name _____ Date _____

SPECIFIC CRITERIA EVALUATION   (Poor 1–Superior 5 / NA)

A. Programming Possibilities   _____

B. Suitability for Intended Audience   _____

C. Comparison with Others   _____

D. Editing/Camerawork/Special Effects   _____

E. Sound/Music   _____

F. Content-Coverage Thoroughness   _____

G. Animation/Dramatic/Live-Action Style   _____

GENERAL EVALUATION   (Poor 1–Superior 5 / NA)

A. Structure   _____

B. Clarity of Presentation (Content)   _____

C. Script   _____

D. Performance/Narration   _____

E. Originality/Creativity   _____

F. Technical Qualities   _____

G. Accuracy of Content   _____

H. Timeliness   _____

I. Usability for Collection   _____

J. Interest Level for Intended Age Group   _____

K. Fills Collection Gap/Curriculum Need   _____

L. Aesthetic Qualities   _____

List specific classes/curricula in which you would use this video: _____

Would you recommend this video to other instructors?   Yes   No

List names/classes: _____

Brief Annotation and Critical Notes: (on verso)

Recommended for Purchase: YES   NO   Possible Reconsideration

SAMPLE COLLECTION DEVELOPMENT, GENERAL SELECTION, VIDEO SELECTION, AND WEEDING POLICIES FOR PUBLIC LIBRARIES

☐ VIDEO COLLECTION DEVELOPMENT POLICY
SKOKIE (ILLINOIS) PUBLIC LIBRARY

The following video collection development segment is excerpted from the larger collection development policy of the Skokie Public Library, Skokie, Illinois. Written by the various Department Heads with assistance from the Coordinator of Collection Development, the policy provides a clear mission, historical selection perspective, current status, and goals toward the collection's future. It was developed using information from the book *Developing Library and Information Center Collections*, by G. Edward Evans. The format is true to the style of a collection development policy, integrating all of the beforementioned elements into a solidified plan rather than tacking a mission statement and long- and short-range goals onto a selection policy.

The wording is at times very specific and at other times very broad, but carefully considers the nonfiction/feature collection proportions and ultimate collection size, and specifically lists selection sources by title. The document has two strong points: It is written in plain language, easily understandable by both librarians and patrons; and it is very simple, successfully documenting and analyzing some very complex and intense decisions, goals, and questionnaire results, and stating them in nonabstract, concrete language.

Specifics to be added, of course, depend on each library's collection. Film genres might be highlighted with a discussion on the extent of collection development within. Acquiring videos for identified patron groups (the hearing-impaired are mentioned in the policy), such as foreign language-speaking groups, particular targeted minorities, or age groups (such as youths or senior citizens), might be

further developed. As a rule of thumb, the verbal detail and collection component breakdowns should increase only in relationship to the current size and the expected growth of any collection (or part thereof), and the expected goals of that collection.

Collection Development Policy
Skokie Public Library
(Excerpts)

Definitions of Collection Levels

The definitions for collection levels used in this plan have been adapted from the collection levels in the American Library Association's *Guidelines for the Formulation of Collection Development Policies* (first edition). Since these definitions are designed for academic libraries, they were modified for use with Skokie Public Library's collection. The definitions were modified to describe the dual nature of public library collections that have materials on subjects that can fit into an academic scheme of learning from introductory through advanced research, and that also have materials on popular, nontechnical, high-interest subjects that do not readily lend themselves to systematic, hierarchical study. For example, subjects such as logic, chemistry, linguistics, architecture, etc., can be studied in an organized manner that leads the learner from a basic level on to a research level of study, and materials can be selected on all of these levels. In contrast, subjects such as cooking, woodworking, fiction, feature films on video cassette, etc., are explored in a less structured manner. The materials selected to support this type of use cover a broad spectrum, but do not necessarily follow a progression of increasing difficulty wherein knowledge at advanced levels builds on that acquired at foundation levels. In areas such as cooking or woodworking, advanced interest and research levels would include material for persons employed in the area or involved at the avid hobbyist level. Two different sets of definitions were written as the criteria for defining the adult and youth

collections. The following definitions are used by the Adult Services Department.

1. BASIC

A highly selective collection that serves to introduce and define the subject, and to indicate the varieties of information available elsewhere. The emphasis is on popular materials and/or materials that provide a general overview. It includes popular titles, significant works or classics, some major reference works, and a few periodicals in the field. Growth and development are kept at a minimal level.

2. GENERAL INTEREST/STUDY

A collection that is adequate to support general interest and initial study; or a popular collection of materials that will have a selection of the important current titles, which are consistently weeded. The emphasis is on developing a collection to meet general community needs. It includes a judicious selection from currently published titles, supported by selected, retrospective, significant titles; a broad selection of works of more important writers; a limited selection of the most significant works of secondary writers; a selection of major journals; and current editions of the most significant reference tools and bibliographies pertaining to the subject.

3. ADVANCED INTEREST/STUDY

A collection that is adequate to support study at post–high school or practitioner levels, or sustained independent study, and that is adequate to maintain knowledge of a subject required for student or occupational needs of less than research intensity; or a popular collection of materials that has a large and diverse number of titles representing many aspects of the subject, and some titles that will be kept for historical value. The emphasis is on developing a comprehensive collection that will support special users in the community, but will also cover the needs of a wide range of users. It includes a broad spectrum of current and retrospective materials; complete collections of the works of more

COLLECTION DEVELOPMENT AND THE SELECTION POLICY

important writers, composers, performers, or artists; selections from the works of secondary writers; a selection of representative journals; and new, specialized, and some older reference and bibliographic tools pertaining to the subject.

4. BEGINNING RESEARCH LEVEL

A collection that includes major published source materials required for independent research or graduate level study; or a popular collection of materials that is so inclusive and extensive that most works in the area are purchased and retained. The emphasis is on extensive and in-depth coverage of a subject, and the development of a specialized collection to serve highly specific and specialized portions of the community. Bibliographies, indexes, and databases of a scholarly or technical nature support research by leading to materials both within and outside the scope of the library's collection. Local materials both of general interest and of a unique and specialized nature should be included. In interpreting the assigned collection levels, the full text of the collection descriptions should be read.

Depth of collection is assigned on a 1 to 4 scale, but can be modified by a plus or a minus. This allows for greater flexibility in evaluating an area, because a minus next to a number means that the collection has less breadth (a range of titles at similar level of difficulty with a duplication of titles to meet need), less depth (a range of titles at different levels of difficulty), and/or lower retention of materials than the numerical definition indicates. A plus next to a number means that the collection has more breadth, depth, and/or retention of materials than the numerical definition indicates.

The ranking of the collections on three levels—past, current, and future—was adapted from the Pacific Northwest Conspectus Worksheets, which have two levels for evaluating collection intensity. Since this is the first time the Skokie Public Library has formally evaluated its collection, it was important to identify at what level the collection had been developed in the past (Past Development Collection Level), at what level selection is currently being done (Current Collection Selection

Level), and at what level the collection should develop to achieve the library's mission (Future Collection Development Level).

M. Jacob
B. Murphy
6/1990

Videocassettes

Description: The video collection consists of a mix of feature films, including current high-interest titles, old classics, and foreign films (40 percent); and nonfiction films, including self-help, educational, performance, how-to, travel, etc. (30 percent). At this time, new purchases are exclusively VHS. Demand for Beta has decreased. Little Beta equipment is being sold, and fewer films are being released in Beta format.

Influencing Factors: The library acquires and makes available videocassettes to serve the general information, educational, and recreational needs of the community. Numerous local video rental stores supply recent releases of the most popular films in greater quantity than the library. Quality films—those that exhibit "appropriateness and expected use and value to the collection through the long term"—are acquired for both adults and children. When available, closed-captioned films are purchased to meet the library's commitment to serve the hearing-impaired. Patron requests for specific videos will be considered if the film is appropriate to the collection for the long term. Changing technology in the video marketplace is a factor to be considered in the long-range development of the collection.

Selection Plan: Besides the standard selection tools, reviewing sources such as *Video Review, Video Librarian, Children's Video Report, Video Software, Variety, New York Times*, and/or other periodicals are looked at regularly. Publishers' catalogs (Video Trend, B&T, MS, Home Vision, Facets) and advertisements are also used to identify current high-interest releases, nonfiction films, and replacements. *Video Source Book, Motion Picture Guide,* and *Videolog* are referred to for retrospective selection.

Multiple (two to three) copies in VHS format are ordered only for high-interest feature films.

Retention and Weeding: The video collection is still growing, and only a moderate amount of weeding has been done. At this point, videos with little or no circulation, and multiple copies of former high-interest features, are considered for weeding. Weeding is an on-going process requiring approximately three or four hours per month. Replacement copies for missing, worn, and damaged videos are ordered only if the quality (appropriateness, expected use, and value to the collection through the long term) of the item warrants it. Sources such as *Videolog*, *Video Source Book*, and publishers' catalogs may be consulted before a title is withdrawn. The circulation statistics for Beta films will be monitored to see if continuing representation of the Beta format in the collection is justified.

Development Plan: The video collection continues to grow, with the emphasis being on the development of a well-rounded collection. Areas to be considered for retrospective development are old classics and/or films that represent outstanding technical and artistic achievement in cinema. A balance (via new titles, replacements, weeding) must be maintained among the three broad video categories (features, nonfiction, and children's). The video collection should grow to approximately 4,000, depending on the space available and new technology, which could supplement or replace videos. This is an area that will have moderate growth.

	PAST COLLECTION DEVELOPMENT LEVEL	CURRENT COLLECTION SELECTION LEVEL	FUTURE COLLECTION DEVELOPMENT LEVEL
Feature Films	1+	2	2
Nonfiction Films	1+	2	2+
Children's Films	1+	2	2

G. Boggs
G. Newhouse
7/1989

☐ COLLECTION DEVELOPMENT POLICY
LAKE COUNTY PUBLIC LIBRARY, MERRILLVILLE, INDIANA

The Lake County Public Library's collection development policy is broad, but clearly written. It provides broad goals (not objectives) with specific statements relating to selection responsibility, collection scope, and collection purpose. However, specific collections (except local history) are not delineated. Selection criteria are, again, very broad. Although it does not address the differences in media formats, the policy does an adequate job of emphasizing quality, basing selection on qualitative and measurable factors (although measurement/evaluation is not discussed). The policy also addresses all pertinent collection development activities, including weeding, reassignment, gifts, and replacement, with specific criteria given for the latter. Intellectual freedom issues (use of the collection by minors) receives substantial coverage, with various ALA documents endorsed; however, the Freedom To View document is not specifically mentioned.

Lake County Public Library
Collection Development Policy

Statement of Objectives

The primary objective for collection development of the Lake County Public Library is to provide the resources and services necessary to meet the educational, recreational, cultural, and informational needs of the population served, in accordance with the broad service goals of the library.

To support the primary objective, library materials are selected, organized, and made accessible in order to meet the diverse needs of the citizens of the Lake County Public Library District.

A branch collection is not as comprehensive as that of the central library. Material is selected according to the needs of the particular community, and in relation to the collection as a whole.

Authority and Responsibility for Collection Development

The ultimate responsibility for the selection of all library materials rests with the director, and, under his/her direction, is given to the professional staff, who are qualified for this activity by reason of education, training, and experience.

Criteria for Selection

Availability, suitability, and quality of the physical form. Suitability of subject, style, format, and use for intended audience. Critics' reviews and information in professional selection aids. Need for balance of subjects within the collection. Need for diverse opinions (minority and majority) on a subject. Reputation of author, publisher, composer, and/or performer. Public demand. Cost.

Collection Maintenance

Weeding—Lake County Public Library is not a library of historical record, except in the area of local history. To ensure a vital collection of continued value to the district, materials that have outlived their usefulness are withdrawn.

Reassignment—Materials that are no longer in active use at a branch may be transferred to the central library or to another branch at the discretion of the professional staff.

Gifts—Gift materials are accepted with the understanding that they will be used or disposed of as the library sees fit. The same criteria for their inclusion in the collection is used as for the purchase of new materials. The library does not provide an evaluation of any gifts for tax deduction or other purposes.

Replacement—The library does not automatically replace all materials withdrawn from the collection. The need for replacement is judged by the age of the material and the existence in the system of more current coverage of the same subject; availability of more recent and/or comprehensive materials, or similar

material in different format; number of additional copies available in the system; public demand for the title; cost.

Use of the Collection

The choice of library materials by users is an individual matter. A person may reject certain items for himself/herself or for his/her family, but he/she does not have the right to restrict access to these materials by others.

Responsibility for materials used by children and adolescents rest with their parents or legal guardians. Library materials are not marked or identified to show approval or disapproval of their contents.

The library takes no responsibility for copyright infringements and other illegal use of library materials by patrons.

Reconsideration of Material Already in the Collection

A patron who wishes to make a formal complaint about a book or other material may fill out a Patron's Request for Reconsideration form, and the matter will be reviewed by the appropriate department head. If the patron is not satisfied with the decision, he/she may appeal through administrative channels to the library board.

Once an item has been selected as qualifying under the selection policies, it will not be removed unless it can be shown to be in violation of these policies.

Intellectual Freedom Statements

The library endorses the following statements as approved by the American Library Association:

Library Bill of Rights (Revised)

Freedom To Read

☐ SELECTION POLICY
AMES (IOWA) PUBLIC LIBRARY

An abridged version of the Ames Public Library's materials selection policy is reprinted here as an example of a generic

policy covering all formats. The policy addresses specific departmental collections and, in the case of the media department, breaks the collection down into various formats, with each format receiving a brief scope statement.

The Ames Public Library materials selection policy is very complete. It possesses a well thought out mission statement; covers selection responsibility; interweaves the library's classification system; and discusses weeding, censorship, gifts, and collection development. However, the Freedom To View, Labeling, and Access for Minors statements are not mentioned, and specific selection criteria for videocassettes are not listed. Also, the current status of the collection in regard to current and future needs is not discussed.

Note: this document has been shortened in order to present only those sections directly or indirectly pertaining to the videocassette collection.

Materials Selection Policy
Ames Public Library
May 18, 1989

I. Mission of the Ames Public Library

The Mission Statement of the Ames Public Library, approved by the Library Board of Trustees, establishes the library's primary mission: to be a community information center. The library provides materials and programs that promote an educated citizenry and enriched personal lives. Materials are selected to help meet the *educational, informational, cultural,* and *recreational* needs of the community. The library is a place of continuing personal enrichment for all persons of the community.

The library provides access to information in the most appropriate formats, whether print or nonprint. Materials are selected in anticipation of and in response to identified community and personal needs. The library represents as many points of view as possible, irrespective of their general social acceptability, to provide a place where anyone may encounter the original, sometimes unorthodox, and critical ideas so necessary in a society that depends for its survival on free competition in ideas.

II. Responsibility for Materials Selection

Ultimate responsibility for materials selection, as for all library activities, rests with the Library Director, who operates within the framework of policies determined by the Board of Trustees. Direct responsibility for each of the collections rests with designated collection managers. The Assistant Director serves as collection manager for the adult circulating collection. The Youth Services coordinator is collection manager for children's and young adult materials. The Technical Services Coordinator is collection manager for reference materials, and the Media Coordinator is collection manager for the adult nonprint materials collection. Other staff members participate on selection committees for particular collections as appropriate, and all staff members are encouraged to suggest titles for purchase. Citizens are invited to offer suggestions, which are considered promptly for possible purchase.

III. Materials Selection Policies

GENERAL GUIDELINES:

The purpose of these materials selection policies is to guide librarians and to inform the public about the principles upon which selections are made. In its selection activities, the library emphasizes its *cultural, educational, informational,* and *recreational* functions.

The library provides a broad selection of materials to communicate the full complexity of the culture shared by the community. The library also collects materials that enable children, teenagers, and adults to educate themselves continually, as a vital supplement to formal schooling. An item has educational value if it contributes to the positive growth of a person, either as an individual or as a member of society. In addressing the cultural and educational needs of the community, the library recognizes the importance to a free society of aware and effective citizens, who are familiar with their past heritage and with the essential issues underlying decisions for the future.

The public library does not need to be, and cannot afford to be, a storehouse of last resort for the world's

great knowledge. Other libraries function to satisfy specialized research needs. But the library recognizes the fundamental *informational* needs of the public in an increasingly complex and technological society, and the unique community role that it plays in providing practical and immediately useful public, personal, and business information. The library provides reference staff and material as the budget will allow, and makes use of specialized reference and interlibrary loan services provided through regional, state, and national cooperative resources.

The library also recognizes the *recreational* reading needs of the community. Materials are selected not only for their permanent value, but also because of community demand. Citizens want to read the novels, be familiar with the ideas, view the video recordings, and hear the audio recordings that are currently popular in the nation's culture. It is the obligation of their tax-supported library to provide such materials, in sufficient quantity to truly meet the demand. The fact that an item will not be popular within a few years is not important in responding to what the public is interested in now.

Selection is a judgmental and interpretive process, involving general knowledge of the subject and its importance; familiarity with the materials in the collection; awareness of the materials available on the subject; and recognition of the needs of the community. Items are selected for various reasons, including permanence of value, currency of interest, diversity of viewpoint, and creative merit, but all items selected should have a reasonable probability of being needed and used by the local community.

Citizen needs are central to the selection process at the Ames Public Library. With finite staff time and materials funds, every purchase is measured in terms of probable use by the public. Procedures for selecting materials and evaluating the collection focus on quickly, accurately, and effectively anticipating public needs, as indicated by subject and title circulation patterns, reserve and interlibrary loan requests, explicit suggestions, observed failures in meeting requests for specific titles or information, and other user-centered measures. The

final and most telling expression of a public policy is through the allocation of funds. The Ames Public Library materials budget is allocated with particular attention to citizen use of the various collections and trends in user demand.

The library does not promulgate particular beliefs or views, nor is the selection of any given book equivalent to endorsement of the viewpoint of the author. Within the framework of the Library Bill of Rights and the Freedom To Read statement, adopted by the American Library Association, the library does provide materials representing all approaches to public issues of a controversial nature. The librarians and trustees are aware that one or more persons may take issue with the selection of any specific item, and welcome any expression of opinion by patrons, but do not undertake the task of pleasing all patrons by the elimination of items purchased under guidance of the policies expressed herein. To provide a resource where the free individual can examine many points of view and make his/her own decisions is one of the essential purposes of the library.

SPECIFIC CONSIDERATIONS:

A. The library recognizes the purposes and resources of other libraries and institutions in the community, and does not needlessly duplicate functions and materials.

B. The library does not attempt to acquire textbooks or other curriculum related materials, except as such materials also serve the general public.

C. Because the library serves a public embracing a wide range of ages, educational background, and reading skills, it provides materials of varying complexity.

D. The library responds to the special characteristics of the community in determining the public need for specific subjects and types of materials.

E. The library provides materials in any format that helps meet its objectives. Formats may include books, periodicals, pamphlets, newspapers, pictures, slides, films, music scores, maps, audio recordings, video recordings, and microforms.

F. Materials that are no longer useful are systematically weeded from the collection and disposed of accordinging to the policy for disposition of library material approved by the Board of Trustees.

G. The library depends upon a variety of resources in evaluating materials to be added to the collection, including reviews, patron recommendations, bibliographies, and media trade information. Bestseller lists and other indicators of potential interest are used to anticipate popular demand.

H. The library emphasizes expedient purchase and processing, so that materials are available at the time public interest in them is high.

I. Collection managers maintain collection development plans that specify the scope, activities, and goals of the collection management process for each collection, within the parameters identified in this selection policy.

J. The selection criteria described in this policy are used in the evaluation of gifts of potential library materials, within the framework established by the gifts policy approved by the Board of Trustees.

K. Citizen concerns about items in the library collection are dealt with according to the procedure set forth in [the Appendices] of this policy.

L. Items that are locally published or produced are evaluated by the same criteria as other acquisitions, such as probable citizen interest and permanent value. Locally created items are not given special consideration simply because of their local connection.

M. The library does not accept individual items or collections, whether temporarily or permanently, for the convenience of the members of particular organizations rather than for the use of the general public.

N. The library maintains separate collections on the basis of format, function, and age of audience. Materials with the same format and audience are integrated into unified collections, relying upon the Dewey Decimal classification system to organize shelf locations by subject. Separate subject collections are discouraged because they are difficult for users to find; they isolate items from their expected place in the

general collection, making browsing less effective in both locations; they are complicated and inefficient to maintain.

MEDIA:

The Ames Public Library Media Department collects, maintains, and circulates nonprint cultural, educational, informational, and recreational material. The department also loans audiovisual equipment to support the media collection. The collection includes formats that communicate through listening, watching, or computing. Although written materials occasionally accompany the audiovisual items, the media materials are largely nonprint, and most require electronic equipment to use.

Formats presently collected by the department include art prints, compact disks, phonograph records, videocassettes, audio cassettes, mixed media kits, computer software, video and Polaroid cameras, and a variety of equipment to support the circulating materials. Because of the long-term investment required to establish a collection in a new format, and the risk of investing in a format that might prove commercially unsuccessful, the decision to add a new format is made neither frequently nor lightly.

Heavy consideration in media selection is given to patron requests, particularly if those requests reflect current trends in audio or video usage. The Media Department emphasizes the currency of its collection, and frequently uses announcements or advertisements in media trade publications in making selections. Criteria for selecting media titles includes whether they meet the needs of the intended audience, popularity and timeliness, patron suggestions, favorable reviews, appropriate format for the subject matter, cost, and contribution to the collection.

Videocassettes are purchased in VHS format only. The collection is composed of theatrical and nonfiction items. Although popular titles are given significant consideration, the theatrical collection emphasis is on foreign films, classics, family fare, and highly acclaimed movies. The nonfiction collection is developed response to citizen demand. Leisure time activities and instructional materials receive the greatest emphasis.

The Ames Public Library also circulates a flyer to patrons that reinforces the collection development policy, makes the public aware of such a policy, and provides a communication vehicle for patrons to suggest videocassette titles and be apprised of their acquisition. Patrons should feel satisfaction that they have a voice in selection and that the library is working to satisfy their needs. In this respect, the flyer is a positive public relations tool.

VIDEO PURCHASE REQUESTS:
The Media Department accepts videocassette requests and gives them heavy consideration when monthly purchase selections are made. All selections are guided by a collection development policy. Briefly, that policy says the library acquires videos that are family entertainment, critically acclaimed films, foreign films, and current, in-demand nonfiction video topics. Because the media budget will support only a small video collection, marginal, expensive, or narrowly focused videos are not cost effective. Library users making a video purchase request can expect a response in four to six weeks.

SAMPLE VIDEO SELECTION POLICIES

The following represent separate video selection policies based upon each library's general materials selection policy.

☐ THOUSAND OAKS (CALIFORNIA) PUBLIC LIBRARY

This policy states a simple purpose and reinforces selection continuity by using premises stated in the library's broader Materials Selection Policy. It also covers the role of an alternative avenue (the Foundation) in selection. Throughout, selection priorities are correlated to budgetary decisions. The policy also provides a purchasing target of nonfiction videos. However, it mentions fiction videos only once, and then without defining classic or providing quantifiable selection criteria for the genres.

52 COLLECTION DEVELOPMENT AND THE SELECTION POLICY

While the above factors are noteworthy, the policy omits several major items:

- It does not describe who makes the selections and the manner in which selections are made, nor does it say who is responsible for selecting duplicates in the Foundation collection.
- It does not describe the shape, scope, or limits of the collection, nor state any goals for selection by genre or subject.
- It does not mention any quantitative selection criteria other than price.
- It does not state who retains control of the Foundation videos in the event of collection dissolution.
- It does not align itself with any Freedom To View or Access policies.

Further, the policy includes several phrases such as "[an] item added to ... [the] collection should reasonably be expected to pay for itself," "high demand," and "items that no longer meet ... needs," yet does not explain how these criteria are to be determined. The circulation policy is apparently included only to form a distinction between the Foundation collection and the regular library collection, and the recycling of revenue from the Foundation is not mentioned. Finally, it is difficult to comprehend the philosophy behind having one copy of a high-demand title available for free and another one available for a fee.

This policy is severely limiting because its premise is attached to negative budgetary constraints, "effectively putting a price on information and recreation needs" by format distinction.

Thousand Oaks Library Video* Policy

The Thousand Oaks Library circulates videos in order that people may educate and inform themselves, and

---

* Video refers to VHS format videocassettes.

also to support their cultural and recreational needs. Selection of all videos added to the collection is based on the Thousand Oaks Library Materials Selection Policy.

Due to an exploding video market and a greatly increased public demand, the library cannot meet all needs immediately. The Thousand Oaks Library Foundation and the Thousand Oaks Library, within the limits of their purposes and budgets, cooperate to provide as broad a spectrum of videos as possible to users.

Library Video Collection

1. The Thousand Oaks Library, with regular materials funds, will purchase videos for the collection for the same reasons it selects and buys books and other nonbook items.
2. Limited budget and high public demand require prioritizing requests. The following will be used as guidelines for selection:
   A. The Thousand Oaks Library will not purchase videos that are primarily designed for classroom use.
   B. Individual videos priced at more than $100 usually will not be considered for purchase. Series for which the price is more than $100 per part will not be purchased.
   C. Nonfiction videos of general information or cultural nature will be the primary purchasing target of the library.
   D. Due to the broad needs of the collection, the Thousand Oaks Library will usually purchase a single copy of a title. In order to augment the library's collection for high-demand nonfiction items, the Thousand Oaks Library Foundation may purchase duplicate copies and make them available to users at their customary fee.
   E. Nonfiction videos that are not high priority for library purchase, but that may have current public demand, may be purchased by the Foundation and supplied to the public through the Thousand Oaks Library Foundation's fundraising project (e.g., wrestling, music videos, etc.).

F. The library will purchase fiction videos of classic or community interest if these materials do not fall within the parameters of Thousand Oaks Library Foundation purchase.
3. Items purchased through the Thousand Oaks Library budget will be circulated free of charge to patrons. Fines will be charged for overdue material.

Thousand Oaks Library Foundation Collection

1. The primary purpose of the Thousand Oaks Library Foundation collection is to serve as a fundraiser for the Foundation's nonprofit projects. Fees will therefore be charged for all items checked out from this collection.
2. The Thousand Oaks Library Foundation video collection must serve a twofold and connected purpose; first, as a fundraiser; second, as an adjunct to the library collection for high-demand items that the library cannot provide through normal budget allocations.

Items added to the Foundation collection must serve both of these functions.

3. Each item added to the Foundation collection should reasonably be expected to pay for itself *and* supply income for the Thousand Oaks Library Foundation.
4. Nonfiction videos will be considered by the Thousand Oaks Library Foundation in order to meet high public demand for access to materials that the library cannot supply.
5. Items that no longer meet the Thousand Oaks Library Foundation's fundraising needs, but that have value to the overall collection, may be transferred to the Thousand Oaks Library's collection. Such transfers must be approved by the Thousand Oaks Library Foundation.
6. Foundation videos that no longer meet Thousand Oaks Library/Foundation needs, but are still in working condition, will be sold to provide revenue to

the Thousand Oaks Library Foundation. Titles sold will be listed and provided to the Thousand Oaks Library Foundation on a regular basis.

This policy will be revised on a biennial basis or as needed. Rev. 10/11/89

☐ FRANKFORT (INDIANA) COMMUNITY PUBLIC LIBRARY

This is an interesting policy. The goal helps to establish the collection's purpose, while the criteria list details quantifiable attributes and provides the collection with a purchase emphasis. Criteria speak to individual titles as well as to the entire scope of the video collection. The policy focuses upon the priority of selecting home videos while recognizing the usefulness of public performance titles. It also serves as a positive public relations document.

On the minus side, the policy does not establish selection responsibility. It fails to recognize that nonfiction and feature videos are different and should be selected using appropriate criteria—indeed, the terms nonfiction and feature are absent. It also does not indicate support for any Intellectual Freedom, Access, or Labeling documents, and presents no collection evaluation or weeding methodology.

Frankfort Community Public Library
Videotape Acquisitions Policy

Goal: To build a distinctive permanent collection of videotape programs that appeal to a broad range of interests and ages. This policy establishes criteria to help focus acquisitions.
Criteria: Videotapes purchased for the library's permanent collection should be

Alternative. The collection should consist largely of programming not readily available from other sources. Movies, music, and television programs are not a priority of the permanent collection, although a

sampling of such programming is made available to patrons through the Indiana Video Circuit.

Interesting. The emphasis should be on programming that is not strictly educational or strictly entertaining, but rather something of both ... that is, interesting. While entertainment programming is not a priority of the permanent collection, programs *about* music, movies, and TV should be included.

Effective. The permanent collection should emphasize programming that is especially well presented in video, and avoid programming that can be handled equally or better by other media. Tax guides, for example, are better left to print, while sports subjects are most effectively presented on video.

Appropriate. Consideration should be given to how tapes in the permanent collection are used, with short-term loan and referencing being most important. Documentaries, for example, are far better served by being accessible to interested individuals in the library than by being randomly broadcast. Dramatized fiction, with little reference value, should be a low priority ... although "video storybooks" should be included in young children's programming as an introduction to reading. In the area of how-to tapes, programs that are more general and informational should be favored over those with detailed step-by-step instructions that must be constantly referred to.

Affordable. To make the collection as diverse as possible, it is necessary to emphasize cheaper, consumer oriented, home-view-only videotapes at this time. Selected programs should be obtained with full rights for library or patron presentation, although such use should remain essentially the province of 16mm film for the near future.

Complementary. New tapes should either enhance the distinctiveness of the collection by adding to areas of emphasis, or purposefully increase diversity. All age groups should be considered, and patrons should be actively consulted. Most importantly, no acquisitions should be made haphazardly.

COLLECTION DEVELOPMENT AND THE SELECTION POLICY 57

☐ BIRMINGHAM (ALABAMA) PUBLIC LIBRARY

This policy provides an excellent example of a policy organized by medium, with specific sections speaking directly to video. By stating that "audiovisual material selection is consistent with the selection policies for other materials," the library reinforces selection consistency throughout its various collections, without having to restate many of the mutual principles set forth in each policy.

This policy illustrates that a document need not be elaborate in order to be effective. It is simple and concise, yet contains almost all of the elements of a good policy. General and specific selection criteria concerning production/technical quality and content accuracy as well as aesthetic qualities are included. The community is briefly mentioned in terms of 16mm and slide collection equipment availability. While collection goals are not specifically delineated, they are implied in the emphasis statement, where a rationale for inclusion is also stated. Intellectual freedom is also advocated. Replacements and gifts are discussed, and previewing is presented as an additional method of selection.

The policy is slightly disorganized and omits some important information. Selection responsibility is not established except in previewing. The entire purpose of the policy is to provide guidelines for purchasing materials. It would seem logical to list specific goals for each collection that focus and drive the overall policy. While the emphasis statement refers to educational and classic types, it does not discuss the current shape of the collection and its direction for the future. The bulk of selection criteria are listed on the first page; however, four professional journals are mentioned in the last sentence, which seems out of place. It would seem more logical to group all selection activities together, establishing selection responsibility and including a general statement about purchasing based on favorable reviews in authoritative, professional review sources. In-house previewing could then be mentioned as an additional selection method, followed by specific criteria for both reviews and previews. Listing specific review journals, other than as

examples, is unwise because doing so may severely restrict selection and cause the policy to appear unnecessarily restrictive to the public. Lastly, weeding and reconsideration of materials are not mentioned.

Birmingham (Alabama) Public Library Media Services Department Selection Policy 1988 Revision

Audiovisual material selection is consistent with the selection policies for other materials for the Birmingham Public Library. Audiovisual materials are chosen primarily for their informational and cultural values for all ages. Content, authenticity, suitability for the intended audience, and similar qualities are subject to careful scrutiny. Special criteria for selection include:

1. Content must be valid and contain no half-truths or generalizations.
2. Subject matter should be either timely or timeless.
3. Material should be presented in a manner suited to its content, with no condescension and no loaded words, avoiding cheapness, preachiness, and coy humor.
4. Material should be considered an art form and should be judged for its style, imagination, originality, and other aesthetic qualities.
5. Material should have the following technical qualities:
   A. Imaginative photography, sense of movement and change
   B. Good, clear, understandable sound
   C. Imaginative narration or dialogue
   D. Good color quality (black and white included)
6. Material should have unity and be a cohesive whole

The important factor in media selection is the probability of use in the area served. While video equipment is more accessible to most organizations and individuals,

we will continue to maintain our 16mm film and slide collections. Additions to these specific collections will be made only after careful consideration and evaluation of their use for large group programming. We will circulate our existing filmstrips, but will not make additions to that collection.

The video collection will meet the same criteria and selection standards as the other materials in this department. The emphasis in the video collection will be educational and classic in scope, with an attempt to collect those items not so readily available at local video stores. In addition to home-use videos for entertainment and education, we are committed to providing materials that are cleared for public performance and available for group showings.

Materials are selected to appeal to all age groups, with the emphasis on out-of-school programming. The library will not attempt to duplicate the collections maintained by various educational institutions in our service area; i.e., school curriculum centers and university media collections. Materials produced primarily for classroom use are not included because, as with other teaching material, they are the primary responsibility of the schools.

The principle of intellectual freedom applies to the selection and retention of all types of library materials. Special-interest materials, such as religious films, are acquired when they are of good quality, acceptable to many denominations, and explanatory rather than persuasive in nature. Replacements will be added when damaged materials are deemed worthy of replacement, according to the selection guidelines and circulation records.

Gifts will be accepted only if the library may dispose of them if their physical condition, obsolescence of the content, or failure to be of sufficient use to the patronage of the library makes them undesirable additions to the collection. They will be evaluated by the same guidelines as new purchases.

It is the policy of this department to preview materials before purchase, whenever possible. This responsibility is usually carried out by the Media Services

Librarian. In those cases where specific subject areas are addressed, another librarian may be asked to preview for content accuracy. Selection is frequently made on the basis of reviews in professional journals. These include *Booklist, Library Journal, Science Review, Video Librarian,* and *Landers Film Review.*

☐ PHOENIX (ARIZONA) PUBLIC LIBRARY

The Phoenix Public Library collection development policy represents a fully-developed selection policy for one format. It describes the VHS medium and presents general levels of collection development and target audience groups. It provides in-depth detail for each category/genre collected, in essence establishing goals (in some instances, quantifiable objectives, such as "20 titles annually") for those respective categories. Also, levels of comprehensive collection development are discussed in a logical fashion.

Specific review sources are mentioned with brief descriptions. The danger in listing such inclusive sources is that they may prove too limiting. Also, new sources are always coming on the scene, and traditional sources may cease publication, merge, or change scope. It is preferable to use general statements, such as "authoritative review sources by noted organizations, publishers, and individuals in the form of books, periodicals, journals, and television programs."

The Phoenix policy is strictly a selection policy; it does not discuss replacement, multiple copies, weeding, or gifts, and does not allude to a larger policy governing these activities. It does not address intellectual freedom concerns, nor provide a form for reconsideration of materials. In the sense that it professes to be a collection development policy, rather than a selection policy, it provides no evaluation methodology. It also does not establish selection responsibility. Overall, the policy is very well organized and logically presented, with in-depth coverage of the elements presented.

Phoenix Public Library
July 15, 1988
Library Staff Circular No. C40.1
Subject: Collection Development Policies—
½-inch VHS Videocassettes

I. Definition of the Medium for the Purpose of Clarifying Selection Responsibility

The videocassette collection will consist of ½-inch VHS videocassette materials. Because it is assumed by the library staff that this format will soon win over competing formats such as Beta in the videocassette market, these competing formats will not be purchased. Within the VHS format, the selector's responsibility will include all subjects, types of programs, and types of information.

II. General Level of Collection Development and the Principle Target Groups

The purpose of the ½-inch videocassette collection is to provide library users access to art and information in a visual format for their home use. Selection begins, however, with the assumption that the library cannot provide free loans of all the videocassette titles that the public would like to view. The selector must consider the other local film and video resources that are accessible to library users in order to avoid unnecessary duplication of holdings. The library does not intend to compete with or undercut the growing and prospering retail businesses that are renting videocassettes of popular feature films. The content of the videocassette collection is broad and spans all age levels. The emphasis of the collection is on obtaining the most critically acclaimed examples of film art available in VHS format. Only those feature films of the highest quality and critical acclaim will be selected. (The library does not collect ½-inch videocassettes specifically for the purpose of supporting the curriculum of local educational institutions.)

III. Aspects of the Videotape Collection That Will Be Developed at a Higher Level than the General One for the Subject

A. THE DOCUMENTARY

Documentary films have been defined as "a creative interpretation of reality." Documentaries of historical importance and those that serve an informational function will be collected.

B. PLAYS AND DRAMATIZATIONS OF CLASSIC LITERATURE

Plays and dramatizations of classic works of literature will be collected if they meet high standards of playwriting, performance, and cinematography. These include PBS series such as the *American Short Story* and *Masterpiece Theater*.

C. FILM STUDY

Only films that have proved to be of long-term or lasting value and have been produced at least 20 years ago are considered film classics and will be collected as examples of film study. These videocassettes should describe or illustrate the history and development of film as a source of information and as an art form, and should be listed in most books on film study. Because these films give an understanding of the history and development of film, they will be purchased regardless of the fact that they may not meet the latest technological standards for picture quality and sound. Videocassettes that have been colorized (changed from their original black-and-white format) will not be purchased unless this is the only format available. Classic silent films will be collected as examples of the earliest stages of filmmaking.

The collection will also include the most important works of acclaimed producers, directors, actors and actresses, or other significant personalities in the film world. Although many of these films were award winners, some of them may not have been well reviewed when they were first released. A number of factors have

made these films important today. For example, critical opinion may have changed or the film may prove to be an example of an important director's early work that sheds light on later productions.

D. LOCAL AND REGIONAL TOPICS

Videocassettes that deal with local and regional topics will be selected when available. Due to the limited number of these films produced, our standards of quality may be lowered to allow acquisition of these specialized videotapes.

E. HOW-TO

How-to tapes have been called "infotainment." A good how-to videotape must present accurate and appropriate material in an informative and entertaining manner. As more and more how-to and do-it-yourself tapes are released, it is important that the selector determine whether the topic of the videotape can be taught or explained better on a tape rather than in another medium.

On occasion, how-to tapes are produced by a specific company, and sometimes these videos may contain a brief commercial or feature a product. Usually, these tapes are less expensive because of this [sponsorship], and they may be purchased if they meet all other criteria for selection.

F. CONCERTS, OPERAS, BALLETS, AND OTHER MUSICAL PRODUCTIONS

Videocassettes of concerts and musical events must meet high standards of sound reproduction and performance. The selector must weigh the importance of the event in the music or entertainment world and determine whether the use of the visual enhances the enjoyment and/or appreciation of the musical event.

G. CHILDREN'S FILMS

The importance of the visual experience in the lives of children is recognized by the library. A videocassette with children as the intended audience must possess and

demonstrate respect for the child's intelligence, taste, and integrity. It should stimulate the child's senses and imagination.

As with other tapes in the collection, children's videotapes should utilize the film medium to its best advantage. Iconographic films, which consist of a series of still images, will be particularly avoided—there are other mediums (filmstrips, slides, and books) that portray this material far less expensively. Programming specifically designed to sell a product (e.g., He-Man, Transformers, and Care Bears) will not be purchased. Care should also be taken with titles in an ongoing series to be certain that new releases are up to the past standards of that producer.

IV. Aspects of the Videotape Collection That Will Be Developed at a Lower Level than the General One for the Subject

A. CONTEMPORARY AMERICAN CLASSICS

Motion pictures that have been produced in America within the past 6 to 20 years and have, over the course of time, gained in importance so that they regularly appear in cinematography texts shall be considered contemporary classics and added to the collection. All films selected should have a three- or four-star rating in at least two best sources listed in Section V. About 20 of these titles will be purchased annually.

B. AMERICAN FEATURE FILMS

Because of the vast number of recent commercial feature films available on videocassette and their general availability at Valley rental stores, the most rigorous criteria for selection will be applied.

1. Features must have at least three excellent reviews by the country's leading film critics.
2. Features must, in the opinion of the selector, be of outstanding merit and importance in the study of film and/or modern society. Whenever feasible, it is suggested that the selector have seen the film prior to purchase.

Features that have won a major award (e.g., [New York] Film Critics [Circle], Cannes, Golden Globe, or Academy awards) should be seriously considered. Only about ten titles in this category will be purchased annually.

C. FOREIGN FILMS

Videocassettes of foreign-made films can be an important source of information on a country and its culture. Because relatively few of these films are released in Phoenix, and these for only a short run, and also because many are not available in Valley rental stores, particular attention should be paid to obtaining a representative collection. All foreign films that have won a major award in their country or ours should be purchased. Foreign films that have received a three- or four-star rating in a best source book should also be collected.

In order to retain the integrity of the original version of a foreign film, the subtitled rather than the dubbed edition should always be purchased.

D. AVANT-GARDE/EXPERIMENTAL FILMS

The selector will, within the limits of budget and general selection standards, collect representative avant-garde and experimental films. These unusual films may be produced on a limited budget by a film institute or a university study group, and because of this, our standards of sound and picture quality may be lowered to allow purchase.

V. The Best Sources of Information for Collection Development in This Subject

A. PERIODICALS

1. AFVA Evaluations
Most precise and discriminating in its reviews. Also covers informational/educational 16mm film and video.

2. Booklist
Audiovisual reviews in which review constitutes approval.

3. Children's Video
Bimonthly reviews of children's videos. Each title contains producer, date, running time, recommended age group, and star rating.

4. Films in Review
Published by the National Board of Review of Motion Pictures. Reviews new films and presents articles on the film industry.

5. Film Quarterly
Published by the University of California, Berkeley. Provides articles on cinema of different countries and in-depth reviews of new films.

6. Library Journal
Audiovisual reviews.

7. Landers Film Reviews
Gives reviews, both pro and con, and covers titles (non-feature) that are available both in 16mm and video.

8. New York Times (Sunday videocassette reviews)
Excellent source for quality, critical, full-length reviews on videocassettes.

9. School Library Journal
Regular audiovisual section. One of the best sources for educational video reviews.

10. Sight & Sound International Film Quarterly
British Film Institute's film journal, providing in-depth reviews of new American and foreign films.

11. Sightlines
Quarterly publication of the American Film and Video Association. Gives reviews, lists awards.

12. Video Magazine
Popular newsstand magazine that not only reviews recent and older features available on video, but also lists monthly a wide variety of titles that are currently available for purchase.

COLLECTION DEVELOPMENT AND THE SELECTION POLICY 67

13. Video Review
Written for the home viewer; offers lengthy evaluative reviews on new video releases.

B. SERVICES

1. Librarian's Video Service
A jobber's annual catalog that preselects for librarians video titles in a wide variety of areas, from how-tos to features. Its special value is that it includes ratings, price, and running time.

2. Videolog
A subscription service, updated on a weekly basis. Gives annotations, release dates, and ratings. Tries to give complete coverage on everything in print, regardless of video format or subject content.

3. Ingram's Video
A weekly listing with annotations of the jobber's new videocassette acquisitions.

C. COMPILED REVIEW BOOKS

1. Kidvid: A Parent's Guide to Children's Video, by Harold Schechter.
Capsule reviews of recommended children's films.

2. Leonard Maltin's TV Movies and Video Guide, edited by Leonard Maltin.
The best browser's guide available. Over 17,500 films discussed, reviewed, and rated.

3. Movies on TV and Videocassette, edited by Steven H. Scheuer.
Similar to the Maltin guide.

4. Roger Ebert's Movie Home Companion, edited by Roger Ebert.
More than 700 full-length reviews, including some documentaries.

5. *Video Movie Guide,* edited by Mick Martin and Marsha Porter.
Similar to Maltin and Scheuer.

Carol Alabaster
Collection Development Coordinator

☐ BALTIMORE COUNTY PUBLIC LIBRARY, TOWSON, MARYLAND

Baltimore County's informal and organizationally unconventional policy covers many topics, including selection, weeding, acquisitions, and branch title/copy distribution. It also addresses collection development, the role of circulation in the entire process, and recycling of videocassette circulation revenue. It does not, however, establish selection responsibility, nor does it endorse any intellectual freedom principles. It also omits a reconsideration-of-materials policy. It is very specific at some levels, broad and ambiguous in others.

Baltimore County Public Library Videocassette Policy

I. The Board designates a Self-Supporting Video Collection, composed of both free and service-charge videotapes, using the following guidelines:

A. Systemwide, all government-issued videos or those in programs supported by the County will be free of charge. These include IRS videos for income tax preparations, and the drug abuse videos from the County's Office of Substance Abuse. As new titles are acquired in this vein or in analogous projects, these videos will be free.

B. At least one copy of every existing and new video title will be designated as a free copy systemwide. In additional, no less than 15 percent of each branch collection will be free, as designated by the branch manager across the entire range of video classifications. All free videos will be labeled No Service Charge on display boxes.

COLLECTION DEVELOPMENT AND THE SELECTION POLICY

C. Receipts from the service-charge videos will constitute the support for the entire collection, and will be placed in a special account. This account will be used to purchase new videotapes and to maintain the collection by defraying associated costs, such as processing supplies, display fixtures, labor and space costs, etc.

II. This policy shall be implemented as soon as possible following its adoption, and will be reviewed at staff or board request.

Adopted by the Board of Library Trustees, April 18, 1988
Revised January 16, 1989

BCPL Collection Development Guidelines for Videocassettes

1. Videocassette (VC) collections are designed to give library users access to materials in a visual format for home use.
2. The VC collection will consist of 1/2-inch VHS format tapes in all library outlets.
3. VC selection should be made to provide for the interests of library users as demonstrated by their use of print materials. Acquisitions will be made in line with the library's basic collection development policy, i.e., to make readily available to Baltimore County residents library materials proportionate to levels of demand and use. A representative collection of high-interest videocassettes is not intended to be competitive with retail rental video businesses. Retail businesses exist that handle every format of materials in the library's collection, e.g., book, phonograph record, audiocassette.
4. Content of the VC collection is broad and spans interests of all age groups. Areas for development are as follows:
    A. *Documentaries* of historical importance that serve an information function
    B. *Plays* and *dramatizations* that have classic appeal and long-term interest

C. *Film study* that describes or illustrates the history and development of the film as a source of information and as an art form
D. *Feature films* of high interest as a result of current reviewing media, and older feature films for comparisons with current films, e.g., theme treatments, director's emphases, and cast performances
E. *Children's films* that add to the visual experience in a child's development
F. *How-to* tapes that present informative material appropriately rendered in a visual way equal to or better than in a print source
G. *Concerts* and other *musical events* for which the visual enhances the enjoyment, appreciation, and understanding of the musical event
H. Tapes of *local* and *regional topic interest* in high demand, with at least a minimum professionalism in quality of production

The following section on selection represents internal policies and procedures, not just general policy. It melds board policy, collection goals, and scope, as well as providing a basic framework for internal procedures for acquisitions and selection.

SELECTION

Videocassettes are acquired through centralized selection using the attached formulas. Videocassettes are ordered every week, and we order approximately 70 new titles per month. Feature films are ordered by the prebook date listed in the vendor catalogs to guarantee receipt on the advertised shipping date. Thus, we receive our copies of titles on the same day the retail/rental outlets receive their orders.

Our video collections comprise 15 to 20 percent informational titles, 25 to 30 percent juvenile titles, and 50 to 55 percent movies (including feature films, foreign films, and classics). Of course, these percentages are flexible and will be altered to reflect industry trends and changing patron interests and demands. New titles are selected using these percentages as a guideline, and our

COLLECTION DEVELOPMENT AND THE SELECTION POLICY   71

collections contain a wide range of materials covering a variety of topics and interests. We purchase titles with all MPAA ratings except X [written before implementation of NC-17 rating]. Titles are considered for addition to our collection on their merit and are neither purchased nor excluded because of their MPAA rating. Any rating information included on the packaging is left as is, and we do not add any other type of rating labels.

New videocassette titles are selected by the staff in the Materials Selection Department with input from the branch staff. Branch staff submit title and subject requests on Materials Information Cards. Requests are researched, and the submitting branch is informed of the action taken.

Our approach to video selection is very similar to our method of book selection. For feature films, we begin by looking at vendor catalogs. Then we look at any reviews, box office sales data, advertising and promotion (available in vendor catalogs), and interest that may be generated by the starring actors. Information on feature films is readily available in vendor catalogs, *Billboard*, *Video Review*, and *Premiere* (to name a few).

In the area of instructional videos, we are working toward developing a comprehensive, interesting collection, paying particular attention to patron requests and subjects/titles that are ideally suited for video. Although there are some reviewing sources (*Library Journal*, *Booklist*, *School Library Journal*, *Video Librarian*), it is at times difficult to locate titles on specific subjects. Selection of titles in this area can require a great deal of searching, and may require previewing.

Although juvenile titles are being more widely reviewed (*School Library Journal*, *Children's Video Report*), it is usually possible to gather enough information from vendor catalogs to make a purchase decision. Our juvenile collection contains feature films, both live action and animated, cartoons, videos of juvenile fiction and easy books, and an increasing number of information titles on a variety of subjects from science projects to skateboards.

We usually purchase videos in the $9.95 to $99.95 price range. Most home video is priced within this range.

72 COLLECTION DEVELOPMENT AND THE SELECTION POLICY

Titles from vendors dealing primarily with the educational market are usually much more expensive ($100–$500), and often include public performance rights. We purchase a small number of these more expensive titles, particularly if they are all that is available to fill a specific need.

Sources (for titles, reviews, and industry information and trends):

1. Vendor Catalogs
2. *Billboard* (reviews; rental and sales charts)
3. *Video Review*
4. *Video Librarian*
5. *Library Journal*
6. *Booklist*
7. *School Library Journal*
8. *Children's Video Report*
9. *Premiere*
10. *Video Software Dealer*
11. *Variety Home Video Directory* (CD ROM)
12. *People*
13. *Video Marketing Newsletter*
14. *Roger Ebert's Movie Home Companion*
15. *Leonard Maltin's TV Movies and Video Guide*

The formulas for number of copies purchased for each branch [presented in Fig. 2.5] are based on percentages

FIG. 2.5 Baltimore County Public Library Partial Videocassette Purchasing Formulas for Branches

GENRE/SUBJECT	AR	CA	CY	DU	ES	LR
1. Special	—	X	X	—	—	—
2. Special	—	X	X	—	—	—
3. Classic	—	X	X	—	—	—
...						
7. Above-Ave. Feat.	X	3	4	—	2	2
...						
11. Blockbusters	4	7	8	—	4	4/5

(BRANCH CODE spans AR–LR)

COLLECTION DEVELOPMENT AND THE SELECTION POLICY

of video circulation. However, we also take into consideration the specific needs and interests of individual branches, and modify the formulas accordingly.

Branch code column numbers represent copy numbers reflecting branch circulation and video budget as a percentage of BCPL's overall video budget.

The genre/subject descriptors represent:

1–2: Special, limited interest, expensive, usually informational.

3–4: Classics, foreign films, most juvenile and informational titles.

5–6: Average feature films (current and older releases), well known classics and foreign films, popular juvenile titles (e.g., *Pee Wee Herman* and *Sesame Street*), older Disney titles, high-interest informational titles (e.g. pregnancy and childbirth and aerobics).

7–10: Above-average feature films, award winners, films with recognizable stars that did moderately well at the box office.

11–13: Blockbusters, top box office hits, new Disney titles. Video equivalent to *New York Times* best-seller list.

WEEDING

Weeding is based on several factors:

1. Condition
2. Circulation: Calculate an average turnover rate for various sections of the video collection. [A turnover rate is obtained by dividing the total circulation of a section (Dewey group, etc.) for a specified time period by the total number of volumes in that respective section during that same time period. Thus, an average circulation can be obtained that can be compared to each individual title's circulation.]
3. Representation: What other titles, if any, are owned? Is this a heavily requested subject? Is this a subject of seasonal interest?

4. Last Checkout Date: Establish a cutoff date when circulation drops significantly. [Towson's Video Weeding Method (Fig. 2.6) delineates various time period sets, then groups title circulation around those sets. A cutoff date is selected at which time weeding occurs. In essence, this method is similar to tracing the standard deviation or the deviation of actual scores from the mean (average).]

Branches adapt the above suggested guidelines to their own situations.

SYSTEM SUPPORT

BCPL has a Video Advisory Committee that meets approximately once a year to discuss the videocassette

---

FIG. 2.6 Towson's Video Weeding Method

1. The first step is to set up a calendar-type chart that contains about six weeks; separate weeks into individual rows.
2. The last due date of each video is then determined, and a hash mark is put in the space where that due date falls.
3. Once ALL videos have been checked, a stark cutoff point at a date, or dates, indicating below-average video circulation can easily be seen.

Example:

8/15–8/21	|||| |||| |||| |||| |||| |||| |||| ||||
	|||| |||| |||| |||| |||| |||| |||| ||||
	|||| |||| |||| |||| |||| |||| |||| ||||
8/8–8/14	|||| |||| |||| |||| |||| |||| |||| ||||
	|||| |||| ||||
8/1–8/7	|||| |||| |||| |||| |||| |||| |||| ||||
7/25–7/31	|||| |||| |||| |||| _____
7/18–7/24	||| _____ CUTOFF POINT _____
7/11–7/17	| _____

NOTE: It should be noted that BCPL has an essentially demand-driven video collection. Towson's Video Weeding Method tracks only the most recent circulation date, not the total number of circulations per title over a given period of time (it is not a frequency-based statistical method). In effect, it uses a timeline with an arbitrary "popularity" cutoff date that targets individual titles for weeding.

collection, policies, and procedures. Additionally, problems, suggestion, etc., can be introduced and discussed at monthly meetings of Managers of Branch Resources.

☐ MODEL VIDEOCASSETTE SELECTION POLICY

The following Model Video Selection Policy was formulated by combining two existing policies from the Seattle (Washington) and the Decatur (Illinois) public libraries.

The Community District Library Board of Trustees hereby adopts the following collection development policy on this date, December 1, 1987. This document will be used as a guide to direct the Library Director and all department heads in the various aspects of collection development, including: selection, acquisitions, and discarding of materials.

Purpose
The library acquires, makes available, and encourages the use of videocassettes to serve general information, education, and recreation needs within the community. The collection strives to complement, rather than to compete with, local video rental stores by offering a different collection focus. Materials in all genres and all subjects will be collected as long as the subject or subject treatment is deemed suitable to the video format. Currently, the collection is very general in subject/genre scope, and does not contain specialized material for the exclusive use of one particular group. Materials are collected on a basic level (i.e., a highly selective collection that serves to introduce and define minor subject matter, and to indicate the variety of information available).

As video matures and comprehensive subject videos and genre depth increase, the library will similarly improve its collection coverage. Materials selection is guided by a general design to maintain a 50/50 split between nonfiction and feature films representing a wide variety of general subjects and genres. The collection does not include materials purchased specifically for school or college curriculum use. The library asserts the fundamentals of intellectual freedom, and purchases

materials representing all sides of a subject/topic when possible. The library endorses the Library Bill of Rights, the Diversity in Collection Development Interpretation, the statement on Labeling, the Challenged Materials Interpretation, Expurgation of Library Materials and Freedom To View statements, and does not label or censure materials. However, the library does provide patron information on the catalog cards in the form of MPAA ratings, content annotations, and audience levels.

Community Served
Videocassettes are selected to serve the broad, general interest ranges of the District, which is medium-sized, with a 60 percent population of white-collar workers and 30 percent of blue-collar workers. Twenty-five percent of the population is black, while 2 percent is Mexican. English is a second language for much of the minority population. Illiteracy is 6 percent overall; 18 percent in the minority groups. Ten percent of the community is under the age of 18. Forty percent of the community has a library card, with more than 42 percent of those registered being female.

However, minority cardholders represent only 12 percent of the total. Latch-key children represent 6 percent of the total school population, and present a service problem in the library after school hours.

Structure
Videocassettes are made available in the AV Department of the Main Library, and through request at the two bookmobiles. Selection of materials is the responsibility of the AV Department Head.

Selection Process
The AV Department employs the AV Department Head to coordinate the selection, acquisition, and discarding of materials within the video collection. Items are considered for collection inclusion based on favorable reviews from authoritative professional selection tools. Regularly scheduled weekly selection meetings are held at which all the department heads gather to discuss and review potential purchases.

Selection Criteria

Generally, the selection of video follows the same standards as for print material; however, videos (composed of moving images) are recognized to have some fundamental differences, and should be evaluated accordingly. Video programs are evaluated as a whole and not on the basis of particular scenes or segments. A work will not be excluded from the collection just because it presents an aspect of life honestly or because it exhibits frankness of expression. An item need not meet all of the criteria to be acceptable. In some instances, materials may be judged primarily on artistic merit, or because of scholarship, or as valuable historic records, or as critical to the information needs of the community. In a few instances, the criterion may be substantial demand.

Because of the great diversity of materials, there is no single set of general criteria that can be applied to all items. Some items are judged primarily in terms of artistic merit or documentation of the times, while others are selected to satisfy the recreational and informational needs of the community. The library encourages purchase suggestions from the public, and will give them serious consideration. Selection decisions are based upon reviews in professional review magazines and books such as *Halliwell's Film Guide, The Motion Picture Guide, Library Journal, Booklist, Video Librarian, Video Review, Video Rating Guide for Libraries, Children's Video Report, Librarian's Video Review,* and others. Currently, only VHS videocassettes are included in the collection.

SELECTION CRITERIA BY SUBJECT OF MATERIAL

In selection of material by subject, consideration should be given to such matters as popular (and timely) demand for the item; relationship of the material to the existing collection and to other materials available on the subject; the likely attention of critics, opinion makers, and the public to the item; its importance as a document of our times; the cost of the item as compared with comparable material on the same subject; and the cost to benefit ratio compared with an alternative expenditure. Acquisition of such material will include videotapes of an informational, cultural, recreational, local

business, and instructional nature for collections that contemplate and emphasize serious use while recognizing also the legitimacy of entertainment purposes. Acquisitions are limited to works for which an acceptable level of quality has been determined in one or more of the following ways:

1. By the opinion of qualified reviewers in recognized, authoritative review sources. At least one positive review is required.
2. Through recognition by prizes, awards, etc., given by critical organizations, institutes, or associations of peers of producing artists, such as the New York Film Critics Circle, the Television Academy of Arts and Sciences, Cannes Film Festival, etc.
3. Materials reissued in video form from filmed material or reproduced 20 years or more after the original production shall be assumed on the basis of longevity of appeal to meet standards for acquisition.
4. Materials that have appeared on Public Television networks.
5. In-house review/preview evaluation by the Department Head.
6. If an artist, in seeking realistic representation of the human condition, includes material that is sexually candid or dialogue with vulgar diction, such inclusion will not be considered reason for rejection if the video otherwise meets standards for acquisition.

General quality criteria include the following:

1. Is of present and potential relevance to community needs.
2. Provides insight into human and social needs.
3. Accurately presents factual information.
4. Is useful for its intended audience.
5. Satisfies public demand resulting from the attention of critics and reviews.
6. Provides high quality performances and accurate content.

COLLECTION DEVELOPMENT AND THE SELECTION POLICY

7. Is produced with technical skill.
8. Provides a presentation most effectively or appropriately delivered by the video format.
9. Provides information or presentation that is unique to or only available in the format.
10. Currency and timeliness of the material. Videos on rapidly changing or ephemeral subjects should not be purchased.
11. Cost effectiveness of one media over another.
12. Weakness of the collection in a particular area.
13. Durability of the physical item.
14. Commercialism must be minimal, not distracting from theme or content.

SPECIFIC CRITERIA: NONFICTION, BUSINESS, CHILDREN'S, YOUNG ADULT, FEATURE FILMS, AND PUBLIC PERFORMANCE VIDEOS

1. Nonfiction—Nonfiction video is purchased when the format provides a useful and eclectic way of presenting information to a clientele. All general subjects will be acquired, with particular emphasis upon cooking, travel, craft how-tos, and sports videos. All video programs advocating exercise or special diets must receive certification, approval, or a favorable review from an authoritative subject source such as The Aerobic and Fitness Association of America or the American Dietetics Association.

2. Business—In association with the local area business reference area, the library will seek to acquire a wide variety of general business-oriented videos on subjects such as interviewing, resume writing, employee motivation and productivity, and management skills. Specific business-related materials are not purchased.

3. Children's and Young Adult—These materials should be useful and relevant to such patrons' everyday needs, interests, and activities. Children's materials will be purchased for the age group ranging from preschool through eighth grade. Special emphasis will be placed on a child's developmental needs for stimulation of imagination and mental growth. Video adaptations of children's books, folktales and fairy tales, animated videos, and concept videos [programs teaching basic

concept skills—such as shape, color, and number recognition—leading to development of specific skills] will also be emphasized. Titles that promote a product or are based upon a toy and used primarily as promotional/advertising vehicles will not be purchased. Young Adult material will emphasize current, popular, lively themes that contribute to the development and pleasure of this group. Also, programs concerning specific timely health, social, and personal issues of interest to young adults will be collected. Programs such as ABC's Afterschool Specials will be included for Young Adults.

4. Feature Films—Features will be purchased to satisfy the public's need for recreational materials, and to serve differing tastes and interests. Owing to the relatively high cost of video materials and limited library budgets, it is impossible for any library agency to adequately satisfy public demand for high-interest feature films. Classics; long-term, popular features and musicals; award winners; and other broad-based genres will be included. English-language features are emphasized; however, foreign film Academy Award winners are purchased in the captioned original-language form (not English-dubbed). Popular, ephemeral music videos will not be included.

5. Public Performance and Off-Air Tapes—Eighty percent of the titles purchased are designated home-use-only, and are purchased through standard vendors or direct from the producer/distributor. However, some titles are recorded off-air (when legally possible) and put into the collection.

Many titles include public performance rights, and these rights are indicated on the physical cassette as well as the videographic record; however, titles for the circulating collection are *not* expressly purchased for those rights. A separate budget has been established for purchasing videocassettes with public performance (non-theatrical exhibition) rights, to be used exclusively for in-house programming—especially for the Children's/YA departments—concentrating on Children's/YA literature adaptations. The library expects to expand this collection into areas of adult interest as well.

Collection Maintenance

FORMAT SELECTION AND MULTIPLE COPIES

Information in diverse video formats will be acquired and made available if the format is judged to be useful in satisfying the immediate and long-range needs of the community. Also, a substantial portion of the community must desire the format. Multiple copies will be provided based on demonstrated and anticipated user interest, availability of funds, and availability of similar items already in the collection.

REPLACEMENT OF MATERIALS

Programs will not automatically be replaced because of loss or damage. Replacement decisions will be based upon:

1. Demand for title (popularity)
2. Number of copies already held
3. Existing coverage of a subject/genre in the collection
4. Availability of newer (more appropriate, more accurate, or better-presented) materials on the subject

Weeding

Weeding or deaccession by virtue of damaged, lost, or not returned items is continuous. The circulation department works in concert with the AV department to visually inspect all videos upon return, and those damaged are sent to the AV department head for deaccession/replacement consideration. In order to maintain active, up-to-date, useful collections, selectors, as assigned, will periodically examine all video materials in terms of relevance to user needs and selection criteria. Last-copy and out-of-print titles will usually be retained if of local historical interest or significance, or if the information they contain is of use to the community and cannot be acquired elsewhere. Other factors to be considered include:

1. Lack of use (as measured by the turnover rate of the genre/subject as a standard).

2. Physical playing condition and age (acquisition date). Videocassettes exceeding 200 circulations are coded with a colored dot. Within weeding parameters, these are the first items to be considered for collection deaccession. Video Damage Condition Reports, included with each tape at the time of circulation, are examined for potential weeding.
3. Accuracy and datedness of information. Not only the information, but the presentation style of that information is important. The Video Damage Condition Reports also flag potential candidates for deaccession relating to subject accuracy and presentation style.

Evaluation

The collection is continually evaluated in terms of circulation performance, currency, content inclusion, scope and depth of coverage, and popularity. All subjects/genres are continually analyzed for subject strengths, weaknesses, and omissions. Patron suggestions also play an important role in evaluation. Continuous weeding and responsible replacement of damaged/lost titles aids in maintaining a collection that reflects changing community needs and library goals.

Gifts

Gift materials will be accepted by the AV department with the understanding that they become the property of the library. They will be evaluated against the same criteria as purchased materials. Donors may not place any special conditions upon the loan or handling of the items. Department Heads will make the final decision on use and other disposition of all donations, and will determine the conditions of display, housing, and access to the materials.

Materials Not Included

Works that include material that achieves its appeal strictly by sensationalism, erotic, scatological, or other cheap exploitive means. Material that is strictly ephemeral in nature and is dependent upon speedy acceptance encouraged by massive publicity will not be acquired.

COLLECTION DEVELOPMENT AND THE SELECTION POLICY

☐ ALABAMA PUBLIC LIBRARY SERVICE

While delineation of the collection by Dewey Decimal categories, genre/subject areas, or departments may aid in the selection process, another method of grouping by type (viewing level, specific audience, or video attributes) may be helpful. For example, a library wishing to serve a hearing-impaired clientele may single out closed-captioned videos in an attempt to focus acquisitions. A specific minority or foreign language–speaking group can similarly be emphasized. This method is especially useful for integrating objectives within specific categories. The Alabama Public Library Service employs such a categorization for its film collection that could easily be adapted for videocassettes.

Alabama Public Library Service Video Selection Policy

The content of the collection will be very broad and will reflect the Alabama Public Library Service's commitment to service to all citizens of Alabama, regardless of social, economic, ethnic, or educational levels. However, because of the film format, there is a need to make statements concerning certain areas represented in the collection. These statements are with regard to

1. The Documentary
Documentary films have been defined as "a creative interpretation of reality," meaning the presentation of information on any subject in such a way that the audience is thrilled and excited, and prepared to accept the information as important and having a bearing on their lives. A top priority in the Alabama Public Library Service's statement of purpose with regard to film is the information function. In light of this statement, the documentary film has a high priority in the total film collection. Additionally, documentaries of historical importance are collected to provide primary source material about the changing mores of man and society.

2. Business Films

Since service to business and industry is an important aspect of the library's objectives, business films will be selected that meet the library's standards of quality and usefulness, and meet the requirements of the state's business community. Films produced solely to train employees for specific activities will not be included in the collection unless they are multipurpose and can be used for a variety of programs.

3. Local and Regional Films

Since the Alabama Public Library Service serves as the resource center for the entire state, the acquisition of films about this area and films made by filmmakers within the state will be given a high priority.

4. Nonverbal Films

Nonverbal films are defined as those films that communicate pictorially, making maximum use of music and special sound effects, and using speech sparingly, if at all. Nonverbal films with appropriate subject, sound, and technical excellence that appeal to many levels of experience, crossing the barriers of age, education, physical handicaps, language, and culture, will be collected.

5. Captioned Films

Recognizing the need of service to those individuals with the physical handicap of deafness within the state, the Alabama Public Library Service will collect captioned films on many topics and issues.

6. Film Study

There is a growing awareness of film as a source of information and as an art form in today's society. Films that describe the history and development of the film, filmmaking, filmmakers, and other significant personalities of the film world are important to the scholar. The Alabama Public Library Service collection will include films in the area of film study to stimulate further study and to provide a frame of reference from which the individual will be better able to judge quality,

to develop critical judgment, and to make his or her own judgments.

7. Feature Films
Feature films, approximately 90 minutes in running time, are motion pictures produced for showing in commercial movie theaters and, more recently, for telecasting. The chief aim of the feature film is to entertain. The Alabama Public Library Service will acquire as available those feature films that enhance the total collection and fulfill the library's statement of purpose.

8. Holiday Films
Films that are solely concerned with a specific holiday and for which there is an acute demand only at the time of those celebrations are termed holiday films. A small collection of holiday films is provided, but since the content of these films limits their use, they will not be considered a high priority in the collection.

9. Children's Films
The importance of the visual experience in the lives of children is recognized by the Alabama Public Library Service. Also recognized is the responsibility to select, circulate, and program films that make a contribution to the full maturing of the child. A film with children as the intended audience must possess and demonstrate respect for the child's intelligence, taste, and integrity. It should contribute positively to the child's self-image and expanding awareness, and stimulate the child's senses and imagination. The film should leave the child with increased understanding and joy in life and things in this world.

Instructional films [i.e., concept films] that teach a specific skill or impart the same type of information contained in a textbook or training manual will not be included unless they serve a variety of purposes. The decision and responsibility for acquiring curriculum-related films for classroom use is the prerogative of the state's public schools.

10. Controversial Films

Areas such as politics, social problems, religion, psychology, science, sex, drug use and abuse, and ethics are subjects on which many opinions have been expressed in the past and are currently being formed and articulated. Alabama as a state is composed of a wide range of peoples, with widely divergent opinions, educational levels, age levels, tastes, and interests. The Alabama Public Library Service has the responsibility to provide films for informational and educational purposes, with the realization that not all individuals will agree with all the ideas or methods of presentation contained in the collection.

While every effort will be made to present all aspects of an issue, excluded from the collection will be any film that has the overall intent to belittle or denigrate the ideas, opinions, or practices of individuals or groups [unless portrayed in an accurate historical context].

11. Sponsored Films

Films funded by organizations and business with a specific aim in mind are referred to as sponsored films. Such films that meet the criteria for film selection and that add scope to the collection will be gratefully accepted by Alabama Public Library Service, provided no stipulations are made governing their use.

Any film with obvious and overt advertising, or any film that solicits funds for any cause or organization, will not be accepted.

☐ WEEDING POLICY
GRANT WOOD AREA EDUCATION AGENCY

The Grant Wood Area Education Agency weeding policy provides an excellent weeding rationale complete with lucid, but not overly restrictive or specific, goals. The policy establishes who will be responsible for weeding, and provides positive, general weeding criteria, referring specifically to four easily measurable variables: curriculum relevancy, copyright date, physical condition, and circulation records. A positive effort has been made to correlate weeding with

selection in the weeding rationale, replacement, and weeding criteria sections. However, a general statement (such as: "Items not meeting current collection goals and objectives and/or specific, current selection criteria will be prime candidates for weeding") would serve to further integrate the two concepts. A section on weeding procedures, which is not a necessary portion of the board-approved policy document, is also included. Within the context of the entire document, the procedures reinforce the policy and demonstrate a logical approach to carrying out the weeding goals in a consistent manner.

While this is an excellent example of a general weeding policy, I feel that the procedures should include a vehicle for teachers to report damages and inappropriate/inaccurate information pertaining to individual titles, such as a damage report. Also, content curriculum relevancy could be more strongly reinforced by mention of any state/local curriculum documents currently in use (as comparison and standardization tools).

Grant Wood Area Education Agency
Weeding Rationale

One of the goals of any good library is to serve effectively by providing relevant, accurate materials and information. Maintaining such a collection requires active and responsible selection and weeding. The Grant Wood Media Advisory Committee, through its Ad Hoc Committee, established to examine current services, has recommended aggressive weeding of collections to maintain content quality.

Weeding is really selection in reverse. Instead of deciding what materials to add to the collection, weeding involves deciding which items should be withdrawn. In developing and maintaining a solid, well-balanced collection, judicious weeding is just as essential as wise selection. Even an occasional mistake in weeding is less serious than the cumulative effect of a cluttered, outdated collection.

Materials in the collections are evaluated on the basis of usage, currentness, content, scope, and depth of coverage. Just as materials should meet the selection criteria if they are to be acquired for the collections, so they should continue to meet these criteria in order to remain in it.

The professional staff is responsible for weeding the collections. Some of these decisions can be made independently with confidence. Other decisions should be made with the help and advice of individuals knowledgeable in specific fields.

The collection should be weeded in order to

1. Keep the collection reliable and up-to-date. Obsolete materials are a source of misinformation and, thus, a disservice to clients.
2. Use shelving, storage, and other space efficiently. Keeping materials that should be weeded is a nonproductive use of space.
3. Allow the professional staff to find materials that need repair or replacement. When the need for repair is detected early, the collection can be kept in good condition at a minimum cost of money and effort.

The two types of weeding used at Grant Wood AEA are defined as follows:

1. *Formal Weeding* of the total collection is completed systematically on an established schedule that is based on catalog release dates. This is an annual process for all collections but the K–12 Student Books Collection.
2. *Informal Weeding* is done continuously. Materials are checked as they are circulated, shelved, or inspected. Inspectors and clerks know which items need repair/replacement, and will forward them on to the professional staff for examination. The professional staff will determine whether the material will be kept or replaced based on the following criteria.

Weeding Criteria

1. CURRICULUM RELEVANCY

Content is unsuitable if it is not related to the curriculum, or the interests of the students, or the professional needs of educators. Materials that are suitable when they are purchased do not necessarily continue to be so. Changes in curriculum as well as changes and advances in various fields and disciplines may also effect suitability. Items are also considered unsuitable if the quality of the production is inferior.

2. COPYRIGHT DATE

Materials that present factual information must constantly be monitored for accuracy. Special attention must be paid to the rapidly changing fields of science, economics, geography, careers, politics, government, technology, etc. In these areas, the useful lifetime of materials may be very limited. (Example: An item that refers to the possibility of landing on the moon in the future.) Items with copyright dates older than 10–15 years, and not considered to be classics, are also considered for withdrawal. This especially includes materials containing sexist attitudes/information, geographically incorrect information, or out-dated clothing or automobiles, etc., that would effect viewer reaction to the material.

3. PHYSICAL CONDITION

Even with careful handling, materials become worn out. Film can only be spliced so many times before it becomes difficult to run through a projector. In addition, films experience color shifting with age.

Titles will not automatically be replaced because of loss or damage. Replacement decisions will be based upon the following criteria: (1) demand for the title, (2) number of copies already held in inventory, (3) existing coverage of a subject/genre in the collection, (4) availability of more current materials on the subject, and (5) age and topic.

4. CIRCULATION RECORDS
Items that have not circulated at all within the last two years, or less than five times within their lifetimes, will be considered for removal.

Weeding Procedures
After a decision has been made regarding what materials are to be withdrawn, the following steps should be taken:

1. Reservable items will be flagged in the reservation system, allowing them to be booked during the remainder of the school year. Circulating items will be noted and removed during the summer months.
2. Damaged items will be discarded as soon as they are replaced with new prints/titles, if it is determined to replace the title.
3. Earlier editions/titles will be discarded when revised, or new editions are received.
4. Items will be disposed of in a discreet manner. Generally, if the materials are not suitable for the AEA collection, they are not suitable for [other uses, such as a school district's or teacher's private collection].

References
Fitzgerald, Ruth. *Evaluating Media Collections.* St. Joseph, MI: REMC 11, 1988.
Scholtz, James C. *Developing and Maintaining Video Collections in Libraries.* Santa Barbara, CA: ABC-CLIO, 1989.
Slote, Stanley J. *Weeding Library Collections—II.* 2d rev. ed. Englewood, CO: Libraries Unlimited, 1982.

SCHOOL LIBRARY MEDIA CENTER SELECTION POLICIES

☐ SURVEYING THE FIELD

The only difference between school library media center and public library selection policies is in the defined goal statement.

COLLECTION DEVELOPMENT AND THE SELECTION POLICY 91

All other principles and cognitive elements apply equally to both types of institutions. Even small school district library media centers are like academic libraries or large departmentalized libraries, in that they receive selection suggestions from a diverse set of people, including faculty, staff, students, and their own staff members.

In 1985, Betty Kemp sent out a questionnaire to 1,000 schools nationwide, with 159 schools, representing 39 states, responding. Although the information is more than five years old, the situation has not changed significantly regarding selection. Following is a brief summary of some pertinent information dealing with school libraries and their selection policies:

- 30 percent of all respondents indicated they did not have selection policies.
- 10 of the 111 schools with selection policies had building-only policies approved by internal staff, with the remainder having district-wide policies approved by either the school administration or the school board.
- 17 of the 48 respondents without policies indicated that their districts were considering writing policies.
- 41 percent of the respondents with selection policies indicated that they had been written between 1980 and 1985, with policy reviews ranging from never to yearly.
- The most popular selection review sources for AV materials were, not surprisingly, *Booklist, School Library Journal, Media & Methods,* and *Library Journal.*
- The majority of schools did not require written reviews for selection. However, 72 percent of the respondents do preview AV materials.
- Over 84 percent of responding schools indicated they do their own ordering, rather than going through a district library services office. Also, most schools ordered directly from AV producers rather than from jobbers.
- Collection weeding was performed on an annual basis by 45 percent of schools.
- Finally, 79 percent of the schools had a formal plan for review of challenged material.[22]

☐ TOWARD A SERVICE PHILOSOPHY

As previously mentioned, the school policy differs from the public library policy only in the service philosophy regarding selection. Collections built to support the instructional programs of K–12 schools are usually expected to meet current needs with high-quality materials. Often materials are selected according to a collection development plan that adheres to district-wide policy while addressing the needs of the individual school.

To emphasize the level of quality expected in the collection, the national guidelines include the following selection criteria:

1. Intellectual content of the material: scope, arrangement and organization, relevance and recency of information, special features, and overall value to the collection.
2. Philosophy and goals of the school district: resources support and are consistent with the educational goals of the district and with goals and objectives of individual schools and specific courses.
3. Characteristics of the user: resources are appropriate for the age, emotional development, ability levels, learning styles, and social development of the students for whom the resources are selected.[23]

☐ A GOAL STATEMENT FOR MATERIALS SELECTION

Following is a goal statement outlining the overall approach to materials selection within the philosophical service structure of a school:

1. Secondary school libraries exist for the support, enrichment, implementation, and supplementation of the curriculum and educational programs of the school system. To that end, books, periodicals and other library resources exist:

A. to provide materials that will stimulate growth in factual knowledge, appreciation of literature, aesthetic values, and ethical standards;
B. to provide a varied and diverse background of information that will enable students to make intelligent judgments in their daily lives;
C. to provide materials presenting a variety of points of view concerning literary and historical issues in order to develop, under guidance, critical examination, thinking, and informed judgment;
D. to provide materials that realistically represent our pluralistic society and reflect the contributions made by groups and individuals to our American heritage;
E. to generate an understanding of American freedoms and a desire to preserve those freedoms through the development of informed and responsible citizenship;
F. to promote a critical appreciation for, as well as skills in, reading, viewing, listening, and learning that will continue as a lifetime source of education and enjoyment; and,
G. to provide a planned program that will arouse in students an interest in books and other types of media, and to broaden this interest through service and guidance in a pleasant atmosphere.

[Part of a policy prepared by plaintiff's attorney Ronald R. Coles for submission in *Sheck vs. Baileyville School Committee* (1982)].

Similar to public library selection policies, school library media center selection policies reflect their building/ district organizational structure as well. In multicampus school districts, collection development activities are usually distributed between individual schools and the district office, possibly with a District Coordinator who supervises the entire operation. In smaller districts, individual building librarians may be responsible for all selection. The activities of these individuals range from gaining knowledge of the curriculum and faculty and student needs, to securing and

routing selection aids to selection committee participants, to previewing (or setting up previews). While maintaining separate print libraries, some districts centralize AV services and materials purchases. A central coordinator must take care of selection and circulation. In other states, school districts cooperate to form regional systems and AV co-ops to utilize staff and budget more efficiently.

The Manchester Community School District provides these general selection objectives:

> In order to ensure that the school media program is an integral part of the educational program of the school, the following selection objectives are adopted:
>
> - To provide materials that will enrich and support the curriculum and personal needs of the users, taking into consideration their varied interests, abilities, and learning styles.
> - To provide materials that will stimulate growth in factual knowledge, literary appreciation, aesthetic values, and ethical standards.
> - To provide a background of information that will enable students to make intelligent judgments in their daily lives.
> - To provide materials on opposing sides of controversial issues so that users may develop, under guidance, the practice of critical analysis.
> - To place principle above personal opinion and reason above prejudice in the selection of materials in order to ensure a comprehensive media collection appropriate for the users.

These are philosophical goal statements rather than measurable objectives, but they serve to set the stage of service for selecting curriculum- and enrichment-based videocassettes.

☐ THE EVALUATION PROCESS

The Los Angeles County Office of Education suggests the following selection implementation process:

Forming a Committee

1. Establish a method for selecting members and a chairperson.
2. Include library media professionals, teachers, subject area specialists, administrators, community representatives, and possibly students.

Gathering Background Information

1. School and district goals and objectives
2. Curricular needs [and enrichment programs]
3. Test data
4. Grade levels
5. Community makeup

Collecting Resources

1. State curriculum frameworks, handbooks, adoption lists, and other publications
2. District curriculum documents and/or County Course of Study
3. Reviews from professional journals
4. Subject area indices and bibliographies

Defining the Committee Process

1. Establish criteria to be used for evaluating each type of material.
2. Develop an evaluation form based on the criteria.
3. Define which materials need to be evaluated firsthand and which can be purchased (subject to district approval, with the right of return) from reliable published reviews and recommendations.[24]

Determining use (or, more aptly put, usefulness for the curriculum), especially in today's low-cost video environment, is a problem, primarily because of the lack of broad-coverage, in-depth, specific subject–defined videocassette review

sources. Using location/access sources, such as *The Video Source Book* or *Variety's Complete Home Video Directory*, proves unsatisfactory because of their dismal subject access. A new review source that provides a comprehensive subject index using standardized Library of Congress subject headings is ABC-CLIO's quarterly publication, *Video Rating Guide for Libraries*. Each issue contains approximately 400 to 500 reviews of both home-use-only and public performance videos.

A company that gathers statistical information on educational and library agencies, Quality Educational Data, estimates that there are more than 1,000 videocassettes for the K–12 environment flooding the home video market, at prices ranging from $12.95 to $89.95. However, many fine programs that would be termed general interest to the public librarian could also be used in curriculum contexts within the schools. Today's video programming should not be limited to 15- to 20-minute programs. The VCR makes it possible to control the learning environment, and, with proper previewing and planning, teaching and learning are concurrently enhanced. The video programming that makes such classroom innovations possible is marked by higher production values and more content breadth than previously available on 16mm film-to-video transfers.

Both the media center and the curriculum will benefit from a finely-tuned, coordinated effort to develop a written selection policy and to implement formal selection/evaluation procedures. Recognizing the rich diversity of subject home video and developing the selection tools and open-minded policies to take advantage of that diversity will enable schools to reap both budgetary and curriculum planning rewards.

☐ SAMPLE SELECTION POLICIES FOR SCHOOL LIBRARY MEDIA CENTERS

The following sample policies include detailed content evaluation and technical quality evaluation criteria. All of the

policies represent AV co-ops or regional school systems rather than individual building-level policies.

Burlington County AVA Policies and Procedures for 16mm Film Selection

Objectives of Selection [Section 103]

The primary objective of the Burlington County Audio-Visual Aids Commission is to implement, strengthen, and assist the educational program of the various school districts that hold membership in the organization. To this end, we reaffirm the Library Bill of Rights of the American Library Association and assert that our reponsibilities are:

> To provide films that will enrich and support the curricula, taking into consideration the varied interest, abilities, and maturity levels of those pupils served in the numerous school districts.
>
> To provide films that will stimulate growth in factual knowledge, literary appreciation, aesthetic values, and ethical standards.
>
> To provide a background of information which will enable pupils to make intelligent judgments in their daily life.
>
> To provide films on opposing sides of controversial issues so that young citizens may develop under guidance the practice of critical thinking.
>
> To provide films representative of the many religious, ethnic, and cultural groups and their contributions to our American heritage.
>
> To place principle above personal opinion and reason above prejudice in the selection of films of the highest quality in order to assure a comprehensive collection appropriate for the users of this film library.[1]

Criteria for Selection and Purchase of Films [Section 104]

SELECTION OF FILMS IS BASED ON:

1. Needs of the individual school districts.
   (Based on knowledge of their curricula.)
   (Based on requests from their administrators and teachers.)
2. Needs of the individual students in those member districts.
   (Based on knowledge of children and youth.)

FILM PURCHASES DEPEND ON:

1. Educational significance.
2. Total quality format.
3. Clarity, adequacy, and scope of presentation.
4. Validity, accuracy, objectivity, up-to-dateness, and appropriateness of presentation.
5. Organization and presentation of contents.
6. Comprehensibility.
7. Potential user appeal.
8. Artistic quality.
9. Reputation and significance of author and producer.
10. Need and value to the collection.
11. Value commensurate with cost and/or need.[1]
12. Unbiased consideration of all races, colors, creeds, sexes, social or economic backgrounds.[2]

Selection Procedures [Section 105]

The responsibility for film purchasing rests directly with the Director of the Burlington County Audio-Visual Aids Commission (or with associates delegated this responsibility by the director).

Administrators, teachers, and students are encouraged to suggest films to be added to the collection; these requests are considered during the selection process.

Reputable, unbiased, professionally prepared selection aids are consulted as guides for the selection of films. Some of the more important tools are:

1. *Booklist*
2. *Media & Methods*
3. *Previews*
4. *EFLA files*
5. *NICEM*

Whenever possible, prospective films are previewed by some of the following individuals or groups:

1. The Director of the Burlington County Audio-Visual Aids Commission and associates whom she chooses.
2. Burlington County Audio-Visual Aids Commission Advisory Committee.
3. Media specialist, AVA coordinators and teachers throughout member districts.
4. Students in member districts.[1]

Acceptance of Free and Gift Materials
[Section 105a]
The Commission shall reserve the right to accept or reject free and donated materials. Each item shall be considered on an individual basis and selection based on accepted professional evaluative criteria as set out in Section 104 and 105.

As with purchased films, decisions on accepting materials shall rest with the Director. In addition to the considerations set out in Section 104 and 105, the Director shall consider the appropriateness of the material format, packaging and contents in relation to the capabilities of the AVA delivery system.[3]

1. Adopted at the November 19, 1974 Commission Meeting.
2. Amended at the December 10, 1975 Committee Meeting.
3. Adopted at the March 10, 1983 Commission Meeting.

California Instructional Video Clearinghouse Evaluation Materials

CALIFORNIA INSTRUCTIONAL VIDEO CLEARINGHOUSE
1990 INSTRUCTIONAL VIDEO EVALUATION FORM

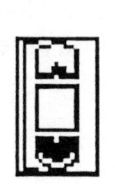

Title
Producer   Copyright   Length
Format   Price
Subject   Grade Level
Preview Identifier

QUALITY ANALYSIS

5 = Exemplary   4 = Desirable (Very Good)   3 = Acceptable   2 = Fair   1 = Poor   0 = Unacceptable

Instructional Design	Logical development of content. Appropriate medium for this content. Presentation design appropriate for grade level. Appropriate use of "talking heads." Suitable instructional support materials.	5 4 3 2 1 0
Content	Accurate, current, thorough, relevant, appropriate for grade level. Can be used across disciplinary boundaries.	5 4 3 2 1 0
Curricular Match	Supports what is commonly taught in schools in this subject at this grade level. Supports instructional themes embodied by California curriculum framework.	5 4 3 2 1 0
Interest	Motivating, actively engages students, intellectually stimulating.	5 4 3 2 1 0
Technical	Supports or enhances communication of content. Visual: focus, color, exposure, true-size relationships. Audio: narration, dialog, background, audio level.	5 4 3 2 1 0

CURRICULAR MATCH

KEY WORDS

LEGAL COMPLIANCE ANALYSIS Meets state legal compliance guidelines: women's roles, ethnic balance, aged, etc.
☐ Yes ☐ No (List the areas of non-compliance on the reverse of this form.)

SENSITIVE CONTENT Contains sensitive content.   If yes, specify any citings on the reverse of this form.
☐ Yes ☐ No Nudity ☐ Yes ☐ No Explicit Sex Material ☐ Yes ☐ No Profanity
☐ Yes ☐ No Excessive Violence ☐ Yes ☐ No Glamorization of Drugs or Dangerous Substances

ADDITIONAL INFORMATION
☐ Yes ☐ No Previewed with students? ☐ Yes ☐ No Do you recommend this for purchase?
☐ Yes ☐ No Could this program be assigned to a student for home viewing (as homework)?

Grade level recommendation _____ Subject area(s) recommendation _____

LOCAL NEED ANALYSIS Circle the number which you feel most accurately describes local need.

0 — 1 — 2 — 3 — 4 — 5
No need   Probable Need   Priority Need

Your name _____ Grade(s) taught _____ School _____ Date _____

#311 90-91 Evaluation 3/1/91 • Video

INSTRUCTIONAL VIDEO

CRITERIA FOR DETERMINING INSTRUCTIONAL QUALITY ANALYSIS RATINGS

INSTRUCTIONAL DESIGN

Organization: Logical development, relatedness of all sequences
Balance of narration and dialog, music and sound effects, background elements
Length of program is suitable for topic and intended audience
Main objectives readily identifiable
Program assists in attainment of objective(s)

Appropriateness: Vocabulary and concepts at user's maturity level
Appropriate use of "talking heads"
Narration, dialog, sound effects, and captions related to subject
Presentation design suitable for grade level
Scope of program appropriate for intended audience

Media-Subject Correlation: Suitable medium for this curricular topic

Special Features: Descriptive notes, user's guide available
Objectives listed in user's guide

CONTENT

Authenticity: Facts accurate and impartially presented
Information up-to-date, useful

Scope: Full coverage of indicated topic
High quality concept development
Relevance for current topic

CURRICULAR MATCH

Supports what is commonly taught in California schools in this subject at this grade level (see state frameworks, model curriculum standards, the Cooperative County Course of Study)

INTEREST

Appeal: Human, sensory, imagination

Believability: Relationship to user's experience, credible

Motivation: Intellectually stimulating
Holds viewer's attention

COMMENTS

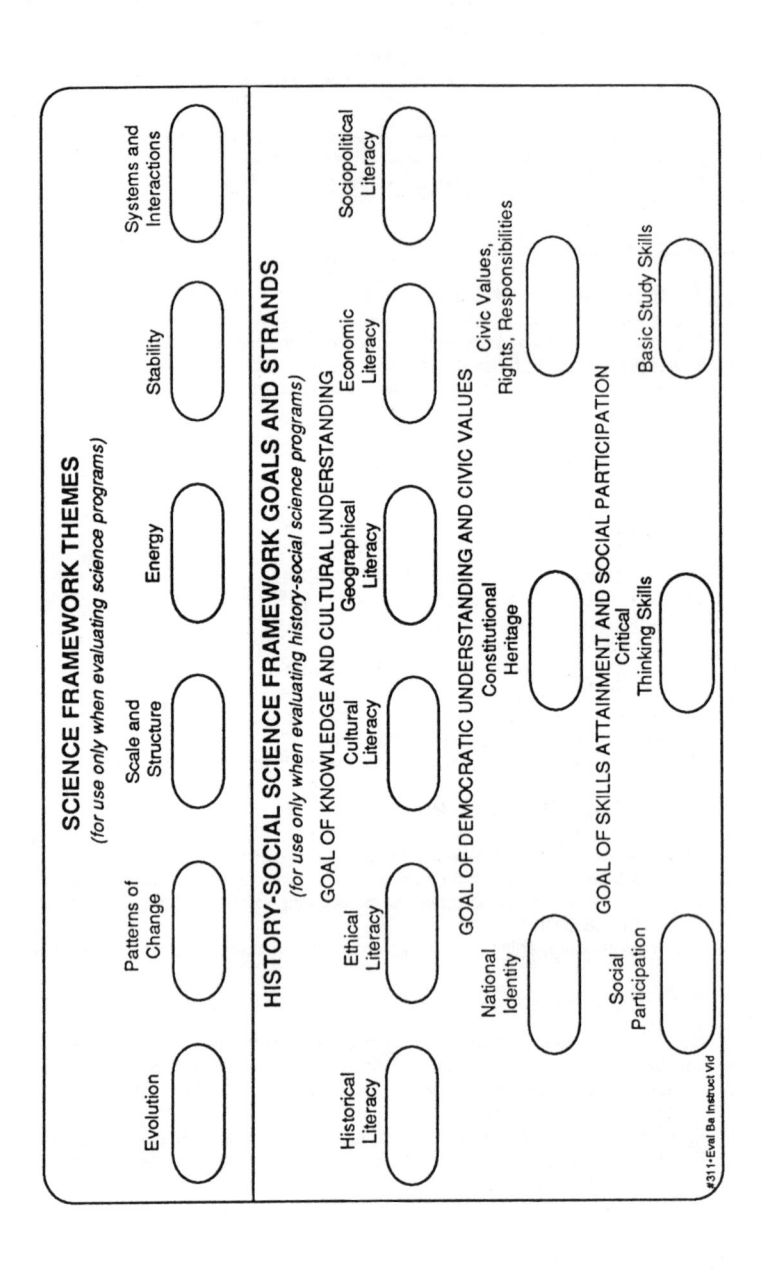

COLLECTION DEVELOPMENT AND THE SELECTION POLICY 103

SCIENCE FRAMEWORK THEMES
(for use only when evaluating science programs)

- Evolution
- Patterns of Change
- Scale and Structure
- Energy
- Stability
- Systems and Interactions

HISTORY-SOCIAL SCIENCE FRAMEWORK GOALS AND STRANDS
(for use only when evaluating history-social science programs)

GOAL OF KNOWLEDGE AND CULTURAL UNDERSTANDING

- Historical Literacy
- Ethical Literacy
- Cultural Literacy
- Geographical Literacy
- Economic Literacy
- Sociopolitical Literacy

GOAL OF DEMOCRATIC UNDERSTANDING AND CIVIC VALUES

- National Identity
- Constitutional Heritage
- Civic Values, Rights, Responsibilities

GOAL OF SKILLS ATTAINMENT AND SOCIAL PARTICIPATION

- Social Participation
- Critical Thinking Skills
- Basic Study Skills

#311 – Eval Ba Instruct Vid

STANDARDS for EVALUATION of INSTRUCTIONAL MATERIALS with RESPECT to SOCIAL CONTENT, 1986 Edition
California State Department of Education
(Education Codes 60040 - 60044)
Abbreviated Edition

Technology resources must comply with these standards. Evaluators must reject programs which contain demeaning labels or role stereotyping. Other criteria in each of the categories must be addressed when appropriate. Note: it may be inappropriate to apply these criteria when examining classical or contemporary literature, music and art, stories or articles having a particular historical or cultural perspective.

MALE/FEMALE ROLES

- No demeaning labels or role stereotyping
- Equal illustrations of male/female figures
- Equal portrayal in occupations and range of career opportunities
- Equal presentation of male/female contributions and achievements
- Equal representation of males/females in mental and physical activities
- Balance of traditional and non-traditional roles
- Equal representation of similar emotions in males/females
  (*i.e.,* fear, aggression, tenderness, etc.)
- Neutral language (*i.e.,* people, persons, men and women, they) preferred

ETHNIC AND CULTURAL GROUPS

- No demeaning labels or stereotyping of minorities
- Displays a fair proportion of diverse ethnic groups
- Differences in customs must not be depicted as undesirable
- Displays minorities in professions
- Shows same socioeconomic ranges for different groups
- Presents minority contributions and achievements
- Equal representation of mentally active, creative roles
- Balance of traditional and non-traditional roles
- Depiction not limited to root culture, but also mainstream of group in U.S.

OLDER PERSONS AND THE AGING PROCESS

- No demeaning labels or stereotyping of older persons
- Displays balanced representation of disabled persons when illustrating human activities
- Balanced presentation of disabled persons with persons of all ages in mental and physical activities
- When appropriate, aging pictured as continuous process spanning entire lifetime

DISABLED PERSONS

- No demeaning labels or stereotyping of disabled persons
- Displays balanced representation of disabled persons when illustrating human activities
- Balanced presentation of disabled persons with persons of all ages in mental and physical activities
- Emotions depicted randomly among characters regardless of ability or disability
- Contributions and achievements of disabled persons depicted, especially when biographies are presented

COLLECTION DEVELOPMENT AND THE SELECTION POLICY

ENTREPRENEUR AND LABOR

- No demeaning or stereotyping of occupations or vocations
- Where appropriate, reference is made to role of both entrepreneur and labor in development of California and U.S.

RELIGION

- No religious practice or belief ridiculed
- Religion, when presented, is presented in objective, non-indoctrinating manner
- Religious diversity reflected in portrayals of contemporary U.S. society

ECOLOGY AND ENVIRONMENT

- Interdependence of people and their environment portrayed
- Appropriate responsibilities of people for creating and maintaining healthful environment portrayed
- Wise use of human and physical resources encouraged

DANGEROUS SUBSTANCES

- Use of dangerous substances not glamorized
- Hazards of use of tobacco, alcohol, narcotics, and restricted dangerous drugs

THRIFT, FIRE PREVENTION, AND HUMANE TREATMENT

- Waste discouraged
- Practices constituting fire hazards not condoned or encouraged
- Inhumane treatment not condoned or encouraged
- Thrift encouraged
- Fire prevention explained and encouraged
- Humane treatment encouraged

DECLARATION OF INDEPENDENCE AND U.S. CONSTITUTION

- These documents should be included in instructional materials for history and social science classes when appropriate for comprehension of students

BRAND NAMES AND CORPORATE LOGOS

- Omit illustrations unless necessary to educational purpose or incidental to scene of general nature
- No prominent use of any one depiction
- Refer to soft drinks generically
- If "fast food" restaurants necessary, use several
- Recreational areas may be mentioned when part of contemporary childhood culture
- Inclusion of corporate names necessary only in very narrow context
- Auto names may be used if fair sampling of different names appear

DIET AND EXERCISE

- Emphasizes foods of high nutritive value
- Emphasizes the value of regular exercise

Grant Wood AEA, Cedar Rapids, Iowa
Grant Wood Area Education
Agency Media Center
Procedure for Materials Selection and
Weeding Policy

Materials Selection

I. The Grant Wood Area Education Media Center hereby adopts the following procedures concerning the evaluation and selection of instructional resources for purchase.

Selection of materials purchased for, or received by the Media Center shall be in accordance with a selection policy that is filed with the DPI by the AEA as part of its proposed program for the Media Center.

II. Materials are to be selected that shall:
  A. Provide for the enrichment and support of the curriculum of schools taking into consideration the varied interests, abilities, and maturity levels of the pupils served.
  B. Provide materials that will stimulate growth in factual knowledge, literary appreciation, aesthetic values, and ethical standards.
  C. Provide a background of information that will enable pupils to make intelligent judgments in their daily lives.
  D. Provide materials representing the many sides of contemporary issues so that young citizens may develop the practice of critical reading and thinking.
  E. Materials shall be chosen to foster respect for minority groups, women, religious and ethnic groups and shall realistically represent our society, along with the roles and life styles available to both men and women today. These materials will be provided to present students with a better understanding of the contributions made by these groups.
  F. Place the principle of freedom to read and view above personal opinion and reason above prejudice in the selection of materials of the highest quality.

III. All materials selected will be consistent with stated principles of selection.

   A. In selecting materials, consideration shall be given to the following:
      1. The media needs of the local school districts.
      2. Provision for weeding or discarding.
   B. In selecting materials, the needs of individual school systems based on knowledge of the curriculums are to be given consideration and shall be covered in two general categories:
      1. Educational Value.
      2. Technical Merit.
   C. Materials for purchase shall be considered on the basis of overall purpose, timeliness, importance of the subject matter, quality of the writing/production, readability and popular appeal, authoritativeness, reputation of the publisher/producer, reputation and significance of the author/artist/composer, producer, etc., format, and price.
   D. Materials shall be selected for their strengths rather than rejected for their weaknesses.

IV. Specific information and recommendations related to the above "general criteria" will be drawn from a variety of sources such as:

   A. Lists of selection tools and judgment of qualified professionals in the field of library science, educational media, and curriculum development.
   B. Recommendations from the professional staff of the Media Center as well as other divisions of the Grant Wood Area Education Agency.

V. Procedure for weeding and discarding

In order to always provide a current, highly usable collection of materials, Grant Wood's professional media staff shall be given the authority to determine which materials shall be weeded based on obsolescence, circulation, and physical condition. Materials will first be considered, where appropriate, for trade in and shall then be disposed of in a suitable and appropriate manner based on the discretion of the Director of Media Services.

VI. Gifts

The Division of Media staff recognizes its responsibility to provide the best instructional materials available to the patrons they serve. Materials are selected for their strengths in meeting curricular needs.

Items that are given to the Division of Media will be accepted with the understanding that disposition of these gifts becomes the prerogative of the Director. These materials may be maintained in the collection if they are deemed supplemental to materials found in the local schools, relate to the media needs of the local schools, provide no unwieldy problem of circulation or storage and be considered on the basis of overall purpose, timeliness, importance of the subject matter, quality of the writing/production, readability and popular appeal, authoritativeness, reputation of the publisher/producer, reputation and significance of the author/artist/composer, producer, etc., format, and price.

VII. Reconsideration of materials

A procedure for processing and responding to criticism of approved materials shall be established and followed. Should a citizen of the school community served by the Grant Wood Area Education Agency raise an objection to the use of an area-provided instructional item, the staff of the Grant AEA Media Center will make every effort to support the local schools' policies in regard to the reconsideration of materials. Should a local district decide they no longer wish to use certain materials found in the Media Center, they may notify the Director of the Division of Media in writing. He in turn will notify the staff who will make every effort to comply with this request. If a local public school district or nonpublic school decides to restrict certain materials, it will be that school's responsibility to administer such restriction. An item will not be removed from the shelf until every public school district and private school served by the Grant Wood Area Education Agency has notified the Director of their desire to have the item removed from the collection.

Delaware-Chenango Board of Cooperative Educational Services Instructional Materials Selection Policies and Procedures

Selection Responsibility

Pursuant to New York Statutes, the legal responsibility for the selection of instructional materials rests with the Board of Education. It is the Board's position that through the exercise of the freedoms set forth in the Bill of Rights an informed choice can take place. If there is to be freedom of speech, of the press, and of assembly, then there must also be freedom to hear, to view, to read, and to discuss. The Delaware-Chenango BOCES will therefore allow free access to a range of instructional materials to insure the realization of these freedoms.

Selection Objectives

The basic objective of materials selection is to provide students and faculty with learning resources that are intrinsic to the implementation of curriculum and/or that have value for diversified interests, abilities, and maturity levels. Selected materials should:

1. Stimulate thinking, provide facts, and contribute to student growth and learning.
2. Contain ideas and information that enable students to make judgments and decisions relating to their daily lives, and responsibilities as citizens.
3. Present a diversity of viewpoints on controversial issues.
4. Include the thinking and contribution of the many cultural, ethnic, and religious groups that constitute society.
5. Portray a variety of lifestyles.
6. Represent a variety of communication formats to provide for individual learning styles and to provide students the opportunity to analyze various media formats critically.

7. Encourage students to read, view, and listen for pleasure and recreation, fostering a life-long appreciation of such activities.

Selection Criteria

Instructional materials shall support and be consistent with the general educational goals of the BOCES. All materials should be selected on the basis of an unidentified need for the materials and the general suitability of the materials to the needs and abilities of those who will use them. In potentially sensitive areas (e.g., race, sex, religion, political theory and ideology), materials should be selected for their strengths and/or significance rather than rejected for their weaknesses. Consideration of the criteria below, where relevant, shall provide the basis for selection of instructional materials. The criteria are not arranged in any particular order of importance.

1. RELATION TO CURRICULUM

Materials should be selected for their contribution to the implementation of the curriculum.

2. RELATION TO EXISTING COLLECTION

The materials should make a contribution to the balance of the individual school collection of materials for which they are selected.

3. INTEREST AND APPEAL

The content and style of the materials should appeal to the interests of those who will use them.

4. ACCURACY AND AUTHENTICITY

The content of materials should be valid, reliable, and complete. Imaginative materials should encourage worthwhile appreciations, attitudes, understandings, and insights.

5. AUTHORITY

Consideration should be given to the qualifications, reputation, and significance of those responsible for creating the material (the author, producer, publisher).

6. COMPREHENSION

The material should be clearly presented in a well-organized fashion. The nature of concepts being developed should be appropriate both to the intended users and the depth of coverage. In print materials, the readability should correspond to the reading ability of the intended users; in nonprint materials, audiovisual representations should correspond to the comprehension level of the intended users. The materials should catch and hold the users' interest and stimulate further learning.

7. PERMANENCE AND TIMELINESS

The materials should be of lasting value and/or should be of widespread current interest or concern.

8. CULTURAL PLURALISM

Students should have access to a current, well-balanced collection of books, basic reference materials, periodicals, and audiovisual materials that depict in an accurate and unbiased way the cultural diversity and pluralistic nature of American society.

9. WHOLE VS. PART

Each item should be approached from a broad perspective, looking at the work as a whole and judging controversial elements in context rather than as isolated parts.

10. RECENCY

In certain subject areas (science and technology, for example), materials should be examined carefully for the currency of the information presented. Copyright date should be used as one indicator of the currency of material.

11. FORMAT

The medium selected to present the material should be appropriate to the content.

12. QUALITY OF WRITING/PRODUCTION

The material should be acceptable mechanically and artistically with each element combining to form an

aesthetically pleasing whole. The material should stimulate growth in factual knowledge and/or literary appreciation. The content should provide adequate scope, range, depth, and continuity while maintaining user interest.

13. TECHNICAL AND PHYSICAL QUALITIES

Print material should be attractively presented with suitable illustrations and graphics. The size and style of type should be appropriate for the intended age level. Audio material should use sound creatively and be clear and free of distortion. The narrator should have a pleasant voice and speak with expression. Visual materials should have good picture quality and be authentic in regard to detail, color, depth, dimension, and size proportions. Original artwork should be reproduced faithfully. There should be sufficient durability to meet the demands of the intended user.

14. COST

The selection of any piece of material, particularly an expensive one, should be seen in relation to the degree of need for the material, the amount of anticipated use, and existing budgetary limitations. The possibility of shared use of materials should be considered. In the event that materials are perceived to be of comparable quality, the materials of least cost shall be purchased.

15. TREATMENT OF CONTROVERSIAL ISSUES

Materials on controversial issues should be selected to represent the fullest possible range of contrasting points of view, to provide a balanced collection of materials on such subjects.

16. TREATMENT OF RELIGION

Materials about religion should be chosen to explain, not to indoctrinate.

17. TREATMENT OF PROFANITY, SEX, AND VIOLENCE

The use of profanity, sexual incidents, or violence in a literary work should not automatically disqualify such

material. The decision should be made on the basis of the work's general literary value, rather than on some isolated parts, and on whether it deals with situations realistically, presenting life in its true proportions.

18. TREATMENT OF HUMAN DEVELOPMENT
Materials on human physiology, physical maturation, or personal hygiene should be accurate and objectively presented.

19. TREATMENT OF BIASED MATERIALS
Materials that unfairly, inaccurately, or viciously treat a particular race, sex, ethnic group, age group, religion, etc., should not be selected unless there exists a legitimate educational purpose—such as analysis, observation, historical development, or interpretation—for the use of such materials.

20. GIFT AND SPONSORED MATERIALS
Gift materials and sponsored materials must meet the same criteria as those selected for purchase. They are accepted with the understanding that, if not suitable, they may be disposed of at the discretion of the school staff members who have received the materials.

PREVIEW FILM EVALUATION REPORT

Date: _____ MPS _____

Please have as many teachers as possible evaluate and return film and evaluation report with regular shipment.

Price _____ Grade Level _____

Title _____ Length _____ B/W _____ Color _____

Producer _____ Produced _____ Subject _____

Evaluated by _____ School _____

Is material presented accurately? _____ Yes _____ No

Is material presented creatively? _____ Yes _____ No

Is material current? _____ Yes _____ No

Does this film eliminate sex bias/stereotyping? ___ Yes ___ No

Do you recommend purchase? _____ Yes _____ No

If purchased, will you use? _____ Yes _____ No

Is the sound: Good _____ Poor _____

Your general estimate of the effectiveness of this film:

Excellent _____ Good _____ Fair _____ Poor _____

Your comments are a valuable guide to purchase.

Will this film support the curriculum in your school?

_____ Yes _____ No

(Please continue comments on other side.)

```
┌─────────────────────────────────────────────────────────────┐
│           Delaware-Chenango BOCES Division of               │
│               Educational Communications                    │
│                                                             │
│  PREVIEW EVALUATION                                         │
│                                                             │
│  Program Number _____ Name _____        │
│                                                             │
│  Program Title _____ School/Building _____      │
│                                                             │
│  Your comments and suggestions are needed so that future film│
│  purchases may be relevant to your classroom needs. Please fill│
│  out this form and return it with the preview print. If more than│
│  one person views this program, please fill out separate evalua-│
│  tions. Thank you!                                          │
│                                                             │
│  This program was viewed by: _____ Myself _____ Students│
│                                                             │
│  _____ Teachers/Administrators                    │
│                                                             │
│  1. How would you rate this program?                        │
│                                                             │
│       1        2        3         4           5             │
│      Ugh!    O.K.    Good    Very Good    Best Ever         │
│                                                             │
│  2. Program could be used in (subjects): _____    │
│                                                             │
│  and general grade level(s): _____                │
│                                                             │
│  3. Would you recommend BOCES buy this program?             │
│                      _____ Yes _____ No │
│                                                             │
│  4. Additional comments:                                    │
│                                                             │
│  _____│
└─────────────────────────────────────────────────────────────┘
```

☐ NOTES

1. James C. Scholtz, *Developing and Maintaining Video Collections in Libraries* (Santa Barbara, CA: ABC-CLIO, 1989), 69.
2. Rose Mary Magrill and John Corbin, *Acquisitions Management and Collection Development in Libraries*, 2d ed. (Chicago: ALA, 1989), 1.

3. Ibid., 1.
4. Ibid., 1.
5. Ibid., 2.
6. Scholtz, 70.
7. Barbara Lockett, ed., *Guide to the Evaluation of Library Collections* (Chicago: ALA, 1989), 1.
8. Bonita Bryant, ed., *Guide for Written Collection Policy Statements* (Chicago: ALA, 1989), 4.
9. Ibid., 5.
10. Phyllis J. Van Orden, *The Collection Program in Schools: Concepts, Practices, & Information Sources* (Englewood, CO: Libraries Unlimited, 1988), 76.
11. Randy Pitman, "Rockefeller Foundation Videocassette Distribution Task Force: Final Report—Library Market" (Bremerton, WA, 30 June 1962, typewritten), 2.
12. Hugh A. Durbin, "Using Policy Statements to Define and Manage the Nonbook Collection," in *Policy and Practice in Bibliographic Control of Nonbook Media*, ed. Sheila Intner and Richard Smiraglia (Chicago: ALA, 1987), 40.
13. Pitman, 2.
14. Elizabeth Futus, ed., *Library Acquisition Policies and Procedures*, 2d ed. (Phoenix, AZ: Oryx Press, 1984), xxii.
15. Scholtz, 159.
16. G. Edward Evans, *Developing Library Collections* (Littleton, CO: Libraries Unlimited, 1979), 216.
17. Stanley J. Slote, *Weeding Library Collections—II*, 2d rev. ed. (Littleton, CO: Libraries Unlimited, 1982), 24–25.
18. Carol Mahon, "Weeding is PR Too," LIPP: *Library Insights Promotion & Programs* 14 (January/February 1987): 3.
19. Slote, 50.
20. Ibid., 65.
21. Ibid., 96.
22. Betty Kemp, ed., *School Library and Media Center Acquisitions Policies and Procedures*, 2d ed. (Phoenix, AZ: Oryx Press, 1986): 28–36.
23. Magrill and Corbin, 47–48.
24. Media Technology Committee, *What Educators Need To Know About Evaluation and Selection of Instructional Materials* (Los Angeles County, California, Office of Education, 1989), 8–9.

3 CIRCULATION AND USE POLICIES AND PROCEDURES

CIRCULATION PROCEDURES

The actual process of circulating videos is no more complicated than circulating other library items; however, some special problems and considerations need to be addressed. Historically, librarians have always treated audiovisual materials, particularly film and video, differently from books:

- Shelving requirements, as well as organizational arrangements, were different.
- Full cataloging and subject/added access was not provided.
- Access for minors was restricted.
- Loan fees were charged.
- Loan periods were short, fines prohibitive, and renewals and reserves rare.

Most of these policies were based on the rationale that this new medium was extremely popular, ephemeral, and expensive. Today, this is not the case; in fact, many books exceed the price of their video alternatives. Libraries should be proactive in establishing circulation procedures, designing them to provide patrons with maximum opportunities for use. These procedures will enhance the attractiveness of

special-interest videos to patrons, and will pave the way for the not-too-distant future, when print and nonprint information will be available in every library through a few simple keystrokes. Pat Lora, Audiovisual Manager for the Toledo–Lucas Public Library (Ohio), oversees a collection that has grown from 100 to almost 20,000 tapes. She describes the possible benefits to patrons:

> Picture the business woman assigned to open a new office in Tokyo. She needs data on the city, the language, the culture. At her library, she finds informational options side by side: books, audiotapes, videotapes. The potential scenarios are endless.[1]

Further, Lora points out, "evolving video information collections are aiding librarians in efforts to mainstream video procedures into those of books, such as providing full cataloging and reserves."[2] With the above statements in mind, it makes sense that librarians start treating video as viable information sources on the same level with print material. Consequently, various circulation and access restrictions should be reassessed and modified. Pat Lora comments on past circulation rules:

- Loan periods are often two days, three days. Why not a week? Do you really think someone can learn a language in two days?
- Interlibrary loan is nonexistent.
- Reserves are rare. Most libraries offer video on a "first come, first served" basis. The reason for this was demand [versus] collection size.... If Danielle Steel warrants reserves, why not Huston, Ford, Spielberg and Weir?[3]

To this list, I would add the following considerations:

1. Circulation loan periods, renewal policies, and limits on the number of videos per patron must be established that accurately reflect the popularity of the medium and give patrons sufficient time to view tapes.

2. Access for minors and age limitations for use of the collection, or any part of it. The intellectual freedom ideology of the library directly impacts the circulation of materials, especially for minors. If the library endorses the ALA Freedom To View document, and the Access for Children and Young People to Videotapes and Other Nonprint Formats document, it should follow a practice of unrestricted access—or risk being labeled a hypocrite. The Access for Children and Young People to Videotapes and Other Nonprint Formats document states the following:

> People who would rather their children did not have access to certain materials should advise their children. The library and its staff are responsible for providing equal access to library materials and services for all library users. Policies which set minimum age limits for access to videotapes ... with or without parental permission, abridge library use for minors.[4]

The Access to Resources and Services in the School Library Media Program document also elaborates upon that philosophy, stating:

> Major barriers between students and resources include: imposing age or grade level restrictions on the use of resources ... requiring permission from parents or teachers, establishing restricted shelves or closed collections, and labeling.[5]

Use of a parental restriction (limitation) form is not an ethical option (even in schools) when library materials are involved. (For a more in-depth discussion of this topic, refer to Chapter 6.)
3. Registration/responsibility, including parental consent cards for video users. If endorsing the two documents described above, parental consent cards are unethical.
4. Overdue fines.
5. Replacement/damage policy. Also, the policy should address patrons who attempt to repair, erase, or otherwise

wise alter/edit videocassettes. (Endorse the U.S. Copyright code.) Damage assessment is part of circulation, weeding, and selection.

Some libraries may find it advantageous to include Video Damage Condition Report Forms (Fig. 3.1) in all circulated tapes. Patrons complete this form and deposit the video in a special drop box or return location. Other libraries would prefer to have the staff inspect each returned video for potential damages. Even in large libraries, patrons tend to be good about informing staff about problems. For this reason, an informal damage log might be a good solution. Essentially, a damage log is a running list of titles that have exhibited problems. Dates and brief problem descriptions are recorded, and titles checked for damage. If the recorded damage is not apparent, or cannot be replicated, the video is put back into circulation. When two or more patrons have the same problem with the title it may be a candidate for deaccession. Some computerized circulation systems may have a section within each bibliographic or circulation record where brief damage notes can be appended to the item.

6. Circulation/loan fees, often called insurance or handling charges. These fees may be illegal in some states and adversely affect/restrict access for minors. In some states, the charging of fees may impose regulatory conditions such as listing the MPAA ratings on every video or not loaning any video not possessing MPAA ratings. If your library endorses the ALA Statement on Labeling, this practice may be an ethical contradiction. Libraries are advised to check with their library legal counsel and their State Attorney concerning these matters.

7. A statement affirming the library's liability limitations for damage to a patron's VCR through the use of any library videocassette, such as: "The library maintains its video collection in good working order, and assumes no liability for damage to patron's VCR through the playing of library videocassettes."

CIRCULATION AND USE POLICIES AND PROCEDURES 121

FIG. 3.1 Model Video Damage Condition Report Form

In order that we may keep the video collection in good condition, please complete this form if you experienced any problems in playing this video. Before completing the form, remember to check your VCR operations manual and all VCR/TV connections, controls, and cables. If you experience problems, don't try to repair the tape—leave the tape at the damage point. Thank you.

Title _____ Call No. _____ Copy No. _____

Description of Problem _____

_____

_____

_____

Circle the terms that best describe the problem:

broken tape   broken case/parts   no sound   no picture

picture rolls, shakes   cannot track   excessive dropout

many distortion lines   twisted/creased tape

Please ask one of our AV staff if you have any questions.

FIG. 3.2 Model Video Damage Log Form

Date	Call No.	Copy No.	Title	Damage Description
____	_____	_____	_____	_____
____	_____	_____	_____	_____
____	_____	_____	_____	_____
____	_____	_____	_____	_____

VIDEOCASSETTE CIRCULATION POLICIES

Videocassette circulation policies are often brief statements, references, or sections of larger policies. This reinforces the consistent application of regulations throughout the range of all library materials.

The first paragraph of a circulation policy simply states to whom the library will loan materials and the types of materials loaned, and endorses some statements on access to materials, such as the ALA's Access for Children and Young People to Videotapes and Other Nonprint Formats (public library) or Access to Resources and Services in the School Library Media Program (school library). The concepts of interlibrary loan and reciprocal borrowing or other circulation agreements should also be generally mentioned.

This paragraph is usually followed by department delineations (if the departments circulate their own items, such as Children's and AV Departments), branch circulation specifics, or sections grouped by format. A large, departmentalized library may let each department house and circulate all its own items, including videocassettes within its own information/subject sphere. Even in libraries where the AV Department is the centralized circulation unit for media, the policy may be broken down by format based on different handling and circulation restrictions, limits, loan periods, and damage considerations.

EQUIPMENT/VCR LOAN

With VCR penetration in the United States approaching 70 to 80 percent, most libraries are finding it unnecessary to lend VCRs; however, some libraries still provide the service. Following are some basic items to consider when establishing a VCR loan policy:

1. Loan/insurance fee.
2. Loan periods—congruent with the videocassette loan period or for a shorter time period?
3. Restrictive loan by age?
4. If the VCR is a recorder/player, the copyright notification pertaining to illegal tape duplication should be affixed.
5. Statement of library's liability limitations for playing personal tapes in library-owned VCRs (this may also be included in the in-house use policy). An example might read: "The library maintains its rental/loan VCR equipment in good working order and assumes no liability for damage to patrons' personal videocassettes. Please report equipment malfunctions on the equipment use card."

    Keep in mind that if this policy is enforced, it may be impossible (and highly unethical) to charge for damages incurred to a library tape played on a library machine as well.
6. Statement of library's and patron's shared liability for equipment damage repair bills—shared liability or single liability?

IN-HOUSE VIEWING

Taking the stance affirmed by Mary Hutchings Reed and Debra Stanek, former ALA legal counsel, it is legal to view home-use-only videocassettes in a private, individual carrel setting within the public library. If libraries wish to offer this service, not only must they provide and maintain equipment, they must also establish and enforce procedures for equitable patron use. Considerations include the following:

1. Reservations of equipment and/or videocassettes—acceptance of telephone calls from both on and off site.

This requires staff time and a scheduling book. An alternate method is first come, first served.
2. Preview-only machines. Historically, this method has failed in public libraries.
3. Number of titles/alternates, or total number of minutes one patron can use a VCR unit.
4. Equipment use fee.
5. Identification required for use, or if video must be an actual checkout.
6. Waiting lists accepted?

SAMPLE CIRCULATION POLICIES

Following are examples of existing library circulation policies, procedures, and consent/responsibility forms. Please note that a library's circulation policy is a direct reflection of its intellectual freedom stance—especially concerning access for minors. Most policies are conventional and limiting, and combine policy and procedures in one document.

> ### Ames Public Library Policy
> ### Statement on Fees and Charges
>
> The Ames Public Library has adopted and subscribes to *The Public Library: Democracy's Resource: A Statement of Principles* as written by the Public Library Association. That document states in part:
>
> > "Public libraries freely offer access to their collections and services to all members of the community without regard to race, citizenship, age, education level, economic status, or any other qualification or condition.
> >   Free access to ideas and information, a prerequisite to the existence of a responsible citizenship, is as fundamental to America as are the principles of freedom, equality and individual rights.
> >   Public libraries were founded and supported by appropriations from tax revenues for very practical

CIRCULATION AND USE POLICIES AND PROCEDURES

reasons: to provide and conserve books and journals economically for community use."

It should also be noted that the Library is empowered by sections 15.7(2), 15.7(6), 15.7(7), and 15.14 of the Ames Municipal Code to make rules and regulations including fines and fees regarding use of the library, its collections and services.

The library may charge fines or fees to encourage compliance with rules that promote fair and equal access to limited resources. As an operating principle, the Ames Public Library will not charge for the use or loan of materials it owns or for the use of Library services. The Library may assess fees or pass through costs for use of resources outside of this institution. Fees may be charged for materials or services that become the property of the user or for actions of the user that cause extraordinary expenses to be incurred by the Library. Fees may also be charged for materials or services that are not basic requirements for access but that serve the user's specific convenience.

AMES MEDIA
MEDIA LOAN AGREEMENT

_____

Expiration Date (four years)

Equipment and software subject to this agreement:

Videocassettes	Projection Screens
Videocassette Players	Microcomputers
Video Cameras	Polaroid Cameras
Overhead Projectors	Carousel Slide Projectors
16mm Films	Enlarging Viewers
16mm Film Projectors	Audiocassette Players

Other (specify): _____

PLEASE PRINT
Name: _____ Date: _____

Address: _____, _____, Iowa _____
     (number) (street) (city)   (zip code)

Telephone Number(s): Home: _____ Work: _____

I HEREBY AGREE:

1. To assume full financial responsibility for loss of, or damage to Library media and/or equipment in my care, from the time such media and/or equipment is borrowed until it is returned to the Library.
2. To assume full financial responsibility for any and all damage to my own media and/or equipment that may occur while I have Library media and/or equipment in my care.
3. To return to the Library all media and/or equipment that I have borrowed on or before the date and, if applicable, time due, or I will pay any and all overdue fines and penalties. [Please note: Fines accrue beginning one hour after certain equipment is due.]
4. To honor any and all copyright and/or performance restrictions. [Please note: Rights to all videocassettes and films are protected by federal law. Under no circumstances shall any videocassette or film in the care of any borrower be duplicated or copied by any process, electronic or mechanical, in whole or in part. Videocassettes and films are loaned only for private use in the home and may not be performed in schools or other public places, or be broadcast, or cablecast without the express written consent of the producer or distributor. The borrower is solely responsible in any legal action that may result from any possible copyright infringement.]

_____
Signature of Borrower

[If the borrower is a minor, under eighteen years of age, parental authorization, below, is required.]

PARENTAL AUTHORIZATION:

I hereby declare myself personally responsible and liable for all the above stipulations, in the name of my minor dependent. I further declare that my minor dependent may borrow, or view in the Library, films that have been rated "PG13" or "R" by the MPAA.

_____   _____
Signature   Relationship

CIRCULATION AND USE POLICIES AND PROCEDURES

MEDIA STATION POLICY

1. A maximum of two people is permitted at each viewing, listening, or computing station.
2. Patrons are allowed a maximum of two hours at each of two media stations per day. Patrons may view only one video, regardless of length, per video station use. During periods of high demand staff may limit a patron's use of media stations to twice per week.
3. Patrons must present their own Library cards when requesting a media station.
4. Patrons are responsible for damage to equipment, materials, and furniture while they are using a media station.
5. AV media stations may be reserved on a same day basis. Reservations will be held for fifteen minutes only past the appointed time.
6. Any behavior deemed inappropriate by Library staff may be cause for immediate loss of media station privileges for a period determined by Library staff.
7. All listening, viewing, and computing must be finished fifteen minutes before closing. At one half hour to closing staff will advise patrons that all activities must be finished in the next fifteen minutes.

Laramie County (Wyoming) Library System VHS Videocassette Information

I. General Information
   A. Laramie County Library System videocassettes are VHS format, and are available for a fee.
   B. The Library System does not have Beta videocassettes. VHS videocassettes will not work in a Beta player. VHS videoplayers are available for checkout for a fee.
   C. Video titles, with a brief description of each, are listed in the AV card catalog.
   D. VHS videocassettes frequently have electronic protection against copying.
   E. All videocassettes are inspected when they are returned.

F. Videocassettes can be damaged if returned in the bookdrop.
G. DO NOT ATTEMPT TO REPAIR A VIDEOCASSETTE.

II. Copyright Law
The copyright law of the United States (Title 17, U.S. Code) governs the making of duplicate videocassette tapes or other reproduction of copyrighted materials. The person making a videocassette is responsible for any infringement.

Patron's Initials _____

III. Circulation
A. You are responsible for the video titles you select. Refunds or exchanges cannot be made because of selection errors.
B. You are responsible for making sure your television can handle the antipiracy device on VHS videocassettes.
C. You are responsible for any damage that occurs while you have a videocassette checked out.
D. YOU ARE RESPONSIBLE FOR THE VIDEOCASSETTES CHECKED OUT ON YOUR LIBRARY CARD FROM THE TIME THEY ARE CHECKED OUT TO THE TIME THEY ARE RETURNED TO THE *MAIN DESK*.
E. DO NOT RETURN VIDEOCASSETTES IN THE 29TH STREET BOOKDROP.
F. Damage to a videocassette because of your attempts to repair it is your responsibility, including the cost of replacing the videocassette if necessary.
G. There is a daily fine of $1.00 assessed for each overdue videocassette. You will be fined for each day from the close of business on the due date through the day the videocassette is returned. Fines *must* be paid before you check out more videocassettes. If you do not pay the fines, your account will be turned over to our Billing Department.

CIRCULATION AND USE POLICIES AND PROCEDURES

MY SIGNATURE ON THIS SHEET INDICATES THAT I HAVE READ, UNDERSTAND, AND AGREE TO ABIDE BY THESE POLICIES WHENEVER I CHECK OUT VIDEOCASSETTES. IT ALSO INDICATES THAT I HAVE RECEIVED A COPY OF THIS SHEET.

Signature _____ Date _____

Please print your name clearly on this line

Videocassettes and Video Player Regulations Santa Monica (California) Public Library

Videocassettes
All videocassettes are in the VHS format, and will not play on Beta equipment.

REQUIREMENTS

1. Borrower must be 18 years old.
2. Borrower must have a valid **SMPL** library card, and must present the card each time a videocassette is borrowed. Borrower must also register in the Film Department.
3. The owner of the library card assumes full responsibility in the event of damage or loss. If a videocassette is damaged, the borrower pays $20.00 toward its replacement, plus $1.00 service charge.

PROCEDURES

1. Videocassettes may be reserved in person or by phone up to one month in advance.
2. Four titles may be borrowed at one time.
3. Videocassettes circulate for one day for $1.00, or two days for $2.00. When the library is closed on Sundays or holidays, the videocassettes are due on the next business day. NO REFUNDS FOR EARLY RETURN.

4. Videocassettes must be returned only to the Film Desk at the Main Library. They must not be left in the Book Return, or a penalty will be charged.
5. There is a $3.00 per day per item late charge. Failure to pick up reserved videocassettes or to return them on time can result in loss of reserve privileges for six months.

RESTRICTIONS

1. Videocassettes cannot be shown where any admission fee, donation, or collection is made.
2. The library is not responsible for determining audience suitability. Please preview to avoid misunderstandings.

CARE OF VIDEOCASSETTES

1. Never store videocassettes near magnetic sources; stereo speakers, electric motors, etc., can erase tapes.
2. Dust, dirt, and fingerprints cause picture deterioration. Never touch the tape itself. Store tape in container provided.
3. Please do not rewind the tapes after viewing.
4. Keep videocassettes away from heat. Do not leave them in auto trunks or glove compartments.
5. Keep player heads clean. Follow manufacturer's instructions for equipment maintenance.

COMMON PLAYBACK PROBLEMS

1. Rolling picture: Adjust vertical hold on TV.
2. Picture tearing: Adjust horizontal hold on TV.
3. Picture wavy: Adjust tracking on video player, or rewind all the way from the end.

Video Players

The video player is available to borrowers who live or work in Santa Monica. Library cards stamped MCLS are not acceptable.

CIRCULATION AND USE POLICIES AND PROCEDURES

REQUIREMENTS

1. Borrower must be 18 years old.
2. Borrower must have a valid SMPL library card, and must present the card each time a video player is borrowed, along with some personal identification (California Driver's License). Borrower must also register in the Film Department. The person whose library card is being used MUST sign for the player at the time it is checked out—no one may be delegated to pick up the video player.
3. The borrower assumes complete responsibility for loss or damage to the player or its accessories.

PROCEDURES

1. Player must be checked out with at least one library videocassette.
2. Player may be reserved in person or by phone up to one month in advance. It may not be borrowed more than once a week nor more than one weekend per month by the same person.
3. The loan period is one day. When the library is closed on Sundays or holidays, the player is due on the next business day.
4. The video player must be reserved separately from the videocassettes. It is not automatically supplied when videocassettes are reserved.
5. Fees: $7.50 for one checkout period. No refund for early return.
6. Library staff cannot carry the player to the borrower's car. A cart is available for borrower's use.
7. There is a $10.00 per day late charge. Always call the Film Department promptly if the player will be late.

Video players donated by The Friends of the Santa Monica Public Library

Videocassette Circulation Policy Schaumburg Township (Illinois) Public Library

Videocassettes

Videocassettes may be checked out by all *Schaumburg Township Public Library cardholders*. There is a limit of one videocassette per cardholder, and a maximum of two per family. Each individual wishing to check out a videocassette must have a video card. Video cards may be obtained at the Audiovisual Desk upon presentation of a Schaumburg Library card. Children under high school age will need a parent's signature on their video card. *Individuals under 17 years of age will not be allowed to check out R-rated videos.* Those under 17 years of age will receive a PINK video card indicating the restriction on R-rated movies.

Most of the videocassettes may be checked out for a period of three days; however, we have a collection of instructional videocassettes that may be checked out for seven days. *Only these instructional (seven-day) videocassettes may be reserved.* Any videocassette may be renewed once, unless the video is on reserve. There is no charge for checking out videocassettes; however, there is an overdue fine of $1.00 for each day the videocassette is overdue. For the convenience of all, there is a 50-cent fine for each videocassette that is not *fully rewound* when it is returned.

The patron who checked out the videocassette is responsible for any damage incurred after it has been checked out to him/her. The patron becomes responsible for the videocassette as soon as it is handed to him/her at the Audiovisual Desk. *Do not leave the videocassette unattended in the library after it has been checked out because it may be misplaced or stolen.*

If it is determined that a damaged videocassette cannot be repaired, then the patron who checked out the videocassette will be held responsible for the cost of replacement of the damaged videocassette.

After a videocassette is returned, it must be processed by the Audiovisual Staff; therefore, only videocassettes

on the shelves in the display cabinets are available for circulation. Videocassettes that have been recently returned are temporarily stored behind the Audiovisual Desk and may not be checked out until they have been processed and returned to the display cabinet. Every effort will be made by the Audiovisual Staff to process the returned videocassettes as quickly as possible.

THE SCHAUMBURG LIBRARY ASSUMES NO RESPONSIBILITY FOR ANY DAMAGE TO YOUR EQUIPMENT WHILE USED IN CONJUNCTION WITH OUR VIDEOCASSETTES.

Damaged Nonprint Material
Phoenix Public Library

I. Policy

It is the policy of the Phoenix Public Library to charge a user a replacement or penalty fee for mutilation or damage to library materials. This policy is established as a protective measure to discourage carelessness or misconduct that results in damage or destruction of library materials. Users are responsible for damage to library audio and video cassettes, and other nonprint items.

It is the policy of the Phoenix Public Library to assume no responsibility for damage to user equipment that occurs when nonprint materials are used. Users are expected to assume responsibility for keeping their equipment in good order to prevent damage to materials.

II. Definitions

A. Repairable damage—Damage that can be repaired with minimal effect on the appearance and/or usability of the material.
B. Damaged beyond repair—Damaged beyond the point where it would be possible or practical to repair the material. This designation is also applied to a set returned with items missing that cannot be found or replaced.

C. Negligible damage—Damage that has little or no effect on the usability of the material and that will not be repaired by library staff. There will be no charges for negligible damage.

III. REGULATIONS

A. "Repairable Damages":
  1. Repair of the following damages will be done by the owning agency. Based on the following schedule, fees for these damages may be assessed and collected by circulation staff at any agency where the item is returned, if the library user wishes to pay at that time. [Charges following damages indicate Adult Audio/All Video and Juvenile Audio charges respectively.]

     Barcode replacement—2.00/1.00

     Label replacement—2.00/1.00

     Replacement of missing or damaged booklet—2.00/1.00

     Lost outer plastic bag—No charge

     Audio outer album*— 2.00/1.00

     Video outer album*—2.00

     Lost phonodisc jacket*—2.00/1.00

     Lost CD outer case*—2.00/1.00

  2. Inspection and repair of the following damages must be done by Central AV. However, it is then the responsibility of the owning agency to bill the library user for damages or repairs, according to the following schedule. [Charges following damages indicate Adult Audio/All Video and Juvenile Audio charges respectively.]

     Audio tape repair/splice—2.00/1.00

     Video tape repair/splice—2.00

---

*Add in barcode and label fees if these are missing with the outer album.

Repair to manufacturer cassette housing —2.00/1.00

Slide remounting—2.00

Replace slide boxes/cases—2.00

Study print relaminating—2.00/1.00

Filmstrip repair/splice—2.00

Sculpture (minimal gluing)—2.00

Framed art: torn backing—2.00
        broken glass—Cost of repair
        frame damage—Cost of repair

3. All videocassettes are considered as adult material and charged accordingly.
4. Total cost of damages plus overdue fees, if any, may not exceed the cost of the item.

B. "Damaged Beyond Repair": Full price of cataloged items, adult and juvenile, as listed in the database. If the user can provide verification that the price listed in the database is incorrect, the verified price will be assessed. Overdue fines are not charged when materials are damaged beyond repair.

1. Fees for an audio or video item that is mangled or clearly damaged beyond repair may be collected by the circulation staff at any agency at the time the item is returned.
2. The library user may replace a cataloged item with a new copy of that title. A $3.00 service charge to partially defray reprocessing costs is assessed the user.
3. Damaged beyond repair generic or uncataloged items will be assessed on the following schedule:

    Generic phonodisc—3.00

    Study prints—2.00

    Study print envelopes—2.00

    Slides—2.00

4. Materials that have been damaged beyond repair and for which the charges have been fully paid remain the property of the City of Phoenix. The user may not keep these materials. It is

understood that these charges are not for purchase of a damaged item, but for replacement of that item.
5. Damaged beyond repair materials will be kept for 28 days for user inspection.
6. If the cassette portion of an audio book set is damaged or lost, the owning agency may
   a. if possible, order a replacement cassette, clearly indicating on the Book Selection Work Slip that the cassette will complete an existing set, or,
   b. charge the user 1/2 the total price of the set, discard the cassette, and either
      (1) send the book to cataloging for deletion and subsequent ADDITEM as a book in CLSI, or
      (2) appropriate staff at the owning agency may delete the cassette and ADDITEM the book in the CLSI.
7. If the book portion of an audio book set is damaged or lost, the owning agency may
   a. order a replacement book, if available, clearly indicating on the Book Selection Work Slip that the book will complete an existing set, or
   b. both the book and cassette may be deleted. The owning agency may charge the user 1/2 the price of the set.
C. "Negligible Damage": Staff will note in pencil on returned materials with negligible damage the type of damage and will date and initial the note so that subsequent borrowers are not held responsible for the damage. No charges are assessed for negligible damages. This category includes

   crayon or pencil marks

   cleaning (all materials)

   study print envelope repair
D. Receipts will be written for all damage charges collected if the total sum is over $5.00. Note that the "For" line includes the title, barcode, and date due of the damaged item, type of damage assessed, and amount of charges collected.

CIRCULATION AND USE POLICIES AND PROCEDURES

E. Partial payments on damaged items will not be accepted.
F. Any questions regarding charges should be referred to the librarian on duty in the appropriate area of the library.

IV. PROCEDURES

A. When a user brings a damaged item to the attention of a library staff person and wishes to pay damage charges immediately, the following procedures apply:
  1. If the damage may be assessed by circulation staff in accordance with III-A1 above, the following apply:
     a. Check item in on CLSI database using process CHECKIN, function OVERDUE ALERT "Y," so that user may pay any overdue fines as well as damage fine, if he/she chooses.
     b. Collect assessed charges, i.e., damage charge plus any fines, as long as the total charge does not exceed the cost of the item.
     c. Write a receipt in accordance with III-D above if the total charge is $5.00 or more.
        (1) If fees are collected by owning agency, proceed to "d" below and "e" below.
        (2) If fees are collected by other than owning agency, send item to owning agency with an AV Damage form (see attached), indicating the nature of the damage and the *amount paid*. Note: Top portion of form *must* be filled out. Owning agency will proceed as follows.
     d. Items with damages repairable by owning agency, listed in III-A1 above, should be:
        (1) checked out to MEND and routed to appropriate staff for repair.
        (2) repaired items will be checked in and returned to public access.
     e. "Damaged beyond repair" items will be discarded by owning agency in accordance with Circular CO2.2 (Branch) and CO2.3 (Central).
  2. If damage must be assessed by Central AV, in accordance with III-A2 above, the following procedures apply:

a. Inform library user that item must be sent to Central AV Services for damage repair and assessment.
b. Help patron to fill out AV Damage form as completely as possible. Note: All lines in top portion of form *must* be filled out.
c. Check item in on CLSI database using process CHECKIN, function OVERDUE ALERT "Y" so that user may pay any overdue fines if he/she chooses.
   (1) Note any overdue fines paid on AV Damage form.
d. Check item out to MEND and send, along with AV Claims Damage form, directly to Central AV Services.
e. AV Services will assess damages, repair if possible, and return item to owning agency with the Damage Assessment portion of the AV Damage form filled in.

B. When a damaged item is returned in the book drop or left on the circulation desk, or the user is present, but no payment is made at the time of return, the following procedures apply:
1. If the user is present, obtain his/her name and barcode number. Using process INQUIRY, function ITEM, note date due and date returned on the AV Damage form. Note user's description of damages and location of problem on item.
2. If user is *not* present
   a. search CLSI using process INQUIRY, function ITEM, for user APATID, date item was due, and date returned;
   b. search CLSI for user details using process INQUIRY, function PATR. Record user's name and barcode number on the AV Damage form.
3. Check item in on CLSI using OVERDUE ALERT "Y"; if item is overdue, log fines.
4. If damages may be assessed by circulation staff in accordance with III-A1 above, the following applies:

CIRCULATION AND USE POLICIES AND PROCEDURES

a. Item returned to *other* than owning agency:
   (1) Record information from steps B1-2 above as completely as possible on an AV Damage form.
   (2) Send item to owning agency, along with AV Damage form, check "Branch Repairable" and "No" by "Damage Fees Collected."
   (3) Owning agency will proceed as follows:
b. Item returned to owning agency:
   (1) Determine type of damage and fees to be charged.
   (2) Making sure that damage cost plus overdue fines do not exceed item cost, enter fees on patron record:

   Using CC Patron, change user status to "S."

   In ADDATA field, enter AV Damage $_____, the barcode, title of damaged item (may be abbreviated), *type of damage*, date, and staff initial.
   (3) Send Notification of Damage form to library user.
   (4) Check item out to MEND and give to appropriate staff for repair.
   (5) After repair is completed, check item in and return it to public access.
      (a) If staff decide that physical evidence of damage should be retained, the AV Damage form, a copy of the Notification of Damage, plus the damaged material (i.e., damaged case) may be filed on the AV Damaged Shelf by user's last name for 28 days.

      If payment is not made in 28 days, discard "physical evidence" and file forms in AV Damaged File by user's last name.
      (b) If damaged material is not retained as evidence, file copies of the AV Damage form and the Notification of Damage

in the AV Damage File by the user's last name.
    (6) After payment is made, enter process CC Patron in CLSI, change user status back to "N," remove information about damaged item from ADDATA field, and discard AV Damage and Notification of Damage forms from the AV Damage File. Also discard these forms and evidence material, if any, from the AV Damaged Shelf.
  5. If damage must be assessed by Central AV Services
    a. complete steps B1-3 above, filling out AV Damage form as completely as possible;
    b. check item out to MEND and send, along with AV Damage form, to Central AV Services;
    c. AV Services will assess damages, repair if possible, and return item to owning agency with the Damage Assessment portion of the AV Damage form filled in.
C. When a repairable damage item is mended by Central AV Services and returned to the owning agency, the following procedures apply:
  1. Check item in.
  2. Using the Damage Assessment information on the AV Damage form, the owning agency will determine if the user is to be billed for repairs.
  3. If the user is to be billed, library staff should
    a. making sure that damage costs plus overdue fines do not exceed total item cost, enter damage charge on user record, using the following procedures:
      (1) Using the process CCPATRON, change the user status to "S."
      (2) In the ADDATA field, enter AV Damage $_____, the barcode, title of damaged item (may be abbreviated), *type of damage*, date of entry, and staff initial.
      (3) Send Notification of Damage to library user.

CIRCULATION AND USE POLICIES AND PROCEDURES

      b. file the AV Damage form plus a copy of the Notification of Damage in the AV Damage File by the user's last name.
      c. return item to public access shelves.
   4. When user has paid damage fees
      a. change user status back to "N";
      b. delete damage notes from the ADDATA field;
      c. discard the AV Damage and Notification of Damage forms from the AV Damage File.
D. When a damaged beyond repair item is returned from Central AV Services to the owning agency, the following procedures apply:
   1. Using the Damage Assessment information on the AV Damage form, the owning agency will determine if the user is to be billed for the material.
      a. Any overdue fines paid and noted on AV Damage form will be deducted from total cost of the item.
      b. Library staff should enter process INQUIRY, function ITEM to find the total number of circulations for the damaged item and note this on the AV Damage form. If the total circulations add up to more than 50, a degree of leniency is recommended unless the damage is clearly a result of negligence. (Note, however, that James Scholtz in *Developing and Maintaining Video Collections in Libraries* states that video cassettes can circulate up to 150 times before needing replacement.)
   2. If the user is to be billed, library staff should
      a. fill out a Notification of Damage form (see attached);
          (1) Send original to user.
          (2) Check item out to the agency AV Damaged Shelf number.
          (3) Attach copy of Notification of Damage plus the AV Damage form to the item and place on the AV Damage Shelf by user's last name for 28 days for the user to examine if he/she so desires.

b. To create the damage charge on the user record, the following procedures apply:
   (1) Using the process CCPATRON, change user status to "S."
   (2) In the ADDATA field, enter AV Damage $____, the barcode, title of damaged item (may be abbreviated), *why item is damaged beyond repair*, date of entry, and staff initial.
   (3) Enter process FINES and delete overdue fines, if any, on item.
3. When the overdue notice to the agency Damaged Item Shelf for the item arrives, circulation staff will
   a. check item in;
   b. discard item, label "discarded," and route to Central AV for reusable parts;
   c. file a copy of the Notification of Damage plus the AV Damage form in the AV Damaged File under the user's last name.
4. When full payment has been made by library user, circulation staff will
   a. check item in;
   b. change user status back to "N";
   c. delete damage notes from ADDATA field.
   d. discard item.
   e. if item is still on the AV Damaged Shelf, pull item, label "discarded," and route to Central AV for reusable parts;
   f. discard forms from AV Damaged File.

CIRCULATION AND USE POLICIES AND PROCEDURES

AV DAMAGE

TITLE _____ ____ BRANCH REPAIRABLE

ITEM BARCODE # _____ Damage Fees Collected?

USER BARCODE # _____ _____ Yes _____ Amt.

_____ No & not entered in CLSI

DATE _____ OVERDUE FINES PAID?

DATE DUE _____ _____ Yes _____ Amt.

_____ No

_____ Material left on desk. Information below not available.

1. Did library user play the tape?

_____ Yes   How many times? _____   _____ No

2. Describe damage to case, tape, or disc. Details: (How did damage occur and location of any damage to tape, e.g., beginning, first three minutes, middle, etc.)

_____

_____

DAMAGE ASSESSMENT

_____ Nothing was wrong. (Played okay in AV.)

_____ Damage has been repaired. No fees.

_____ Fee damage(s). Repaired _____

Note: Fee per each repair (splice or housing repair) or per each replacement (barcode, label, outer album, jacket, booklet)

$2.00 Adult audio and all video
$1.00 Juvenile audio (LSC-L50.6, III-A)

_____ Damaged beyond repair. Cost of item.

_____ Item damage cannot be removed.

_____ Item has been recorded over.

_____ Item is old and worn out. Do not bill the user.

OTHER: _____

Please feel free to contact Debbie Veldhuis (2-4797) if you have questions.

VIDEO CIRCULATION BY SCHOOL LIBRARY MEDIA CENTERS

No circulation policies were submitted by school libraries for the compilation of this book, and only one school library sent a policy dealing with teacher use of videocassettes that are not owned, broadcast, or recommended by the district. The Los Angeles Unified School District has an excellent policy regarding use of these videocassettes, which also directly relates to the educational exemption in the copyright law for showing home-use-only videocassettes, and the use of home-taped, off-air programs used by teachers in schools. These

---

NOTIFICATION OF DAMAGE FORM

Dear _____ (User Barcode _____)

The following library material has been returned to the library in a damaged condition:

Title _____

Item Barcode _____

Date Due _____ Date Returned _____ Returned at _____

Type of Damage _____

Charge _____

The damaged item will be held for 28 days at the _____ _____ Library for you to examine if you so desire.

You may pay the charge for this item in person at the Central Library, any of the branch libraries, or the Bookmobile. Please bring this notice with you if you pay in person or enclose it with payment made by mail.

If you have questions about this notice, please call Circulation Services: _____

---

topics will be covered in more detail in Chapter 4: Copyright Issues and Policies.

Traditionally, schools have restricted access exclusively to students, administration, and faculty. In many libraries, media has further been restricted to in-library use only. Although community members pay school taxes, they are usually restricted from borrowing school materials.

Many schools schedule media and the corresponding viewing equipment for classroom use well in advance of the use date, as well as providing walk-in circulation service.

These differing service philosophies and practices need to be clearly stated in a policy in order to avoid misunderstandings. When the Access for Children and Young People to Videotapes and Other Nonprint Formats, and Access to Resources and Services in the School Library Media Program statements are endorsed by school media centers, the use of parental permission forms to restrict access to library materials used in the classroom (even by teachers, librarians' agents) should be considered contradictory to the ideology set forth in those documents (see Chapter 6 for a complete discussion).

Also, in a similar manner, parental permission forms for video programs taped off-air by the library, even if legally copied and retained (ten-day retention period), are contradictory to the philosophy set forth in the beforementioned ALA documents, because they originate from the school library media center. The only case in which this contradiction would not arise is if the teacher taped an off-air program at home and used it in the classroom. Legally, the teacher can use the video within the ten-day retention period; however, unless board policy specifically states, the video would not enter the jurisdiction of the library, and would be, in effect, exempt from the ethics of the ALA documents.

An important consideration in the writing of a school library circulation document is the following question: Do legally obtained and/or privately taped videocassettes automatically fall within the scope and jurisdiction of the school library, even though they are not a permanent part of the school media center collection? If the answer is in the affirmative, school librarians would be burdened with monitoring media use in the classroom. Perhaps the situation would best be resolved by having the school board adopt a policy defining this type of use and placing the burden of classroom use directly on the teacher rather than on the library.

Business/commercial interests are currently making their way into the school community in the form of short news programs with commercial messages specifically targeting children and young adults; e.g., Whittle Communications' Channel One, a 12-minute news program inter-

spersed with two minutes of commercials. Satellite transmissions are videotaped by local schools in the morning and played back during the day. Media centers need to develop policies delineating selection and use of those materials in a captive-audience atmosphere. Gordon Conable, chair of the ALA Intellectual Freedom Committee, states that:

> Curriculum content is an extremely sensitive issue.... In many instances, Whittle's programming is becoming part of the school day for every child in a district without having to meet the established educational criteria and existing selection process that all other required materials go through.[6]

The ALA Council has adopted a resolution stating that the selection of such services must be made within the established guidelines of written selection policies, without regard to gifts or premiums.[7] Furthermore, the ALA recommends that all schools and libraries have written policies regarding materials selection to ensure that resources are appropriate to the educational program and the school community. Particular concerns about the service cited by the ALA include the following:

1. Forced viewing by students.
2. The appropriateness of commercials in the classroom.
3. Whether quality of content could be relied on.
4. The influence of private commercial concerns on school curricula and news reports.[8]

It should be noted that Whittle Communications allows a prescribed portion of the commercials to be deleted for rebroadcast. However, if the satellite taping function, commercial deletion, and rebroadcast functions fall under the jurisdiction of a library endorsing the Library Bill of Rights, the deletion of commercials is censorship or expurgation, and highly unethical.

Currently, the use of videocassette features by classroom teachers is under scrutiny by many communities such

as Albuquerque, New Mexico, where a librarian and a teacher were suspended for not following policies in showing the feature *Catch-22*. Previously, some parents had questioned the teacher's classroom showing of the feature *The Last Temptation of Christ* in a high school world history class, although she had followed school policy.[9] Primarily, this problem is an extension of the intellectual freedom conflict and the use/interpretation of MPAA ratings. The Los Angeles Unified School District has outlined policies relating to this use, providing parental consent letters and explicit MPAA rating guideline explanations.

☐ NOTES

1. Pat Lora, "Getting Ready for the 21st Century: Media Moves into Library Mainstream," *Wilson Library Bulletin* 64 (April 1990): 31.
2. Ibid., 32.
3. Ibid., 31.
4. American Library Association Council, "Access for Children and Young People to Videotapes and Other Nonprint Formats," *Newsletter on Intellectual Freedom* 38 (September 1989): 156.
5. American Library Association Council, "Access to Resources and Services in the School Library Media Program," *Newsletter on Intellectual Freedom* 39 (March 1990): 39.
6. American Library Association Public Information Office, "ALA Urges Caution on Use of Channel One" (press release, Chicago, March 1990, typewritten), 1.
7. Ibid., 1.
8. Ibid., 1.
9. Charlene Money, Albuquerque Public Schools, Albuquerque, New Mexico, telephone conversation with author, 17 April 1990.

4 COPYRIGHT ISSUES AND POLICIES

This chapter will discuss some of the copyright issues that both public and school librarians face in maintaining a circulating videocassette collection or production/off-air taping service. It will also present a number of copyright policies illustrating how libraries handle copyright problems.

The (use and abuse) of copyrighted videocassettes by libraries and schools is one of the most hotly debated issues in the library field today. Copyright concerns are magnified somewhat because of the nebulous nature of the law (specifically, the lack of case law to contest those issues), and the lack of knowledge of specific copyright terminology. Librarians must be knowledgeable enough about the copyright law to interpret it and protect themselves while keeping their best interests in mind. This section will address the following questions and concerns:

- How is the copyright law defined?
- What do the terms private, home use, public performance, and public domain mean?
- How may videocassettes be used in semipublic and educational institutions under the "fair use" section of the law?
- Can libraries show videocassettes in-house to individuals and small groups?

149

- Can libraries tape programs off-air, and how long may they keep them?
- What is meant by off-air taping; does it include cable transmissions and pay TV channels such as HBO and Cinemax?
- Can libraries tape from satellite transmissions?

COPYRIGHT DEFINED

Copyright is the exclusive legal right to reproduce, publish, and sell the matter and form of a literary, musical, or artistic work. Copyrights are issued by the federal government, and are not necessarily honored worldwide; in many cases, copyright holders must apply for several different copyrights if they wish to market the product in other countries. Essentially, the U.S. copyright law provides limits of use for the work, as a whole, in part, or in reproductions (photocopying) by people other than the copyright holder. A copyright is valid for the life of the copyright holder plus 50 years. Copyrights are not necessarily automatic by virtue of the act of writing, producing, or publishing.

Before the advent of prerecorded videocassettes, the VCR, and computer software, copyright was fairly straightforward, but these new technologies have muddied the waters significantly, and copyright law has failed to keep up with the times. For example, off-air taping is guided by congressional committee guidelines established in 1979, before VCRs, cable television, and home satellite dishes were common.

Where copyright leaves off, contractual law begins. The copyright law does not specifically mention terms such as "home use only" and "public performance." These are terms relating to the negotiated use rights of videocassettes. Until the advent of prerecorded videocassettes, neither the motion picture industry nor the educational film industry even considered separate rights for the home video and public performance markets; today, such multirights contracts are complex and commonplace.

THE COPYRIGHT ACT OF 1976

The Revised Copyright Act of 1976, Title 17 of the U.S. Code, Sections 101–810, which took effect on January 1, 1978, regulates the use of all copyrighted materials, including videocassettes. A brief outline of some of the law's basic concepts, with sections enumerated, is shown below:

SECTIONS	OUTLINE
101	basic definitions of terms used throughout
102–104	works protected by copyright
105	U.S. government works excluded
106	right of fair use
108	reproduction by library or archives
109	effect of transfer of a particular copy
110	performances and displays for nonprofit organizations
111	secondary transmissions
118	noncommercial broadcasting
401–406	notice of copyright
501–506	copyright infringement
504	innocent infringement by libraries

A rule known as the first-sale doctrine regulates the copyright ownership of most materials. Generally, copyright controls over the ownership of the physical medium terminate after the first sale of each copy. Translated, this means that the copyright holder would not receive any revenue from rentals such as video store rental transactions. However, the first-sale doctrine does not apply to prerecorded videocassettes. For example, libraries purchase a wide range of educational and entertainment videotapes for in-library use and for lending to patrons. Copyright makes the distinction between ownership of a physical object and ownership of the copyright; therefore, guidelines are necessary to define the extent to which all types of libraries can use prerecorded videocassettes.

PUBLIC PERFORMANCE AND PUBLIC DOMAIN

One of the major questions librarians ask is, "What is a public performance video, and how does it differ from the rental store (home-use) type?" A public performance video is, generally speaking, any title for which licensing fees (or contractual arrangements by a distributor) have been paid so that it may be shown in public. In the past, especially with motion pictures, short- or long-term leases, or single performance contracts, were negotiated. Today, videocassette producers primarily provide two options: blanket licenses, covering specific titles from specific producers for unlimited showings; or public performance rights on a per-title (per-copy) basis, purchased when the videocassette is purchased.

Single-showing and per-title public performance rights can be arranged, but librarians must be careful to get such agreements in writing from the copyright holder. Usually, public performances of videocassettes fall into one of three categories:

- theatrical exhibition
- nontheatrical exhibition
- fair use/educational exception (classroom use)

Theatrical exhibition deals with the showing of the video when an admission is charged, while nontheatrical exhibition exclusively limits group performances to non–admission-charging (including donation) situations. Section 101 of the law defines public performance as a performance taking place anywhere "open to the public or at any place where a substantial number of persons outside of a normal circle of a family and its social acquaintances is gathered."[1] Therefore, it is illegal to show a home-use videocassette to a group of people other than in a family (home) setting.

The 1976 revised copyright law includes sections 106 (right of fair use) and 110 (performances and displays for nonprofit organizations), which extend performance rights

COPYRIGHT ISSUES AND POLICIES

to specific educational settings. Specifically, this applies only to schools and academic institutions; public libraries are not considered educational institutions by law. In-classroom performance of a copyrighted (home-use-only) videotape is permissible under the following conditions:

1. The performance must be either by instructors (including guest lecturers) or by pupils;
2. The performance must be in connection with face-to-face teaching activities;
3. The entire audience is involved in the teaching activity;
4. The entire audience is in the same room or same general area;
5. The teaching activities are conducted by a nonprofit education institution;
6. The performance takes place in a classroom or similar place devoted to instruction, such as a school library, gym, auditorium or workshop;
7. The videotape is lawfully made, i.e., the person responsible had no reason to believe that the videotape was unlawfully made.[2]

The only instance in which a home-use-only videocassette could be used in a group setting within the public library would be if it were used in conjunction with an education program conducted in the library's public room, following the seven requirements listed above.[3] In order to qualify as a nonprofit education institution, the library educational program must meet the following criteria:

1. Do students receive frequent reading, field, or laboratory assignments, for which they are held accountable?
2. Do instructors assign grades based on papers, examinations, oral reports, and other reliable measures of pupil performance?
3. Are grades reported to parents, guardians, employers, or other responsible parties?
4. Are transcripts of students' grades available to other educational institutions?

5. Does the course lead to a recognized degree, diploma, license, or certificate?[4]

Because public libraries are not nonprofit education institutions by law, they cannot legally utilize home-use-only videocassettes for public performance showings for story hours, adult programming, film festivals, or the like. Similarly, education institutions are also limited in their use of home-use-only videocassettes. They can only be used within the classroom setting, under face-to-face teaching situations. Showing home-use-only videos as extracurricular activities, for entertainment or other purposes not in conjunction with a course of study, is illegal.

Many public libraries have expressed concern over trying to determine which videocassettes have public performance rights and which ones do not. Generally speaking, videos with public performance rights will state such rights on the video case/container or pre-title frame. Home-use-only videos, however, may not be as obvious; frequently the copyright notice on the videocassette case/container or pre-title frame consists only of a generic FBI copyright warning.

Companies such as Films Inc. have complicated matters further by offering two-tiered pricing, one for public performance (or education/institutional) and the other for home use. Price used to be a fair indicator of whether a video carried public performance rights or was for home use only, but that is not the case today. Quality videocassettes with public performance rights sell for from $9.95 up to $800, while the range for home videos consistently falls between $14.95 and $89.95. The problem is further exacerbated by the fact that many videocassette distributors (and producers) do not know which rights they hold (if any). Therefore, sending a letter to Baker & Taylor asking for public performance rights for the videocassette *Who Framed Roger Rabbit?* is futile, because Baker & Taylor has no authority to grant public performance rights. When in doubt, contact the *copyright holder* for permission (in writing).

Public domain titles are titles in which the copyright protection has run out or has never existed. Several companies,

COPYRIGHT ISSUES AND POLICIES

such as Video Sig in Sunnyvale, California, have fairly good quality public domain feature and documentary titles for sale at extremely reasonable prices. These titles can legally be shown in public performance, transmitted over broadcast/cable television, and/or duplicated.

Library videocassette collections should be delineated by public performance and home-use-only categories. This can be done in a variety of ways, including:

- notations on the catalog card or on-line catalog
- colored or symbol stickers
- a predetermined alphamnemonic code placed on the videocassette spine/container, possibly in association with the call number
- separating the public performance collection physically from the home-use-only collection

The St. Louis (Missouri) Public Library prints a flyer describing their videocassette services that also includes a brief statement on copyright.

Copyright

"For Home Use Only" means just that!

Without a separate license from the copyright owner, called "Public Performance Rights," *it is a violation of Federal law* to exhibit pre-recorded videocassettes outside of a family residence or at a place where a substantial number of people are gathered beyond the family members or a close circle of friends. This is regardless of whether an admission fee is charged or not. Even performances in semipublic places such as clubs, lodges, businesses, camps, day care centers, senior centers, schools and libraries are "public performances" and subject to copyright control. This applies to profit making organizations and non-profit institutions alike. For such performances to be legal, public performance authorization from the copyright owner must be obtained.

> There is one exception. This is the so-called "face-to-face" teaching exemption found in Section 110 (1) of the copyright law. In this case the performance is legal if it is conducted by a teacher or student, and occurs in the course of a face-to-face teaching activity in a nonprofit educational institution, classroom, or similar place of instruction. Noncurriculum programs do not qualify for exemption.
>
> Televising a prerecorded tape is not allowed. In addition, any temporary videotaping or copying for later playback of copyrighted materials readily available by rental, lease, or license is an infringement of copyright and not fair use.

PUBLIC PERFORMANCE AND BROADCAST RIGHTS

Obtaining public performance rights and closed-circuit or cable/broadcast rights can sometimes be difficult. Many libraries have printed purchase orders stating "videocassettes purchased on this P.O. will be used for private home use and for nontheatrical exhibition to groups in both curricular and noncurricular settings." This statement implies that fulfillment of the purchase order gives the library or school the right of public performance (schools are exempt under the fair-use teaching exemption only for curricular use); however, this practice would, most likely, not be upheld in a court of law.

Most videocassette distributors do not have the copyright authority to grant public performance rights. Such a situation is analogous to a person writing on an automobile purchase order, "I will drive this car 80 mph." The fact that the dealer has sold the car with the knowledge that the purchaser will exceed the legal speed limit does not make the dealer liable for the purchaser's illegal actions, because it is not within the dealer's power to modify the speed limits. Contributory negligence in these one-party contractual forms is not a factor; responsibility of legal use rests solely

COPYRIGHT ISSUES AND POLICIES 157

with the purchaser, and ignorance of copyright does not serve as a rationale for illegal use. It would be advisable to include public-performance and home-use purchase objectives in the selection policy—possibly providing measurable purchase objectives for specific genres and/or subject areas or percentages of the entire collection. The selection of these titles can then be easily tied into the circulation and copyright policies.

Most film and video producers do not automatically grant closed-circuit/broadcast transmission rights upon purchase—these rights must be negotiated separately, as part of the purchase or afterward. Most often, the rights are not blanket (all titles of one producer), but negotiated by individual title per one-time showing. The Media Services Department of the University of Utah initially contacts distributors/producers by telephone to make the request for clearance, then sends a letter restating the verbal agreement, which includes the following conditions:

1. Closed circuit transmission will be limited to those network reception sites that are located on campus.
2. Programs will only be used as part of the curriculum in regular accredited classes.
3. No editing will be allowed.
4. Programs will be played in their entirety including credits.
5. Transmission time will only be announced to members of the classes for which the program is scheduled.
6. Provisions of the Copyright Act will be strictly observed.[5]

OFF-AIR AND SATELLITE TAPING

The Copyright Act itself does not specifically address the issue of off-air taping. In 1979, a federal negotiating committee deliberating the off-air taping issue developed an eight-point consensus document (detailed in the following sample policies) concerning the application of the fair-use doctrine to the recording, retention, and use of television broadcast

programs for educational purposes. The committee recommended specific retention time periods and use of recordings in nonprofit educational institutions.

It should be noted that off-air refers specifically to antenna-received broadcasts (and simultaneous cable retransmission). This specifically eliminates taping from channels such as Discovery, A&E, HBO, Cinemax, Showtime, Disney, and other pay-TV and cable-only channels. Nonprofit educational institutions seeking off-air taping rights should contact the specific channel for taping and retention permission (on an individual program basis).

Schools encounter many instances in which the librarian or teacher will tape a program at home and use it in a class. When the video is brought to school, it falls under the school's jurisdiction and, as such, is subject to the same retention laws as copies made on school equipment. Thus, the legality of the copy is at question; if the teacher taped a program from HBO at home to use in class, it would probably not be considered a legal copy—especially if the sole reason for copying it was for school use.

The congressional committee guidelines make no provisions for educational taping of televised channels received via satellite and decoder/descrambler units. Except for legally authorized educational channels, taping from satellite transmissions is illegal.

Memphis Schools use the following labels affixed to school owned VCRs:

Warning!
Guidelines for Video Recording
and Classroom Use

"OFF-AIR" RECORDING A television program may be copied off-air and may be used once by an individual teacher in relevant classroom instruction for a period of up to ten (10) days following broadcast. *After the 10-day period, the recording must be erased.*

RENTED/PURCHASED VIDEOTAPES Tapes marketed for the home video market, when rented or purchased by schools, *can only be used in face-to-face instruction in a regular classroom.*

Rented/purchased videotapes may never be copied unless the rights or license-to-copy has been purchased.

IMS [Memphis Schools] VIDEO TAPES IMS videotapes that *may not* be copied will be identified with a DO NOT COPY label. IMS video tapes that *may be copied* will be so identified—but *must be erased on the expiration date printed on the cassette.*

IF IN DOUBT, DON'T COPY—YOU ARE RESPONSIBLE

DEVELOPING A COPYRIGHT POLICY

Janis H. Bruwelheide outlines the benefits of having a library copyright policy:

1. It will provide protection for staff, faculty, administration, and the governing body ... [helpful in] avoiding [costly] litigation.
2. The policy provides direction for adhering to the law (PL 94-553) and its interpretations.
3. The policy states that employees can refuse to do tasks which are possibly infringements of the law.
4. To avoid legal problems by sticking to the law and interpretations as diligently as possible.[6]

Common copyright policies contain the following:

1. An opening statement that the governing body endorses the Copyright Act of 1976 and other pertinent laws.
2. A section defining legal fair use, and specifying that illegal use or duplication will not be allowed (Sections 107, 108, 117), as well as a section about using

library equipment legally. A strong warning concerning willful violation and subsequent responsibility should be placed here.
3. A section delineating administrative procedures, including designation of a copyright officer who monitors and records use of videocassettes and equipment.
4. A mandate that warning notices be posted on or near all photocopying/recording equipment.
5. The actual body of the policy. This might explain the nature and purpose of each collection, and how copyright is viewed, such as photocopying for print, off-air copying for acquisition when legally applicable, etc. Many policies include a list of questions and answers about what is illegal and legal. This is followed by either appendices (containing all pertinent portions of the Copyright Act) or a manual that informs readers about copyright and gives specific examples. The San Diego County Office of Education has an excellent booklet entitled *Off-Air Video Recording Issues and Answers*, which is reprinted below in full as a sample policy.

Within this section, specific examples for fair use might be given by media type with guidelines for use. Also, step-by-step procedures, including sample forms, for the following activities should be outlined: authorization of privately taped videos; use of rented/purchased videos other than library- or school-owned videos; obtaining licensing agreements; requesting a program be taped off-air; and monitoring compliance. Copies of all warning notices and statements should be supplied.
6. A clear statement of do's and don'ts.[7]

SPECIFIC APPLICATIONS OF POLICY

Videocassettes are just one aspect of a total copyright policy, which also includes print material, photocopies, use of fax machines in transmission of copyrighted materials under the fair-use clause, copying of sound recordings, and the 1980 Computer Software Copyright Act. Copyright expert Dr. Jerome Miller stresses that:

COPYRIGHT ISSUES AND POLICIES

> Libraries and/or librarians are not liable for copyright infringements on the part of individual patrons. A staff member can inform (and in the case of library-owned VCRs, should probably affix a copyright warning to the machine) a borrower about copyright laws—specifically, injunctions against duplicating and [home-use] . . . but is under no obligation to challenge or cross examine a patron concerning intended use of the program.[8]

However, Mary Hutchings Reed reminds librarians that

> If a librarian learns that a patron is borrowing videotapes and using them for public performances . . . while there is no clear duty to refuse to lend, there is a point at which a library's continued lending with actual knowledge of infringement could possibly result in liability for contributory infringement.[9]

With the above statements in mind, and considering the way in which most public libraries use/collect videocassettes, it would probably be sufficient for most public libraries to provide one policy statement endorsing the 1976 Copyright Act and acknowledging home-use-only and nontheatrical exhibition videocassettes within the collection.

Off-air taping can be a source of many free collections, retained for the life of the tape. For example, National Geographic allows the off-air taping of all its National Geographic Specials (with lifetime retention). Public libraries should acknowledge this form of acquisition in their selection policy, but also endorse the 1979 Off-Air Videorecording Guidelines.

Many schools and public libraries are developing community/student television channels with the assistance of local cable television stations. When a library is involved in this type of activity, its policies need to be broader and more in-depth. Topics that should be included in this type of policy include endorsement of all of the above documents, plus a discussion about obtaining broadcast licensing agreements for all or parts of programs used on-air, plus the retention (archivist) functions relating to the selection policy.

Some additional sources that may help librarians concerning the issues of videotape copyright are listed below.

AIME (Association for Information Media and Equipment)
P.O. Box 865
Elkader, IA 52043

A clearinghouse for information on copyright, among other library topics. AIME supplies some copyright policies and publishes a monthly newsletter.

Ivan R. Bender and Jerry Hazelmeier, *Copyright: What Every School, College and Public Library Should Know*. Association for Information Media and Equipment (AIME), 1987. 16mm film, $65.00; videocassette, $25.00. Distributed by Films Inc., 108 Wilmot Rd., Deerfield, IL 60015. 25 min.

The program covers five points: What is copyright?; fair-use; face-to-face teaching exemption; off-air videotaping guidelines; and situations and questions. This would be an excellent introduction for educational administrators.

Virginia Helm, *What Educators Should Know about Copyright*. (Phi Delta Kappa Educational Foundation, Eighth and Union, Box 789, Bloomington, IN 47402), 1986. Pamphlet. 90 cents.

This pamphlet is an excellent layman's overview of the copyright law as it pertains to AV materials. The fair-use doctrine is covered, as well as do's and don'ts for educators.

Dr. Jerome K. Miller, *Video/Copyright Seminar, 1987*. (Copyright Information Services, 440 Tucker Ave., P.O. Box 1460, Friday Harbor, WA 98250), 1987. Audiocassette, $24.95.

This tape covers the pros and cons of showing videos in public, school, and college libraries; loaning videos for home, school, and organizational showings; off-air and satellite videotaping; and preparing a school district video copyright policy. Also included in the package is a seminar outline, an

educational video copyright policy outline, relevant texts of the Communications Act and the Fair-Use Guidelines, and information from the Television Licensing Center.

Charles Vlcek, *Copyright Policy Development: A Resource Book for Educators*. (Copyright Information Services, 440 Tucker Ave., P.O. Box 1460, Friday Harbor, WA 98250), 1987. $17.95.

A step-by-step guide to writing and implementing institutional copyright policies. Six outstanding school and college copyright policies are included as examples, along with a lengthy discussion concerning satellite recording.

SAMPLE COPYRIGHT POLICIES

The following is a composite model policy.

Model School District Policy

Guidelines for Use of Copyrighted Video Programs

In order to comply with the revised Copyright Act of 1976 as it applies to the use of copyrighted audiovisual programs, it is the policy of the School District to abide by the following guidelines. The School Board prohibits all staff, faculty, and students from copying/misusing school materials not specifically allowed by either the (1) copyright law, (2) fair-use guidelines, (3) educational exemption, (4) licenses or contractual agreements, or (5) other written permission. Each building librarian has been designated as the copyright monitor and will report all violations in writing to the building principal. It is presumed that all faculty, staff, and students will follow the copyright laws diligently. The School Board disapproves of unauthorized supplication/illegal use of copyrighted material. Employees who willfully disregard the copyright policy are in violation of said policy at their own risk, and must assume all liability.

I. Instructional Use

The School District is a nonprofit educational institution by definition of law, and therefore can use home-use-only videocassettes in classroom settings only under certain conditions (as stated in sections I and II). It is the policy of the library to purchase curriculum-based and enrichment materials in part on faculty suggestions. Whenever possible, and within certain budgetary limitations, the library tries to acquire videocassettes with nontheatrical public performance rights. However, this is not always possible. To this end, the library also purchases home-use-only videocassettes, rents videos from local/national agencies and businesses, acquires videocassettes through interlibrary loan, and tapes off-air when legally possible.

PUBLIC PERFORMANCE

Video programs displaying the public performance restriction sticker (PP) can be used for any school function providing no admission charge is levied.

HOME-USE-ONLY

"For Home Use Only" means just that! Without a separate license from the copyright owner, called public performance rights, *it is a violation of federal law* to exhibit prerecorded videocassettes outside of a family residence, or at a place where a substantial number of people are gathered—beyond family members or a close circle of friends. This is regardless of whether an admission fee is charged. Even performances in semipublic places such as clubs, lodges, businesses, camps, daycare centers, senior centers, schools, and libraries are public performances, and subject to copyright control. This applies to profit-making organizations and nonprofit institutions alike. For such performances to be legal, public performance authorization from the copyright owner must be obtained.

There is one exception. This is the so-called "face-to-face" teaching exemption found in Section 110 (1) of the copyright law. In this case the performance is legal if it is conducted by a teacher or student, and occurs in the course of a face-to-face teaching activity in a nonprofit

COPYRIGHT ISSUES AND POLICIES 165

educational institution, classroom, or similar place of instruction. Noncurriculum programs do not qualify for exemption.

Televising of a prerecorded tape is not allowed. In addition, any temporary videotaping or copying for later playback of copyrighted materials readily available by rental, lease, or license is an infringement of copyright and not fair use.

II. Conditions for Use of Home-Use-Only Videos

The following guidelines apply only to those copyrighted video programs used in the classroom that display the home-use-only restriction (HSO).

1. The performance must be by instructors (including guest lecturers) or by pupils; and
2. The performance must be in connection with face-to-face teaching activities; and
3. The entire audience is involved in the teaching activity; and
4. The entire audience is in the same room or same general area;
5. The teaching activities are conducted by a non-profit education institution; and
6. The performance takes place in a classroom or similar place devoted to instruction, such as a school library, gym, auditorium, or workshop; and
7. The videotape is lawfully made; the person responsible had no reason to believe that the videotape was unlawfully made.

Copyrighted home-use-only video programs MAY NOT be used when:

1. They are used for entertainment, recreation, or enrichment programming in group/individual situations within the library.
2. They are shown in a situation before an audience not confined to students and/or not directly a part of an instructional program, such as an awards banquet or a sporting event.
3. An admission fee is charged.

Instructors utilizing rented videocassettes are responsible for their legal classroom use. Privately taped video programs must be registered with the library before classroom showings (shown only on school equipment), guaranteeing that the 45/10 consecutive day retention period is followed.

III. Off-Air Videotaping

The school library media center is the only entity authorized to produce off-air video copies (except when privately taped videos are used). The instructor must contact the librarian at least one day in advance of the program time by submitting Form A (see attached). Off-air is defined as broadcast television received via antenna or simultaneous cable retransmission. It does not include pay channels such as HBO, A&E, Cinemax, Showtime, and Disney.

All off-air videotapes will be used according to the following guidelines:

1. Off-air recordings may be made only at the request of an individual teacher for systematic instructional purposes. No broadcast program may be recorded off-air more than once at the request of the same teacher, regardless of the number of times the program may be broadcast (within the 45–calendar day retention period).
2. A broadcast program recorded off-air may be retained for 45 calendar days, after which time the tape(s) must be erased.
3. An off-air program is limited to two showings per class: it may be shown once to students for relevant classroom activities, and once more for necessary instructional reinforcement during the first 10 consecutive school days beyond the 45-day retention period. (Consecutive school days are school session days—not counting weekends, holidays, vacations, examination periods, or other scheduled interruptions.)
4. After the first 10 consecutive school days, the recordings may be viewed only by teachers for evaluation purposes.

COPYRIGHT ISSUES AND POLICIES 167

5. If several teachers request videotaping of the same program, duplicate copies may be made, but the use of all copies will follow the above restrictions.
6. Recordings need not be used in their entirety, but they must not be altered from their original content or combined (edited) with others to form anthologies.
7. All videotapes must include the original copyright notice.

All School VCRs have the following label affixed:

Warning!
Guidelines for Video Recording
and Classroom Use

"OFF-AIR" RECORDING   A television program may be copied off-air and may be used once by an individual teacher in relevant classroom instruction for a period of up to ten (10) days following broadcast. *After the 10-day period, the recording must be erased.*

RENTED/PURCHASED VIDEOTAPES   Tapes marketed for the home video market, when rented or purchased by schools, *can only be used in face-to-face instruction in a regular classroom.*
  Rented/purchased videotapes may never be copied unless the rights or license to copy has been purchased.

IMS VIDEO TAPES   IMS videotapes which *may not* be copied will be identified with a DO NOT COPY label. IMS videotapes that *may be copied* will be so identified—but *must be erased on the expiration date printed on the cassette.*

IF IN DOUBT, DON'T COPY—YOU ARE RESPONSIBLE

If the school library media center cannot record the program(s) for an instructor, that instructor may privately record the programs desired, provided Form A is filled out and submitted to the media center after recording. All privately recorded off-air programs aired for classroom use immediately become educational-use programs, and, as such, must follow the above guidelines. It is emphasized that the private copy must be legally acquired.

FIG. 4.1 Model School District Form A: Request for Off-Air Program Taping

Date form submitted:_____
Title, channel, date, and time of program(s) requested:
    TITLE   DATE   TIME(S)   CHANNEL FORMAT

1.

2.

3.

4.

5.

Recorder's signature: _____

List classes, periods where programs will be used (numbers match titles above):

1.

2.

3.

4.

5.

_____ Instructor will be recording these programs.

Instructor's signature: _____

Would you recommend any of these titles for purchase? [List titles and attach preview/evaluation form(s)]

COPYRIGHT ISSUES AND POLICIES

Following are sample copyright policies from actual libraries:

Reproduction and Use of Copyrighted Materials (Nonprint/Print) Grossmont Union High School District

It is the intent of the Governing Board to delineate, enforce, and abide by the provisions of the current copyright laws as they affect the District and its employees.

Copyrighted materials, whether they be non-printed or printed, may not be duplicated without first receiving written permission from the copyright holder or complying with guidelines presented in administrative regulation ECHC-R.

The District does not sanction illegal use or duplication in any form. Employees who willfully violate the district's copyright position do so at their own risk and assume all liability-responsibilities.

Adopted: 3/6/78

LEGAL REFS.:
United States Code, Title XVII
County Counsel No. 79-2638/CLD
County Counsel No. 78-0011/RBH

Reproduction and Use of Copyrighted Materials (Nonprint/Print)

The local unit chief administrator is responsible for the enforcement of the provisions of this regulation. He/she will identify an individual to act as a liaison person for staff information (inservice), control of approval process (written and verbal), and the maintenance of written

records relative to the duplication and distribution of copyrighted materials.

Off-Air Video Taping

District Instructional Media Services operates an off-air video tape recording service for District schools. This service is available 24 hours a day, seven days a week and includes all channels (except pay channels such as HBO, Showtime, Disney, etc.) that are carried on network or cable as well as instructional television with the San Diego County Office of Education (ITFS). The primary purpose of these procedures is to permit use of off-air video tape in face-to-face instruction and enable staff to preview instructionally related materials for possible acquisition through purchase, lease, rental, or free-loan agreements by the District. These guidelines enable teachers to replay television programs within a specified period of time.

To help prevent problems involving copyright violations on the part of the District or District employees, off-air taping of audio-visual materials shall be accomplished under the following conditions and comply with the Governing Board Policy ECHC:

1. Any teacher desiring that an instructionally related program be taped by the District for classroom use shall complete a "Request for Off-Air Video Taping" form (Exhibit ECHC-E). Such requests must be signed, which in effect is an agreement to abide by the provisions of this regulation. If a school elects to video tape at the local unit, a similar form must be used. An individual may use video programs taped at home as long as he/she complies with the policy and regulations adopted by the Governing Board regarding its use.
2. Unless otherwise authorized by the associate superintendent or his/her designee, all video tape recordings of network programs shall be erased no later than 45 days after the taping of the requested program. Instructional television programs broadcast over ITFS by the San Diego

COPYRIGHT ISSUES AND POLICIES 171

County Office of Education can be retained for the entire year (consult the County Instructional Television Guide for details).
3. Individuals who wish to retain programs beyond the 45 day period need to complete and return the preview evaluation portion of the "Request for Off-Air Video Taping" form to District Instructional Media Services for each program video taped. District Instructional Media Services will be responsible for requesting permission to use or retain copyrighted television programs beyond the 45 day retention period. Video tapes of commercial programs may only be retained with written approval of appropriate copyright holders.
4. Copyright law and cable franchise agreements exclude the District from recording or using pay channels, such as "Showtime," "HBO," "Disney," etc., for classroom instruction. This provision covers any program broadcast by pay channels and intercepted through the use of cable channels or satellite dish. Exceptions may be authorized by the associate superintendent or his/her designee, and some "pay programs" may be available for legal acquisition.
5. Use of off-air recordings made from a satellite dish must conform to the 45 day retention period established for broadcast or cable programming.
6. A taped program shall not be exchanged with other schools in the Grossmont Union High School District or other school Districts without approval of the associate superintendent or his/her designee.
7. The taped program shall not be used for public or commercial viewing.
8. The taped program shall be used for the specific curriculum application for which the request was intended, and no other curriculum application is authorized.
9. Published lists of authorized video tape libraries shall be prepared and maintained for each local site.
10. Video tape programs that fall under the State's Sex Education Codes 51550, 51820, and 51240

may only be used following the established parent notification and material review process.
11. Off-air recordings need not be used in their entirety, but the recorded programs may not be altered from their original content. Off-air recordings may not be physically or electronically combined or merged to constitute teaching anthologies or compilations.
12. The principal of each school site is responsible for establishing practices that will enforce this policy at the school level. (See ECHC-E)[2].
13. The legal or insurance protection of the District will not be extended to employees who violate copyright laws. In the event said employee is found guilty of violating existing copyright law by administrative law judge, judge or jury, or a combination thereof, the employee will be required to remunerate the District in the event of loss due to litigation.

Letters of Request for Information to Major Networks or Producers

A request for information as to the availability of a television presentation, which has been determined to be of educational value for classroom use through teacher preview, shall be made to the appropriate major television network (e.g., NBC, ABC, CBS). Information requested will include the following (see Exhibit ECHC-E)[1]:

1. Agency holding distribution rights to educational institutions
2. If and when the program will be available to the educational market
3. Type of film or video format to be used
4. Procedure for purchase, rental, or lease agreement

Requests to Networks or Producers for Permission To Tape or Retain Copyrighted Works

Although some producers allow nonprofit organizations to reproduce their materials, they must first review the status of their copyright to determine whether or not

COPYRIGHT ISSUES AND POLICIES

they have the power to grant permission. Regardless of the standard policy a producer may have regarding the granting of duplication rights, each request requires a careful checking of the exact materials to be duplicated. Therefore, requests to producers for permission to duplicate copyrighted audio-visual materials shall include the following information:

1. Correct title of the material
2. Exact description of the material to be used (i.e., test, visuals, soundtrack, etc.)
3. Type of reproduction
4. Number of copies to be made
5. Use to be made of reproduced materials: If the material is a video cassette, specify whether the intended use involves single receiver playback or multiple receivers. If the intended use involves transmission of the material, specific information should be supplied as to the method of transmission; whether radio or television, open or closed circuit. In such cases, many license agreements require that the number of students in the intended audience be stated.

Rental, Purchase, and Use of Video Tape

Copyright law and County Counsel opinion specify the following guidelines for the rental and purchase of video tapes. Due to the changing nature of the video industry these guidelines assure the District will remain in compliance with copyright and contract law provisions.

1. Use of feature length video tapes must be part of a systematic course of instruction and not for entertainment or recreation, and their use must take place in a classroom or similar place devoted to instruction.
2. The purchase or rental of feature length or educational video tapes will be coordinated by the associate superintendent or his/her designee.
3. Use of video tapes must be made from legitimate copies.

4. Local schools may transmit video tapes over their closed circuit television systems for face-to-face instruction.

Computer Software Copyright Regulations
It is the intent of the Grossmont District to adhere to the provisions of the copyright laws in the area of microcomputer programs.

1. District employees will be expected to adhere to provisions of Public Law 96-517, Section 7 (b), which amends Section 117 of Title 17 of the United States Code to allow for the making of a back-up copy of computer programs. This states that " . . . it is not an infringement for the owner of a copy of a computer program to make or authorize the making of another copy or adaptation of that computer program provided
   a. that such a new copy or adaptation is created as an essential step in the utilization of the computer program in conjunction with a machine and that it is used in no other manner, or
   b. that such a new copy and adaptation is for archival purposes only and that all archival copies are destroyed in the event that continued possession of the entire program should cease to be rightful."
2. When copyrighted software is used on a disk sharing system, efforts will be made to secure this software from copying.
3. Illegal copies of copyrighted programs may not be made or used on school equipment.

Los Angeles County Office of Education Guidelines on Copyright

3450* Copyright

3451* Office Copyrights
Any material or work that is intended for use, distribution, or publication and that is developed by an

employee within the scope or as a result of his or her employment shall be claimed as the sole property of, and may be copyrighted, licensed, trade secreted, or patented by the County Board of Education. (EC 1044, 1045, 32360)

(Adopted 4-25-77)
(Revised 4-8-80)
(Revised and renumbered 3-22-88)

3452* Use of Copyright-Protected Material
It is the intent of the Board that the County Office of Education adhere to the provisions of the U.S. Copyright Law. All County Office of Education staff shall comply with the provisions of the law. Any staff member who willingly violates the Copyright Law shall be held personally liable for infringement and may be subject to disciplinary action. Copyrighted material shall be treated as the property of the copyright holder, with all rights and limitations specified in the law.

Section 107 of the law allows educators "fair use" of copyrighted material, meaning that limited numbers of copies of portions of copyrighted works for classroom, scholarship, or research purposes may be made without infringing on copyright. County Office of Education staff shall adhere to the fair use guidelines established in the regulations for printed materials and off-air video recordings.

Fair use guidelines have not yet been developed for software; therefore, staff shall adhere to restrictions in regulation 3452.3R on duplication of software.

The classroom uses allowed under the fair use doctrine for print and video shall be deemed to apply to use by County Office staff in instructional or training settings for the public education clients served by the office. (Title 17, U.S. Code)

(Adopted 3-22-88)

3453* Use of Proprietary Software Products
It is the intent of the Board that the County Office of Education adhere to the provisions of copyright law

(Title 17, U.S. Code) and publishers' license agreements, including trade secret provisions, in the area of proprietary software products. (Proprietary products are those made or marketed by persons having exclusive manufacturing and sales rights, who may or may not be the copyright holders.) Therefore, persons may use or cause to be used on office computing equipment only software that is included in one of the following categories.

    a. Public domain (i.e., uncopyrighted) software
    b. Software covered by a licensing agreement with the software author, authors, vendor, or developer, whichever is applicable (A licensing agreement is a legal contract authorizing use of the software.)
    c. Software purchased by the office, with a record of the purchase on file
    d. Software purchased by the user, with a record of purchase available for office verification
    e. Software donated to the office and officially accepted by the Board
    f. Software being reviewed or demonstrated by the users in order to reach a decision about possible future purchase, license, or acceptance of a donation

Prohibited

1. Copying more than one work or two excerpts from a single author during one class term or per workshop or series of training sessions
2. Copying more than three works from a collective work or periodical volume during one class term or per workshop or series of training sessions
3. More than nine instances of multiple copying for distribution to students during one class term or in one workshop or series of training sessions
4. Copying used to create or replace or substitute for anthologies or collective works
5. Copying of "consumable" works such as workbooks, standardized tests, answer sheets

Note: These prohibitions do not apply to current news magazines and newspapers.

(Approved 3-22-88)

3452.2R Off-Air Video Recording

To help ensure compliance with the law, the following notice shall be posted on all video tape recorders in use in the office:

Warning: Federal law provides severe civil and criminal penalties for the unauthorized reproduction, distribution, or exhibition of copyrighted motion pictures, video tapes, or video discs.

The following guidelines were developed to apply only to off-air recording by nonprofit educational institutions.

Permitted as Fair Use

1. A broadcast program may be recorded off-air simultaneously with broadcast transmission (including simultaneous cable retransmission) and retained by a nonprofit educational institution for a period not to exceed the first 45 consecutive calendar days after date of recording. Upon conclusion of such retention period, all off-air recordings must be erased or destroyed immediately. "Broadcast programs" are television programs transmitted by television stations for reception by the general public without charge.
2. Off-air recording may be used once by individual teachers, consultants, or other trainers in the course of relevant instructional or training activities and repeated once only when instructional reinforcement is necessary in classrooms and similar settings, during the first 10 consecutive work days in the 45-calendar-day retention period.
3. Off-air recordings may be made only at the request of and used by individual teachers, consultants, or other trainers and may not be regularly recorded in anticipation of requests. No broadcast program may be recorded off-air more than once at the request of the same teacher, consultant, or other trainer, regardless of the number of times the program may be broadcast.
4. A limited number of copies may be reproduced from each off-air recording to meet the needs of

teachers and other trainers under these guidelines. Each such additional copy shall be subject to all provisions governing the original recording.

5. After the first 10 consecutive work days, off-air recordings may be used up to the end of the 45-calendar-day retention period only for evaluation purposes (i.e., to determine whether or not to include the broadcast program as part of ongoing training activities—in which case permission from the producer would be required).
6. Off-air recordings need not be used in their entirety, but the recorded programs may not be altered from their original content.

Prohibited

1. Off-air recording in anticipation of teacher or other staff member requests
2. Using the recording for instruction after the 10-day use period
3. Holding the recording for weeks or indefinitely because—

   units, workshops, or training sessions requiring the program concepts were not held within the 10-day use period

   an interruption or technical problems delayed its use

   another teacher, consultant, or trainer wishes to use it

   of any other assumed "legitimate" educational reason
4. Physically or electronically merging or combining off-air recordings to constitute instructional anthologies or compilations
5. Using off-air recordings or programs rented or purchased from a video store for entertainment during the work day or evenings (This constitutes a public showing for which special fees must be paid.)
6. Using owned equipment for making or playing back copies that are not legally required

(Approved 3-22-88)

Carmel Clay Schools
Copyright Policy

It is the intent of the Board of Education of Carmel Clay Schools to adhere to the provisions of the current copyright laws and congressional guidelines.

The Board recognizes that unlawful copying and use of copyrighted materials contributes to higher costs for materials, lessens the incentives for development of quality educational materials, and fosters an attitude of disrespect for law that is in conflict with the educational goals of this School Corporation.

The Board directs that Corporation employees adhere to all provisions of Title 17 of the United States Code, entitled "Copyrights," and other federal legislation and guidelines related to the duplication, retention, and use of copyrighted materials.

The Board further directs that:

1. Unlawful copies of copyrighted materials may not be produced on Corporation-owned equipment.
2. Unlawful copies of copyrighted material may not be used with Corporation-owned equipment, within Corporation-owned facilities, or at Corporation-sponsored functions.
3. The legal and/or insurance protection of the Corporation will not be extended to employees who unlawfully copy and use copyrighted materials.

Employees who make and/or use copies of copyrighted materials in their jobs are expected to be familiar with published provisions regarding fair use and public display and are further expected to be able to provide their supervisor, upon request, the justification under Sections 107 or 110 of USC 17 for copies that have been made or used.

Employees who use copyrighted materials that do not fall within fair use or public display guidelines will be able to substantiate that the materials meet one of the following tests:

1. The materials have been purchased from an authorized vendor by the individual employee or the Corporation and a record of the purchase exists.
2. The materials are copies covered by a licensing agreement between the copyright owner and the Corporation or the individual employee.
3. The materials are being reviewed or demonstrated by the user to reach a decision about possible future purchase or licensing, and a valid agreement exists that allows for such use.

Though there continues to be controversy regarding interpretation of the copyright laws, this policy represents a sincere effort to operate legally. All school employees will be provided with copies of this policy and accompanying rulings.

Adopted 1-27-86

Guidelines for Use of Copyrighted Materials

Copyright is the exclusive right that protects an author, composer, or programmer from having his or her work published, recorded, exhibited, translated, or reproduced by way of copies and other versions, except by permission. The purpose of copyright is to encourage the development of new and original works and to stimulate their wide distribution by assuring that their creators will be fairly compensated for their contributions to society.

Current American copyright law is embodied in Title 17 of the United States Code. Works of authorship include, but are not limited to, the following categories: computer programs; dramatic works, including any accompanying music; literary works; motion pictures and other audiovisual works; musical works, including any accompanying words; pantomimes and choreographic works; pictorial, graphic, and sculptural works; and sound recordings.

The law affects classroom practices and necessitates that educational staff examine:

WHAT they copy

HOW MUCH they copy

COPYRIGHT ISSUES AND POLICIES

the PURPOSES for which they copy

the CONDITIONS under which they copy

Of special interest to educational staff are the "fair use" doctrine and the accompanying congressional guidelines, that stipulate what may and may not be copied for use in schools and classrooms.

The following pages explain some highlights of the law and its accompanying guidelines. The guidelines, while not law, were generated in response to questions. They will be modified by future court decisions and legislative action. However, they are an interpretation of the law as developed by congressional sub-committees.

If there are questions not covered by these pages, staff members should contact the Office of Media Services.

COMPUTER SOFTWARE

A teacher may:

make one archival or back-up copy of a copyrighted program. The school must keep this copy in storage and may only use the copy if the original has been damaged and has been sent to the publisher for repair.

adapt a copyrighted program from one language to another for which it is not commercially available or add features to a program to better meet local needs.

write the publishers of copyrighted programs in order to obtain permission to use the software in a manner that could be a violation of the copyright law.

A teacher may not (without the express permission of the software publisher/copyright owner):

make multiple copies of copyrighted software (or a locally produced adaptation or modification), even for use within a school or school district.

make replacement copies from an archival or back-up copy.

make copies of copyrighted software (or locally-produced adaptation or modification) to be sold, leased, loaned, transmitted, or even given away to other users.

load a copyrighted program into several computers or a network from the same diskette and use them simultaneously.

make multiple copies of the printed documentation that accompanies copyrighted software.

SUGGESTIONS:
Remember that WITH PERMISSION FROM THE COPYRIGHT OWNER the above prohibitions may be removed ... or at least significantly modified.

A teacher should be skeptical of those who say, "Go ahead and copy; nobody will ever know." The teacher will know. Illegal copying of software is theft of the software authors' and publishers' legitimate right to produce income from their efforts.

The cost of necessary multiple copies of software should be included in the budget for educational projects. Buying enough will relieve the temptation to make unauthorized copies. The Office of Media Services will make every effort possible to provide funds for worthy projects. Teachers may discover that the school system already has several copies of the software needed; these could be gathered together for a project.

Teachers may inquire from OMS about special licenses available from software companies that allow the user to make and use multiple copies at reduced cost. It is necessary to follow the guidelines set up by the license so that software publishers will be encouraged to provide them to schools.

VIDEOTAPES

RECORDING TELEVISION BROADCASTS
The guidelines were developed to apply to off-air recording by nonprofit educational institutions.

An individual teacher may:

record a broadcast program off-air simultaneously with broadcast transmission (including simultaneous cable re-transmission) and retain it for a period NOT TO EXCEED THE FIRST FORTY-FIVE (45) consecutive calendar days after the date of the recording.

COPYRIGHT ISSUES AND POLICIES

Upon conclusion of such retention period, all off-air recordings must be erased or destroyed immediately. "Broadcast programs" are television programs transmitted by television stations for reception by the general public without charge. The 1984 ratification of the Brussels Satellite Convention—a public law agreement obligating states to suppress the unauthorized distribution of satellite-derived signals without the consent of the originating organization—provided Congress with the opportunity to pass legislation affirming the right of the private viewers—that is, HOME VIEWERS ONLY—to receive satellite signals without fear of violation of U.S. law, so long as no further distribution of the received signals takes place.

use off-air recordings once in the course of relevant teaching activities and repeat them once only when instructional reinforcement is necessary, in classrooms and similar places devoted to instruction within a single building, cluster, or campus, as well as in the homes of students receiving formalized home instruction, during the first ten (10) consecutive school days in the forty-five (45) calendar day retention period. "School days" are school session days—not counting weekends, holidays, vacations, examination periods, or other scheduled interruptions—within the forty-five (45) calendar day retention period.

make off-air recordings at the request of and for use by individual teachers. Off-air recordings may not be regularly recorded in anticipation of requests. No broadcast program may be recorded off-air more than once at the request of the same teacher, regardless of the number of times the program may be broadcast.

reproduce a limited number of copies from each off-air recording to meet the legitimate needs of teachers under these guidelines. Each such additional copy shall be subject to all provisions governing the original recording.

after the first ten (10) consecutive school days, use off-air recordings to the end of the forty-five (45) calendar

day retention period only for teacher evaluation purposes, i.e., to determine whether or not to include the broadcast program in the teaching curriculum. The recording may not be used in the recording institution for student exhibition or any other nonevaluative purpose without authorization.

use only a portion of an off-air recording. Off-air programs need not be used in their entirety, but the recorded programs may not be altered from their original content. Off-air recordings may not be physically or electronically combined or merged to constitute teaching anthologies or compilations.

NOTE: All copies of off-air recordings must include the copyright notice on the broadcast program as recorded.

Each school is expected to establish appropriate control procedures to maintain the integrity of these guidelines.

In January 1984, the U.S. Supreme Court ruled, in the so-called Sony Betamax case, that the videotaping of television programs off the air for home use is not a violation of copyright law. Some educators contend that the Court said it is now all right for a teacher to tape any program at home, carry it to school, and use it in a classroom. "Anyone who thinks this is making a grave mistake," says Kenton Pattie, who heads the Government Relations Department of the International Communications Industries Association. "There is absolutely nothing in the 82-page decision to support this contention." Carmel Clay Schools is accepting the Senate Committee Guidelines that a program *may be taped at home or school* for use, BUT PLAYED ONLY ONCE, plus one time for reinforcement. *Permission to retain and use again*, however, must be obtained from the copyright holder.

USING COPYRIGHTED VIDEOTAPES:

A teacher may:

use in face-to-face instruction a videocassette PURCHASED BY THE SCHOOL even though it bears a

COPYRIGHT ISSUES AND POLICIES 185

warning label FOR HOME USE ONLY. The key is that the tape is INCORPORATED AS PART OF THE SYSTEMATIC TEACHING activities of the program in which it is being used.

use for instructional purposes a RENTAL VIDEOCASSETTE bearing the FOR HOME USE ONLY label if the program is used as a part of planned, systematic, direct instructional activities.

A teacher may not:

use either a purchased or rental video program labelled FOR HOME USE ONLY in other than planned, direct, instructional activities. The program may NOT be used for entertainment, fund-raisers, nor time-fillers. Any use, other than instructional, must be negotiated at the time of purchase or rental, usually in the form of a licensing agreement.

make an archival or back-up copy of a copyrighted film or videotape.

LIBRARIES AND STUDENTS HAVE ADDITIONAL PRIVILEGES OTHERS DO NOT

A student may:

tape a recording to use as background music for a slide production to be USED IN CLASS. (Since a class effort might be appropriate at a later time as a media fair project or as part of a public display, either inside or outside the classroom, the student is advised to develop an original composition or to use music from a production library or other sources for which the school has obtained a license and copyright permissions.)

tape a song from a record owned by the student in order to provide music for a class photography project. The program may be shown at no charge to a parent group. However, if the record is owned by a parent, or if admission will be charged, taping the song would be an infringement.

use an opaque projector to enlarge a visual from a book or magazine onto a poster. (An outline map of

the U.S., the states, and rivers may not be copyrighted. These are considered public domain. The colors and details, however, are copyrighted. Any commercial map may be used to generate merely an outline map.)

A student may not:

be directed to violate copyright in behalf of a teacher.

donate student photocopies (that incorporate copyrighted material) to become part of a school's collection.

A library may:

copy unpublished works (print and phonorecords) for purpose of preservation and security.

copy print materials or phonorecords to replace damaged, deteriorating, lost, or stolen copies if replacements cannot be obtained at a fair price. A music teacher may preserve or replace library copies when not available for purchase.

reproduce for a patron (student, staff, or member of the community) a single copy of one article or small part of a work to become the property of the patron for the purpose of study or research. (In an effort to promote material the library may also reproduce a single copy of an article or a page of a book for all teachers.) THE COPY MUST DISPLAY THE COPYRIGHT WARNING.

photocopy for the purpose of inter-library loan. However, the following inter-library loan restriction applies: MORE THAN SIX COPIES OF AN ARTICLE from a periodical (not a single issue, but over a year) shall be considered excessive and interpreted as an evasion of purchase of said periodical.

The library media specialist and the media staff are protected from copyright infringement violation by users of equipment under their jurisdiction if every duplicating machine is posted with a copyright warning to the effect that "the use of this machine to reproduce copyrighted material beyond the legal fair use is

COPYRIGHT ISSUES AND POLICIES 187

punishable by fine and/or imprisonment of the user."

These guidelines will, from time to time, be revised. However, as in many other areas of the profession, copyright law interpretation is continuously changing. Staff must comply with any court decisions or changes in the law that pertain to use of copyrighted materials in the educational setting.

REQUEST FOR PERMISSION TO COPY

Date _____

Office of Media Services
Carmel Clay Educational
 Services Center
P.O. Box 2099
Carmel, IN 46032

Person/School making request

_____

TO: Permissions Department

Dear Permissions Department:

We request permission to copy the following copyrighted materials:

Materials to be copied:

Number of copies to be made:

Copy medium:

Use of copies:

Anticipated date of first use:

Distribution of copies:

If we have not heard from you within 30 days, we shall assume the permission to duplicate has been granted.

Thank you for your cooperation. I an enclosing a copy of this request for your files, signed by me, and a self-addressed envelope for the return of this request.

_____
(Signature)

COPYRIGHT ISSUES AND POLICIES

```
                    PRODUCER REPLY
     Title _____ Date _____

     _____

     Permission granted _____
                              (Signature)

     Permission denied _____

     Conditions or details: _____

     _____

     _____
```

California Instructional Video Clearinghouse
Excerpted from the Handbook for
Review Committee Members
Copyright Guidelines

Exclusive Rights of the Copyright Owner

The copyright owner has five basic rights. Violation of any of these rights is an infringement of the copyright law.

The copyright owner has the right to . . .

reproduce the work

prepare derivative works

perform the work

display the work

distribute the work

But What About Fair Use?

Congress has given the five exclusive rights to the copyright holder, but Congress also added some limitations. If there were not limits on the owner's rights, it would

not be possible to copy anything for any reason without the owner's permission. Some of these limits are outlined specifically in various Sections of the law. Other limits are relegated to the broad interpretations under Fair Use.

"Fair Use" has been the cry educators have used when copying for instructional purposes. Educators have a tendency to lump all copying done in the school setting under the banner "fair use" because schools are nonprofit and the copying is done to teach students. "Fair use" is often used as an excuse for copying rather than a well thought out reason for copying. Fair Use is part of the copyright law.

Section 107 of the 1976 Copyright Act discusses four factors that determine whether copying can be done legally. All FOUR of the factors must be considered in determining fair use. All FOUR criteria must be met before copying of any material is allowed. The law does not give one factor more weight over another. However, the courts have generally placed the most emphasis on the last factor, while the second factor is generally accorded the least importance and is also the most unclear of the four.

1. The purpose and character of the use, including whether such use is of a commercial nature or is for nonprofit educational purposes.
2. The nature of the copyrighted work.
3. The amount and substantiality of the portion used in relation to the copyrighted work as a whole.
4. The effect of the use upon the potential market for or value of the copyrighted work.

The four factors are explained below.

PURPOSE AND CHARACTER OF THE WORK

If the purpose for copying does not fall into the categories of criticism, comment, news reporting, scholarship, or research, it is not a fair use. The fair use guidelines are not to be interpreted as any sort of not-for-profit or educational "carte blanche" for copying.

NATURE OF THE COPYRIGHTED WORK

"Where the nature of the copyrighted work is more in the nature of a collection of facts than in the nature of a creative or imaginative work, alleged infringers have greater license to use portions of such work under the fair use doctrine than they would have if creative work were involved." *(New York Times Co. v. Roxbury Data Interface, Inc.)* In other words, copying a news magazine article (factual) is more likely to be allowed under Fair Use than copying a short story (creative).

AMOUNT OF THE WORK USED

The use of an entire work, in other words, wholesale copying, can NEVER be a fair use, even in cases where the infringer had no intent to infringe. Copying a large portion of a work or the "essence" of a work is an infringement.

FAIR USE SUMMARY

Copying parts of or entire works for use in a classroom cannot be done simply because the purpose is educational. The Fair Use statute is used to determine the legality of copying when the instance of copying is not addressed in the other sections of the Copyright Act. In other words, first look to the Copyright Act and the accompanying guidelines for the permission to copy. If the copying is not specifically prohibited, it MAY be allowed under Fair Use.

Guidelines for Education or Classroom Copying of Books or Periodicals (Not Musical or Audiovisual Works)

There are guidelines established to help educators decide when copying print materials is allowed. *Guidelines for Classroom Copying in Nonprofit Educational Institutions* was written by educators, authors, and publishers and is part of the legislative history of the Copyright Act. The guidelines are not a part of the law.

The guidelines are prefaced by the statement: "There may be instances in which copying which does not fall

COPYRIGHT ISSUES AND POLICIES

within the guidelines stated below may nonetheless be permitted under the criteria of fair use."

SINGLE COPYING

Teachers may make single copies of a chapter of a book; an article from a periodical or newspaper; a short story, essay, or poem; a chart, graph, diagram, drawing, cartoon, or picture from a book, periodical, or newspaper to teach a class.

MULTIPLE COPYING

Multiple copies (one copy per pupil in a course) can be made if it meets the criteria of brevity, spontaneity, and cumulative effect and if each copy contains a notice of copyright.

1. Brevity—A complete poem printed on no more than two pages or an excerpt from a longer poem not to exceed 250 words copied in either case.
   A complete article, story, or essay of less than 2,500 words or an excerpt from prose less than 1,000 words or 10% of the work, whichever is less, but in either event a minimum of 500 words to be copied. One chart, graph, diagram, drawing, cartoon, or picture per book or periodical issue.
2. Spontaneity—Copying is done by the teacher when there is not a reasonable length of time to request and receive permission to copy.
3. Cumulative Effect—The copying is only for one course, and only nine instances of multiple copying per course during one class term is allowed. Not more than one short poem, article, story, essay, or two excerpts may be copied from the same author, nor more than three from the same collective work or periodical volume during one class term.

SPECIAL WORKS

Short works such as children's books are often less than 2,500 words. These works cannot be copied as a whole; but an excerpt of not more than two published

pages containing not more than 10% of the words found in the text may be reproduced.

PROHIBITIONS TO SINGLE OR MULTIPLE COPYING
You can't copy:

to substitute for purchase or replacement

workbooks, exercises, standardized tests, or answer sheets

the same item by the same teacher term after term

if it is directed by a higher authority

if there is a charge to students beyond the photocopy cost

to create, replace, or substitute for anthologies, compilations, or collective works

Guidelines for Videotaping

OFF-THE-AIR RECORDING
Guidelines for Off-the-Air Recording of Broadcast Programming for Educational Purposes is a product of Congressman Robert Kastenmeier's committee and is not part of the law. It does serve as the authority for taping off-air for educational purposes.

1. The guidelines apply only to off-air recording by nonprofit educational institutions.
2. Videotapes may be kept for only 45 calendar days after the recording date. The tapes must be erased after this time.
3. The videotape may be shown to students only during the first 10 school days after the recording date. It may be repeated once for reinforcement. (Points 2 and 3 are the 45-10 rule).
4. Off-air recordings may be made only at the request of an individual teacher and not in anticipation of a teacher request. The same teacher can request the program be recorded only once.
5. If several teachers request the same program be recorded, duplicate copies may be made.

COPYRIGHT ISSUES AND POLICIES 193

6. After the first ten school days allowed for showing, the recording may only be used for evaluation purposes.
7. Off-air recordings may not be edited or combined with other recordings to create an anthology or a new work.
8. All copies of the recording must contain a notice of copyright as a broadcast.
9. Schools are expected to establish the appropriate controls to ensure compliance with these guidelines.

The above guidelines and the law do not address the situation of a teacher who videotapes a program off-air at home and then uses the videotape in the classroom. A review of the literature indicates that the teacher should follow the above guidelines to comply with the spirit of the law.

PUBLIC BROADCAST SYSTEMS

Public Broadcasting Service, Public Television Library, Great Plains National Instructional Television Library, and Agency for Instructional Television allow educators to videotape their programs off-air under these conditions:

1. Recordings may be made by students or teachers in accredited, nonprofit educational institutions.
2. Recordings may be used only for instruction in a classroom, lab, or auditorium. (Not restricted to one classroom or one teacher.)
3. Recordings may not be shared outside of that school.
4. Recordings may be used as often as needed for seven days and must then be erased.

"FOR HOME USE ONLY" VIDEOTAPES

Rented videotapes often carry the warning "FOR HOME USE ONLY," which raises the question of whether the rented videotapes may be used in the classroom. If the videotape has been cleared for public performance, there is no problem using it in the classroom.

The gray area revolves around whether a classroom is a public place. The debate over this question will continue until a court case resolves it. In the meantime, a review of literature INDICATES that a teacher COULD show a home-use-only videotape in a classroom with the reasoning that educators have the right to display or perform works in face-to-face teaching situations. A review of the literature indicates that the videotape must meet an instructional goal and not be entertainment for the students.

Display, Performances, and Copying Other Audiovisual Works

If there were no exceptions to the five exclusive rights of the copyright owner (the rights to reproduce, prepare derivative works, perform, display, and distribute the copyrighted work) no audiovisual materials could be used in a school. The material would be displayed or performed and would violate the copyright law.

To protect educators when using copyrighted audiovisual materials in a class, the following conditions must be met:

YOU MAY USE AUDIOVISUAL MATERIALS WHEN

1. It is shown as part of the instructional program.
2. It is shown by students, teachers, or guest speakers.
3. It must be shown in the classroom, studio, workshop, library, gym, auditorium.
4. It must be shown in a face-to-face teaching situation or in the same building or general area.
5. It must be shown only to students or educators.
6. Copyright notice must be included and it must be a legitimate copy.

YOU MAY NOT USE AUDIOVISUAL
MATERIALS WHEN

1. It is for entertainment or recreational purposes and unrelated to a teaching activity.
2. It is transmitted by radio or television from an outside location (such as closed circuit from another building).

COPYRIGHT ISSUES AND POLICIES

3. It is shown to an audience other than students or teachers, even when students or teachers are present.
4. You may not use an illegally acquired or duplicated copy.

GUIDELINES FOR COPYING MUSIC

The guidelines for educational uses of music are not a part of the law but are helpful in determining when copying music is allowed.

COPYING FOR PERFORMANCE

Emergency copying is allowed only if the purchased copies are not available for a performance. The photocopies must then be destroyed.

COPYING FOR ACADEMIC PURPOSES

Single or multiple copies of excerpts may be made if less than 10% of the whole work and if it is not a performable unit such as a selection, movement, or aria.

Purchased music may be edited if the fundamental character of the work is not distorted or the lyrics altered or added if none exist.

A single copy of an entire performable unit can be made if it is out of print or unavailable except in a larger work. It can't be used for performance.

A single recording may be made for aural exercises or tests and may be retained by the school or teacher.

A single copy may be made as a free service for the blind.

A single copy of a student performance may be made for study and for the archives.

A single copy may be made for preservation or replacement in the library when copies are not available for purchase.

COPYING THAT IS PROHIBITED

You can't copy to create, replace, or substitute for anthologies, compilations, or collective works.

You can't copy to avoid purchase.

Questions and Answers

The answers to these copyright questions are based upon the opinions of experts in the copyright area whose writings have been reviewed for this publication.

COPYING FROM BOOKS AND PERIODICALS

Q. May a teacher make a transparency from a book?
A. Yes, this falls within the guidelines of single copying for classroom use.

Q. Can a teacher duplicate materials and put them on reserve at the library?
A. Yes, if the copying is spontaneous and if copying falls under guidelines for education or classroom use of books and periodicals or is a fair use.

Q. A teacher finds an O. Henry short story that would fit into a unit to be taught next week. Can multiple copies be made for the class?
A. Yes, since it was the inspiration of the teacher and also meets the requirement of brevity. The copies can't be used next term.

Q. Can a teacher make copies from a workbook?
A. No, workbooks are consumable materials and can't be copied.

Q. Some materials are marked as follows: "All rights reserved. No part of this book may be reproduced or utilized in any form or by any means, electronic or mechanical, including photocopying, recording, or by any information storage and retrieval system, without permission in writing from the publisher." Can this material still be copied for education purposes?
A. Yes, fair use would still apply.

Q. A teacher ran across a book that has no copyright notice. Can copying be done freely in this instance?
A. No one can be certain that a work is in the public domain unless a notice states that reproduction is permitted. When in doubt about copyright status, ask permission to copy or contact the Copyright Office.

COPYRIGHT ISSUES AND POLICIES

Q. How strict are the Guidelines for Classroom Copying?

A. The purpose of the guidelines is to state the minimum and not the maximum standards of educational fair use. There may be instances where copying doesn't fall within the guidelines but is permissible under the criteria of Fair Use.

COPYING MUSIC

Q. In order to avoid damaging records, the media center has made cassette tapes for circulation.

A. This is not allowed because a) it is a substitute for purchase of possible replacement copies and b) copying of an entire work is not allowed.

Q. A teacher is making a sound/slide presentation and wants to use several popular songs as background. Is this allowed?

A. Using portions of songs (less than a performable unit) is probably allowed; however, using an entire song is not.

Q. The music teacher has changed the lyrics of a song to be presented at the Spring Banquet in order to be more contemporary. Can 30 copies be made for the choir?

A. No, altering or adding lyrics changes the fundamental character of a work and is not allowed under the copyright guidelines.

Q. Several students forgot their music the night of the band performance. Can copies be made just for use that night?

A. Yes, emergency copying to replace purchased copies is allowed. The duplicates must be replaced by the originals.

Q. A teacher wants to make a cassette copy of a Beethoven record in the media center so that the music can be stopped and started easily. The cassette will be used for the final exam in music.

A. Yes, one copy of the record can be made for exams or aural exercises and may be retained by the school or teacher.

COPYING AUDIOVISUAL MATERIALS

Q. The school only has one slide projector. Since the school has several filmstrip projectors, can some of the slides that the school owns be converted into filmstrips?
A. No, this type of copying is prohibited. Even though the school has purchased the slides, the right to copy the slides was not purchased.

Q. A couple of teachers have some filmstrips that they would like to combine into one. They will make only one copy that will be for instructional purposes.
A. This is not allowed under the guidelines. Written permission must be obtained.

COPYING OFF-THE-AIR

Q. Can a school tape a movie off-air and use it in the classroom?
A. Yes, if: a teacher specifically requests the copy be made, a notice of copy is included, it is shown to students within ten school days, it is erased within 45 days (unless you want to preview it at a later date for possible purchase), and it is used for instructional rather than entertainment purposes.

Q. Can a teacher tape a movie at home and show it in a class?
A. Yes, following the guidelines in the previous answer.

Q. Can a media specialist videotape a program that the science teacher may want to use in class?
A. Not really. According to the guidelines, the teacher must request that a specific program be videotaped.

COPYRIGHT ISSUES AND POLICIES

Q. Can a teacher show last Sunday's Walt Disney cartoon during a rainy recess?
A. No, the videotape must be used for instructional not entertainment purposes.

Q. Can the school show a group of parents and students a recently televised program on drugs?
A. Probably not. The presence of parents constitutes a public performance.

Q. Can a program taped off-air be transmitted to several classrooms via closed circuit?
A. Probably. Closed circuit may be considered similar to a face-to-face teaching situation. The question comes in when the transmission is from one building to another.

USING HOME-USE-ONLY VIDEOTAPE

Q. Can you use a videotape in a class if it was rented at a video store?
A. Probably. The question arises if showing a video to a group of students constitutes a public performance. The experts differ. You can probably show the videotape if it is for instructional, not entertainment purposes.

Q. Can you make a copy of a videotape that was rented if it is used only once and within the ten days?
A. No, copying an entire work that you do not have permission to copy is a violation of the copyright law.

Off-Air Video Recording Issues and Answers
San Diego County Office of Education

Distributed and developed in cooperation with:
Instructional Media Committee of the Area VI County
Assistant Superintendents for Instruction and Directors of Curriculum

Reprinted By
San Diego County
Office of Education 9-88

COPYRIGHT ISSUES AND POLICIES

Recent advances in technology have created unforeseen dilemmas for educators in the area of copyright law. The video recorder is an example of a technology which has an increasing impact on school systems. It has become a valuable instructional tool, if used appropriately, in the hands of dedicated classroom teachers.

While quick and easy access to a variety of broadcast programming has an immediate and compelling appeal, the use of such programming in the classroom carries with it a clear legal and moral responsibility to respect the protections provided in copyright law. Recent federal court decisions have made it quite clear that unlimited use and retention of off-air video recordings, without requesting permission or paying licensing fees, is a clear violation of the intent of the law.

Educators must be aware of their rights and responsibilities regarding this complex issue. It is important to understand that there are federal guidelines which provide for limited copying and retention of off-air video recording for a specified time period. In addition, the Fair Use provisions of copyright law permit limited use of copyrighted materials for educational purposes without permission or payment of fees.

The attached document has been developed by a committee of educators to provide districts with suggested strategies for revising existing policy or formulating a new policy on copyright. It provides a legal basis for the need, clarifies specific issues that should be included when developing a policy statement, and suggests practical ways to implement the policy and regulations.

The need for districts and counties to develop a copyright policy as a basis for maintaining legality has recently taken on a sense of urgency. The proliferation of home recording units, combined with the state's efforts under AB 803 to expand videocassette recorder (VCR) use in the schools requires that all educational agencies address this serious issue in the immediate future. In addition, recent AB 803 guidelines require that educational agencies have in place a copyright policy which applies to microcomputer software. It would be in their best interests to develop a comprehensive copyright statement which addresses the copyright issue for all instructional technologies.

It is our intent that the attached document will be of use in the initial planning required to develop an effective policy statement and accompanying regulations.

It is important to note that the recommendations expressed herein represent the informed opinions of the authors but do not constitute legal advice.

Chair: Donald S. Lake, Los Angeles County Office of Education

Committee Members: Dorothy Baird, Los Alamitos USD
Robert Bell, San Bernardino County Superintendent of Schools Office
Sue Quinn, Los Angeles USD
Kitty Salinas, Montebello USD
Ray Stansbury, Grossmont UHSD
Joseph White, Ventura County Superintendent of Schools Office

Distributed and developed in cooperation with:
Instructional Media Committee of the Area VI County Assistant Superintendents for Instruction and Directors of Curriculum

PART I

Use of Video Recordings in Educational Settings: Copyright and Evaluation Concerns

Recent advances in media technology promise to have a significant impact on classroom instruction. The proliferation of home video recording units has made it easy and inexpensive to record off-air programs for playback in home and school.

The use of video recordings for educational purposes has two major implications which must be addressed by policymakers. First is the issue of copyright. What can educators legally record and use for instruction? There are many questions and "gray areas" regarding the Fair Use provisions and federal guidelines for use of off-air programs. Second is the issue of evaluation. Most districts have established policies for evaluating materials for instructional use. Media materials often undergo a rigorous process involving teacher and administrative input prior to being approved for classroom use. However, video recordings taped at home by well-intentioned educators may circumvent these established evaluation procedures and leave districts and county offices open to potential criticism or legal action from members of the community. Thus, unsupervised off-air video recording has serious policy implications for all educational agencies.

Copyright Concerns

The federal Copyright Revision Act of 1976 (PL 94553) is designed to protect for a limited time the creative works of authors, artists and others, including the producers of instructional media. Without such protection there would be little incentive for creative people to continue to produce.

The Fair Use provisions of the law permit limited use of copyrighted materials for educational purposes without permission or payment of fee. In 1981, a congressional committee chaired by United States Representative Robert W. Kastenmeier issued guidelines which delineated the acceptable boundaries of Fair Use of off-air video recordings for educational purposes. While the guidelines do not carry the force of law, they represent a reasonable attempt to define the copyright Fair Use provisions for educators. The Fair Use guidelines are as follows:

COPYRIGHT ISSUES AND POLICIES 203

Guidelines for Off-Air Recording of Broadcast Programming for Educational Purposes (*Congressional Record*, October 14, 1981)

1. The guidelines were developed to apply only to off-air recording by nonprofit educational institutions.

2. A broadcast program may be recorded off-air simultaneously with broadcast transmission (including simultaneous cable retransmission) and retained by a nonprofit educational institution **for a period not to exceed the first forty-five (45) consecutive calendar days after date of recording.** Upon conclusion of such retention period, all off-air recordings must be erased or destroyed immediately. "Broadcast programs" are television programs transmitted by television stations for reception by the general public without charge.

3. Off-air recording may be used once by individual teachers in the course of relevant teaching activities, and repeated once only when instructional reinforcement is necessary in classrooms and similar places devoted to instruction within a single building, cluster or campus, as well as in the homes of students receiving formalized home instruction, **during the first ten (10) consecutive school days in the forty-five (45) day calendar day retention period.** "School days" are school session days - not counting weekends, holidays, vacations, examination periods, or other scheduled interruptions - within the forty-five (45) calendar day retention period.

4. **Off-air recordings may be made only at the request of and used by individual teachers, and may not be regularly recorded in anticipation of requests.** No broadcast program may be recorded off-air more than once at the request of the same teacher, regardless of the number of times the program may be broadcast.

5. A limited number of copies may be reproduced from each off-air recording to meet the legitimate needs of teachers under these guidelines. Each such additional copy shall be subject to all provisions governing the original recording.

6. After the first ten (10) consecutive school days, off-air recordings may be used up to the end of the forty-five (45) calendar day retention period only for teacher evaluation purposes, i.e., to determine whether or not to include the broadcast program in the teaching curriculum, and may not be used in the recording institution for student exhibition or any other non-evaluation purpose without authorization.

7. Off-air recordings need not be used in their entirety, but the recorded programs may not be altered from their original content. Off-air recordings may not be physically or electronically combined or merged to constitute teaching anthologies or compilations.

8. All copies of off-air recordings must include the copyright notice on the broadcast program as recorded.

9. **Educational institutions are expected to establish appropriate control procedures to maintain the integrity of these guidelines.**

It is understood that these guidelines do not cover all the problems an educator may encounter. Part II of this document suggests questions and answers on a number of related issues.

Evaluation Concerns

1. Sound educational practice, as well as several provisions of the Education Code, require that all instructional media materials be carefully evaluated and approved before being used in the classroom.

2. Proper review and evaluation helps to assure the quality and effectiveness of materials used for instruction. In addition, this process safeguards against criticism and legal action. Districts should review their procedures for the evaluation of classroom materials and design a process which protects employees and students.

3. Materials which fall under the requirement of 51550, 51820 and 51240 of the Education Code (sex education) are particularly vulnerable to community criticism. Individual teachers who use such materials without informing parents and providing the opportunity for review are subject to loss of their teaching credentials.

PART II

Some Questions and Answers About Copyright

What is the responsibility of the Board of Education?

The Board of Education is ultimately responsible for any copyright infringement by any employee. The lack of a clear policy makes school boards vulnerable to legal action even though they may have had no prior knowledge of the copyright violation. The best defense against legal action is for educational agencies to adopt and enforce a clearly defined policy statement with accompanying regulations addressing the specific issues.

What are the responsibilities of the site and district administrator?

Site and district administrators can be held legally responsible for the illegal actions of their staff members. **Staff members who knowingly or unknowingly violate copyright laws place administrators in legal jeopardy.** Consistently enforced administrative regulations which reflect board policy are the best protection for administrators. These regulations should be periodically presented to staff members as a reminder of their rights and responsibilities under the law.

What are the responsibilities of teachers and other staff members?

It is the responsibility of any teacher to provide materials that have a direct relationship to the curriculum in a format that contributes most effectively to achievement of educational goals and objectives. It is also the responsibility of the teacher or staff member to follow district policy and abide by the law. While the need for using whatever is available and appropriate at the "teachable moment" is recognized as valid, and while the television medium may be especially suitable for this purpose, this does not excuse the teacher from other constraints. Teachers may be held personally liable for deliberate violations of the copyright law. Perhaps more important is the role model a teacher presents as a law-abiding citizen. There are reasonable provisions for *limited* use of copyrighted television broadcasts in the classroom.

May any staff member use an off-air recording of a television broadcast in the classroom?

The Federal Copyright Revision Act (PL 94-553) allows for Fair Use of copyrighted material for educational use and sets forth criteria for such Fair Use. These criteria are subject to interpretation. To help clarify these issues, a committee of representatives from education and the film and television industry met for several years to recommend federal guidelines for Fair Use of off-air video recordings in education. (See p. 2-3.) The guidelines are *not* part of the copyright law and have not been tested in court, but they have been accepted by most of the educational community and some of the commercial interests.

What other requirements guide the use of off-air video recordings?

District and state requirements for evaluation of instructional materials must certainly be applied. For example, the state Education Code requires notification of parents and guardians of minor students when instructional materials are to be used that deal with sensitive issues involving sex education or sexually transmitted diseases.

May off-air recordings from a personal home video library be used in the classroom?

Fair Use provisions of the copyright law and the federal guidelines suggest that this use is permissible. **Repeated** use of copyrighted material in educational settings without the owner's permission is in violation of these guidelines. Written permission must be secured from the copyright owner if the teacher wishes to use a video recording in subsequent semesters.

May an educator record and use off-air recordings made from subscription TV services, such as HBO?

No, any such service must be negotiated contractually between the user and the owner of such a service.

Many tapes available for sale or rent from local video stores have labels stating "Not for public performance," "For home use only," or something to that effect. May a teacher legally use these in the classroom?

Legal use is permitted in a classroom or similar place devoted to instruction in face-to-face teaching activities.

May a rented tape be used in a recreational, entertainment, or fund-raising event at school?

No, not without a public performance license.

COPYRIGHT ISSUES AND POLICIES

Does the nonprofit status of the public schools exempt them from many limitations in the copyright law?

Schools are exempt under some conditions, but nonprofit educational status does not relieve educators of the responsibility to uphold the copyright law. The Fair Use doctrine and off-air video guidelines were developed to balance the legitimate needs of educators against the rights of copyright holders.

How can an administrator prevent violations of the law?

It is the administrator's primary responsibility to inform teachers of their rights and responsibilities within the law. This includes not only copyright law, but requirements within the Education Code for selection of educational materials and for parental consent before presenting materials on sex education and sexually transmitted diseases. Some administrators require teachers to complete simple forms providing title, length, and general content of programs recorded off-air and used with their classes.

Does a locally produced program presented on a cable channel fall under standard copyright restrictions?

Yes. Cable companies themselves must be careful to observe copyright law, and creators of locally originated programs may wish to retain rights.

Are there any programs broadcast which can be retained?

Yes. There are regional educational television networks that have purchased licenses allowing their subscribers to record and use specific programs for the duration of the contracts negotiated by the regional educational agency. Lists of programs may be obtained from regional ITV agencies.

Is it permissible to record programs using a satellite antenna?

There is much debate on this question. Presently it appears that such recording falls under the Fair Use provisions of the copyright law and federal guidelines for off-air recording. Legal interpretations covering satellite recording will be forthcoming in the near future.

What other materials besides video recordings are covered under the copyright law?

Print materials of all types, musical scores, self-published materials, computer software, sound recordings of all types, photographs, etc., are protected.

PART III

Positive Steps an Educational Agency Can Take

- Develop and have adopted a Board policy addressing district responsibility for compliance with copyright laws and regulations.

- Develop administrative regulations for implementing the Board-adopted copyright policy.

- Establish procedures for the use of on-site administrators in monitoring the legal and appropriate use of all instructional materials in the classroom.

- Provide all employees with information about their rights and responsibilities under copyright law.

- Review existing policies for evaluation and selection of materials and revise or adjust to accommodate new technologies.

- Set an example. Avoid making personal excuses for circumventing copyright law -- for print materials as well as for video recordings, computer software, or materials in any format.

The copyright forms on pages 8 through 11 are provided by Grossmont Union High School District, San Diego County, and Los Alamitos School District, Orange County. These samples illustrate how two districts monitor and validate the taping of video for classroom instruction based upon an established district policy. Sample forms can be adopted or modified for district use.

COPYRIGHT ISSUES AND POLICIES

Request for Off-Air Video Taping

I, the undersigned, having requested the _____ (name of agency) to video tape the following program(s) within the parameters of the policy set forth by the Governing Board, _____ (date) am aware of said policy (see reverse side) and agree to accept responsibility for the use and erasure of this material to prevent any infringement of copyright law in lieu of expressed written approval of the copyright proprietor.

Title of Program to be Copied _____

Date of Program _____ Date Program is Needed _____

Time of Program _____

Length of Program _____ Station or Channel _____

Special Instructions _____

Preview and Evaluation

Would you recommend this material for purchase?
_____ YES, High Priority
_____ YES, Low Priority
_____ NO

In what *specific* subject area(s) could this material be used? _____

Is the material accurate and authentic? _____ YES _____ NO

This material could be used in _____ College Prep _____ Applied Arts _____ Remedial Classes

Do present district films adequately cover the subject areas? _____ YES _____ NO

Do you want the video tape of this program to be retained until information regarding the sale, lease, free loan, or rental of this material is obtained? _____ YES _____ NO

Overall evaluation (summary, use, etc.) AND/OR reasons for requesting retention of tape: _____
_____
_____
_____
_____
_____

Video Tape Status - Office Use Only

_____ Available   Format: _____ 16mm _____ ¾" _____ ½" VHS   Date _____

                   Price _____

_____ May be retained indefinitely.

_____ May be kept on an indefinite basis, pending updated information on the program's future availability.

_____ Must be erased immediately.

_____ May be kept permanently on a licensed basis.

"Adopted from materials developed by the Grossmont Union High School District"

COPYRIGHT ISSUES AND POLICIES 211

VIDEO RECORDING USAGE REQUEST
(Office rental)

Date _____

Teacher's name _____ School _____

Title or description of program _____

Network producer (if known) _____

I am requesting permission to use the above program in my classroom(s) on _____
(date)

I consider this material appropriate and important for the following reasons:
_____
_____

If this program has been recorded off-air, I affirm that it will be erased according to Fair Use interpretations of federal copyright regulations.

_____
(Signature)

(See back of this form for checklist of state instructional materials requirements)

Adopted from materials developed by the Los Alamitos School District

Legal Compliance Evaluation

Desirable	Undesirable
Male and Female Roles	
____ No male or female stereotypes	____ Male or female stereotypes
____ Wide variety of occupational roles for both men and women	____ Unbalanced presentation of either male or female roles
____ Mentally and physically active roles given to both sexes	____ Domination by one sex of physically and mentally active roles
____ Sexually neutral language	____ Exclusion of female references
Ethnic and Cultural Groups	
____ Fair representation of cultural groups	____ Demeaning labels for minority groups
____ Appreciation for differences in life style	____ Value judgments as to cultural life styles
____ Representation of minority groups in variety of occupational roles	____ Minority groups depicted in stereotyped roles
____ Balanced, accurate historical presentation of ethnic and minority groups	____ One-sided historical presentations involving ethnic and minority groups
Entrepreneur and Labor	
____ Appreciation for contributions of all types of work	____ Demeaning references either to laboring or entrepreneur roles
____ Accurate presentations of roles and functions of laborer and entrepreneur	____ Biased representation of roles of entrepreneur and laborer
Ecology and Environment	
____ Accurate presentation of influences on human and other resources	____ Inaccurate, biased presentations about human resources and the environment
Dangerous Substances	
____ Treatment of use of alcohol, drugs, tobacco factual and not glamorized	____ Biased representation of value and use of dangerous substances
Religion	
____ Presentations of religious ideas in non-doctrinaire manner	____ Takes advantage of opportunity to encourage or discourage religious belief
____ Reflection of cultural diversity	____ Certain religious beliefs or practices held up to ridicule

Prohibitions also exist within the Education Code regarding the use of materials that describe, illustrate, or discuss human reproduction, sexually transmitted diseases, or related matters. (51550, 51820, 51240)

"Adopted from materials developed by the Los Alamitos School District"

☐ NOTES

1. Jerome K. Miller, *Using Copyrighted Videocassettes in Classrooms and Libraries* (Salem, MA: Copyright Information Services, 1984), 16.
2. Mary Hutchings Reed and Debra Stanek, "Library Use of Copyrighted Videotapes and Computer Software," *American Libraries* 17 (February 1986): special pull-out section, A.
3. Ibid., B.
4. Miller, 28.
5. Judith A. Gaston, editor, "Professional Interchange," *Sightlines* 23 (Spring 1990):
6. Janis H. Bruwelheide, "Practically Speaking: Do You Have a Copyright Policy?," *School Library Journal* (March 1989): 129.
7. Ibid.
8. Miller, 48.
9. Reed and Stanek, D.

5 INTELLECTUAL FREEDOM ISSUES AND POLICIES

PRINCIPLES OF INTELLECTUAL FREEDOM

The ALA's *Intellectual Freedom Manual* defines intellectual freedom as

> the right of any person to hold any belief whatever on any subject, and to express such beliefs or ideas in whatever way the person believes appropriate.... [However, that] freedom becomes virtually meaningless when accessibility to such expression is denied to other persons. [It is] manifested in the freedoms of speech and press dictates of the First Amendment, [and] forms the bulwark of our constitutional republic.[1]

Intellectual freedom affects many library policies, including circulation, access for minors, selection, and censorship. The best approach to handling complaints is to develop a policy and formal complaint procedure before a complaint arises, rather than as a consequence of any complaint. Also, all library staff should be knowledgeable about the complaint procedures and their implementation. The American Library Association's Office for Intellectual Freedom offers the following guidelines for librarians dealing with complaints:

1. Maintain a materials selection policy. It should be in written form and approved by the appropriate governing authority. It should apply to all library materials equally.
2. Maintain a library service policy. This should cover registration policies, programming and services in the library that involve access issues [an extension of the circulation policy].
3. Maintain a clearly defined method for handling complaints. The complaint must be filed in writing and the complainant must be properly identified before action is taken. A decision should be deferred until fully considered by appropriate administrative authority. The process should be followed, whether the complaint originates internally or externally.
4. Maintain in-service training. Conduct periodic in-service training to acquaint staff, administration, and the governing authority with the materials selection policy and library service policy and procedures for handling complaints.
5. Maintain lines of communication with civic, religious, educational and political bodies of the community. Library board and staff participation in local civic organizations and presentations to these organizations should emphasize the library's selection process and intellectual freedom principles.
6. Maintain a vigorous public information program on behalf of intellectual freedom. Newspapers, radio and television should be informed of policies governing resource selection and use, and of any special activities pertaining to intellectual freedom.
7. Maintain familiarity with any local municipal and state legislation pertaining to intellectual freedom and First Amendment rights.[2]

It is important to realize that following these practices will not preclude receiving complaints from pressure groups or individuals, but should provide a base from which to operate when these concerns arise. Elizabeth Futus performed a survey of public libraries in the United States in 1983, and found that 87 percent had intellectual freedom policies in

force, with 42 percent experiencing materials challenges within the past five years.[3] Most librarians feel that intellectual freedom concerns deal directly with access rather than selection activities, although the two activities are connected. Many items are collected by libraries, but until an item is accessed (i.e., circulated) there seems to be little controversy.

ACCESS FOR MINORS

The issue of access for minors is a hotly debated topic, especially regarding videos and films, and is a direct extension of intellectual freedom concerns. Libraries are confronted with a two-sided problem; on one side community pressures obligate them (to a degree) to acquire popular feature video titles, but the same community also exerts pressure to restrict their access.

A survey of 33 libraries done by Randy Pitman for *The Video Librarian* in 1986 revealed that 28 restricted access by children, with 24 libraries setting a flat restriction of 18 years or older.[4] Within the Northern Illinois Library System, a multitype library system consisting of 115 member libraries in northwestern Illinois, 28 out of 30 public libraries with video collections possess some type of age restriction. These ranged from age 13 (at which an adult card is issued) to age 18 and up. Many states have enacted access-for-minors statutes, and some prohibit libraries from loaning certain videos to minors.

The issues regarding access for minors are as follows:

- Should children have access to all library videos?
- What role should the librarian play in this access, and how does the materials selection policy enter into the picture?
- Should libraries use MPAA (or other) ratings, and more importantly, what is the importance (access consequence) attached to using such ratings?

The ALA's Access for Children and Young People to Videotapes and Other Nonprint Formats—An Interpretation of the Library Bill of Rights, states that "the library and its staff are responsible for providing equal access to library materials and services for all library users."[5] The ALA interpretation indicates that totally free access is the only option, unless prohibited by law, and that it is the parents—and only the parents—who may restrict their children—and only their children—from access to library materials and services.[6]

The interpretation recognizes that librarians cannot act in loco parentis, and supports the exercise by parents of their responsibility. It should be noted that, according to the philosophy outlined in both the Access to Resources and Services in the School Library Media Program, and Access for Children and Young People to Videotapes and Other Nonprint Formats statements, providing minors with library cards allowing parental signature for use of various materials may be unethical. The implication is that the burden of intellectual restriction falls solely upon the parents, and the library's only responsibility is to provide equal access to library materials and services.

The key to providing free access to materials for children consists in having clearly stated policies for collection development, selection, and circulation, as well as adopting a formal "challenged-materials" process. Librarians emphasize the role of literacy in helping people to recognize full human potential and become functional members of contemporary society. However, visual literacy is becoming as important as print literacy. Critical viewing skills are essential as viewers are forced to synthesize rational thought, emotions, and experiences (memory). Moving visual images are, to a degree, more powerful than the written word because, in order to synthesize the written word, one must be able to understand the denotation and connotation (context) of those words. Also, the power the words evoke comes from an internal understanding or "bringing the experience to a personal level." By contrast, the moving visual medium places the depth of experience in external control; in effect,

the viewer is seeing an interpretation of an experience through another's eyes.

Human maturation occurs on physical, emotional, cognitive, and psychosocial levels. Children pass through progressive stages of reading ability, motor skill coordination, cognitive ability, and emotional understanding as they grow. Why not levels of visual understanding as well? This argument is presented, not in defense of restricting access for minors, but rather to emphasize the differences between print and the moving visual images of film and video. A statement of this nature, indicating that libraries recognize the power of video, used in association with an unrestricted access for minors policy, may help emphasize the parents' responsibility in providing guidance for their children, while upholding the precepts of intellectual freedom at the same time.

MPAA RATINGS

Conjunctive with the access for minors issue is that of displaying MPAA ratings on library video titles. The ALA stance is clearly opposed to this practice; however, Joseph W. Palmer offers some cogent thoughts on this matter:

> It does seem to me that including MPAA ratings in catalog records does not necessarily mean that [the library endorses] or will enforce them; it could be viewed as merely providing patrons with easy access to information they want. If censorship may be defined as denying information that people want, because you disagree with it or you consider it dangerous, is not the refusal to provide [it] . . . a kind of censorship?[7]

Palmer goes on to cite Ranganathan's "laws of librarianship," saying that librarians should do everything they can to assist patrons in locating any materials they need and want, rationalizing that the MPAA ratings fall into this category.[8] Actually, ALA's Access for Children and Young People to Videotapes and Other Nonprint Formats statement does state that libraries may display MPAA ratings:

> This material may include information provided by video producers and distributors, promotional material on videotape packaging, and ... (MPAA) ratings if they are included on the tape or in the packaging by the original publisher.... Marking out or removing ratings information from videotape packages constitutes expurgation or censorship.[9]

Furthermore, the *Anglo-American Cataloguing Rules*, (2d revised edition, 1988) provides a specific place in the note area for "audience" (7.7B14)—implying an intended audience level.[10]

THE PUBLIC LIBRARY

Public libraries may want to include the following statement as part of the censorship section of their selection policy:

> ### Censorship and Materials Reconsideration
>
> The choice of library materials by users is an individual matter. Responsibility for access restrictions on library materials for children and adolescents rests with their parents and/or legal guardians. While a person may reject materials for him/herself and for his/her children, he/she cannot exercise censorship to restrict access to the materials by others. While the Library Board recognizes the differences between media and print, and the power of visual images as compared with print, it also supports intellectual freedom and endorses the following ALA documents, in part: Library Bill of Rights; Freedom To View; Statement on Labeling; Access for Children and Young People to Videotapes and Other Nonprint Formats; and Restricted Access to Library Materials. However, the Library Board recognizes its social responsibility to the community, and provides a vehicle by which parents can restrict (limit) their minor children's reading, viewing, and listening; otherwise, free access to all library materials is assumed, regardless of age.

> Citizens wishing to register complaints or concerns about specific library materials should complete the Request for Reconsideration of Library Materials form, available from the library information office (Central Library) or from branch heads. A formal reconsideration process involving the citizen and library will follow, as delineated in the materials reconsideration procedures.

☐ PUBLIC LIBRARY RECONSIDERATION PROCEDURES

In all types of libraries (public, school, and academic) authority and responsibility emanate from the governing body or board. The formal reconsideration procedures will reflect the degree of authority that body has bestowed upon the library staff. It is the librarian's task to gain the authority, interpret the policy, and define and delineate the procedures so that they accurately reflect that policy, but do not present needless bureaucratic obstacles for patrons or staff.

Regarding intellectual freedom concerns, the object is conflict resolution, not a final solution. Both parties may be unsatisfied with the outcome, but agree to discontinue the conflict. Governing bodies are ultimately responsible for their policy actions, but by their very nature should delegate authority and responsibility to specifically educated staff. Delegation implies support, which should be consistently supplied throughout the reconsideration process.

Reconsideration procedures vary greatly according to the structure of the organization. In small and medium-sized public libraries, the director may meet with the citizen to resolve the complaint. In other instances, the department head may initially meet with the complainant. These informal meetings should not be overlooked. The vast majority of complaints can be amicably resolved using personal conferences, whereas a shift to a more formal procedure might inflate the problem.

If the informal method does not work, a formal procedure must be initiated. This usually involves a report from a materials evaluation committee, and an eventual decision by

the director or board if necessary. In some organizational structures, it may be wise to shield middle management from this decision task at the outset, resolving it at the upper management level. In larger, more diverse libraries, the department and/or branch head should always be involved in the process. Also, it is wise to employ a committee in this review process. It is vitally important that the reconsideration procedures delineate, in a chronological fashion, who does what when. Notification of the results to the complainant should also be outlined and timelines provided for the entire process. Notification should be verifiable (e.g., by certified mail). The procedures should include a time period during which the challenged material cannot be subject to reconsideration by the same group (or any other group) again. It is also important that the challenged materials be kept on the shelves during the reconsideration process.

Videos, because of their form, do not reveal their contents easily. Most print reconsideration forms have a statement such as: "To what in the book do you object? Please cite specific page references." The task of analyzing visual information through words is difficult even for professional reviewers, therefore a closed screening of the challenged video, with the complainant present, might be a good idea. Following is a Model Public Library Request for Reconsideration Form for Visual Media.

FIG. 5.1 Model Public Library Request for Reconsideration Form for Visual Media

Please print legibly or type

Title _____

Call Number _____

Producer (if known) _____

Reconsideration Initiated By _____

Street Address _____

City, State, Zip _____ Ph. _____

Complainant represents:

_____ self

_____ organization or group (identify)

1. Where did you acquire the item in question? (Please specify library, branch, department and/or specific collection.)

2. Did you view/listen to the item in its entirety?

　　Yes　　No

If No, what parts? _____

3. What do you believe to be the general theme, intent, or subject coverage of this item?

4. To what in the item do you object? (Be specific: describe visual scenes/segments; contents; lyrics/narration/dialogue; characterization; technical or other aspects.)

5. Who was affected, and in what harmful way, by viewing this item?

6. Are you legally responsible for the person affected?

　　Yes　　No

7. For what age group would you recommend this item?

8. What do you feel might be the result of viewing this item?

_____

_____

_____

9. Is there anything good (or of redeeming quality) about this item? (Please be specific, as in No. 4.)

_____

_____

_____

10. Are you aware of published reviews/evaluations of this item? (Please cite references or append reviews.)

_____

_____

_____

11. What would you like the library to do about the item?

_____ Withdraw it from the library/branch completely.

_____ Place it in a more age-appropriate collection in the library.

12. In its place, what item of equal value and intent would you recommend putting in the collection?

_____

_____

_____

13. Do you wish to make an oral presentation to the Reconsideration Committee?

    Yes   No

If Yes, please contact the library director.

Estimated time for presentation _____

_____   _____

Signature of Complainant   Date

Formal action may require a closed, in-house screening of media by committee and complainant (when it is a legal option). NOTE: Please feel free to attach additional material, references, or any other pertinent information.

SCHOOL LIBRARY MEDIA CENTERS

The school library media center collection bears a direct relationship to the school's instructional curriculum. However, the collection should also be reflective of student needs and interests, serving to extend the core curriculum; or provide bridges from one subject to another, or between levels of increasing complexity. Most public libraries possess a mission statement, and to a large degree know the diversity of the public they serve. In short, they have a purpose in collection development. School libraries are more focused and defined in terms of audience served and materials selection. In contrast to public libraries, they often do not possess mission/purpose statements. This lack of intent or purpose in collection development may be one underlying cause of many censorship complaints.

School librarians and administration must seek to inform teachers of their selection policies and materials use, as well as providing ongoing in-service training and bibliographies of newly purchased enrichment materials. Indeed, all teachers should be involved in the selection of materials on some level. The collection development policy reflects organizational intellectual freedom ideals, and while having a policy in place will not eliminate censorship complaints, it may avert them to some degree. At the least, complainants will realize that the challenged material was acquired in a preconceived, logical fashion and not on a whim.

Policies regulating use of media, such as copyright policies, must be enforced. In most schools, it is not the acquisition of materials that originates censorship challenges; rather, it is the use of that material by teachers and librarians. Just as in public libraries, while the challenged materials are in the reconsideration process, they should be kept on the shelf and/or in use. Likewise, librarians and teachers using the material should not be suspended. Schools, like public libraries, must recognize and foster the parents' right to restrict viewing. Aggressive communication efforts by schools can be instrumental in educating and informing parents about school materials, curriculum, special programs,

and new library materials and their positive use in the classroom. Communication vehicles are numerous, and include: school and local newspapers, special flyers and bibliographies, school cable television channels, parent workshops, and local organization/business presentations.

Schools face some unique problems related to intellectual freedom. The first problem is in defining the extent of jurisdiction for the school library program. That is, what effect will the intellectual freedom constraints imposed by the library endorsing the ALA statements have upon the teachers? If the library is in charge of copying off-air programs for school use, then the video is a temporary part of the library's collection. The Access to Resources and Services in the School Library Media Program statement says:

> Major barriers between students and resources include: imposing age or grade level restrictions on the use of resources, . . . requiring permission from parents or teachers, establishing restricted shelves or closed collections, and labeling.[11]

If teachers use library materials in the classroom, and the library endorses the Access to Resources and Services in the School Library Media Program, and Access for Children and Young People to Videotapes and Other Nonprint Formats statements, then, ethically, they cannot send out permission letters. To the extent that the library oversees school off-air taping, this would also apply to such legally made copies, except those made at home by teachers and used in the classroom. However, if the school interprets videos duplicated or taped off-air at home to be under the auspices of the library policy, then permission slips for these tapes would also be unethical.

As in the case of the public library, it is the responsibility of the teacher to direct students' learning and inform parents of the methods and instructional materials they are using. Permission slips play a vital role in that information function—serving as a two-way communication vehicle, and possibly averting problems before they start. In a similar

manner, age/grade level labeling (even as suggested guidelines) in the selection process, or as a result of a challenged-materials committee decision, is contradictory to the ALA documents.

A new problem that has entered the schools is the use of commercial educational television. Whittle Communications, for example, gives schools free video, televisions, and satellite reception equipment in turn for playing a 12-minute news program with two minutes of interspersed commercials. Programs are broadcast daily, videotaped, and rebroadcast during the school day. If the library is in charge of videotaping these programs, then the expurgation of these commercials (even if legally permissible) is a form of censorship and expurgation.

☐ SCHOOL LIBRARY RECONSIDERATION PROCEDURES

Schools need more diverse reconsideration procedures than public libraries do, because so many distinct groups and individuals must be represented: administration, students, teachers; school librarians; parent groups; and the complainant. In large school districts with much diversity among individual schools, each school may need its own review committee (even if the media collection is centralized off site).

Committees are presented with the dual problem of evaluating the challenged material not only for the specific use, but also for subsequent use by other teachers, often representing different subject areas and grade levels. The rational approach would be to limit the committee evaluation to the specific instance, and let the teachers use their educated judgment on subsequent subject or age-appropriate use. However, some schools may want the committee to provide a subject/grade level range that could be used as a guide by teachers in determining use. The committee procedure might be applied after the item has been acquired but before it has been used in the classroom. Perhaps screenings could be arranged in the teacher lounge, with all faculty members evaluating the material for usefulness and class appropriateness.

Librarians should obtain and keep in-house preview forms and published reviews of newly acquired media requested by teachers. The preview forms can be similar to public library evaluation forms, with additional qualifiers asking "How does this item fit into your class structure?" and "How and for what classes will you use the item?" This information would prove invaluable to the librarian in assessing the degree of usefulness and priority for purchase. Multiple use materials (used in more than one class or by more than one teacher) should have a greater purchase priority over single-use items in term of budget allocation.

☐ PARENTAL RESTRICTION OF MATERIALS

As part of the challenged-materials policy, teachers and librarians should develop a procedure whereby parents can exercise restriction of library/classroom materials. Upon receiving a written parental restriction notice, it may prove beneficial to contact the patron on an informal basis to explain the nature and use of the material and discover the reason for the restriction. Items to be addressed in the procedure section include the following:

1. Who may register a complaint.
2. Who should be notified when a complaint is received.
3. Whether complaints must be in writing.
4. A form for the complainant to complete and sign. (This form should be slightly different depending upon the medium in question.)
5. Procedures for handling the complaint when the complainant is unwilling to fill out the form. (The common practice is either to put the person on the board agenda, or to drop the matter based on the patron's unwillingness to comply with the requirements.)
6. Who should review the complaint and how it is handled. Usually, the governing body endorsing the selection policy should be the review board. However, a special committee of board members can also be established. This section should also discuss who is to inform the

INTELLECTUAL FREEDOM ISSUES AND POLICIES 229

complainant of the action taken, and how the information is delivered.
7. How challenged materials are handled during this process—will they remain in use, be removed, or be placed in a special area?
8. Time limits for the whole process, and whether any item can go through the process more than once within a specified time period, whether instigated by the same or different individuals or groups.
9. Appeal procedures.

The following is an example of a model challenged-materials policy.

Model Challenged-Materials Policy and Procedures for Schools

Initial Policy Statement
The choice of library materials by users is an individual matter. Responsibility for restrictions on access to library materials for children and adolescents rests with their parents and/or legal guardians. While a person may reject materials for him/herself and for his/her children, he/she cannot exercise censorship to restrict access to the materials by others. While the School Board recognizes the differences between visual media and print, and the power of visual images as opposed to print, it also supports intellectual freedom and endorses the following School Library Association (SLA) and American Library Association (ALA) documents: School Library Bill of Rights; Library Bill of Rights; The Student's Right to Read; Freedom To View; Statement on Labeling; Access for Children and Young People to Videotapes and Other Nonprint Formats; and Restricted Access to Library Materials.

By nature of our constitutional republic and in line with First Amendment rights, any adult resident or resident organization of the school district may challenge learning resources used in any of the district's

educational libraries on the basis of appropriateness for all students. This procedure is designed for the purpose of considering the opinions of those persons who were not directly involved in the initial resource selection process. However, it is the policy of the School Board to support and respect both the initial library materials acquisitions decisions (which are presumed to be valid), and the individuals to whom that role and selection/use authority has been delegated and entrusted.

Procedures for Dealing with Challenged Materials
A. Complaints regarding instructional materials used in the district's educational program shall be forwarded to the teacher responsible for that use. Complaints arising from use of media center materials shall be forwarded to the Media Specialist in that school. If classroom use, rather than personal student use (not teacher-specified) is involved, the teacher responsible for that use will also be involved in the complaint procedure. These individuals will try to resolve the issue informally by contacting the complainant.

1. The individual(s) initially receiving the oral complaint shall explain to the complainant the school's selection procedure, criteria, and the qualifications of those persons selecting the material.
2. The individual(s) initially receiving the complaint shall explain the particular place the challenged material occupies in the educational program, its intended educational usefulness, and additional information regarding its use.

B. Request for Reconsideration
In the event that the person making an objection to material is not satisfied with the initial explanation, he/she should request a Materials Reconsideration Form, available from any school district office, along with a copy of the school district's reconsideration procedures. The form should be completed and signed by the complainant, and submitted to the office of the school in which the challenged material is being used. Within five business days of the filing of the form, the Principal,

or the person designated by the Principal, shall submit the matter to the Reconsideration Committee in the respective school. The committee shall recommend disposition to the Principal within 60 business days from the submittal of the completed materials reconsideration form.

C. The Reconsideration Committee

The Reconsideration Committee shall be made up of eleven members:

- All the department chairpersons
- A school library Media Specialist familiar with school library policy
- One member of the administrative staff
- Three members of the community, appointed annually by the executive committee of the parent/teacher/student association
- Two high school students (1 male, 1 female), selected annually from and by the student advisory committee

D. Committee Procedure and Jurisdiction

1. The committee will meet initially to distribute copies of the completed Materials Reconsideration Form; distribute available previews and reviews; and distribute copies of the challenged material, or arrange for group/individual screening in accordance with the United States copyright laws (Section 110).
2. The committee will completely read, view, or listen to the item in question, and obtain all pertinent in-house preview evaluations and published reviews. Passages or segments shall not be pulled out of context, and the committee evaluation shall be made on the material as a whole.
3. The committee will hold at least one other meeting that will allow the complainant and the teacher(s) (if any) using the challenged materials to present brief oral presentations. The meeting will be previously advertised and announced to the public, and

any member of the public may attend and comment upon the challenged material at issue. All parties will be given appropriate notice of Reconsideration Committee meetings.

4. From the initial receipt of the completed Materials Reconsideration Form until the final decision by the School Board, the challenged material shall not be removed from the library or classroom, nor placed upon any restricted shelf, nor in any other manner be made unavailable to students. Continued classroom use will also not be curtailed. Notwithstanding any other provision contained herein, no restrictions of any kind or manner may restrict any student from reading, carrying, or otherwise possessing on school grounds, the challenged material utilized by the student for his/her own personal use.

5. The committee's final decision will be one of the following alternatives:

- To take no removal action
- To remove the challenged material from the library only
- To place it in a more age-appropriate collection within the district
- To remove all or part of the challenged material from the total school environment
- To restrict/remove the material from specified classroom use
- To restrict/remove the material from all classrooms
- To allow students to use alternate titles (list to be provided by the committee)
- To provide subject/grade-level indicators for the material as guidelines for future use

E. Any committee decision must be arrived at by a three-fourths majority vote.

F. Any decision to sustain a challenge shall not be interpreted as a judgment of irresponsibility on the part of the professional involved in the original selection or use of the material.

INTELLECTUAL FREEDOM ISSUES AND POLICIES 233

G. Requests to reconsider materials that have previously been before the committee must receive approval of a majority of the committee members before the material will again be reconsidered. Every reconsideration request shall be acted upon by the committee.

H. Committee members directly associated with the selection, use, or challenge of the challenged material shall be excused from the committee during the deliberation on such materials. The Principal may appoint a temporary replacement for the excused committee member, but such replacement shall possess the same general qualifications of the person excused, as far as possible.

I. In the event of a severe overload of challenges, the committee may appoint a subcommittee of members or nonmembers to consolidate challenges and to make recommendations to the full committee. The composition of this subcommittee shall approximate the representation on the full committee.

J. Committee deliberations shall be audiotaped, and minutes kept by the administrative secretary. The committee chairperson (to be appointed by the Principal annually) will provide a written summary of key points, and the recommendation to the board.

K. The School Board shall adopt the recommendation of the committee absent of any clear and convincing proof that the committee findings were capricious or arbitrary. That adoption will be administratively final and legally binding. At that time the Board President will direct the Board Secretary to draft a letter notifying the complainant of the Board's decision. It will be sent registered mail on the next business day.

L. If not satisfied with the decision, the complainant may request that the matter be placed on the agenda of the next regularly scheduled meeting of the Board. At that time, the Board may ask the Superintendent to investigate the matter further, appoint a Board committee to investigate the matter, or render a decision.

M. Any person dissatisfied with the decision of the Board may appeal to the State Board of Education pursuant to state law.

N. Individual Parental Restriction

In accordance with the ALA's statement on Access for Children and Young People to Videotapes and Other Nonprint Formats, and the Library Bill of Rights, the School Board recognizes the right of parents and/or legal guardians of minor students to absolutely restrict said student from reading, viewing, or listening to any specific library or classroom resource. The parent/guardian may exercise this right by advising, in writing, the librarian or specific classroom teacher involved that specific materials (name by title) be made unavailable to the student. One copy of this restriction will be placed in the student's file; a second copy will be given to the student by the librarian/teacher; and the original will be retained by the librarian/teacher.

The written restriction shall be effective only during the academic school year in which the restriction was received, and will become null and void on the last day of the academic year. Should the student attain the age of 18 years during the academic year in which the parental restriction is in effect, that restriction will become null and void on the student's birthdate.

FIG. 5.2 Model School Library Request for Reconsideration of Materials Form

---

Please print legibly or type.

Title _____

Call Number _____

Producer (If Known) _____

Reconsideration Initiated By _____

Street Address _____

City, State, Zip _____ Ph. _____

Complainant represents:

_____ self

_____ organization or group (identify)

1. Where did you acquire the item in question? (Please specify school building, library, and/or specific collection)

_____

2. Are you aware of how this item is being used in the school library and/or classroom?

     Yes   No

If Yes, please describe (specify class, teacher, and instructional method)

_____

_____

_____

3. Did you view/listen to the item in its entirety?

     Yes   No

If No, what parts? _____

_____

_____

_____

4. What do you believe to be the general theme, intent, or subject coverage of this item?

_____

_____

_____

5. To what in the item do you object? (Be specific: describe visual scenes/segments; contents; lyrics/narration/dialogue; characterization; technical or other aspects.)

_____

_____

_____

6. Who was affected, or in what harmful way do you think students will be affected, through the use of this item?

_____

_____

7. Are you legally responsible for the person affected?

    Yes   No

8. For what age group would you recommend this item?

_____

9. What do you feel might be the result of viewing this item?

_____

_____

10. What is there of educational or redeeming value in this item? (Please be specific, as in No. 5.)

_____

_____

11. Are you aware of published reviews/evaluations of this item? (Please cite references or append reviews.)

_____

_____

12. What would you like the School Board to do about the item?

_____ To remove the material from the library only.

_____ To place it in a more age-appropriate collection within the School District. (Please specify age grouping or grade level.)

_____

_____ To remove all or part of the challenged material from the total school environment.

INTELLECTUAL FREEDOM ISSUES AND POLICIES 237

_____ To restrict/remove the material from specified classroom use.

_____ To restrict/remove the material from all classrooms.

_____ To allow students to use alternate titles.

_____ To provide subject/grade-level indicators for the challenged item as a guideline for future use.

13. In its place, what item of equal value and intent would you recommend putting in the collection?

_____

_____

14. Do you wish to make an oral presentation to the Reconsideration Committee?

     Yes   No

If Yes, please contact the School Principal's office.

Indicate estimated time for presentation _____

_____   _____

Signature of Complainant   Date

Formal action may require a closed, in-house screening by committee and complainant (when it is a legal option).

Routing:

Complainant

Reconsideration Committee members/Reconsideration Subcommittee members

School Principal

Superintendent

Board of Education

NOTE: Please feel free to attach additional supporting material, references, or any other pertinent information.

It is important that only options that the School Board is willing and able to carry out (keep in mind the endorsement of various ALA documents) be listed as complainant

choices (see question number 12 on the model reconsideration form).

Many school libraries may choose to use a Simple Complaint Card (illustrated in Fig. 5.3) as a documentation device before initial contact is made by the teacher or librarian, in an attempt to resolve the complaint without Reconsideration Committee action.

FIG. 5.3 Model Simple Complaint Card

Date _____ Title of Material/Item Challenged _____
_____

Classroom/Situation Item Was Used In _____
Name of Teacher/Librarian Using Item _____
_____

Complainant's Name _____
Complainant representing Self _____
Organization (name) _____
Address _____
Telephone _____
Description of Complaint (Reason) _____
_____
_____
_____
_____

Complainant Signature _____
Teacher/Librarian Use:
Results of Initial Contact _____
_____

Complainant took Request for Reconsideration Form
        Yes   No
Teacher/Librarian Signature _____
Date _____

INTELLECTUAL FREEDOM ISSUES AND POLICIES

Also, it may be useful to acknowledge the receipt of the Request for Reconsideration Form by sending a letter to the complainant. This letter also documents the initiation of formal procedures and the responsibilities of all parties involved.

☐ USE OF NONSCHOOL MATERIALS

Because of the wide availability and low purchase/rental cost of home-use-only videocassettes, many schools also encounter situations in which the teacher wishes to use videocassettes (legally obtained and used) acquired from nonrecommended sources outside of the school district—such as tapes purchased or rented from a local video outlet or tapes brought from home. The Los Angeles Unified School District has such a policy, which is specifically designed for feature films used in the classroom, and discusses the MPAA ratings in depth (see also Chapter 4).

FIG. 5.4 Model Response to Complainant

Dear _____ ,

Thank you for completing the formal Request for Reconsideration of Materials Form, in which you questioned the use of

_____ in _____ school(s). We appreciate your concern, and wish to assure you that we will give the matter serious consideration. The filing of this form starts a formal review process that is described in detail in the Materials Reconsideration packet you received with the form. You will be notified of the Board's decision and resultant action taken concerning disposition of the item by the Board within ____ days.

I am sure you understand the complexity of providing materials suitable to the maturity, needs, interests, and abilities of all students on all grade levels. This is a continuous task of re-evaluation, and an important responsibility that often requires direction and guidance from the parents of our students.

Sincerely,

_____
Principal

This policy also includes an excellent example of a letter to parents requesting permission for their child to view the specific tape being shown in the class. A sample form, to be completed by the teacher and submitted to the school principal, is also included. This form serves as a verification tool for all parties, showing how and why the item will be used in the classroom.

SUMMARY

In an attempt to avoid censorship problems, many public libraries are restricting access to videocassettes by minors. Many schools practice preselection censorship in an effort to circumvent problems. The profession of librarianship is admirable for its stance and enforced ethics concerning intellectual freedom, and this stance should not be undermined. The development of both a sound collection development policy and a sound materials reconsideration policy and procedures will assist in diluting, but not eliminating, censorship attempts.

Some additional resources include the following books:

1. Frances M. Jones, *Defusing Censorship: The Librarian's Guide to Handling Censorship Conflicts* (Phoenix, AZ: Oryx Press, 1983).
2. Office for Intellectual Freedom of the American Library Association, *Intellectual Freedom Manual*, 3d ed. (Chicago: ALA, 1989).
3. John Robotham and Gerald Shields, *Freedom of Access to Library Materials* (New York: Neal-Schuman Publishers, 1982).
4. Linda Schexnaydre et al., *Censorship: A Guide for Successful Workshop Planning* (Phoenix, AZ: Oryx Press, 1984).

☐ NOTES

1. Office for Intellectual Freedom of the American Library Association, *Intellectual Freedom Manual*, 3d ed. (Chicago: ALA, 1989), ix.

INTELLECTUAL FREEDOM ISSUES AND POLICIES

2. Office for Intellectual Freedom of the American Library Association, "Dealing with Concerns about Library Materials" (American Library Association, Chicago, 12 January 1983, press release), 1–2.
3. Elizabeth Futus, ed., *Library Acquisition Policies and Procedures*, 2d ed. (Phoenix, AZ: Oryx Press, 1984), xxviii.
4. Randy Pitman, "Access by Minors/Collection Management Questionnaire: The Results," *The Video Librarian* 1 (November 1986): 1.
5. American Library Association Council, "Access for Children and Young People to Videotapes and Other Nonprint Formats," *Newsletter on Intellectual Freedom* (September 1989): 156.
6. Ibid., 156.
7. Joseph W. Palmer, "Audiovisuals of Professional Interest: A Column of News and Reviews," *Catholic Library World* 61 (March/April 1990): 202
8. Ibid., 202.
9. American Library Association Council, "Access for Children," 156.
10. Michael Gorman and Paul W. Winkler, eds., *Anglo-American Cataloguing Rules*, 2d ed., rev. 1988 (Chicago: ALA, 1988), 197.
11. American Library Association Council, "Access to Resources and Services in the School Library Media Program," *Newsletter on Intellectual Freedom* (March 1990): 39.
12. American Library Association Council, "Access for Children," 156.

APPENDIX A
Freedom To View

The Freedom to View, along with the freedom to speak, to hear, and to read, is protected by the First Amendment to the Constitution of the United States. In a free society, there is no place for censorship of any medium of expression. Therefore these principles are affirmed:

1. To provide the broadest possible access to film, video, and other audiovisual materials because they are a means for the communication of ideas. Liberty of circulation is essential to insure the constitutional guarantee of freedom of expression.
2. To protect the confidentiality of all individuals and institutions using film, video, and other audiovisual materials.
3. To provide film, video, and other audiovisual materials which represent a diversity of views and expression. Selection of a work does not constitute or imply agreement with or approval of the content.
4. To provide a diversity of viewpoints without the constraint of labeling or prejudging film, video and other audiovisual materials on the basis of the moral, religious, or political beliefs of the producer or filmmaker or on the basis of controversial content.
5. To contest vigorously, by all lawful means, every encroachment upon the public's freedom to view.

[This statement was originally drafted by the Freedom to View Committee of the American Film and Video Association (AFVA), formerly the Educational Film Library Association, and was adopted by the AFVA Board of Directors in February 1979. The statement was updated and approved by the AFVA Board of Directors in 1989, and endorsed by the American Library Association Council at its Midwinter Meeting, 10 January 1990.]

APPENDIX B

Challenged Materials: An Interpretation of the *Library Bill of Rights*

The American Library Association declares as a matter of firm principle that it is the responsibility of every library to have a clearly defined materials selection policy in written form which reflects the *Library Bill of Rights*, and which is approved by the appropriate governing authority.

Challenged materials which meet the criteria for selection in the materials selection policy of the library should not be removed under any legal or extra-legal pressure. The *Library Bill of Rights* states in Article 1 that "Materials should not be excluded because of the origin, background, or views of those contributing to their creation," and in Article 2, that "Materials should not be proscribed or removed because of partisan or doctrinal disapproval." Freedom of expression is protected by the Constitution of the United States, but constitutionally protected expression is often separated from unprotected expression only by a dim and uncertain line. The Constitution requires a procedure designed to focus searchingly on challenged expression before it can be suppressed. An adversary hearing is a part of this procedure.

Therefore, any attempt, be it legal or extra-legal, to regulate or suppress materials in libraries must be closely scrutinized to the end that protected expression is not abridged.

[Adopted 25 June 1971; amended 1 July 1981; amended 10 January 1990, by the ALA Council.]

APPENDIX C

Expurgation of Library Materials: An Interpretation of the *Library Bill of Rights*

Expurgating library materials is a violation of the *Library Bill of Rights*. Expurgation as defined by this interpretation includes any deletion, excision, alteration, editing, or obliteration of any part(s) of books or other library resources by the library, its agent, or its parent institution (if any). By such expurgation, the library is in effect denying access to the complete work and the entire spectrum of ideas that the work intended to express. Such action stands in violation of Articles 1, 2, and 3 of the *Library Bill of Rights*, which state that "Materials should not be excluded because of the origin, background, or views of those contributing to their creation," that "Materials should not be proscribed or removed because of partisan or doctrinal disapproval," and that "Libraries should challenge censorship in the fulfillment of their responsibility to provide information and enlightenment."

The act of expurgation has serious implications. It involves a determination that it is necessary to restrict access to the complete work. This is censorship. When a work is expurgated, under the assumption that certain portions of that work would be harmful to minors, the situation is no less serious.

Expurgation of any books or other library resources imposes a restriction, without regard to the rights and desires of all library users, by limiting access to ideas and information.

Further, expurgation without written permission from the holder of the copyright on the material may violate the copyright provisions of the United States Code.

[Adopted 2 February 1973; amended 1 July 1981; amended 10 January 1990, by the ALA Council.]

APPENDIX D

Access to Resources and Services in the School Library Media Program: An Interpretation of the *Library Bill of Rights*

The school library media program plays a unique role in promoting intellectual freedom. It serves as a point of voluntary access to information and ideas and as a learning laboratory for students as they acquire critical thinking and problem solving skills needed in a pluralistic society. Although the educational levels and school programs effectively shape the resources and services of a school library media program, the principles of the *Library Bill of Rights* apply equally to all libraries, including school library media programs.

School library media professionals assume a leadership role in promoting the principles of intellectual freedom within the school by providing resources and services that create and sustain an atmosphere of free inquiry. School library media professionals work closely with teachers to integrate instructional activities in classroom units designed to equip students to locate, evaluate, and use a broad range of ideas effectively. Through resources, programming, and educational processes, students and teachers experience the free and robust debate characteristic of a democratic society.

School library media professionals cooperate with other individuals in building collections of resources appropriate in the developmental and maturity levels of students. These collections provide resources which support the curriculum and are consistent with the philosophy, goals, and objectives of the school district.

Resources in school library media collections represent diverse points of view and current as well as historical issues.

While English is, by history and tradition, the customary language of the United States, the languages in use in any given community may vary. Schools serving communities in which other languages are used make efforts to accommodate the needs of students for whom English is a second language. To support these efforts, and to ensure equal access to resources and services, the school library media program provides resources which reflect the linguistic pluralism of the community.

Members of the school community involved in the collection development process employ educational criteria to select resources unfettered by their personal, political, social, or religious views. Students and educators served by the school library media program have access to resources and services free of constraints resulting from personal, partisan, or doctrinal disapproval. School library media professionals resist efforts by individuals to define what is appropriate for all students or teachers to read, view, or hear.

Major barriers between students and resources include: imposing age or grade level restrictions on the use of resources, limiting the use of interlibrary loan and access to electronic information, charging fees for information in specific formats, requiring permissions from parents or teachers, establishing restricted shelves or closed collections, and labeling.

Policies, procedures, and rules related to the use of resources and services support free and open access to information.

The school board adopts policies that guarantee students access to a broad range of ideas. These include policies on collection development and procedures for the review of resources about which concerns have been raised. Such policies, developed by persons in the school community, provide for a timely and fair hearing to assure that procedures are applied equitably to all expressions of concern. School library media professionals implement district policies and procedures in the school.

[Adopted 2 July 1986; amended 10 January 1990, by the ALA Council.]

APPENDIX E

Access for Children and Young People to Videotapes and Other Nonprint Formats: An Interpretation of the *Library Bill of Rights*

Library collections of videotapes, motion pictures, and other nonprint formats raise a number of intellectual freedom issues, especially regarding minors.

The interests of young people, like those of adults, are not limited by subject, theme, or level of sophistication. Librarians have a responsibility to ensure young people have access to materials and services that reflect diversity sufficient to meet their needs.

To guide librarians and others in resolving these issues, the American Library Association provides the following guidelines.

The *Library Bill of Rights* says, "A person's right to use a library should not be denied or abridged because of origin, age, background, or views."

ALA's *Free Access to Libraries for Minors: An Interpretation of the Library Bill of Rights* states:

The "right to use a library" includes use of, and access to, all library materials and services. Thus, practices which allow adults to use some services and materials which are denied to minors abridge use based on age. . . . It is the parents—and only the parents—who may restrict their children—and only their children—from access to library materials and services. People who would rather their children did not have access to certain materials should advise their children. The library and its staff are responsible for providing equal access to library materials and services for all library users.

Policies which set minimum age limits for access to videotapes and/or other audiovisual materials and equipment, with or without parental permission, abridge library use for minors. Further, age limits based on the cost of the materials are unacceptable. Unless directly and specifically prohibited by law from circulating certain motion pictures and video productions to minors, librarians should apply the same standards to circulation of these materials as are applied to books and other materials.

Recognizing that libraries cannot act in loco parentis, ALA acknowledges and supports the exercise by parents of their responsibility to guide their own children's reading and viewing. Published reviews of films and videotapes and/or reference works which provide information about the content, subject matter, and recommended audiences can be made available in conjunction with nonprint collections to assist parents in guiding their children without implicating the library in censorship. This material may include information provided by video producers and distributors, promotional material on videotape packaging, and Motion Picture Association of America (MPAA) ratings *if they are included on the tape or in the packaging by the original publisher* and/or if they appear in review sources or reference works included in the library's collection. Marking out or removing ratings information from videotape packages constitutes expurgation or censorship.

MPAA and other rating services are private advisory codes and have no legal standing.* For the library to add such ratings to the material if they are not already there, to post a list of such ratings with a collection, or to attempt to enforce such ratings through circulation policies or other procedures constitutes labeling, "an attempt to prejudice attitudes" about the material, and

---

*For information on case law, please contact the ALA Office for Intellectual Freedom. See also: Statements on Labeling and Expurgation of Library Materials, Interpretations of the Library Bill of Rights.

ACCESS FOR CHILDREN AND YOUNG PEOPLE

is unacceptable. The application of locally generated ratings schemes intended to provide content warnings to library users is also inconsistent with the *Library Bill of Rights.*

[Adopted 28 June 1989, by the ALA Council.]